C3 CORVETTE 1968-1982
HOW TO BUILD AND MODIFY

Chris Petris

CarTech®

CarTech®

CarTech®, Inc.
838 Lake Street South
Forest Lake, MN 55025
Phone: 651-277-1200 or 800-551-4754
Fax: 651-277-1203
www.cartechbooks.com

© 2013 by Chris Petris

All rights reserved. No part of this publication may be reproduced or utilized in any form or by any means, electronic or mechanical, including photocopying, recording, or by any information storage and retrieval system, without prior permission from the Publisher. All text, photographs, and artwork are the property of the Author unless otherwise noted or credited.

The information in this work is true and complete to the best of our knowledge. However, all information is presented without any guarantee on the part of the Author or Publisher, who also disclaim any liability incurred in connection with the use of the information and any implied warranties of merchantability or fitness for a particular purpose. Readers are responsible for taking suitable and appropriate safety measures when performing any of the operations or activities described in this work.

All trademarks, trade names, model names and numbers, and other product designations referred to herein are the property of their respective owners and are used solely for identification purposes. This work is a publication of CarTech, Inc., and has not been licensed, approved, sponsored, or endorsed by any other person or entity. The Publisher is not associated with any product, service, or vendor mentioned in this book, and does not endorse the products or services of any vendor mentioned in this book.

Edit by Paul Johnson
Layout by Monica Seiberlich

ISBN SA247P
Item No. 978-1-61325-469-1

Library of Congress Cataloging-in-Publication Data

Petris, Chris.
  C3 Corvette / Chris Petris.
      pages cm
  ISBN 978-1-61325-033-4
  1. Corvette automobile--Performance. 2. Corvette automobile--Customizing. 3. Corvette automobile--Maintenance and repair. I. Title.

TL215.C6P394 2014
629.28'722--dc23

2013035435

Written, edited, designed and Printed in the U.S.A.
10 9 8 7 6 5 4 3 2 1

Title Page: The Street Shop chassis is a "roller," ready for body installation. I tried a set of C5 Corvette headers hoping that they might fit; unfortunately, they come too close to the transmission. Street Shop has pre-bent fuel and brake lin to make a very tough part of the project much easier. I prefer to make my own because I have all the required tools; this can be pricey for one-time use. The chassis can be put in the corner until your Shark is ready for the transformation.

Back Cover Photos

Top Left: A custom fuel tank mounting frame was fabricated out of 1-inch, 20-gauge square tubing to drop the tank as far as possible. This allowed a talle fuel tank for longer stints on the Hot Rod Power Tour. Rick's Hot Rods built our tank from our drawings and a cardboard replica. That's right; a cardboard replic was assembled and then shipped to them to ensure a perfect fit. There is nothir like an exact replica to make sure everything fits.

Top Right: This Vintage Air Front Runner big-block application with a front engi mount plate worked out well with our crank trigger ignition. The engine mount plate was made from the same-thickness material as the trigger wheel to keep tl system in alignment. A ground strap should be installed at either of the alternator through-bolts. The surface conditioning of the components prevents a good ground, and possible charging system issues can occur.

Middle Left: This early Shark is receiving a modified T-5. It is a tight fit with the non-removable transmission crossmember. Another issue is the shifter location; placing the shifter stick in the center of the tunnel requires either a custom console or no console. By the time you find a re-buildable unit and buy all the upgrade transmission internals (mainshaft and countershaft gears) to help it har dle some real torque, you can buy a ready-to-go unit that handles the pressure.

Middle Right: This reproduction carrier for Eaton differentials is available for a Shark. Eaton made the differentials for General Motors. This is a heavy-duty replacement with high-tension Posi-Traction springs and the latest carbon-disc Posi-Traction clutch packs. The only thing you need to do for years to come is change the fluid. The bearing and seal kit does the job right for a total rebuild of the differential assembly.

Bottom Left: A set of 2001 Camaro LS exhaust manifolds were used for the engine installation because they fit close to the engine, clearing the frame rails. This GM LS crate-engine harness was routed onto the engine before the body installation to check fitment while it was easy to access the engine. You need to integrate the engine harness with the Shark's original harness. The best possible solution for the novice is to use an engineered wiring system from a company such as Painless Performance, which has intimate knowledge of the LS engine requirements and the Shark body you are using.

Bottom Right: SPC has fully adjustable upper control arms that can be easily adjusted for maximum positive caster up to 10.5 degrees. The control arm pivot shafts are fixed: no fiddling with shims that can come loose in a race environmer The hex adjusting sleeves and lock nuts make the changes quick and simple. Lo nuts are used on the sleeve ends and should be checked regularly for proper 45 ft-lbs of torque.

PGUK
63 Hatton Garden
London EC1N 8LE, England
Phone: 020 7061 1980 • Fax: 020 7242 3725
www.pguk.co.uk

Renniks Publications Ltd.
3/37-39 Green Street
Banksmeadow, NSW 2109, Australia
Phone: 2 9695 7055 • Fax: 2 9695 7355
www.renniks.com

CONTENTS

Acknowledgments	4
Introduction	5

Chapter 1: Engine Modifications 6
   Inspection and Testing 7
   Intake Manifolds 10
   Cylinder Heads 12
   Camshaft Selection and Installation 16

Chapter 2: Crate Engine or LS Engine? 19
   Crate Engines 19
   Crate Sources 20
   LS Engines 21
   LS1 Install 25
   Engine Setup and Tuning 33

Chapter 3: Power Adders 34
   Nitrous Oxide 34
   Nitrous Flow Control 38
   Supercharging and Turbocharging 40
   Superchargers 40
   Turbochargers 42
   Intercoolers 43

Chapter 4: Performance Fuel Systems 44
   Carburetors 44
   Carb Sources 45
   Fuel Injection 49
   EFI Manufacturer Options 50
   Wiring 51
   Fuel System 53
   Aftermarket Fuel Tanks 56
   Fuel Lines 60

Chapter 5: Exhaust Systems 62
   Headers 63
   Exhaust System Obstacles 69
   Catalytic Converters 70
   Mufflers 70
   Kit Options 71

Chapter 6: Performance Cooling System 73
   Cooling System Design 73
   Radiator Choice 75
   Tube Requirements 75
   Coolant Flow Rate 77
   Cooling Fans 77
   Ancillary Cooling Systems 81
   Cooling System Tips 83
   Accessory Drive Systems 83
   Aftermarket Kits 86

Chapter 7: Transmissions and Drivelines 88
   Manual Transmission Technology 88
   Transmission Gearing 89
   Transmission Options 90
   Clutches 94
   Automatic Transmissions 97
   Modify or Swap? 98
   The Ultimate Swap: A 4L60E 101
   Transmission Installation 102

Chapter 8: Driveline 105
   Differential 106
   Axle and Driveshaft 115
   Universal Joints 115

Chapter 9: Aftermarket Chassis Installation 117
   Do You Need One? 117
   Three Project Examples 118
   Prep for Body Removal 120
   Body Cushion Removal 122
   Lifting the Body 123
   Suspension and Drivetrain Installation 126

Chapter 10: Chassis Modifications 129
   Damage Inspection 130
   Front Suspension and Steering 130
   Rear Suspension 139
   Springs 143
   Shocks 143
   Coil-Over Kits 144
   Anti-Roll Bars 145
   Chassis Stiffening and Bracing 146
   Alignment 146

Chapter 11: Brake Upgrades 148
   Calipers 149
   Disc Pads 151
   Disc Brake Rotors 151
   Brake Bias 155
   Brake Boosters 155
   Brake Fluid 158
   Brake Bleeding 158
   Performance Brake Kits 158

Chapter 12: Wheels and Tires 161
   Wheels 161
   Wheel Fitment 164
   Wheel Upkeep 164
   Tires 166
   Tire Balancing 167
   Tire Wear 168

Chapter 13: Interior Upgrades 169
   Seat Belts 169
   Rollbars 170
   Roll Cages 172
   Seating 172
   Gauges 173
   Steering Wheels 174
   Pedal Pads 175
   Safety Equipment 175

Source Guide 176

ACKNOWLEDGMENTS

After my many years of modifying and enhancing Corvette drivetrain components it made sense to share all that I have learned. As a GM fan owning and driving many Shark Corvettes, this book became the perfect medium to convey my experiences.

I was very fortunate to have understanding parents who let me pursue what made me feel comfortable to work on. Later on, my lovely wife, Hope, let me keep the dream going while we raised our two beautiful daughters, Stacy and Stephanie. What many regard as a hobby has been my life, trying to build the perfect Corvette for both street and track experiences. Too few of us can do what we love and I have been very fortunate to experience that every day.

A true friend and associate Andy Bolig helped me to convey my thoughts onto paper and how to use a camera many years ago. Andy, many thanks are due; I couldn't have gone this far without your help.

The team at CarTech, especially Paul Johnson, deserve much of the credit for being so helpful and understanding through my learning curve as a book author. Thanks guys.

A special thanks to Charlie Mornout for letting me use his 1973 Corvette convertible for many of the photos.

All my love goes out to Hope, Stacy, and Stephanie for hanging in there and being so much help throughout my career. You are a huge part of my success.

INTRODUCTION

The Corvette C3 is the longest-running Corvette generation in history. Few other models have had an illustrious life span of 14 years and even fewer still have bridged three distinct decades in automotive history. As many know, the C3 was an evolution of the C2. The C3's suspension, brakes, steering, and chassis were carried over from the C2. But the classic C2 Stingray had the propensity for body lift at speed, and that meant loss of control. The C3 is much more aerodynamically efficient. The Mako Shark concept car that evolved into the C3 cured the body lift problem of the C2 and became an unmistakable car and in the minds of many, the quintessential Corvette.

A Brief History of the C3

The C3 was released in 1968 when muscle car wars were reaching a fevered pitch. Many of GM's best small- and big-block powerplants were installed in the Corvette. The high-performance 350-ci models fitted with Muncie 4-speed provided exceptional performance in a nimble chassis for sterling handling. But with a big-block engine, the C3 delivered titanic performance and excellent road-holding characteristics to reassert the Corvette as an "all muscle" sports car. From 1968 to 1974, the C3 Stingray received several renditions of the 427-ci engine and most produced horsepower from 400 to 500.

At the top was the L88 engine. It was strictly built for racing, produced 430 hp, and carried a high-flow 4-barrel carb, aluminum heads, a unique air-induction system, and a 12.5:1 compression ratio. For 1971 General Motors slotted the new LT-1, a 350-ci V-8 that had been installed in the 1970 Camaro Z28. This was apex to Gen I small-block performance and technology, featuring solid lifters, forged steel crankshaft, aluminum intake, 4-barrel carburetor, 4-bolt main block, 11:1 compression ratio, extruded pistons, high-lift camshaft, and low-restriction exhaust. The LT-1 certainly stood up to the competition on the road and at the track.

In 1971–1974, General Motors installed the 454-ci engine that pumped out gobs of torque, which made it an ideal street engine and magnificent in stoplight-to-stoplight sprints. For 1972, Chevy offered the 454-ci LS6 engine in the Corvette, which spun out 425 or more gross hp. But by 1974, the nation was reeling from the energy crisis, rising insurance rates, and a general negative public perception of high-performance cars; the muscle car era came to unceremonious close. And with it, the Corvette morphed from a high-performance sports car into a grand touring car.

From 1975 to 1979, the C3 continued to soldier on in this brave new era with a low-compression and much lower horsepower engine. In fact, Chevy promoted the 1975 Corvette as "a more efficient Corvette," and it carried CDI ignition and, of course, a catalytic converter, which further dampened performance. Dual exhaust pipes were routed to a single converter and split into individual pipes at the rear, and this certainly choked off the car even more. Bumpers were no longer chrome. In a *Car and Driver* test, the C3 accelerated from 0-60 in 7.7 seconds, which wasn't terrible, but it was much slower than previous years.

When the 1980s dawned, the muscle (or high-performance) cars started to make a slow rebound and the Corvette was one of the highest-performing American cars you could buy from that era. The Corvette was much more refined in its final years. Chevy engineers shaved weight off the vehicle. The Shark was fitted with thinner body panels and an aluminum Dana 44 independent rear suspension and differential assembly. The new lighter unit replaced the stronger cast-iron GM 10-bolt IRS differential. The old cast-iron intake gave way to the aluminum intake manifold and new tubular stainless-steel exhaust manifolds. In 1981, there was only one powerplant available, a 350-ci engine that produced 190 hp. In 1982, the last year of the C3, it could muster a 0-60 mph time of 8.1 seconds.

Building the Perfect Beast

Many of the C3s built from 1975 to 1982 are readily available and quite affordable, but more importantly, these are not rare, high-value collector cars so an owner should not regret modifying one. Without having the luxury of a crystal ball, it's unlikely that the later C3s will ever attain high collector values. The reason is that these cars are not rare, don't have a racing pedigree, nor are fitted with special high-performance equipment. On the other hand, this is the very reason that the C3 is the ideal platform for a high-performance build. You can completely transform the performance of these grand touring sports into an aggressive, fine handling, responsive, and quick sports car.

This book will be your guide for selecting the best performance package for a particular budget and application. Remember your Corvette performs as an entire package; if you upgrade certain parts or components, it affects a related component group. If your engine produces much more horsepower than stock, then the stock transmission and rear axle are most likely inadequate and must be upgraded. A massive number of high-performance engine parts is made for the Chevy engines installed in these Corvettes. Transmission options abound as well. The aftermarket has embraced the C3 and a full selection of chassis, suspension, steering, and brake products are offered to enhance, improve, and transform performance. With the right combination of parts and the correct building procedures, a common C3 can produce performance that rivals a modern sports car.

A variety of high-performance engine parts can be fitted to the low-compression smog-controlled 350-ci V-8 engines. High-compression aluminum heads from Dart, AFR, RHS, or a number of other manufactures, and in conjunction with a high-lift hydraulic roller cam and intake improvements, can dramatically improve the performance of these engines. Fitted with the right combination of high-performance parts an engine that made 165 hp stock can now make 300 hp or much more. Of course, all-aluminum blocks, high-performance valvetrain parts, aluminum intake, and more-efficient carbs are available. You can also upgrade to a particular tubular header exhaust system that not only saves weight, but also efficiently scavenges spent exhaust gas for increased performance.

Many 1975-1982 Corvettes were fitted with the TurboHydramatic 350 transmission, Muncie 4-speed, and BorgWarner T-10 manual transmission. These transmissions were adequate for the stock engine. However, if you are building a high-performance engine that produces 300 hp or more, you need a stout transmission to effectively transmit the power to the wheels. Tremec makes a variety of manual transmissions in 5- and 6-speed options, which not only transmit more horsepower, but also have an overdrive gear so they are much more fuel efficient on the highway. The Tremec T-5, TKO, and T56 series transmissions can be installed on the C3. In almost all cases, the transmission crossmember must be modified or replaced to fit the new transmission to the chassis. And a hole for the shifter must be cut in the transmission tunnel, but these swaps can be completed with some careful planning, welding, and a minimal amount of fabrication. A variety of automatic overdrive transmissions can be installed in the C3 as well.

The C3 suspension and chassis were carry-overs from the C2 so it's essentially 50-year-old technology, and there's obviously a lot of room for improvement. I comprehensively cover your options so you can realize the best handling for your C3. The stock stamped-steel control arms can be replaced with tubular chromemoly arms that are camber adjustable for specific setups. In addition, you can install coil-over shocks, stiffer springs, and heavy-duty anti-sway bars to substantially improve road holding and steering response. I discuss your suspension, spring, and shock options for applications, such as high-performance street, autocross/road race, and drag racing. I also cover coil-over shock conversion kits to take front suspension to the next level. In addition, if you're seeking to eliminate the traverse rear spring and convert the rear suspension to coil-over spring setup, I explain the specifics for making this conversion a reality. When performing suspension upgrades, you want to put a bigger tire and larger contact patch on the road. I will go into the complexities and procedures for flaring fenders to accommodate larger tires and wheels.

I have gone to great lengths to cover all the systems and components of the car, so you can enjoy the ultimate driving experience from your C3. I also provide practical cooling system, interior, electrical, and other upgrades for your car. No other car will ever capture the character and allure of the classic Shark but, you are not stuck with the C3's stock equipment package. This book is your gateway to higher performance.

CHAPTER 1

ENGINE MODIFICATIONS

You have an enormous number of options for engines and engine modifications. Most Sharks are equipped with the small-block Chevy, and an almost infinite number of heads, cams, intake, exhaust, ignition, rotating assembly, and other performance part are available. You can build anything from a mildly modified street engine to a race engine. If you have or want to install a Chevy big-block, the number of modifications is nearly as extensive and diverse.

I spent many of my early years pulling cylinder heads and replacing camshafts on a long weekend or two, looking for more power. Sometimes the correct decision was made in haste, and other times a decision was made in haste and a crucial step was missed. Proper and methodical planning is key to any engine project and most automotive projects. You need to develop a clear goal and work back from that to the beginning of the project so all the engine parts are compatible and complementary. But you also need to plan out each crucial step along the way so every step is completed correctly and professionally. Not having a clear goal always costs additional time and money; not evaluating the engine health can set you up for a major disappointment.

Your current engine should go through an evaluation and inspection process to determine what direction to proceed. Your engine may be in questionable health: adding performance pieces could add the death blow to an already worn-out engine. Mileage is usually a factor to take into account when engine health is considered. When the early Shark odometers turned over at 100,000, often the engine was in need of a rebuild. You need to perform an engine compression and/or leak-down test to determine whether the engine needs to be rebuilt. Cylinder compression is an important measurement of overall engine health. Leak-down testing is the best way to check for excessive crankcase pressure (blow-by, as it is often called), valve sealing, and head gasket integrity. As piston rings and cylinder walls wear, combustion gases are forced into the crankcase, creating the excess pressure. A good indicator of worn rings is seeing a steady puff of smoke belching from the valve cover's PCV valve grommet.

Observing the oil pressure, especially once the engine coolant temperature reaches more than 180 degrees, is an important step in determining the

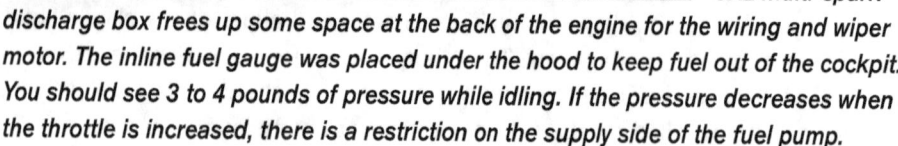

This 1977 Shark received a GM crate engine with many custom components. The K&N air filter resides atop the Professional Products 52007 dual-plane Vortec intake manifold. The use of the small-cap MSD distributor with 6AL multi-spark discharge box frees up some space at the back of the engine for the wiring and wiper motor. The inline fuel gauge was placed under the hood to keep fuel out of the cockpit. You should see 3 to 4 pounds of pressure while idling. If the pressure decreases when the throttle is increased, there is a restriction on the supply side of the fuel pump.

ENGINE MODIFICATIONS

The light blue fog around this slightly tired small-block's PCV valve grommet is not too concerning, as engines wear, piston ring blow-by increases. Severely worn engines have a constant puff of very easily seen blue smoke: engine overhaul is necessary at that point.

Remove the spark plugs for the compression and leak-down testing. Be careful with the spark plugs as you remove them. Use a Sharpie to write the cylinder number on the insulator as you remove them. As you proceed with the evaluation, the plugs provide clues to help determine the engine's health. For the best results, the throttle should be held wide open while the engine is turned over five to six full revolutions per cylinder. This maintains testing uniformity.

Place a screwdriver in the throttle linkage so the butterflies are held wide open. This ensures that the throttle position is the same for every bore and that the compression and/or leak-down test is accurate. A black, oily deposit on the spark plugs is an indication that the rings may be worn excessively.

Record the compression readings. Any low cylinder readings on the compression test are confirmed during the leak-down test. You are looking for a balanced compression test with the cylinders within 10 percent of each other.

Use a leak-down tester for the ultimate engine cylinder performance test. Thread the leak-down tester into each cylinder. The gauge on the right side of the tester informs you that this cylinder has 4 percent leakage. New engines are in the 2 to 8 percent leakage range; heavily worn engines are above 15 percent.

The leak-down test also indicates cylinder balance. If there is more than a 10 percent difference in any cylinder, rough engine performance can be expected. If you find that the leakage is severe enough to be audible, check for escaping air out the intake or exhaust. Also look at the radiator filler for possible bubbles in the coolant from a blown head gasket. Be careful when connecting the air supply; if the crankshaft rotates your hand or other body part could possibly be caught in a pinch point.

engine's rotating components' health. With fresh oil, you should see 15 to 30 psi at idle with the pressure rising to a minimum of 50 to 60 at high RPM. On an extremely hot day, oil pressure may run as low as 10 to 15 psi at idle, and that is normal. However, the pressure must rise as RPM increases. Low steady oil pressure in the 25- to 30-psi range at high RPM is a warning. It is a clear indication of worn internal rotating components. Big-block engines have different oil pressure requirements from idle to wide-open throttle (WOT). Your big-block should idle with at least 30 psi; 35 to 40 is preferred for performance-use engines. Once the throttle is opened, you should see a minimum of 60 to 75 psi as you near the engine's redline.

Inspection and Testing

A good procedure to determine engine health begins with a compression test to see if there are any variations in cylinder pressure. Variations in pressure could indicate leaking valves, blown head gaskets, or bent connecting rods. As you proceed to the leak-down test, you can determine if the low pressure is due to internal leakage or short connecting rods. When connecting rods bend, rod length gets shorter; consequently, cylinder volume is added and compression ratio drops. Make a note of the cylinders with lower pressure, as it is imperative to determine which cylinder is out of factory spec.

In some cases, something as simple as incorrect valve adjustment causes the problem. Removing the rocker arms during the leak-down test verifies the misadjusted valves if you record the findings from each test. Your spark plugs also indicate a worn engine if they have black crusty deposits. Black insulators warn you that the engine was running too rich, possibly washing the oil off the cylinders and causing excessive piston ring wear.

Parts Compatibility

Now that your engine's health has been determined, you should consider its reliability factor as parts are chosen. Factory engine rotating components are typically adequate for up to 400 hp. If horsepower rises above 450, it's tough on the bottom end, so don't expect original-equipment rotating components

CHAPTER 1

Engine Evaluation

An old mechanic's tale goes like this: "Now that the valves are sealed up, the compression was raised and the extra pressure hurt the bearings." When a cam and cylinder heads have been installed, yet the engine failed, 99 percent of the time the culprit is dirt and debris. The engine was not properly cleaned, and debris lodged in the oil pump pick-up tube. When you look at the oil pressure gauge all looks well, but the limited oil volume from the debris-choked oil pick-up is starving the main and connecting rod bearings. To ensure positive results for all your hard work, I recommend removing the oil pan for a thorough cleanup after major engine work is performed.

Another excellent reason for pan removal concerns the timing cover. The front oil pan seal is incorporated into the timing cover. Because of this design, the timing cover requires forceful removal. Once the front cover bolts are removed, you pull the cover forward at the top and insert a screwdriver at the cover to the oil pan area to pry the cover out of the oil pan's front seal. Chances are good that the timing cover is damaged from the screwdriver as it forces the cover out of the pan's front seal.

When it's time to re-install the cover, you must modify the corners of the oil pan seal retainer and straighten the areas bent up by the removal process. Once you prep the cover you must force it back into place. After the cover installation you often find an oil leak from the displaced front oil pan seal during the installation process. Removing the oil pan is a win-win situation, making the task easier and preserving the bottom end of your engine after all that hard work. ■

It's relatively easy to remove Shark Corvette oil pans. The idler arm's two 9/16-inch hex-head bolts and nuts can be unbolted from the chassis to provide clearance for pan removal. Once unbolted, the steering linkage drops down enough to remove the pan.

Remove the 1975–1979 Shark's Y-pipe on the exhaust system. Because the bolts and nuts have been heat cycled so many times, use a thread lubricant. If that is not effective, use a propane torch to heat the fasteners. Use a ratchet and socket to remove the nut; use a wrench to hold the head of the bolt.

If you have factory spark plug wire shields that are retained under the rear upper engine mount bolt and rear spark plug shields, they must be removed to gain access to the center pan bolts.

I also find it easier to remove the starter to gain access to the pan bolts that are alongside the starter. After you remove the starter, remove the bellhousing dust cover from manual transmission–equipped Sharks. The automatic transmission–equipped car's torque converter shield must also come out because it goes over the oil pan's rail at the rear, making it difficult to access the rear oil pan bolts.

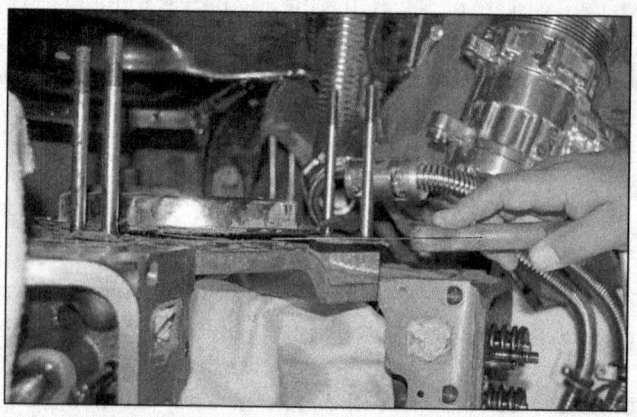

As gasket materials are manually scraped or removed with air-powered devices from the engine's surfaces, a vast amount can end up in the bottom of the oil pan. Care must be taken to limit the amount of debris that enters the oil pan. You must be sure to remove all debris and contaminants from the oil pan. Gasket and sealer remnants can easily clog the oil pump's pick-up tube, which can lead to outright engine failure. This is usually the case after major engine work is performed and the engine fails soon afterward.

ENGINE MODIFICATIONS

If you find gritty debris in the oil pan and on the oil pump pick-up screen, often the main and connecting rod bearings have been damaged even though the oil filter does remove the majority of particles. As the debris builds, the bearings starve for lubrication and begin to fail. At that point it is a great idea to remove a few rod and main bearing caps to examine the bearings for deep scoring into the bearing's copper core layer.

If you find the bearing is more copper than aluminum in color, it is worn excessively. If all looks well, the oil pan and all attaching pieces should be washed in a mineral spirits or water-borne solvent. Make sure to get the underside of any baffles cleaned where debris builds and sticks out of sight. The best cleaning solution is to have your local engine machine shop hot tank dip the pieces for a thorough cleaning.

By the way, that should not be the final cleaning for your parts from the machine shop: a rinse with a good dish detergent is recommended. This may end your plans to hotrod the existing engine but saves you a lot of aggravation down the road.

to live long. As horsepower increases, reliability decreases. Now it's time to make some choices.

Cylinder heads, camshaft, and compression largely determine the final power output of any given engine. At least 95 percent of an engine's power is determined by the Big Three—this has been the rule in the past, and it will hold true in the future.

Essentially, engines are air pumps that perform best when the air entering and exiting the engine occurs as rapidly as possible. Installing high-flow aftermarket cylinder heads while using the factory intake and exhaust manifolds limits the cylinder head's airflow design advantages. Installing a high-flow intake and exhaust with factory cylinder heads also produces minimal power gains. In addition, using the factory camshaft with new aftermarket performance pieces limits power gains as well. It should be evident that you need to select compatible and complementary components because the engine works as a system and the function and operation of one component directly affects another. You need to figure out the best intake manifold, cylinder heads, and camshaft for your application. Changing multiple components is another way to go until you hit something that "works" but that is costly and time consuming. I simply do not have the space to provide all the relevant options and combinations of engine parts for a wide range of C3 powerplants. *How to Build Max-Performance Chevy Small-Blocks on a Budget* by David Vizard and *How to Build Big-Inch Chevy Small-Blocks* by Graham Hansen are two excellent resources. They go into detail on building max-performance and stroker small-block Chevy engines.

Virtual Dyno Testing

You can back up the component manufacturers' recommendations by using testing software, such as Virtual Engine 2000, which has proven to be very accurate. This product lets you input pertinent data, and then a virtual dynamometer pull is performed, showing you what power gain or loss the new component has contributed. The dynamometer software lets you check all the performance engine components you install, including the intake manifold, camshaft, exhaust system, and cylinder heads.

Desktop Dyno Engine Simulation is another virtual resource to ensure the cor-

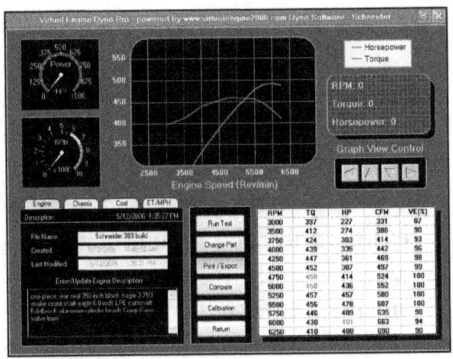

This Virtual Engine Dyno software makes plenty of good sense to avoid extra work and wasting your hard-earned dollars. You can record each parts change and archive the dynamometer run until you find what works best. This really works well and is very close to the actual engine torque and horsepower output.

rect performance parts combination. The same premise applies: input your engine data and test your performance parts choices. One advantage is that the Desktop Dyno software allows nitrous-oxide testing; at the other end of the spectrum fuel mileage can also be determined.

You can start component testing before the first wrench is turned. You need to know some very specific engine information for the most accurate end

CHAPTER 1

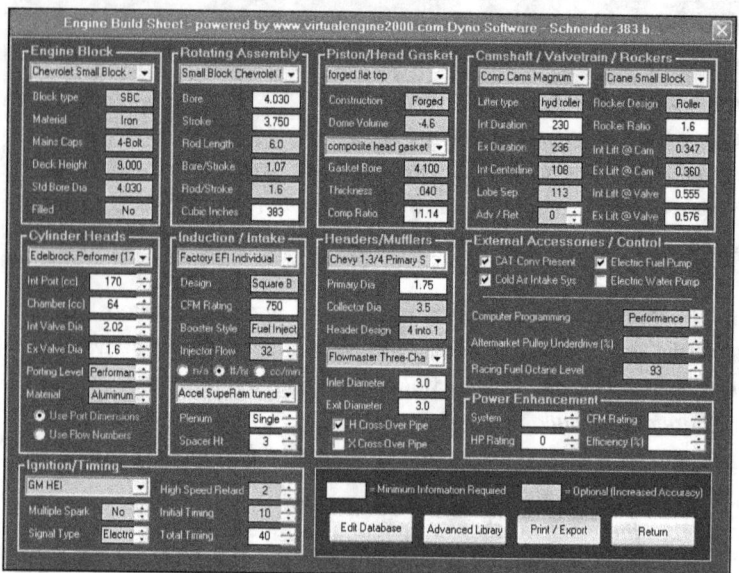

Be sure to input the correct information. You must be extra careful so you have better accuracy on the dynamometer run. Compression means a lot in the final power output numbers, and that is the toughest information to obtain. Valve clearance cut-outs affect piston dome volume, so you need to precisely calculate the clearance spec. Aftermarket piston manufacturers provide precise numbers; stock flat-top GM pistons are -9.2 cc if they have four valve clearance cut-outs.

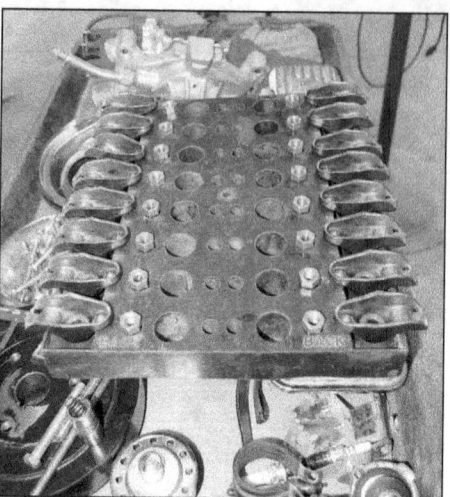

Organization is the key, with an undisturbed area to store the pieces as they are removed. I prefer a mobile cart to set the removed pieces on. Next, I evaluate the pieces to decide whether they require cleaning or replacing. I make it a policy that any piece that will be replaced is removed from the cart when the new one arrives, and only the required pieces for assembly are on the cart. When the job is completed, there should be no pieces left on the cart. If there are, I know that something was left out. The valvetrain tray is a good organizational tool. If you plan to reuse any of the pieces, they should stay in the same location they have worn into.

results. Keep in mind that guessing and inputting incorrect data can result in huge disappointments, or a major surprise with excellent power gains. Engine bore size, stroke, and combustion chamber volume can be found in factory service manuals after verifying your engine's build codes. After you have taken some time to get acquainted with the software, figuring out the correct pieces is easy.

Intake Manifolds

An enthusiast often first installs an aftermarket aluminum intake manifold. Intake manifolds are typically single- or dual-plane design. Single-plane intakes typically have shorter, higher-angled runners (intake tracts) making the power band come in later, allowing higher RPM capabilities. Dual-plane intakes have longer and typically smaller-diameter intake runners, which enhance torque as they prevent reversion of incoming air while restricting high-RPM airflow.

If you want to make good torque at low RPM, dual-plane intakes are the ticket. If high-RPM horsepower is your game, select a single-plane intake manifold.

The tough part of making an intake manifold decision is all the factors to consider. Larger-cubic-inch engines can provide plenty of torque with single-plane intakes, depending on many factors. Engine compression and camshaft selection, for instance, affect the torque output and, more important, when peak torque occurs. The smart plan is to carefully examine the possibilities and heed the manufacturer's recommendations on the combinations that work.

The trick is balancing optimum intake performance with available underhood clearance when using factory hoods. In my experience, Shark owners rarely opt to install an aftermarket hood because they want to retain the factory look. Few single-plane intake manifolds fit under a stock hood. Typically, dual-plane intakes sit much lower in the engine valley and allow the carb to fit under the stock hood. You need to select the entire intake package to clear the stock hood or you need to select an aftermarket hood that's compatible with your intake package. That means the intake manifold, air cleaner, and yes, even the wing nut and air cleaner stud need to fit under the hood.

How to Measure Hood Clearance

Many GM and aftermarket intake manifolds are available. Each Shark is individual as body support cushions wear and hood clearances get tighter. The front-end bodywork often sags over time, which can be seen at the upper fender to door clearances. The gaps widen and the hood becomes closer to the air cleaner. You need to ensure that there is enough clearance between the air cleaner and the hood.

ENGINE MODIFICATIONS

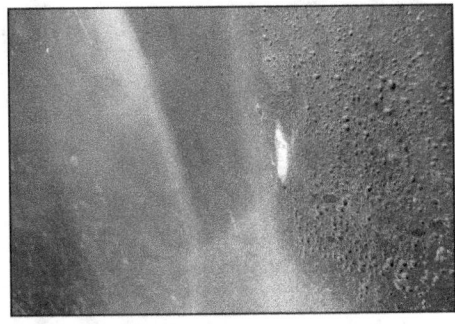

This is the telltale sign that the air cleaner is right there, just slightly touching the hood on deceleration. Remember that the engine does move around, and you need at least 1/2-inch wiggle room to keep the hood from getting chewed up. The center of the hood is raised slightly, so the air cleaner wing nut and stud usually have enough room if the circumference of the air cleaner top cover misses the hood. Never just drop the hood until you know that there is adequate clearance. Lower the hood slowly and then push it down to lock it.

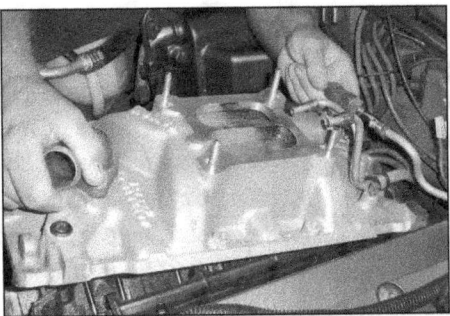

I installed this slightly raised dual-plane intake on Project Shark Attack with a Holley throttle body fuel-injection system. I prefer to use Fel-Pro steel laminate core intake gaskets for easy trimming of the port openings and long-term sealing. Intake manifolds squirm around on the cylinder heads as they heat and cool. In the long term this tears away at composite gaskets. The 383-ci engine had more than 400 ft-lbs of torque and made 403 hp at 5,500 rpm: not too bad for an all-around play toy.

The only way to do that is to measure from the engine block intake manifold sealing surface to the hood. This determines whether there is adequate clearance. Aftermarket intake manifold manufacturers such as Weiand, Edelbrock, and Professional Products have fitment measurements on their websites, including how-to-measure instructions.

Once hood clearance is determined and a manifold is purchased, always check again for clearance before dropping the hood for the first time.

Replacing the Intake

The replacement of an intake manifold on the big- or small-block Chevy engine is one of the easiest mods to perform. Keeping things clean is the key; preparation and then torquing the intake bolts in sequence ensures a tight seal with no oil leaks.

Intake Manifold Installation

1 Match Intake Ports on Cylinder Heads

I am beginning to port- or gasket-match this intake to a set of Patriot cylinder heads. This engine will be run at 6,500 rpm and above often. The port on the right is quite a bit smaller and would be fine for a low-RPM high-torque engine. If you plan on using out-of-the-box cylinder heads, one of the main concerns is to make sure the intake port is smaller than the cylinder head port to avoid airflow disturbance as the intake air and fuel enter the cylinder head. If the cylinder head ports are larger than the intake port, there is no need to do any machining if you plan on keeping the RPM below 5,500. Unless you just have to have matching ports, you don't feel any performance gain.

2 Prep for Gasket Install

I am prepping the cylinder head and engine block end surfaces for gasket installation. As you see, I have stuffed each port with paper towels to keep debris out of the engine. Previously the same blue towels were lying in the valley area to collect debris. If any debris falls into the lifter valley, take some time and remove it to avoid filling the oil pump pick-up tube with junk. I use naphtha, brake cleaner, or alcohol to wipe down all surfaces before placing the gaskets on the engine.

CHAPTER 1

3 | Seal Engine Top End

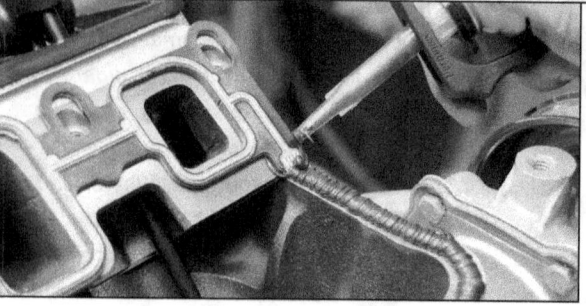

Hot oil-resistant silicone sealer is used at the front and back of the intake manifold for the best sealing.

Before we put the gaskets in place on this Racing Head Service cast-iron Vortec cylinder head, a dab of silicone is placed in the corner of the cylinder head and engine block below the gasket. Then silicone sealer is applied in a 3/16- to 1/4-inch bead ending approximately 1/4 inch up the intake gasket at the corners to prevent oil leakage. Not only does oil leak out, unfiltered air in the engine compartment can be drawn into the engine.

4 | Torque Intake Manifold

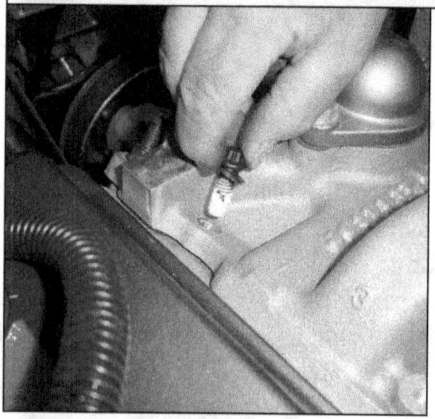

Proper sealing and torquing of the intake manifold are important if you want to avoid intake leaks and prevent distorting or breaking your aluminum intake. This Weiand intake on an early small-block requires bolt sealing to prevent oil from wicking up the bolt threads. I also apply Never-Seez to the outer four bolts to prevent rust or corrosion from forming in the threads if the intake gaskets weep coolant over time.

Torque the intake manifold to the supplier's recommendation, which is 35 to 40 ft-lbs. Take the extra time and read the instructions. Tighten the bolts in sequence and torque the intake bolts to their specs. Tightening sequence is equally important to avoid a cracked or broken intake flange. I use the tightening sequence for a preliminary hand tightening to seat the manifold, then go back and do the final torque. For the most part the tightening sequence starts at the center and works outward, alternating across the intake.

Cylinder Heads

Consider the following when selecting heads. Cast-iron cylinder heads are capable of making plenty of power for many reasons, including excellent thermal efficiency. Aluminum cylinder heads dissipate heat quicker, which drops combustion chamber heat, lowering their thermal efficiency. Cast-iron cylinder heads are much harder to port match and maximize flow with the denser material; because of this, few people use them as performance pieces. Aluminum cylinder heads are lighter weight, and the easy-to-modify intake tracts have made them very popular. Always consider the cylinder head's combustion chamber size and piston configuration that affect your engine's compression ratio. Higher compression ratios make more power and require higher-octane fuels.

Racing Head Service has a couple of cast-iron cylinder head options. The 64-cc combustion chamber yields a 9.90 to 10.10:1 compression ratio, depending on the piston-to-deck height. Pistons can also be purchased with two or four valve reliefs, which affects compression ratio. When your compression ratio approaches 10.0, you must use premium pump gas and pay close attention to ignition timing. I keep total ignition timing at 36 degrees or less to prevent pre-detonation (spark knock).

Small-Block Cylinder Head

Original-equipment GM small-block heads have angled valves relative to the block deck. If you look at the top of the cylinder block, the valves are angled 23 degrees inward at the top toward the intake manifold area. Race-bred small-block cylinder heads have 18-degree valve angles, and the intake ports are not raised as high. This allows a smoother transition for incoming air into the cylinder head. The 18-degree heads require many extra pieces and are impractical when using a stock lower end with a cylinder head/cam change. In this section I only discuss the 23-degree version.

The 1968–1974 OEM Shark small-block (and big-block cylinder heads, by the way) has cast-in valveseats and valveguides. When unleaded fuels were introduced in 1975, valveseat temperatures were elevated, requiring tougher materials to withstand the heat. From 1975 on, General Motors installed replaceable hardened seats in its cylinder heads to handle the unleaded fuels.

If you choose a set of pre-1975 GM cylinder heads for your project, expect to spend extra on machining and installation of hardened seats.

Excessive valveguide wear has been an issue on 1968–1982 GM heads. As the guide wears, it must be machined out and an aftermarket valveguide installed. Knurling is a less expensive alternative machine operation performed to tighten the valve in a worn valveguide. The cost of knurling is considerably less than replacing 16 valveguides. This is a temporary fix at best and not recommended for long-term performance use.

Check with your local machine shop about the cost; in the majority of cases, modifying original cylinder heads comes close to the cost of purchasing a set of aftermarket or GM performance cylinder heads. Your pre-1975 cylinder heads still have the same airflow rates and need a lot of work grinding on cast iron to achieve any dramatic results.

GM's small-block performance aluminum cylinder head with D-shaped exhaust port is in plentiful supply and can be found on 1986 to late-1991 Corvette L-98 engines. General Motors designed the L-98 aluminum cylinder heads for the Tuned Port Induction (TPI) engine that made high torque at low RPM. The Corvette's L-98 engine was breathing hard at 4,500 rpm because of the intake design, so the heads do not flow big numbers at high RPM. L-98 cylinder heads are good for 400 hp with plenty of torque in excess of 400 ft-lbs at or below 5,000 rpm. The L-98 cylinder head is relatively inexpensive and can be readily found at swap meets, so this makes them a deal unless you're after high-RPM horsepower. To make high-RPM horsepower, they require plenty of porting work.

There is also a concern with the L-98 head's limited valve-opening clearances, requiring extra pieces to make them compatible with high-lift camshafts. It makes sense to run the budget numbers before buying a used set of L-98 heads and then prepping them for high RPM with a high-lift camshaft.

General Motors made a really great-flowing OEM cast-iron cylinder head for use on 1996–1999 truck applications. The same Vortec cylinder heads were available from GM Performance Parts (now Chevrolet Performance) as an aftermarket replacement part. The Vortec heads had an improved combustion chamber, promoting better flow with a slight change in spark plug placement for better combustion. The heads are easy to spot because of their intake manifold retention bolt configuration. All Gen I non-Vortec cylinder heads use 12 bolts at a 90-degree angle to retain the intake to the cylinder heads. When the Vortec cylinder heads were introduced in 1996, 8 bolts at a 72-degree angle fastened the intake manifold onto the heads.

As you can imagine, when using GM Vortec heads the intake manifold must be replaced. The Vortec heads flow much better at low valve lift numbers than the late-1986–1991 Corvette L-98s, allowing horsepower to approach 480. General Motors redesigned the Vortec cast-iron head with taller, narrower intake runners and dual-bolt patterns with two port sizes (PN 25534421 for the small port and PN 25534431 for the large port). If you don't mind a little extra weight, the Vortec head saves you a few dollars with airflow numbers approaching CNC-ported aluminum heads.

Big-Block Cylinder Head

GM big-block cylinder heads came in a large number of configurations on the early Shark, including oval-intake port for standard-performance and rectangular intake port for high-performance versions. Open and closed combustion chamber versions were also intermingled among oval- and rectangular-port cylinder heads. Oval-port intake runner volume is less than that of a rectangular port. Oval-port heads produce better low-speed torque output while hindering high-RPM power. Closed-chamber cylinder heads have less combustion chamber volume, which increases the compression ratio. Open-chamber big-block cylinder heads have better airflow characteristics with unobstructed valves.

The GM rectangular big-block cylinder head was offered in various aluminum versions. These special high-performance aluminum cylinder heads made it into limited production on Shark Corvettes with RPO L-89-optioned 427-ci engines. Casting integrity plagued the early big-block aluminum heads, so few were used

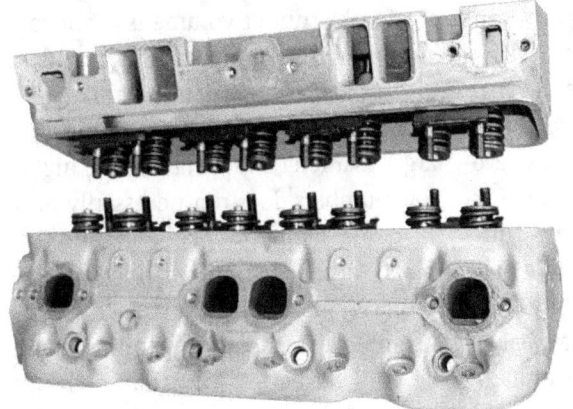

The aluminum L-98 cylinder head found on the 1987–1991 Corvette provides exceptional torque for street performance below 5,500 rpm. These are widely available and reasonably priced. They come with screw-in rocker studs, so they can handle higher revs and help provide accurate valve actuation. Porting does help and the D-shaped exhaust ports help flow. One thing to watch for is valve lift: .500 is the maximum lift for the camshaft, or valvespring retainers begin hitting the valveguides.

CHAPTER 1

This is one of the best values on a healthy engine. These 305-cc intake runner cylinder heads were installed on a 427-ci engine for my 1969 Shark. The 117-cc combustion chamber and factory 435-hp pistons had the compression at 10.0:1. The first dyno test was with a stock set of iron big-block heads and OEM 435 flat-tappet camshaft. I was pleased with the 460 hp at 6,000-rpm pull. The next pull was after changing the stock big-block rectangular heads to these AFR replacements: an astonishing 540 hp at 6,500 was recorded.

in production or sold over the counter. These heads are rare pieces and best suited for high-end restorations.

You should consider buying a set of aftermarket high-performance heads that's suited to your performance package rather than using limited-production Shark cast-iron big-block cylinder heads in a high-performance application. Let someone use the hard-to-find early big-block heads on a numbers-matching restoration.

Aftermarket Cylinder Head

Most aftermarket cylinder heads are aluminum castings. However, cast-iron cylinder head companies, such as Racing Head Service, offer some excellent-flowing iron heads that save you a few bucks. Although cast-iron heads are heavier than aluminum heads, the cost savings may steer you that way. Ultimately, a Shark's front-to-rear weight balance is most important for handling. The majority of us cannot use the available power, and anything that improves handling makes better sense.

In most cases aftermarket cylinder heads have larger valves than stock heads to maximize airflow. They raise the intake port at the manifold area and modify the intake runner volume, maximizing the airflow into the intake valve area. Combustion chamber design is optimized to swirl the incoming air and fuel mixture for the best homogenous flow into the engine's cylinders.

Spark plug placement is also optimized for the best possible flame travel during the fuel's ignition process.

Valveseat science has also grown tremendously, with five-angle seat machining replacing the three-angle seat formation that was used for many years.

Intake runner volume is a hot topic in the high-performance community. As with a small-diameter straw, it takes more effort to draw through it than with a larger-diameter straw. Having the highest flow numbers does not necessarily mean the best overall power combination. Low intake runner volume helps low-RPM torque by increasing the velocity of the incoming air into the cylinder. On the big end, though, it can hurt high-RPM power as a restriction.

Choosing the correct intake runner volume requires camshaft, intake, and vehicle usage info. A correctly set up intake, cylinder head, and camshaft features a single-plane intake for up to 7,000 rpm use, and a long-duration camshaft with 210-cc intake runner volume cylinder heads on a 350- to 383-ci engine. The opposite end of the spectrum is a dual-plane intake for a maximum of 5,500 rpm, and a mild camshaft with 180-cc intake runner cylinder heads maximizing low-RPM torque for 350-ci engines.

A few manufacturers of ready-to-bolt-on performance cylinder heads make your task easier when it comes time to find the maximum horsepower. One of the top performers is Airflow Research (AFR). Great-flowing small- and big-block cylinder heads are what AFR is about, through many years of flow testing and tweaking for the most available power. Patriot Performance cylinder heads are another choice at excellent prices for the performance gain. Edelbrock has a number of options for both big- and small-block engines. They all have good products that provide out-of-the-box performance gains. The smart move is to contact them and see what they have to offer, then use their specifications for a run on your Desktop Dyno or Virtual Engine 2000 software. Don't forget the intake manifold/hood clearance restrictions; that excellent-flowing cylinder head may not work as designed if the intake manifold is prohibiting airflow.

Cylinder Head Installation

The installation of heads typically takes a few days. Cleaning alone can take three to four hours when done properly but time spent cleaning makes the difference in keeping your engine alive for the most possible miles. Cylinder head gaskets affect sealing, compression ratio, and possibly valve-to-piston clearance. You need to pay particular attention to any recommendations the manufacturer provides.

ENGINE MODIFICATIONS

Cylinder Head Installation

1 Prep Block for Head Installation

This original 1969 Shark 350-hp engine had good compression and minimal leak-down, making it a good candidate to replace its original cast-in valveseat heads for a set of new, high-flow cylinder heads. This cleaning step is often missed during the installation phase. Thirty-two of the 34 head bolt threads are subjected to coolant, which prevents a proper tightening. The grit between the threads makes it feel as if you torqued the bolts to 65 ft-lbs, but in reality the threads are tight, not the cylinder heads. A 7/16-14 thread tap is used for the cleanout. Be careful when cleaning the top row of bolts; the tap can bottom out and break.

2 Verify Trueness of Machined Surfaces

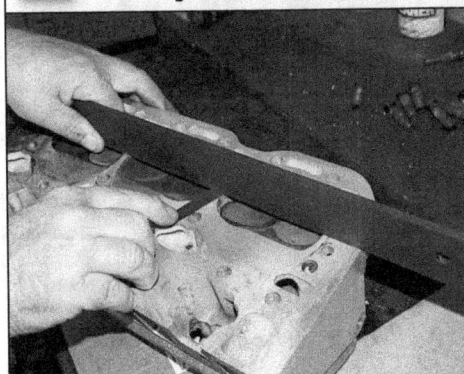

Central Tools provides precision measuring and testing tools such as this straightedge being used to check for cylinder head damage. The first step in checking the cylinder head for any distortion is to clean any carbon and gasket material from the surfaces. I left half of the cylinder head sealing surfaces as they came off the engine to show that there is quite a buildup of material that affects the testing procedure.

The most common areas of distortion are between the cylinders. Place the straightedge lengthwise across the head surface. Insert a feeler gauge between the straightedge and the surface of the head. The .002-inch feeler gauge is being used to see if this cylinder head requires machining. The engine block should also be checked for any discrepancies, or you will pay the price in repeated head gasket failures.

3 Prep Engine Block

Fairly new cotton T-shirt material works well for wiping down the block surfaces before gasket installation. But you need to be sure the rag is lintless, because you don't want the fiber of the rag to get inside the engine and cause damage or potential failure. Coarse rags may leave behind lint on a recently machined cylinder head deck. Here, naphtha or brake cleaner removes any grease or oil left behind from piston installation. Any oil left behind prevents gasket material sealing, creating plenty of extra work when you find that the heads have to come off for another set of gaskets.

4 Install Cylinder Heads

The task seems simple enough: Pick up the cylinder head and set it on the engine block. Aluminum heads make the job easier, but they, like cast-iron cylinder heads, can cut the head gasket or put a serious ding in it that will cause grief later. Try to set the head level and on the alignment pins, moving it around until it seats on the pins. If a sharp edge cuts into the gasket you could be doing this all over again. Combustion leaks can occur: once they do, they can do severe damage to the engine block and/or cylinder heads.

CHAPTER 1

5 Torque Cylinder Heads

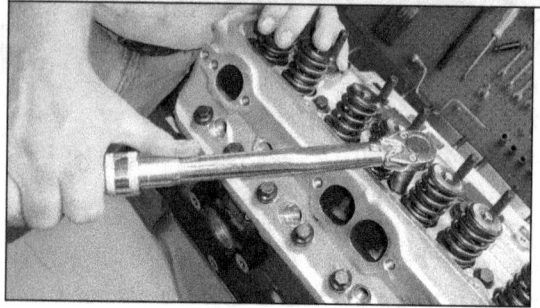

This is serious stuff here, especially if you plan on putting some extra squeeze in the cylinder with nitrous or a supercharger. Torque the cylinder head bolts in sequence starting at 25 ft-lbs for the first pass, then another pass to 50 ft-lbs before tightening them to the cylinder head manufacturer's recommendations. I have used this procedure for many years on supercharged and nitrous-equipped engines without gasket failure. Take the time to go over all the bolts one final time after you have done the final pass, torquing the heads to the manufacturer's recommendations.

Camshaft Selection and Installation

As I mentioned earlier, using virtual dyno testing with computer software gives you information in addition to that from the manufacturer, but now it is time to make the selection.

In my mind, swapping a camshaft is less work than swapping the cylinder heads. Performing both operations at the same time makes plenty of sense because the labor overlaps and these components are interdependent. Again, cleanliness is the best policy, and torquing the fasteners is important.

This is a typical camshaft swap item. Don't forget the camshaft assembly lube, which most camshaft suppliers include.

Camshaft Swap

1 Remove Harmonic Balancer

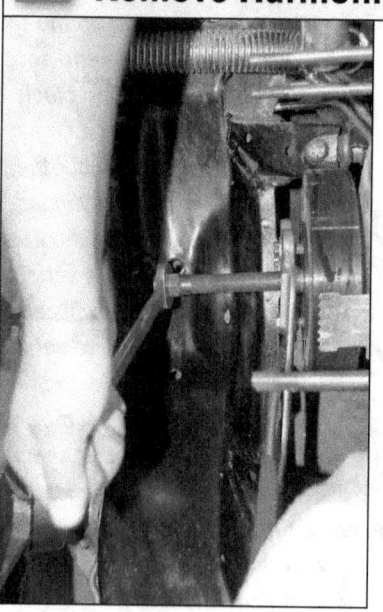

Harmonic balancer removal is the first step in camshaft removal and installation. The Shark's crossmember is in the way, making it difficult to use anything but this long wrench to slowly force the balancer off the crankshaft. To avoid removing the transmission's torque converter cover to hold the crankshaft during balancer removal, use large channel-lock pliers to hold on to the balancer removal tool.

2 Remove Timing Gear

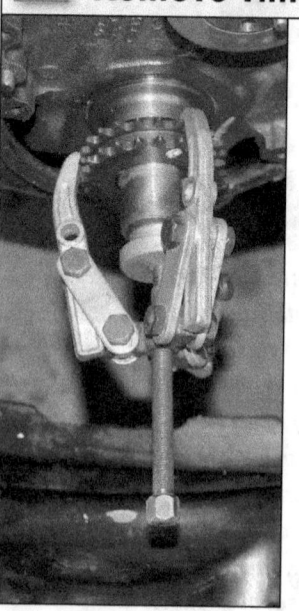

The small- and big-block crankshaft timing gear is pressed on, requiring a puller to remove it. This three-jawed puller does a good job of easing it off. I try to avoid applying heat with the gear in place, as crankshaft main bearing damage can occur. I also use a stop on the end of the crankshaft to avoid damaging the crankshaft balancer's threaded hole during puller use. It is a good idea to change this gear even if the replacement chain and gear match the one in place: wear occurs and slack timing chains alter timing and performance.

ENGINE MODIFICATIONS

3 Remove Valve Lifters

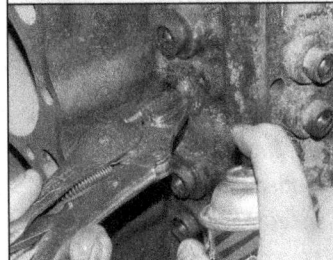

Valve lifters can be very tough to remove from high-mileage engines for two reasons: sludge buildup and mushrooming of the lifter where it rides on the camshaft. My first suggestion is to use carburetor or throttle-body cleaner to soften the oil sludge deposits. Spray the cleaner on the sides of the lifter, then work the lifter up and down to knock off the sludge. This cleaning and working the lifter up and down can take awhile.

If you feel that you need a hammer to get the lifter out, it is time to rethink the plan. Either the lifter is mushroomed on the bottom, or the sludge is so bad the engine will not live much longer even if you clean it up. Lifter bore damage can occur if a mushroomed lifter is forced out of the engine block. In that case you need more machine work than a typical rebuild. Bite the bullet and go through the engine, or get that crate engine you were considering.

4 Install Camshaft

You can use a cam installation tool. Instead, I use this long number-two Phillips screwdriver. When guiding the cam into the cam tunnel, keep the camshaft lobes from cutting into cam bearings as you work the camshaft out and it is seated into the correct position. Slowly move the camshaft to keep the lobes of the camshaft away from bearing surfaces. You can rest the cam on the bearing surfaces to regain a good grip if necessary as the camshaft is removed or installed. The lifters interfere with the cam during installation, so leave them out. The fuel pump needs to be removed to allow the fuel pump pushrod to fall away from the camshaft lobe.

5 Install Camshaft Retainer Plate

This is a 1987 or later small-block with factory roller lifter camshaft. Position the camshaft retainer plate on the block. Squirt some Loctite on the screws and torque them to 20 ft-lbs. Early engines (non-roller lifter) do not require a camshaft retaining component unless a retrofit camshaft is installed. High-performance engine builders use a roller bearing under the camshaft gear and a roller button that rides on the camshaft timing cover to keep the camshaft from moving around at high RPM.

Follow your camshaft manufacturer's recommendations regarding the use of a retaining component on roller lifter camshaft retrofits.

6 Degree the Camshaft

You need to degree the camshaft. High-performance engine builders pay careful attention to camshaft timing on every build, and so should you. This is an effort to extract every possible bit of power out of an engine. The use of computer testing software may have indicated that retarding the camshaft timing added horsepower at the top end where you really want it; degreeing the camshaft is the only sure way to know where the camshaft is sitting.

7 Install Harmonic Balancer

I am a strong believer in this harmonic balancer installation tool as opposed to using a big hammer to pound it in place. Lisle makes an inexpensive version without a bearing under the forcing nut: it works well for someone doing one or two balancer installs per year. Major automotive parts chains also rent them at a reasonable cost, or you can buy one for about $45. Apply a light film of Never-Seez on the balancer's inner hub to aid installation, and make sure to apply lubricant to the front crankshaft seal to avoid burning up the seal at startup.

CHAPTER 1

8 Adjust Valve Lifter

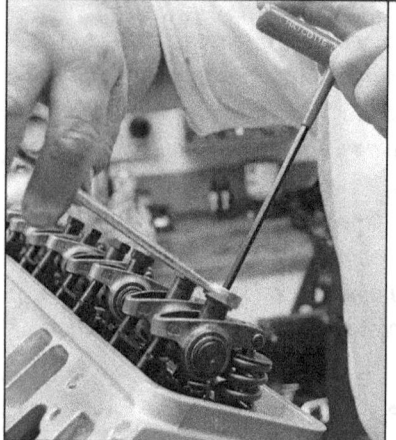

My favorite way to adjust lifters is to do it while the manifold is off. When it's done this way, it is much easier to feel the load on the pushrods as the rocker nuts are tightened down. With each cylinder at top dead cylinder (TDC) on the compression stroke, this can be determined by placing the balancer on TDC for cylinder number-1 to begin with. As you watch the number-1 cylinder's valves during crankshaft rotation, look for the number-1 cylinder's intake valve to open then close. When that intake valve closes, begin watching the balancer. As the TDC mark on the balancer matches the zero on the timing cover tab, you are now at the cylinder number-1 TDC.

Both valves can be adjusted on that cylinder. Rotate the balancer 90 degrees and adjust the next cylinder in the firing order, which would be number-8. Repeat the procedure using the firing order until all the valves are adjusted.

The rocker arm adjusting nuts are tightened until the pushrod just begins to have drag on it while trying to rotate it. Once you feel the slight drag, turn down the nut is an additional 3/4 of a turn to center the lifter. All too often the rocker nuts are left loose to avoid lifter pump up at high RPM. But you cannot leave them loose because they beat up the valvestems and can cause them to fail at high RPM.

9 Seal Oil Pan

I highly recommended one-piece rubber oil pan gaskets to avoid oil leaks. Apply two beads of hot oil-resistant silicone at the front and back of the oil pan to seal up any imperfections at the corners or in the oil pan itself. Once you apply the silicone to the gasket, put the gasket into the proper position as soon as possible. Within 10 to 15 minutes, the silicone provides good bite to the block surface. If the silicone gets too dry, it skins over and does not grip the metal or gasket. Have all the bolts and required tools ready nearby to keep moving once the pan is put into place.

Once you have all the work completed, you need to fill the crankcase with the proper engine oil and set up the engine for tuning. If you choose a flat-tappet hydraulic or solid lifter camshaft, you need to be very careful about what oil you put in the crankcase. Zinc has been phased out of engine oils as of 2007, which requires you to use a zinc additive to prevent cam lobe wear.

Joe Gibbs Driven Break-In Oil and others on the market have ZDDP. This additive can be found in engine oils designated as off-road or race blends. The story is the Feds want catalytic converters to last 100,000-plus miles, and the zinc was contaminating them. Engine oil manufacturers, such as Brad Penn, have multiple viscosities available with the proper zinc blended into each quart for long camshaft lobe life.

Kirban Motorsports has ZDDP in 4-ounce bottles to add to your favorite motor oil. Synthetic motor oils for late-model engines do not have zinc and do not protect your camshaft; you must use the zinc supplement. The best policy is to check the contents of the oil before you drop it in the engine; no zinc, no go.

Ignition timing should be checked as soon as the engine fires up. Connect your timing light and set the base timing to 8 to 10 degrees. If possible, use a timing light that allows you to check the ignition timing advance. If the ignition timing is retarded, high exhaust heat occurs. This can damage valves and also blister the ceramic coating off of a nice set of shiny headers. The timing should be checked to make sure it advances as the RPM rises. If so, lock the distributor down and let the engine reach operating temperature.

CHAPTER 2

CRATE ENGINE OR LS ENGINE?

Crate engines are typically the most cost-effective way to add horsepower with minimal labor. The same goes for transplanting an LS-series engine into your Shark, and you could conceivably save a few bucks buying in bulk, so to speak. You have many crate engine options, including Chevy small-block and big-block. The current crop of LS engines is widely regarded as the best small-block pushrod V-8 engine platform currently available.

Crate Engines

When someone says he or she is looking for a crate engine, the term covers a broad spectrum. To begin with, the simplest form of crate engine is the "short-block," which consists of the engine block, rotating crankshaft, and piston assembly. Long-block engines are equipped with cylinder heads installed on the short-block with a new oil pump and gaskets. In addition, you can buy "dressed" long-blocks that have an oil pan, timing cover, intake manifold, water pump, and sometimes an ignition distributor. Fully dressed engines are available with all of the aforementioned pieces, including a carburetor and plug wires. Due to the Shark's hood and engine compartment restrictions, few fully dressed crate engines are ready to drop in, unless it's a special order, if that is even possible.

True crate engine suppliers have few options available, to keep costs in line. When custom components are added, production slows, adding cost to the unit. Chevrolet Performance (formerly GMPP, General Motors Performance Parts) has a limited number of crate engines that simply and easily install into a Shark. Each crate engine has been specifically built to GM's standards and dyno-tested to ensure uniformity. You can go for a mild 290-hp version, or go to the opposite extreme with the ultimate 700-plus-hp big-block engine. The majority of short- and long-block crate engines work with the Shark or Corvette C3 applications. The fully dressed engines work, but some of the parts, such as oil pans, may need to be replaced in order to fit in the chassis.

I have installed many of the very popular Chevrolet Performance ZZ4 350-ci replacement engines in C3s. These engines pump out 355 hp with 405 ft-lbs of torque. The assembly comes with an intake manifold, water pump, oil pan, and HEI distributor. The pre-1974 Sharks, however, cannot use the supplied HEI distributor because it doesn't have mechanical tachometer drive capabilities. The 1975–1980 Sharks can benefit from the fresh HEI distributor, though, as it is a direct replacement for the factory distributor.

In addition, the long-style water pump is not compatible with any Sharks. General Motors used short water pumps

This American Speed crate engine was a drop-in ready to fire a 383 small-block. The 1979 Shark's owner had the engine configured per his requirements: plenty of torque with regular gasoline. The dynamometer tested 383, had 401 hp, and 450 ft-lbs of torque. Hooker Super Competition headers were used to make sure all the available horsepower could be utilized.

CHAPTER 2

and the accompanying accessory brackets on all Sharks.

The intake manifold may have hood clearance issues on 1968–1972 Sharks.

The oil pan with the ZZ4 assembly fits in the frame but sits lower due to the deeper sump. I replace the supplied oil pan with a later 1987–1991 Corvette oil pan to gain ground clearance.

If a ZZ4-350 is in your future, reselling the pieces may help offset the cost of the crate engine a bit.

Big-block engines always make a statement. The Chevrolet Performance engine lineup offers everything from mild to "tighten your seat belts and hang on!" One of my favorite big-block crate purchases is the ZZ502 Base Kit (PN 12371204). It's a build-it-yourself kit with an assembled rotating assembly (short-block). The oval-port cylinder heads provide the engineered components you need to deliver 502 hp. The rotating assembly comes with a forged-steel crankshaft, aluminum pistons, hydraulic roller camshaft, and oil pan. You have to bolt on the supplied cylinder heads and add the required pieces to make it Shark friendly. The beauty is that all the supplied components work in the Shark chassis, and you get to be a part of the engine build.

Remember to factor into your budget all the ancillary items, such as motor mounts and flywheel or flexplate. I cannot stress enough how important it is that the ancillary items be replaced. Too often crate engines are installed with worn-out carburetors and distributors in place. This causes so many problems because the engine does not run correctly. Many projects end up being sold for this very reason; the engine never runs as intended or the vehicle leaves the owner on the side of the road one too many times.

Crate Sources

All of the following companies have many years of engine building experience, making them worthy of consideration as the time comes near to pull the trigger. Always make sure the engine builder is aware of any power adders that you may be considering. They will adjust compression ratios and most likely recommend tougher rotating components to withstand the added stress. Not mentioning that you may be installing power-enhancing components such as nitrous, supercharging, or turbocharging can be disastrous, and result in a huge hole in the side of the engine block and some important pieces hanging out. If any warranty is still in effect when the big bang occurs, chances are that it will not be honored.

Edelbrock offers a two-year warranty with unlimited mileage. Chevrolet Performance and American Speed cover complete engines for two years or 24,000 miles. The advantages to using the crate engine are all the new pieces used in the construction of the assembly and a warranty to provide a secure feeling knowing that a company is standing behind the product. Most performance-engine warranties are abbreviated versions of a standard engine warranty due to "performance use." It's good to know Chevrolet Performance, Edelbrock, and American Speed stand behind their products.

Chevrolet Performance

Stroking a small-block Chevrolet has become very popular. Chevrolet has stepped up with numerous 383-ci crate engines. More cubic inches mean more torque from the long connecting rods in small-engine-block architecture. This equates to less weight under the hood and power that rivals a big-block, so your Shark handles much better. Chevrolet Performance's ultimate 383 is the ZZ383/425 that features a 4340 induction-hardened forged crankshaft, heavy-duty powdered-metal connecting rods, fast-burn cylinder heads with 2.00/1.55-inch valve diameters, and hydraulic roller lifter camshaft. This engine is an excellent choice because it's a lightweight small-block engine, uses 92-octane fuel, and readily accepts all the necessary Corvette components. It produces 449 ft-lbs of torque, which provides plenty of grunt when coming out of a corner. As with the ZZ4 small-block, the oil pan should be changed and the long-style water pump not used.

Edelbrock

Edelbrock has a crate engine program similar to Chevrolet Performance, building specific dynamometer-proven engines. Their program has ascending performance levels, starting with a non-advertised horsepower or torque output E-Street 350-ci long-block.

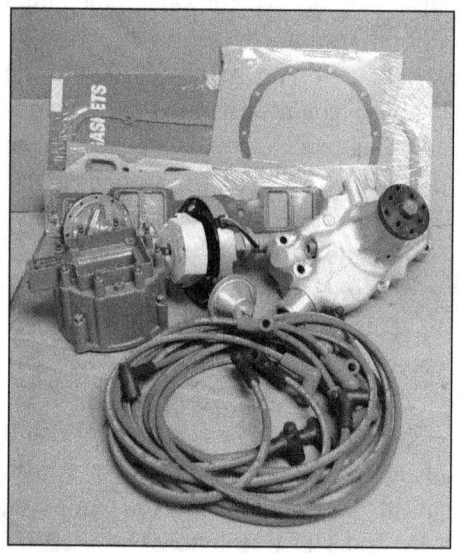

These components are as important as the engine itself. Leaving them off your parts list can lead to frustration and added expense. All too often excessively worn engine support pieces are installed on a fresh engine, causing it to run poorly. Parts such as these can be found for sale at some very good cost savings because the owner did not install them, or installed them incorrectly.

CRATE ENGINE OR LS ENGINE?

The next step up uses the E-Street 350-ci long-block with their intake manifold and carburetor having an advertised horsepower rating of 315 with 381 ft-lbs of torque. This Edelbrock E-Street crate engine (PN 45080) is a drop-in for any Shark; the intake manifold clearance is not an issue, and it comes with a Performer series carburetor. The supplied MSD distributor works with 1975 and later Sharks because they do not require a mechanical tachometer drive. Edelbrock also offers multiple configurations of 383-ci crate engines, so be very careful of intake manifold dimensions or a raised hood may be required.

Edelbrock big-block crate engines are high-output units starting with 676 hp for the carbureted version and 697 hp for the EFI version. The 10 available big-blocks are 555-ci Dart iron blocks, with a healthy Scat forged-steel crankshaft as a base with Edelbrock cylinder heads. These engines require hood or engine placement modifications to fit into any Shark. Available crate engine oil pans and other ancillary components may not work in the Shark chassis. Some of the available Edelbrock crate engines use Chevrolet Performance ZZ4 short-blocks with Edelbrock cylinder heads; it's just a matter of preference.

American Speed

American Speed builds crate engines with an individualized approach, asking what your goals are, and then recommends a base engine that can be modified to fit your application. Using a single source for the info may be a better fit for the first-time performance builder to keep the project on track and goals met. This is the absolute quickest, simplest way to achieve your goals with minimal labor. Depending on your working environment this may be the way to go; building engines in the driveway is tough, and the results are usually less than mediocre.

LS Engines

Chevrolet reinvented the small-block with the LS series of engines. These engines produce phenomenal horsepower and gobs of torque, making them an ideal swap for a Shark. An LS engine fits nicely in the Shark's engine bay without major body and/or chassis modifications.

LS1 engines were introduced in 1997, placing them with the fifth-generation Corvette. The Camaro and Firebird received them for the 1998 model year.

The first-design 345-hp LS1 engine received an update in 2005, increasing the cubic inches to 346; it was designated LS2. At 400 hp and 400 ft-lbs of torque, the LS2 is one potent factory engine for any performance Shark.

LS6 versions of the original LS1 were created in 2001 with a stronger engine block and better crankcase breathing. LS6 cylinder heads were designed with better flow and sodium-filled valves for high-RPM use. LS6 intake manifolds were redesigned LS1 pieces for better flow. Other internal engine improvements were made to increase the original LS6's horsepower to 385; in 2002 405 hp was achieved.

LS2s were then trumped by LS7s with 427 ci for 2006 ZO6 Corvettes. LS7 internals are good for long life at high RPM with forged steel crankshafts and titanium forged connecting rods.

Even the lowly 1997 LS1 has plenty of power, making it an excellent transplant in a Shark. And the fuel economy is astounding.

New or Used?

The LS engine has been installed on GM vehicles for more than 15 years, and millions of these engines have been built. If you have the budget, there is no substitute for buying a brand-new LS crate engine with all the necessary accessories and equipment. The majority of Chevrolet Performance engines available are ready to drop in, with oil pan, intake manifold, valve covers, and most electronics.

Edelbrock is another source for drop-in 416-ci LS engines with an E-force supercharger pumping out more than 700 hp. It's a complex install, because you need to install and route all the plumbing and equipment for the intercooler. This is beyond some first-time installers' mechanical ability. The cost of the installation is not for everyone, either.

A new LS crate engine is the safest bet and also the most costly. Don't forget that you will be buying many individual pieces to install with your crate engine. The cost of these parts can quickly add up. Another alternative is buying the used engine and then modifying it with the right camshaft, cylinder heads, and intakes.

Here's a tip: before you install the engine, hang it on an engine stand and change the camshaft and intake for some serious power gains. Get crazy and change the cylinder heads for the ultimate power gain and then put it in the engine bay.

Your other option is to buy a salvage-yard engine from a reputable supplier. A complete engine that includes the wiring harness and drive-by-wire pedal and all peripheral equipment is called a "take-out." Most have been run-tested and some companies offer a money-back guarantee if the engine exhibits any problems within a 30-day time period.

With that being said, keep in mind that many used engines are pulled from wrecked vehicles. Aluminum engine blocks (or cases, as General Motors calls them) do not always hold up well in crashes and may have sustained serious damage. I have seen broken areas on LS engines at the bellhousing, especially around the starter. LS engines subjected

CHAPTER 2

Oil Pan Considerations

You need to determine oil pan depth and acceptable ground clearance before installing a crate engine in the chassis. Most crate engines come with an oil pan that hangs too low to the ground and could become damaged or destroyed on common public roads. The oil pan on most crate engines will likely fit in the chassis and come very close to the steering linkage and usually 2 inches lower than the original Shark's engine oil pan.

Ground Clearance

General Motors installed oil pans with adequate ground clearance until 1975. In that year, catalytic converters came on the scene and exhaust Y-pipes were required at the engine side. The company installed general small-block oil pans, so the C3 oil pans were no longer Corvette-only deeper-sump oil pans. Possibly the thought was there is a Y-pipe protecting the oil pan from a frontal hit, so why worry?

Corvettes sit low for the best possible center of gravity while still traversing a wide range of roadways. In addition, many C3s are lowered, so you need to use the oil pan that keeps it at the same height as the front crossmember. The idea here is that the bottom of the oil pan should sit no lower than the front crossmember. If a collision with the road surface occurs, the front crossmember takes the beating, not the oil pan.

Your Corvette's ride height is determined by a couple of factors. Number one is the front spoiler or ground effects that use a lowered splitter for frontal down force. The limiting factor is passing over speed bumps or driveway rises without breaking the front nose pieces. With that being understood, clearance from the front crossmember to the pavement ends up being a minimum 3 to 4 inches away. Of course you can go lower, but any road variation can cause the frame to scrape, especially when the suspension is oscillating over a rough road. Big-block engine oil pans need all the room they can get to keep from scraping the pavement. General Motors does not offer many options for the big-block pans. For that matter, aftermarket pans also have limited shallow-sump oil pan selections.

Main Seal Type

The small-block engine has a couple of requirements for ordering the correct oil pan. You need to determine whether your engine has a one- or two-piece rear main seal. In 1975 the front oil pan–to–timing cover seal was changed to a thicker rubber strip that has remained the same for all small-block engines. In addition, in 1980 General Motors moved the dipstick from the driver's side of the engine to the passenger's side.

Oil Starvation

Oil slosh and oil starvation from high-speed cornering is another consideration. Under high-speed cornering, oil is forced up and away from the oil pump pick-up tube. If your engine does not have adequate oil supply when it needs it, serious engine damage is the result.

An oil pan may not seem like a performance item. In reality, it is a key component for keeping your performance engine alive. Corvette Central has the correct-depth oil pan sump for early Shark engines with original baffles to keep oil splash off the crankshaft. This is an important component for C3s that are driven aggressively, because this pan provides adequate ground clearance to keep you from bottoming out the pan and damaging some important internal pieces.

CRATE ENGINE OR LS ENGINE?

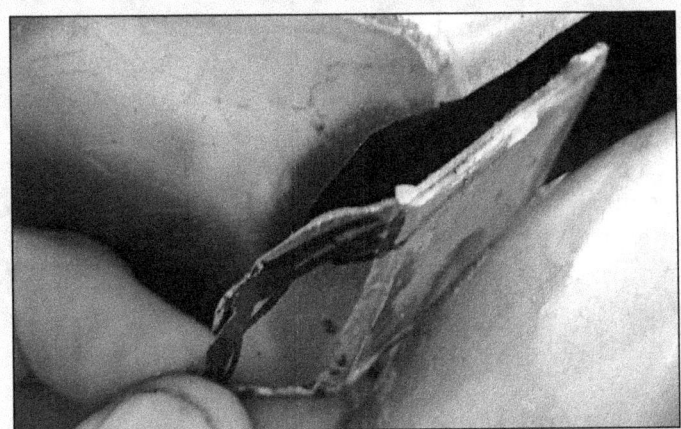

I found one clearance issue with Hooker headers (PN 2134) and the Canton small-block oil pan. One tube of the passenger-side header hits the pan, requiring pan or tube modifications. You can hammer this header tube so the oil pan clears it, but you do not want to damage the tube. In addition, I did not like the idea of the hot header tube resting on or coming within in thousandths of an inch of the oil pan, so I removed a section of the pan and welded a piece in with an inward radius. I suggest checking the header fit before installing the engine if you are going to use any aftermarket oil pan.

Foaming also occurs as the oil interrupts the spinning crankshaft, creating more problems with oil-starved main and connecting rod bearings.

Investing in the correct oil pan for your application is critical. If you don't select a compatible oil pan with adequate ground clearance for the application, you are risking catastrophic engine failure.

Racing Types

Most road or drag race oil pans offer additional oil handling capacity, providing longer engine life under harsh conditions. First, increasing oil capacity lowers the oil's overall temperature; in turn, this keeps the oil viscosity higher while keeping the main and connecting rod bearings cooler with less chance of bearing wear. Second is the handling part of the equation. It is important to keep the liquid in control during high-g-force launches or cornering. Drag-racing oil pans use baffles to keep the oil from rising into the path of the crankshaft with deeper sump pans. I know this contradicts my earlier statement that the oil pan should be no lower than the front crossmember, but in the drag racing world this does not matter because serious drag cars are not street driven.

Road race oil pans have compartments on each side of the pan to increase oil capacity, with doors to control oil rise depending on the particular cornering requirement.

Canton offers the ultimate wet sump oil pan for your road-race or high-performance small-block for the C3. This 8-quart pan for early and late small-blocks with multiple ports available for temperature senders and supercharger oil return lines if necessary. The windage trays and baffles keep the oil around the sump where it needs to be during high-RPM cornering. You can use your old-school AC Delco starter if you prefer: it does get tight, though, and an aftermarket gear reduction starter is recommended.

In addition Canton is the only company that makes an ultra-clearance oil pan for the big-block and the Corvette racing community. This big-block pan allows the most road clearance while retaining 8 quarts of much-needed engine oil for high-speed cornering or hard launches. Think of this as an investment: one piece of road debris could destroy your engine with the oil sump sitting below the Shark's front crossmember.

Oval track oil pans, on the other hand, control oil rise for left-hand turns. It is very important to use the oil pan for your particular application, or oil starvation can result.

Additionally, many performance oil pans require or recommend baffles that are held in place with main bearing studs to seal off the pan from the crankshaft area. You do not absolutely have to change the oil pan but it makes good fiscal and mechanical sense to use the proper oil pan on your new crate engine. ∎

to corrosive atmospheres (salty roads, for example) can make it very difficult to remove the starter. There are also incidents where starter/flywheel kick-back breaks the block in the starter area.

Look over the engine carefully; many used parts suppliers do not work with you concerning engines with broken cases after you have had the engine for a few weeks or longer.

When pursuing a used take-out engine, purchase the complete engine package, sensors, harness, and Powertrain Control Module (PCM) to avoid incompatibility issues. As the LS engine has evolved, General Motors updated and changed the engine management systems, using different crankshaft position sensors. The major changes were the Gen III engine built from 1997 to 2003 that featured a crankshaft reluctor with 24 teeth and the Gen IV engine released in 2004 with a 58-tooth reluctor wheel. These later reluctors are not compatible with one another and as a result, the 1997–2003 PCM is not compatible with a 2004 and later engine. Each generation requires matching pieces for the entire package to operate.

There have been many other differences as LS engines have evolved.

A good source of further information is *How to Build Performance LS1/LS6 V-8 Engines* by Will Handzel. If you plan to buy used assemblies from various suppliers or assembling them piecemeal, you need to read up on the changes that have occurred for compatibility and obtaining maximum performance.

Interchange Notes

An LS engine swap is not terribly difficult to perform. Often one of the most challenging parts of the install is integrating the electronics and wiring into the chassis. In addition, the fuel system requires an electric pump and possibly a fuel return line to make things work.

The LS engine architecture changes require specific components to mate to Gen I small- or big-block drivetrain components and secure the engine into the chassis. Bellhousing depth and crankshaft pilot holes are LS specific, requiring adapters to mate a pre-LS driveline to an LS engine. Engine mount configuration also requires adapter plates to use the original Shark engine mounts. Engine accessory brackets are another area that requires some thought.

Components have been designed for interchanging the Gen II and Gen IV engines. Lingenfelter Performance, for example, has a module that allows the use of the 24- or 58-tooth crankshaft reluctor with any GM operating system. However, it makes more sense to buy the complete package unless you are well versed in the operating systems. If you adapt one system to another, this requires extensive wiring changes that most people are not capable of doing. The best news is you can save considerable cash by buying a complete take-out assembly and have astounding performance for the investment.

Like the Gen III and Gen IV LS engine, 4L60E automatic transmission internal sensors and electronics have evolved. The 4L60E or electronically controlled auto transmission was introduced in 1992 for use in the Camaro and pickup trucks behind a Gen I or II engine with a removable bellhousing. The next major change came in 1997 when the 4L60E was placed behind the LS engine along with major electronic control changes, preventing the use of the earlier PCM for engine and transmission control. By late 2004 the 4L60E had a reluctor placed on the transmission's input shaft to measure internal transmission slip speed.

This is why it is very important to use a complete engine and automatic transmission assembly with the accompanying PCM to make the swap as easy as possible. If you find a deal on separate components, it takes a lot of homework to make sure each component is compatible with the PCM. The best plan here is to take the assembly and serial number from the transmission and engine to the local Chevy dealer parts department and ask if they can decode it for you.

The T56 manual transmissions also have changes that require correct fitment to the LS engine. It comes down to whether the T56 was installed on an early engine or on an LS engine. Early T56s have a longer input shaft than the LS versions. There are no changes in the electronics in early- to late-T56 transmissions. A couple of different clutch configurations were used (pull or push style), and to make it interesting the pre-LS flywheels were dampened, eliminating clutch disc springs. This can become particularly challenging if you find a perceived deal with a bunch of engine and transmission pieces in multiple boxes and try to decipher whether they will work.

This is why I highly recommend that you purchase the whole package (engine, transmission, complete harness, and PCM) from the same vehicle. You can then verify that all these major

This GM LS6 crate engine is a perfect fit in this 1981 Shark. The engine comes with a drive-by-wire throttle body and for the most part is ready to run. General Motors installed a fifth-generation Corvette oil pan that must be changed to fit the Shark chassis. The fuel system does not require a fuel rail return line connection to make the install easier in the old-school chassis.

components are compatible with one another and you won't have to modify and customize them to work together.

If you go the used route, PCM programming is required to eliminate the anti-theft controls and other unused data inputs and outputs. For instance, if you decide to install an LS while retaining your original Muncie 4-speed or Turbo 400, the PCM programming is modified for the early transmission. On the engine side of the programming, there is no need for the secondary oxygen sensors to monitor the catalytic converters and they are programmed out. Each application requires specific modifications and also requires custom programming from someone well versed in the swap and the PCMs operation.

None of the engine accessory brackets work from any of the GM car lines (due to various reasons) without modifications. If you find an engine without any accessory brackets, the cost may be deducted from the sale depending on the seller, plus it gives you a wider range of prospective engines. Although your engine supplier may say the brackets are not negotiable, they are valuable and can be sold separately if necessary. Do not leave them behind.

LS1 Install

A buddy of mine did one of the first LS Shark transplants I know of in his garage at home. An Internet search found a reputable salvage dealer who had a 38,000-mile LS take-out from an F-Body (Camaro/Firebird). Charlie purchased the complete assembly engine, transmission, wire harness, and PCM destined for his 1973 convertible Shark. One very good reason to choose the F-Body LS engine is the oil pan assembly fits into the Shark chassis as is. (The C5 Corvette version has wings on the lower oil pan section, requiring an F-Body-style replacement.)

Charlie has owned this 1973 Shark for several years and has made a number of driveline changes, including a tuned port engine swap early on. While the engine was being fitted into the engine compartment, the wire harness and PCM were sent to Speartech for the necessary changes, making it a plug-and-play harness swap. The PCM was modified, eliminating the anti-theft and other serial data lines that were no longer used. The real beauty of the swap was that the 4L65E's electronic-shifted overdrive transmission was part of the original complete take-out. This procedure eliminated the concern over what depth bellhousing and crankshaft pilot was required. Additionally, all the original harness connections and shift calibrations could be used.

Often, the most difficult phases of almost any project are the wiring, accessory drive, plumbing, and exhaust system requirements. Any electrical wiring project usually has most of us ready to say "uncle" no matter how simple it is. If you've spent some time wiring a previous car and are familiar with electronics, you may be able to perform the modification of the wiring harness yourself. On the other hand, if you're not that skilled in automotive wiring, you should have an expert in the field modify the harness for you and then you can install it. After the harness and PCM have been modified, you need to install the connectors in the correct sensors.

The PCM requires a 12-volt battery and a couple of 12-volt ignition supply wires. As the harness manufacturer recommends, the ground circuits of the PCM should be carefully installed on the engine or chassis. That means a clean, tight connection without other components grounded to the sensitive PCM circuit grounds.

Connection of the ancillary components should be discussed with the harness modifier so the proper wires can be identified and tagged for simple connection once you receive the harness. There are various inputs to the PCM concerning the A/C clutch for proper idle control and cooling fan relay(s) if you decide to use an electric cooling fan. Cruise control input (vehicle speed sensor) wiring is also part of the PCM harness that should be discussed whether you are using a new cruise or original system. It comes down to putting together a comprehensive plan to make your task easier. The harness modification time is the same no matter how many wires you require to be identified, within reason.

Wiring

You need to route the wiring away from hot surfaces and sharp edges that can damage the harness insulation coating. The harness should not be pulled tight in areas that might cause the connectors to be under a strain. If the wiring harness is under stress, this leads to premature failure and electrical problems. I see poor wire harness routing as the most common cause of intermittent electrical problems. Also check the original forward lamp harness for adequate alternator wiring. Most 1968–1979 Sharks had 30- and 65-amp alternators with puny 12-gauge alternator output wiring.

Determining a particular-year Shark's alternator output is impossible. The alternator has most likely been rebuilt numerous times and, if the owner requested, upgraded to a higher amp output. This makes it even more important that the wiring is adequate for the alternator's output.

An electrical specialty shop can determine the output if you want to use the existing alternator. I always upgrade that to a minimum 8-gauge wire, depending on the owner's other electrical upgrades. Integrating the cooling fan power supply into the original forward lamp harness is

CHAPTER 2

Wiring modifications are important for the best performance of your engine and electrical system. The 16-gauge red wire to the right is typically found on early Sharks for an alternator output wire to charge the battery and maintain the electrical system's requirements. The center 8-gauge red wire replaces the 16-gauge wire, using a much better crimp with heat shrink to reinforce the terminal connection.

Depending on what year Shark you are working with, the alternator supply wire may go to a connector near the bulkhead connector and then connect to the starter as in the early cars, or go directly to the starter, which is preferred. The black wire is a ground wire and must be connected directly to the alternator for the best possible charging-system performance.

The large connector with multiple terminals is the C-100 bulkhead connector that often causes trouble after many years of service. When doing any performance work, check this bulkhead electrical connector for corroded or burned terminals. In many cases the harness should be replaced due to corrosion or high heat from poor connections.

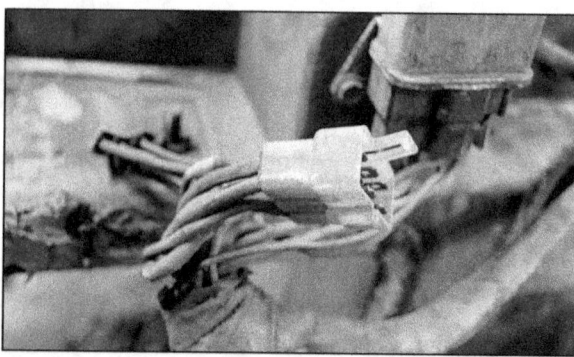

Starting with late-1977 Shark Corvette production, General Motors used a starter extension harness to make engine installation even easier. This six-terminal white-bodied connector connected all the high-amperage wires that ran to the starter in an easy-to-access location near the high blower relay. This connection fails on the majority of Sharks due to poor-fitting terminals: in many cases it melts down completely. The Shark's entire electrical load goes through this connector, and the best policy is to eliminate it. I generally cut the connector off and solder the wires together for a permanent connection.

You can save a few bucks if you find an LS take-out engine from a 1998–2002 Camaro or Firebird. The alternator and brackets work in the Shark chassis without modification. One thing to consider is rebuilding or replacing the alternator. If you choose this setup, changing the alternator on the side of the road would not be good. It must come out the front: the lower control arm prevents it from dropping down and out.

a good idea while you are upgrading the alternator wiring (see Chapter 6).

Accessory Drive

General Motors placed all the accessory components in an alternate position on the 1998–2002 LS-equipped F-Bodies compared to the original Shark pieces, making that the obstacle to overcome. The 1997–2004 Corvette LS engines have the alternator and power steering pump in the same position as the Shark, although the A/C compressor is mounted low on the passenger's side and does not clear the Shark's chassis crossmember. Of course, the crossmember can be modified for the low-mount compressor to save a few bucks; this is where smart money dictates using an aftermarket bracket. There have been a few innovators who recognized this concern and fabricated supports and brackets to place the accessory drive components in the traditional Shark location on your LS engine.

KWiK Performance has a well-engineered kit that uses GM accessory components. I installed their LS accessory component pieces on a Corvette I built for the One Lap of America race in 2012. The earlier system on the LS engine had struts to adjust belt tension with all kinds of pieces bolted together and poor

CRATE ENGINE OR LS ENGINE?

Simple, flat-steel conversion plates from Speedway Motors (PN 91618016) were used to mount the LS Engine. These place the engine in the same position as the original small-block. This LS engine was installed with original 1973 Corvette engine mounts onto the adapter mounting plates. The rearmost LS engine bolts were used for the adapter plates onto the engine. I suggest using interlocking or urethane mounts that cannot come apart. Remember that these conversion plates use metric bolts. It is also a good idea to clearance the conversion plates to allow removal of the large Allen-head coolant drain plug for future engine servicing.

Note the factory-installed Firebird/Camaro oil pan on this used LS take-out engine. This oil pan came on the engine and works in all Shark chassis. The 1997-and-up Corvette oil pans do not fit because of their side wings, which allow slightly higher oil capacity. Pace Performance has an all-in-one package (PN PAC-8771) that includes an oil pan (PN 12628771) and the attaching parts to convert any LS1, LS2, LS3 LS6, L92, and most truck engines to fit in the Shark chassis. The $309 kit saves the hassle of finding a junkyard assembly. Most salvage yards do not sell an oil pan from a running engine to be destroyed; many times the pan has been damaged.

pulley alignment. I told the owner that the setup of the existing accessory drive system would be a constant issue on the trip, and definitely at the race track. He said that was funny because the belt had already come off and he installed a second one.

The One Lap of America race is a true test of endurance. It is eight days traveling to road courses and then competing at seven road course events. The entry held together and showed no sign of abnormal belt wear over the entire event.

Plumbing

Connecting the power steering and air-conditioning compressor hoses takes some plumbing knowledge and some patience to properly install. A couple of the most common problems here are not supporting the tubing or hoses properly and/or incorrect hose use. Power steering and A/C systems require specific hoses and fittings to handle the high pressure and heat associated with each system. Check the items you are using carefully for compatibility.

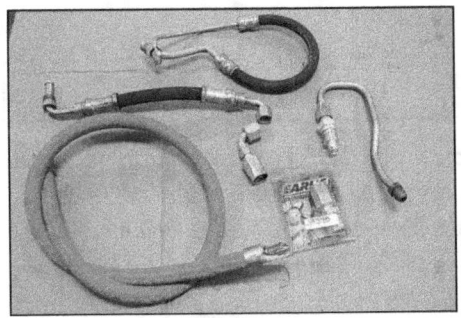

If you install a Borgeson integral power steering box or decide to use a different power steering pump hose, the connection is critical. The hose at the top is a replacement factory-style hose for the 1968–1979 Shark. The hose to the left is a custom hose assembly from NAPA and is a good alternative for a quick, easy fix to a modified power steering pressure hose.

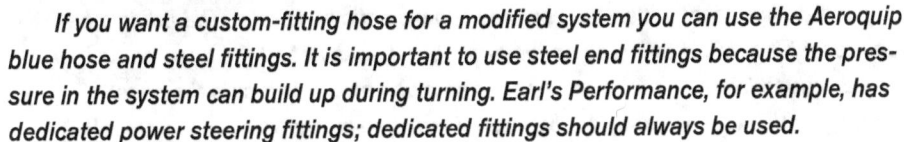

If you want a custom-fitting hose for a modified system you can use the Aeroquip blue hose and steel fittings. It is important to use steel end fittings because the pressure in the system can build up during turning. Earl's Performance, for example, has dedicated power steering fittings; dedicated fittings should always be used.

The tube and fitting at the bottom right is a custom assembly to connect the power steering pump to the power steering hoses.

I often find a long run of power-steering steel tubing coming out of the pump with no support. Over time the tube cracks, leaving you in the worst possible situation on the side of a desolate road. Always look for possible pinch or

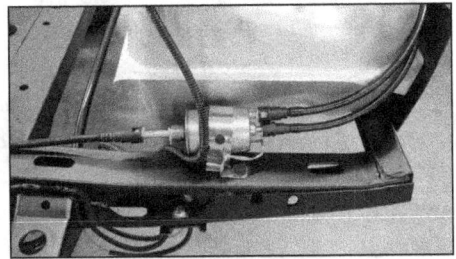

Installing a 2000–2003 Corvette fuel filter makes the return line side of the 2000-and-up fuel system installation simple. Place the fuel filter close to the tank, one line in from the pump, and one line returning fuel to the tank at one end of the filter. The other end of the filter has the fuel line out to the engine while maintaining 65 psi in the fuel system. If you happen to have an earlier 1997–1999 LS engine, the same filter works by placing it close to the engine and running the fuel return line into the filter. These filters are pricey due to their dual purpose, regulating fuel pressure as it filters the fuel before it enters the engine.

chafe points that the hoses can be subjected to; otherwise your pride and joy could spring a major leak. Never leave hoses or tubing on headers or exhaust pipes. Applying insulation helps, but do not expect any insulated hose to stay in constant contact with hot exhaust without some damage.

Your LS swap requires a high-pressure pump and some supply tubing modifications to feed the new-found power. The 1997–1999 LS engines required fuel system return lines; 2000 and later LS engines used a modified fuel filter, housing the fuel return system internally. Using the 2000 Corvette fuel filter is the easiest way to overcome the installation of the return line. As with other plumbing, make sure you route the fuel lines away from heat as much as possible, and avoid hose damage from sharp edges. (Chapter 4 covers the fuel system in detail from the fuel tank forward.)

There are a couple of other items to overcome concerning the LS engine's metric gauge fittings and heater hose outlet configurations. Then there is the throttle cable connection, which is going to require a different cable for the LS installation.

LS Engine Installation

1. Connect Oil Pressure Sensor

This was the first time I had seen this trick (breaking out the center section of an original oil pressure sensor) to install a 1/8-inch NPT (National Pipe Thread) male thread fitting for the 1973 Shark's original mechanical pressure gauge. Tap into the center of the sensor using a 1/8-inch NPT-pipe-thread tap to install the mechanical oil pressure gauge fitting. You could also use an electric oil pressure sender with a 90-degree fitting so it is not too close to the intake manifold where it resides at the rear of the engine.

Adapter fittings are available with straight metric threads converting them to NPT for the LS engine. Be careful when installing adapter fittings: they need to be snugged down. Do not over-torque them. They are delicate and break easily if over-tightened. One inadvertent bump and the fitting can break off, causing oil to be pressure fed out of the engine.

2. Place Power-Steering Pump

The same power steering pump and brackets can be used from the 1998–2002 Camaro/Firebird LS take-out engine. The integral power steering reservoir makes the job a little easier. Although the pump's pulley is close to the upper control arm there is plenty of clearance. Installing the power steering hoses is also easier with this setup.

3. Reconfigure Heater Inlet and Outlets

You need to do a fair amount of conversion work to correctly install an LS engine in a C3. For example, the original heater hose fittings are too close to the upper control arm to work. The easiest fix is to remove the straight hose fittings and install threaded fittings. You must have access to a 3/8- and 1/2-inch NPT pipe tap to thread the ports. Then thread in the AN aluminum NPT male pipe adapter with swivel fitting setup. This application uses a 45-degree swivel fitting and push-on hose that's identified by the yellow plastic hose stop. The fitting's barb design requires a bit of effort to install on the hose, but it does not let the hose go as it digs into the barbs under pressure. Using a hose clamp can cause leaks as the clamp applies so much pressure it cuts the hose.

You need these pipe taps to thread the water pump, which can be costly. In this case it may be smarter to have your local machine shop handle this. Always use a tapping lubricant for aluminum or any threading. Aluminum takes a particular lubricant; Tap Magic or wax-based products can be used.

4 Connect Radiator Hoses

Factory water inlets have a 90-degree fitting, so they do not fit the lower radiator hose. This Jegs water inlet offers a solution: a water inlet and a rubber radiator hose filler connection adapter. The original water inlet is removed and the replacement is installed along with an early small-block thermostat of your choice. These parts allow you to use the original Shark modified lower radiator hose. The original 1973 Shark's lower radiator hose was cut shorter for the connection. This is also the thermostat housing and requires the correct thermostat to fit the aftermarket inlet.

5 Install Fuel Line Adapter

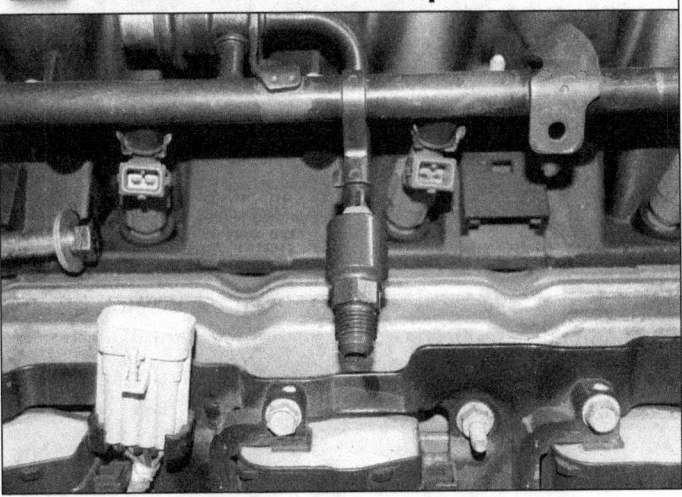

This simple Russel Performance fuel line adapter fitting (PN 644000) makes it easy to connect a -6 hose to an LS engine fuel rail. The original GM hose is a push-on that is held in with a spring to capture the tube. A piece of flexible hose suitable for gasoline that can withstand at least 200 psi should be used for the connection to the frame-mounted fuel line. Although the fuel system pressure should never exceed 100 psi for any reason, doubling the hoses burst pressure is a safety factor.

6 Install Fly-by-Wire Accelerator

If you decide to go fly-by-wire you need this accelerator pedal assembly with built-in accelerator position sensors. General Motors also used a TAC module for this assembly to function and is in the 1997–2004 Corvette and 2010 and later Camaro LS engine installations. The benefit is that the pedal can be installed in just about any configuration and wired easily. Your original Shark accelerator pedal is held in place with two 1/4-inch bolts: they are removed and an aluminum plate is fabricated to connect the new accelerator pedal to the existing mounting area on the firewall.

7 Install Throttle Cable Bracket

As a fly-by-wire alternative, this 1998–2002 Camaro throttle cable bracket works fine with a Lokar universal accelerator cable to connect the throttle. If you decide to use a 700R4 that uses a mechanical throttle valve cable, you have to come up with a modified bracket and throttle body lever. This bracket is for the accelerator cable and cruise only. Note the water temperature sending unit below the throttle lever; the 1/2-inch NPT male thread does not screw into any of the LS engine's available cooling system ports. To remedy this, use a 1/2-inch NPT tap to thread the water pump's upper flat area and then install the original 1973 Shark's coolant temperature sender.

CHAPTER 2

Exhaust System

Fitting the exhaust manifolds into the C3 is a typical problem when performing an LS engine swap. Corvette LS cast-iron manifolds are the only choice at this time, due to the lack of available direct fit headers.

Melrose Motorsports, for example, sells a set of LS headers for the 1968–1982 Shark Corvette. When bolted to an LS engine, these headers complement the engine and neatly fit the C3 chassis. These are true ready-to-install pieces.

You can install 1997–2004 Corvette LS long-tube headers in a C3. They bolt in place, clearing any engine compartment obstructions. However, these headers are positioned so closely together that they encroach on the center transmission tunnel. The 1997–2004 Corvette's rear-mounted transmission allows the exhaust pipes to come together right after the bellhousing, requiring modifications to the headers for them to fit under the car. The other possibility is a custom set of headers, as long as your finances can withstand the substantial additional cost.

A trip to a local exhaust shop is required to connect the Corvette manifolds to the original Shark's exhaust system. The 1973 models had 2½-inch exhaust flowing to the rear bumper through Magnaflow mufflers. Exhaust systems for the LS are covered in Chapter 5, including the header sizing specifications.

The whole used take-out package concept saved a lot of money over finding individual pieces and putting them together. In addition, I knew all the parts were compatible. Stress was also minimized by not trying to procure the myriad of small pieces required to make all the systems come together and work in harmony. The results were apparent immediately; the horsepower and torque gain were phenomenal, with fuel mileage that rivaled a late-model vehicle. Although the swap is controversial to some who want that original look, one ride would make the numbers-matching Corvette fanatic think twice. This is the way Sharks were intended to be driven.

Engine Removal

Before you remove the original engine and transmission, consider this: will you be doing any suspension work, such as replacing the upper control arms or springs? Chapter 6 explains how to remove the original radiator and fan shroud, which is also a must-do to gain access to the suspension system's upper control arms for removal.

If your plan is to do the front suspension, cooling system, and engine replacement all at once, you first remove the radiator, fan shroud, upper control arms, and then the engine. Once the engine and transmission are out, it is difficult to compress the coil springs for front suspension disassembly. You may want to hold off on doing those three separate steps until you have all the pieces set aside. If finances don't allow you to do them simultaneously, consider doing the radiator and suspension first and the engine later.

The engine removal and crate engine install takes at least four or five days if all goes well. Most likely you will need extra time to clean up pieces and the engine compartment before the crate engine is set into place.

You can do the swap in your garage at home with just a few pieces of equipment. You can use an engine hoist or "cherry picker" to pull the engine out. Shark Corvettes are sitting close to the ground, so the transmission needs support and access during the engine's removal.

Chevy Small-Block Engine Removal and Installation Tips

1 Prepare to Remove Engine

All Sharks with power steering have this lower support bolted to the two vertical engine block mounting bosses. They can be difficult to see. The easiest way to remove the pump is to take the two long bolts out of the support from the front. One 9/16-inch hex-head nut holds the pump against the adjuster at the backside; this also requires removal. Removing the bolts holding the support to the pump is not necessary once the two front bolts are out and the rear nut is removed. The pump drops down and lays on the frame, out of the way.

Because of the difficulty of installing these bolts, General Motors rounded the ends into a bullet point. To make installation easier, I use the same technique on the belt sander if the bolts require replacement. A bench grinder also works to round the end of the bolt; after the grinder or belt sander use a wire brush to knock off any edges that have built up.

CRATE ENGINE OR LS ENGINE?

2 Remove Engine Mounts

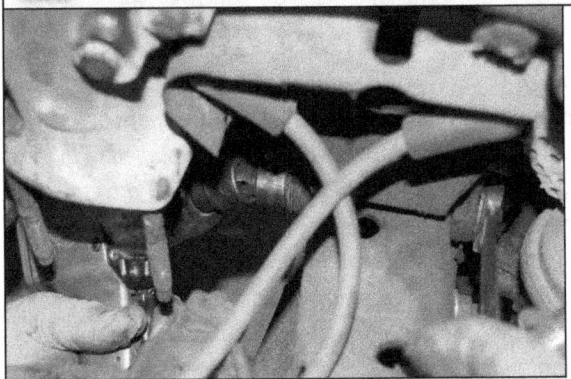

The passenger-side engine mount through-bolt is being removed using a 5/8-inch hex-head universal impact socket and an 11/16-inch closed end wrench. The 11/16-inch nuts are supposed to be locking nuts. Using a ratchet and socket can be quite difficult for removal; wrenches with ratcheting ends make the task easier if no air tools are available. Note the exhaust down-pipe has been removed before working with the engine mount bolt and nut. Another tip is to remove the starter to gain better access at the bolt side. After the engine mount bolt is removed, you can then remove the fuel hose from the supply line to fuel pump. Be prepared: the fuel tank is higher than the fuel pump. When the hose is removed, fuel keeps flowing until the tank is dry. I clamp the hose with a specially designed hose clamp that will not damage the hose. Alternatively, a 3/8-inch bolt can be inserted into the hose and clamped. Make sure you position the hose clamp on the smooth section of the bolt. Chances are if the clamp is positioned on the threads fuel still seeps out. This is a serious matter and can cause a devastating fire if not handled properly.

3 Remove Engine

General Motors used this foam-rubber seal to keep hot air out of the transmission tunnel starting in 1976 after a year of dealing with catalytic converter heat. The foam seal is sandwiched between the transmission tunnel and the transmission case. One of the last things to do is remove the transmission bellhousing bolts. If you see this seal you are working with a virgin Shark. Most likely few of these seals were ever put back in place during any transmission service. The seal makes it difficult to access the 9/16-inch hex-head bolts that attach the transmission to the engine. If the seals become hard and difficult to remove, I just tear them out. Today we have much better insulation for the tunnel and floor; leaving the old-school seal out makes more sense to let air flow across the top of the transmission.

4 Prep for Installation

This later ZZ4 small-block engine uses an external balance flex-plate. It is being torqued to the prescribed 65 ft-lbs to prevent rear main seal leaks. Over-torquing the flexplate or flywheel bolts distorts the one-piece crankshaft seal area. Early two-piece rear main seal small-block and big-block engines use an internal balance flywheel or flexplate that is not affected because the flywheel flexplate mounting flange is separate from the seal area. Applying red Loctite to the bolts is always a good plan after cleaning the threads and threaded holes with brake cleaner.

To the right of the socket is a locating dowel that presses into the crankshaft. It is recommended that one be used in all performance applications to prevent the flywheel from rocking back and forth, eventually wearing away at the bolt threads.

5 Install Engine in 1979 Shark

The ZZ4 350-ci engine is one of the most popular and one of the first crate engines offered by Chevrolet Performance, which makes it a well-known popular engine for many applications. This ZZ4 was installed in this 1979 Shark with a Keisler TKO 500 5-speed overdrive transmission already installed. Note the adjustable engine lift fixture to safely control the engine's angle as it is lowered into place. Because of the Shark's long nose, pay careful attention to the cherry picker's leg length; if you run the boom out all the way a tipping condition can occur. Always make sure the manufacturer's recommendation for leg length positioning matches the boom position.

6 Install Engine Mounts and Plug Wires

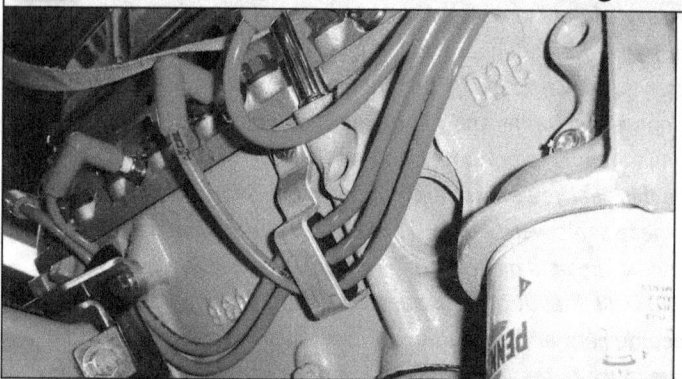

This 1979 Shark has Energy Suspension urethane engine mounts that take the place of the factory mounts. These mounts are recommended for those who like to leave the line hard. They are designed to keep your engine in place even if the urethane breaks away. You will notice that I prefer to install the plug wires under the exhaust; I do not like the look of wires all over the place under the hood. Shark headers and exhaust manifolds work best with the plug wires in this position; they suffer less heat damage over the long run. Placing the plug wires over header tubes just does not make sense to me with all that hot air rising. I am all about being neat, though, and believe the plug wires must be retained for long life. You also may notice that plug wires five and seven are on opposite ends of the plug wire retainer to minimize the chance of crossfire from the plugs' firing next to each other in the firing order.

7 Install Engine Mounts and Fuel Pump

On this crate complete engine, one of the first concerns was whether the fuel pump fittings would hit the frame. During engine installation be sure check this area carefully; most aftermarket fuel pumps are larger in diameter and come very close to the frame rail. On a positive note, the Edelbrock fuel pump allows you to reposition the lower section of the fuel pump for the best fit in your application. I removed the lower section and made sure the lines would connect without hitting the frame. The stainless-steel braided fuel supply hose also proved to be a problem; the long sweep elbow fittings were in the way of the lower hose. If you decide to install the pump after engine installation, make sure the engine mount bolt comes in from the backside of the engine or you will have to remove the fuel pump for bolt removal.

8 Install Engine Shield and Dipstick Tube

Depending on the application, I prefer to use the factory plug wire shielding if possible. This header-equipped engine allowed the use of the lower shields. These shields keep expensive high-quality spark plug wires in good condition for up to 100,000 miles, even in performance applications. The wires are not subjected to direct header heat and are left alone. The more you move the wires, the better chance there is of breaking the inner graphite core.

This later engine uses a dipstick that bolts to the block: some bolt to an exhaust manifold or header bolt, which can get you in trouble. Always verify that you are using the correct-length dipstick, and then check it for accuracy when the oil is full. I have fixed many engines by simply draining the additional oil and installing the correct-length dipstick. One engine had 12 quarts of oil in a 4-quart oil pan; no one thought that it was odd that the engine required so much oil to hit the full mark on the dipstick.

9 Install Starter and Flywheel

Gear reduction starters are the best choices for header and large-sump oil pans. They install easier and crank better under high-heat loads. General Motors used two different starters for all small-block engines; if the mounting boltholes are inline it is for a small-diameter 153-tooth flywheel or flexplate. Staggered bolthole-mounted starters are for large-diameter 168-tooth flywheels and all big-block applications. Aftermarket starters typically do not use the staggered bolt mounting; they can be configured for either-diameter flywheel with the inline boltholes.

When you install the starter's wiring you have a couple of different possibilities in wiring colors. Violet always goes on the inside terminal of the original starter, so it is connected to the aftermarket starter's small terminal. If you have a yellow or tan wire it is for a points-equipped distributor and has no connection on the aftermarket starter. You either have to go to electronic ignition or keep your old-school starter. You also have a black wire with a 3/8-inch eye terminal: this is the ground wire for the passenger compartment fan and wiper motor. It must be connected to the starter mounting bolt or to the transmission-to-engine mounting bolt; I prefer the latter.

Engine Setup and Tuning

Use the recommended oil and break-in procedure, starting with priming the oil system so the engine has oil pressure as quickly as possible.

If you are swapping in a crate engine use the manufacturer's recommendation concerning the timing specifications and idle speeds. It is always important to check and adjust ignition timing carefully to prevent extreme cylinder heat during engine break-in. You absolutely do not want to have retarded ignition timing as your headers will be glowing red. On the flip side, too much advance causes spark knock that can take out a piston very quickly.

LS engines are ready to go; no worries on timing, idle fuel mixture, or idle speed. The engine's break-in procedure really concerns limiting the amount of time that the throttle is held at one continuous speed. Long periods with the throttle held in one position build engine heat and the piston rings take longer to seat. Accelerating the engine helps to put pressure on the piston rings, which allows them to conform to the cylinder walls more quickly. Check for coolant, oil, or fuel leaks, then get ready for your first drive with your new engine.

CHAPTER 3

POWER ADDERS

Power adders have been used since the earliest days of the automotive industry, and they continue to be a popular method for boosting engine performance cost effectively and reliably. Supercharging (forcing air into the engine) to boost compression was one of the first engine power adders. Turbocharging followed, which used exhaust flow to rotate an air compressor, thereby saving precious horsepower that the supercharger required to add power. Nitrous oxide came later; this uses a compressed gas that could be quickly installed for an instantaneous addition of power.

All of these power adders were used to increase engine output without major engine modifications. Any of them can be installed on a relatively stock engine to dramatically increase power. For instance, no rolling or rough idle; everyone knows that a radically cammed high-horsepower engine is under the hood. Certainly there are radically built engines designed to optimize the power adders, but the majority of people using them want a stealthy way to be heard. Due to the high cost of supercharging and turbocharging, along with the cumbersome components and plumbing required, some opt for nitrous oxide to get its relatively inexpensive power boost.

Nitrous Oxide

The simplest power adder is nitrous oxide (NOS). It's a cryogenic gas composed of nitrogen and oxygen molecules that have increased oxygen weight, providing a rapidly expanding cool dense air charge into the engine's cylinders. Stuffing more oxygen into the combustion chamber allows you to hang more fuel on those oxygen molecules, and adding more fuel means adding much more power. NOS gives you the best engine performance increase for the cost.

As the dense nitrous oxide charge rapidly expands, engine compression is enhanced and it can add up to 250 hp without major engine modifications. Doubling your available horsepower, even if it is in short bursts, is something to celebrate. A properly calibrated nitrous system with a full bottle provides an exhilarating acceleration, much like a supercharger boost coming in. Something else to consider: many nitrous kits have discreet components to keep it your little secret that you have an engine enhancer onboard. You can install these systems in a couple of days.

Kit Types

There are two types of nitrous kits: wet and dry systems. The dry system sprays nitrous only, through a single nozzle into the intake system. Dry systems rely on electronic engine fuel controls to compensate for the additional

This is your best shot at fitting a supercharger under a Shark factory hood. A low-rise dual-plane intake manifold, such as the Edelbrock 2700 series on a small-block, is the ticket. Each Shark may have different engine-to-hood clearances. Check the fit of the system before buying anything. The Vortec supercharger kit provides 8 to 10 pounds of boost, immediately gaining an impressive 75 to 100 hp.

POWER ADDERS

fuel requirements of nitrous. Preferably the nozzle is placed before the mass air flow sensor; keep in mind, the Shark Corvette never used a mass air sensor for electronic fuel control. Although easy to install, fuel enrichment when in nitrous boost is difficult to tune and engine damage can result from a lean fuel condition. Dry nitrous systems capable of boosting up to 50 hp can be safely used with a carburetor. These low-horsepower-boost nitrous systems are used in a stealthy situation for a couple of tenths of a second drop in a quarter-mile blast.

Wet systems work well with carbureted engines that do not have the electronically capable fuel compensation. Additional fuel is sprayed, along with the nitrous, into the intake manifold below the carburetor. The wet fuel aids in fine-tuning the introduction of nitrous. More plumbing and components are required to control the fuel flow while providing much higher horsepower output.

Availability

Before you decide on nitrous as your power adder, check the availability of nitrous in your area. If there are no local speed shops, many drag strips have fill-up stations on-site. You can expect six to eight quarter-mile passes from one bottle; after that, the pressure drops off in a 10-pound bottle with a 150-hp shot kit. Many long-time nitrous users have two or more extra bottles available, especially for a long weekend of racing. There is absolutely no worse feeling when you expect the nitrous to kick in, only to find that you have an empty bottle. As with any addiction, you need to feed it and be aware of your nitrous bottle's fill level.

Nitrous oxide's reputation is one of those love-it-or-hate-it power adders. Many performance enthusiasts have trepidation concerning the rapidly expanding gas' effect on internal engine parts. Rightly so. You hear about intake manifolds blown off the engine or, worse yet, an engine scattered all over the pavement from the use of nitrous. Intake manifold design is another important factor: single-plane intakes are recommended for proper nitrous and fuel distribution. Dual-plane intake manifolds have upper and lower levels distributing the fuel, air, and nitrous that often cause lean and rich cylinders, with possible engine damage resulting. This holds especially true with 150-hp-and-up NOS kits, which most likely means a raised hood to use a taller single-plane intake manifold on your engine. So much for a stealthy NOS system that you could catch someone off guard with.

This wet nitrous kit has a fuel and nitrous spray bar with adjustable orifices for properly mixing the horsepower-enhancing ingredients. All of the pieces are in one box ready to make some serious power gains in one afternoon. You can expect a conservative 75- to 100-hp increase without engine damage if you follow the instructions and carefully install the system. As horsepower levels increase it's not the NOS system that causes problems; it's the engine's rotating components that cannot stand the stress.

Nitrous and Engine Health

Properly working systems with conservative horsepower enhancement do not damage your engine. But the nitrous setup needs to be properly calibrated to each engine so the engine isn't subjected to excessive heat and fails. The addition of any power adder, whether it is supercharging, turbocharging, or nitrous, raises the engine's cooling system requirements due to the compression boost. If your cooling system is in good condition and the engine is running below 200 degrees (unless you are caught in traffic for extended periods of time), 100 hp or less is fine. If the shot of nitrous creates more horsepower, it also creates more heat. Excessive cylinder heat is death to pistons and, in some cases, the engine cylinders themselves when in boost. If the cooling system is marginal, take care of that before adding any additional pressure to it.

You need a baseline to figure what you can expect from your power adder and the engine dynamics. Applying a 200-hp shot of nitrous to a base Shark's L-48 190-hp engine with 100,000 miles is risky and catastrophic engine failure may result. A 200-hp-and-above nitrous kit should have a fresh engine with forged pistons, race-quality bearings, and a forged crankshaft for long-term repeated use. However, a 150-hp shot of nitrous is borderline proving to be risky for stock engines with more than 50,000 miles that have had minimal maintenance. Supercharged or turbocharged engines are more susceptible to engine damage at the 150-hp level because the power adder is always on-line.

Typically, Chevy small- and big-block engines safely handle a 100-hp shot of nitrous for many trips down the drag strip and road miles. This means that the same small- or big-block is perfectly fine with the typical 8 to 10 pounds of boost associated with a turbo or supercharger installation.

CHAPTER 3

This Holley booster fuel pump is being installed on top of the passenger-side frame rail using an aluminum bracket. The supplied rubber-coated clamps and rubber sleeve for the fuel pump keep it quiet to some degree. The bracket is then bolted onto the frame rail; I found it works best to have the mounting bolts on the side for simple pump removal if required. With the body off the Shark, it is obvious that the pump is as close as possible to the bottom of the tank. This prevents loss of fuel suction as the fuel level drops; electric pumps push fuel well, but they do not draw fuel as efficiently. Minimum 12-gauge wire should be used to wire the pump, due to the long run from the front of the Shark to the back end.

Many early Shark distributors can have more than 42 degrees of timing. I have seen some with as much as 58 degrees at WOT or, as I call it, the big bang factor. You should have the distributor tested on a distributor machine; they are dinosaurs and few shops have one but the test is good for your engine's best performance.

The ideal is 8 to 10 degrees of base timing. When the engine is idling, I prefer to use a vacuum advance to advance the timing to 20 to 22 degrees. Depending on the engine, most boosted with nitrous are limited to 32 to 34 degrees. Engine compression and boost level determine whether timing should decrease as boost rises. The cost of the test is very reasonable, considering the outcome if the timing is not correct.

The most important part to remember while out cruising with any power-adder system installed is monitoring the engine temperature carefully. Getting stuck in traffic then blasting your way out at full throttle as soon as the road clears can cost you big. Stay calm, let the engine cool down for a mile or so, and once the temperature has leveled off at a safe number (200 degrees or less) you can step into it.

Timing and Fuel Supply

What about the ignition distributor? Is it controlling timing advance properly and does the engine have an adequate fuel supply? Since you are adding cylinder pressure, additional fuel is required to prevent burned pistons from an extremely lean condition. Pay careful attention to the nitrous system manufacturer's recommendations concerning fuel requirements.

To put things in perspective, you could possibly double the horsepower output of your Shark's engine. So a base 210-hp engine could end up with a 200-hp nitrous kit installed that requires almost twice the fuel that the original engine used. Even if the stock fuel system is functioning correctly, it does not mean that the system can handle the additional fuel flow for the nitrous.

The stock fuel pump for a carbureted engine does not provide enough extra fuel flow for a dry nitrous system with more than 125 hp. Booster electric fuel pumps are recommended for all carbureted dry or wet nitrous installations. The carburetor's fuel filter should be changed and fuel lines should be inspected for any cracking or rot that impedes fuel flow (see Chapter 7).

The most important thing to do is read the installation instructions for the kit you are installing before taking out the wrenches.

Bottle Placement

You need to figure out where to install the nitrous bottle. The 1968–1977 Shark coupe's rear compartment is one place to keep it out of sight. The 1968–1975 convertibles have limited room for bottle placement when the top is lowered. Of course, you can keep the bottle out of the compartment when the top is down. The 1978–1982 Sharks have plenty of room for the bottle in the rear compartment. The bottle becomes very hot if the vehicle is left out in the sun. A bottle blanket is strongly recommended to keep direct sunlight off the bottle, plus it can conceal your power adder. Summit and Jegs, for example, have many bottle blanket options in a variety of colors and with insulation keep the temperature in check.

Although I have seen bottles installed in the Shark's spare tire compartment with some ingenious planning, I don't recommend this location because you need to drop the spare tire holder every time a fill-up is required. If you go this route, make sure the spare tire holder is secured well; the original single spare tire drop-down bolt could have your stealth system on the pavement for all to see.

There are also 10-ounce bottles for a one-time run or just enough to get you the edge at the top end. These small bottles can be placed just about anywhere. It's best to have multiple bottles, though, to enjoy more play time.

POWER ADDERS

Nitrous Filters

Nitrous filters are as important as engine oil filters in preventing major internal engine damage. Here's a possible scenario.

Either the nitrous screen or fuel filter is not used, and a couple of small pieces of debris lodge in the nitrous solenoid. You go to start the engine and a loud bang follows. You open the hood after you see some smoke. You find the air cleaner element blown out and the carburetor's throttle blades stuck open. Nitrous has leaked past the solenoid and ended up in the intake, so it gets sucked into the engine when it's started.

Catastrophic engine damage can result if a lethal mix of fuel and nitrous ignite. A leaking fuel solenoid can do plenty of damage also as it slowly fills up the crankcase with fuel. In the best-case scenario the engine is running way too rich. In the worst-case scenario it goes boom as the fuel ignites in the crankcase.

Always use the available filters and screens.

A few words of caution: do not use Teflon tape unless you are very careful to keep the tape out of the fitting; apply it after the first couple of pipe threads. The tape can plug the nitrous and fuel supply tubes or fittings. Most nitrous kit manufacturers do not recommend Teflon tape because of potential careless application. Using liquid Teflon may seem safe, but that too can clog screens.

This NOS fuel and nitrous solenoid setup on a highly modified big-block is hidden at the rear of the engine. Where's the ignition distributor? To make sure the supercharged big-block had plenty of spark and was well controlled, a crank trigger ignition was used. Place the solenoids low and out of sight if possible. The Earl's fuel filter is mounted on the solenoid plate to keep things tidy and easy to service if required. The aluminum lines are custom bent using tubing benders and careful handling. The aluminum tubing bends and also kinks easily making it delicate to work with. NOS supplies the red-and-blue fitting nuts; they should be used to distinguish fuel from nitrous. Serious high-performance applications use aluminum tubing. Street-driven vehicles need to use steel or stainless-steel tubing to withstand the rigors of everyday driving. Race-prepped Sharks are checked before each event for wear, cracking, and general health before subjecting the vehicle to race abuse, which makes aluminum lines a favorable choice.

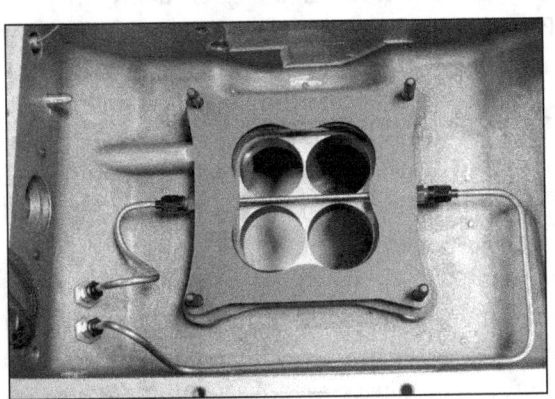

The plumbing for this big-block Vortec supercharged engine had to be carefully planned so the nitrous and fuel lines could be connected to the NOS plate, which was sandwiched between the Holley throttle body and intake manifold. Because the pressurized area lacked visibility, I chose stainless-steel lines for the connection from the solenoids to the plate. The -3 AN tube nut fittings were used at each line and then a 37-degree flare was applied to the lines. A tubing bender was used to configure all the fancy radius lines. (I recommend using some inexpensive carbon steel lines to practice with to get the feel for the correct measurements in the radius.) The -3 AN bulkhead fittings were used to keep supercharged pressure in and provide a neat line installation. The two aluminum lines connect to the bulkhead fittings that supply the fuel and nitrous.

CHAPTER 3

This 1982 Shark has the premium NOS kit installation with Performance On Demand (POD) remote bottle opener, heater, and safety controls. Tank placement is critical to use as much nitrous as possible under acceleration with the bottom of the tank pointing downward and toward the passenger's side of the compartment. This is a safety device that purges the tank if pressures exceed 3,000 psi out of the passenger compartment. The POD controller is placed close to the tank for all the required connections. Once the location is determined, all components must be securely fastened to avoid a projectile in the passenger compartment.

You need a helper to install a fender washer, lock washer, and nut from the bottom side. The differential is within a couple of inches of the rear deck so check the bottom side before stabbing a long drill bit through this area. Drilling and cutting holes for the blow-off, supply line to engine, and mounting screws is easily done in the fiberglass deck area.

The Holley throttle body is installed with some additional plumbing required for external vacuum signals. Aluminum tubing was used for the vacuum lines because the tubing would not be under high pressure. The front line goes through a bulkhead fitting to the fuel pressure regulator for the electronic fuel-injection system. The rear line is used for a vacuum or pressure signal to the supercharger system's dump valve to control boost. When the supercharger is spooled up, both of these vacuum lines also have pressure in them and help regulate fuel pressure. All of the throttle body sensors are sealed and use sealed connectors to provide accurate signals to the engine controller. It is also very important that the throttle cable does not hang up on the linkage. If it does the top must come off and that is not quickly done.

Be very careful if working in an enclosure such as this. Any leaks can be catastrophic.

Once the bottle location is decided and in place, install the supplied nitrous steel braided covered tubing along the frame rail up to the engine area. Keep the braided hose away from any moving pieces and always remember that the braided hose acts like a saw on just about anything it rides up against and has movement.

Plate System

Installing a plate system is not difficult. In most cases the carburetor is removed. The NOS plate is set in place and the carburetor is installed with fresh gaskets. Solenoids are used to control nitrous and fuel flow. They should be placed as close to the plate as possible. They can be out in the open or hidden at the rear of the intake, depending on how proud you are that nitrous is on your engine. Plumbing the solenoids requires some thought to keep the lines from rubbing or leaking.

Nitrous Flow Control

Controlling the nitrous is critical for long engine life. Applying nitrous just above idle can be a major problem as the engine bogs down and fills with excess fuel. Feeding nitrous at three-

NOS plate in place with solenoids.

quarter throttle once the engine RPM is above 3,000 is recommended. The engine's momentum makes a smooth transition to nitrous without any hiccups that might cause engine damage.

Old-school systems used a switch on the shifter and provided the driver with total control. However, if you mistakenly triggered the switch, you could burn down your engine in short order. I recommend using the carburetor throttle activated micro-switch for all installations.

Electronic fuel-injection systems can use the throttle body's throttle position sensor to control the nitrous flow. Use a main electrical cut-off switch to completely shut down the system when not in use. The nitrous and fuel solenoids require adequate wiring to support their high-amperage draw.

Ignition System

The ignition system has high-voltage requirements and is taxed from the added cylinder boost pressure. Sharks from 1968 to 1974 have points and condenser distributors. Certainly they do work and have worked for many years before electronic ignition was introduced as a factory-installed component. Replacing a points-type distributor or converting it to electronic ignition is highly recommended for high-RPM and boosted engines.

Points wear over time, causing late timing and ultimately backfiring, which we dealt with in the early days. Today we no longer need to adjust the points on

POWER ADDERS

Always use an arming switch for your NOS system to prevent unintended operation. The switch can be placed in a readily accessible location for quickly shut down if necessary. This particular switch requires that the upper lever be raised then the toggle switch moved to the on position. If you need to shut down the system quickly the upper lever is pushed downward, immediately closing the toggle switch. The switch is installed inline with the main power supply to shut off all NOS electrical components, so it must be a high-amp switch or a relay for the nitrous and fuel control solenoids.

a regular basis, and ignition performance stays at high-accuracy levels.

The tachometer drive is another obstacle and extra cost on the 1968–1974 Sharks, but there are distributors available that drop in, such as the Summit brand HEI or Mallory 75 series HEI distributor. Both units have in excess of 40,000 volts available at high RPM and offer highly accurate ignition timing tuning for your boosted engine.

Crane Cams and Pertronix make electronic ignition conversion kits to save a few bucks and provide more accurate timing for your stock distributor. The kits fit in the stock points location, and you can use your original tachometer drive. Coil replacement is recommended with either of the kits for the best available spark voltage.

You have to be extra careful, though, with the factory distributor's centrifugal advance system: they can be very close to 50 degrees at WOT due to worn components. Do not feed any nitrous to your engine until you have checked the ignition system's total advance. The same goes for a supercharged or turbocharged engine; ease the RPM up and make sure it does not go beyond 36 degrees. The 36-degrees figure is for 100- to 125-hp nitrous and supercharged or turbocharged engines with 6 to 8 pounds of boost.

Distributor Replacement

Replacing the distributor with a high-performance unit is the best move. Often you have just as much invested in converting the ignition control and modifying the timing advance as you do in an all-new distributor. The current distributors can be easily adjusted for proper timing and are far more accurate over the entire RPM band. Keep in mind ignition timing is critical, and even a new distributor may require timing advance correction. Thirty-two degrees of total advance is recommended for the typical small-block: that is, feed nitrous in excess of 150-hp shot, supercharged, or turbocharged with 10 psi or higher.

You have plenty of options for distributor replacement with the 1975–1982 Sharks, although the original HEI design distributor is a very good unit. The Performance Distributors DUI assembly, for example, is based on the original GM HEI distributor. When the ignition system requires high-spark voltage, the DUI unit works very well and the large cap prevents crossfire, which is very important while in boost. This product is for a 100- to 125-hp nitrous system and also works well with a super or turbocharged engine with 6 to 8 pounds of boost.

High-output ignition coils with premium-quality spark plug wires are also recommended. Be extra careful when choosing the ignition-coil-specific OHM resistance. Coils are required for the typical aftermarket ignition conversion. The same goes for the spark plug wires; having the correct resistance is important to match the distributor and coil output requirements. As nitrous, supercharging and turbocharging levels increase, so do the ignition timing control system requirements. Staged timing increments are important when nitrous is at the 150-hp-plus level. Boost controls along with staged ignition timing advance are also highly recommended as turbocharging and supercharging exceed 10 pounds of boost. As nitrous or boost is applied, ignition timing is retarded a few degrees at a time to avoid detonation while still providing enough advance to prevent backfiring from retarded timing. Distributor accuracy is also very important to avoid a hiccup and scattered engine components. Many choices are out there for the boosted engine with performance distributor requirements.

For example, the Pro-Billet line of MSD distributors is a race-bred distributor that requires a separate ignition box to control timing and has a rev limiter, which is always a good idea on a highly boosted engine. Multiple-spark discharge helps performance and it provides higher spark output voltage throughout the RPM band.

Mallory has a number of products from a basic high-output distributor to a high-performance system with a distributor, control box, and coil. On supercharged and turbocharged applications, I prefer to use MSD's latest billet distributor with a 6AL-2 ignition box to plot out the entire ignition timing curve from idle to WOT on my PC. This box works well with nitrous too, using an input from the nitrous-on switch while providing high-output spark voltage all in one unit.

Ignition System

The most important thing to consider is using the manufacturer's complete system and their recommendations, especially relating to the ignition coil and plug wires. Contact your favorite ignition supplier and explain the goals you have in mind. You usually have one chance at getting this right; precise ignition and timing control are very important for long engine life.

Properly gapped new spark plugs should be installed for tuning purposes. Spark plug gaps can be kept at .045 inch as long as the ignition system has a minimum of 40,000 volts available under cylinder pressure.

Once the system has been installed, use the recommended jets for the desired horsepower enhancement. Run the engine for a period and use an entire bottle of nitrous. Pull the spark plugs and examine the insulator and electrode. If any major spark plug electrode or porcelain damage is occurring, stop using the nitrous until you add fuel or modify the ignition timing.

Supercharging and Turbocharging

The use of turbochargers or a supercharger has multiple benefits with noticeable horsepower gains, very drivable from idle to WOT being the most significant. You can easily add 100 hp to a stock engine without fear of engine damage, enjoy a smooth idle, and that set-you-back-in-the-seat feel when boost comes in. You can use these power adders for road racing, autocrossing, drag racing, and spirited driving without worrying about running out of nitrous in the middle of a long run or while out on a hot lap.

The tough part of installing either of these power adders is space limitations and the lack of any specifically engineered kits on the market. It has been many years since Corvette specialty shops have been involved with any supercharging or turbocharging on Shark Corvettes. If you decide to use either one of these power adders, many areas require custom fabrication. From an engineering standpoint the supercharger is going to be easier than the turbocharger to install. Connecting the turbocharger to the exhaust in an already cramped engine compartment is where the difficulty comes in.

Superchargers

Mechanically driven superchargers can produce a verified 80 to 100 hp in street trim. Race trim superchargers can boost horsepower into the high triple digits, depending how much you want to spend. This, of course, depends on the boost pressure and supercharger design. Superchargers also use some additional fuel and rob some of the horsepower due to parasitic drag.

Roots superchargers use rotors to compress the incoming air, then force it into the engine. These superchargers work well at lower engine speeds and produce boost right off idle, plus they look aggressive. As engine speeds increase, airflow and boost efficiency drop off. One major drawback is lack of available clearance under the Shark hood; the Roots supercharger must be mounted directly on top of the engine.

There is only one option to stuff a Roots supercharger under the Corvette hood. Start the project with an LS crate engine, install a Magnuson supercharger that has an integral intake manifold, and use a big-block Corvette hood. The next obstacle is plumbing the air intake system because of the Shark's lack of space around the radiator and core support. Roots-style compressors also require plenty of knowledge in proper fueling and ignition timing to prevent an intake backfire. While not as spectacular as a Top Fueler losing a blower, any Roots-style compressor backfire can ruin your day with massive engine or vehicle damage. Roots-type superchargers are typically used on show cars for that visceral look, as they protrude through a cut-out in the hood. Not too practical for any street/strip application; they are destined for the drag strip or show circuit.

Centrifugal superchargers use internal impeller fans to build boost. This requires higher engine RPM to build boost, but once they get going they are quite efficient as engine RPM increases. Their universal design allows more placement options while maintaining a stock hood if that was required. Gear drives are used to speed up the impeller fan to obtain the typical 8 to 12 pounds of boost. Most street-driven vehicles (that are actually driven) often keep the boost level at 12 or below. Early gear drives had very noticeable gear whine; today they are virtually undetectable until engine RPM is increased.

It is possible to stuff a ProCharger or Vortec under the hood of your carbureted Shark and have A/C. Using an aftermarket or big-block hood makes the task a bit easier but it is not absolutely required. The ProCharger supercharger uses an air inlet that attaches to the carburetor where the traditional air cleaner sits, often called a hat style, whereas the Vortec unit supplies the compressed air to a box that the carburetor is mounted in. The box presents a couple of issues. Hood clearance is questionable even with a big-block raised hood. The ProCharger's air inlet allows the use of a stock small-block hood if you desire. In addition, you can adjust the carburetor while the engine is running. The carburetor-in-the-box style requires a lot of lessons to figure out just what to do. Anytime an adjustment is required, the carburetor box cover requires removal. What may sound and feel good with the top off usually is not good once it is all buttoned up and under pressure again.

Chances are the idle air mixture requires tweaking on hot humid or cold dry days; while adjusting you must consider the carburetor has pressure

POWER ADDERS

Vortech has a full line of centrifugal superchargers in various trim levels for street, serious street, and race applications. Some are for sustained use on road courses while others have helical cut gears that operate quietly for stealthy Saturday night cruising. They also have a self-contained unit that does not require an oil feed or drain-back lines, which eases installation. Once you feel that you have an idea of your needs, call Vortech to discuss the plan. They make a difficult job easier by helping you choose the correct unit for your application from the multitude of combinations available; they've tackled just about every supercharger installation you can imagine.

This Weiand 142 series Pro-Street supercharger is a low-profile assembly that allows the use of an original Rochester Q-jet carburetor. Of course the carburetor requires modifications and tuning (see Chapter 4). This Pro-Street supercharger can boost performance 25 to 40 percent depending on the application. It has CARB exemption so it is 50-state emissions legal. The supplied pulleys and original equipment carburetor must be used to keep it legal in all 50 states. The visceral look is there, especially with an open hood, which is about the only option for a Shark application even though this supercharger is considered low profile. Weiand has 10 small- and big-block kits including the time tested 6-71 that produces 11 to 12 psi of boost.

entering instead of normally open to atmosphere air bleeds, skewing the settings. Albeit slight, the pressurized air at idle does require some getting used to during tuning. The carburetor boxes have adjustment plugs to access the idle fuel mixture adjusting screws; if you are lucky that may be all that is required for tweaking the tune. Once you get the hang of how the pressurized air changes the carburetor settings it gets easier. Another thought is, no matter what centrifugal unit you prefer, you can substitute the carb-in-a-box air inlet for a hat style to make tuning easier.

To make the tuning task easier and prevent engine damage, a purpose-built carburetor is suggested. Modifying your existing carburetor is possible, but it requires a lot of homework to make it all come together.

Holley has new out-of-the-box carburetors built specifically for supercharged or turbocharged engines. A larger needle and seats with specific floats to prevent collapsing and provide adequate fuel under boost are part of the design. Screw-in air bleeds are utilized for tweaking the idle under pressure, along with manifold pressure referenced power valves for accurate fuel flow under boost. Four corner idle mixture screws are installed to balance the cylinders more efficiently at idle and when the throttle is cracked open. They also come in 600- to 950-cfm air flow for a wide range of supercharged applications. These are perfect for the first-time supercharger endeavor with all the inherent concerns addressed for pressurized installations.

Suppliers such as AED Performance specialize in one-off blow-through carburetors for those who have high-horsepower applications requiring custom tuning. When you get into the 175-plus horsepower enhancement range with your pressurized application, a custom carburetor is required. As you approach the 200-hp range, fuel pressure must rise to ensure adequate fueling at high RPM. Approximately 1 pound of pressure per pound of boost after 10 psi is necessary.

This is when the game gets serious, and the books should come out for a thorough understanding of all the fuel requirements.

Both Vortec and ProCharger make brackets to bolt the supercharger in place on the big- or small-block Chevy engine. The tough part is finding or designing and fabricating the accessory drive brackets if you want A/C and power steering. Of course you need to have the alternator and water pump installation worked out at the very least. You also have to figure out the pulleys that work with the modified accessories. Depending on your situation, you may be able to find GM accessory brackets and components that work; it comes down to spending the time to research the possibilities. You do not have to use Corvette accessory brackets as long as they align the belts and the hood closes.

Plumbing the air intake and compressed air out to the carburetor is all on you, requiring fabrication and a great imagination. Long sweeping bends are required to obtain the most out of the system. Ultimately, once the air intake is close to the front of the Shark the real engineering feat comes in. There is very limited room for any air inlet to pass through the radiator core support to draw cool air from the front of the Shark. The installation of an intercooler is a huge help in making serious power, while preventing engine damage.

Placing an intercooler in front of the radiator as well as routing the plumbing is a difficult task. Depending on the supercharger's manufacturer, it may require an oil feed and drain-back line to the oil pan. While installing a centrifugal supercharger is a difficult project, my recommendation is to consider these aspects and examine the customer gallery photos of 1968–1980 Camaro installations, because the C3 and the Camaro have similar engine compartment restraints.

Turbochargers

Early on, turbochargers were known for a substantial lag time at low RPM. Today's high-tech turbochargers have minimal lag as they spool up and provide boost.

The turbocharger is two systems in one, and requires more plumbing and fabrication than a supercharger installation. An exhaust inlet comes from the exhaust manifold/s along with an outlet that connects to the exhaust system; this spins the turbo fan. On the forced induction side, an air inlet must be used, which then requires a pressurized connection to the intake system.

Twin turbochargers are desired but not mandatory; they balance the exhaust flow without restricting it, whereas a crossover pipe is used on single turbocharger installations to connect the manifolds, creating some restriction. The twin turbo installation requires more complex plumbing, connecting the exhaust system and plumbing the two air outlets. Finding a place for two air filters that draw cool air with the myriad of turbocharger support pieces also requires careful planning. I feel that the turbocharger is the best choice, considering the power enhancement capabilities. Unfortunately, it takes a lot of hands-on fabrication and dollars to be successful.

Designing and fabricating a one-off turbocharger system is not for everyone, unless you understand plumbing as well as engine intake and exhaust systems.

Greenwood Turbochargers

John Greenwood built four turbocharged Sharks: three were considered production models and one was the mule for testing. The Greenwood turbocharged Sharks used a custom exhaust manifold cast by Air Research for the turbo connection to the exhaust along with a waste gate. To utilize maximum exhaust pressure, a crossover exhaust pipe was routed to the manifold that the turbo sat on. Air-conditioning was out of the question, with very limited space on the passenger's side of the engine where the turbo resided. Like the supercharged installation, an air inlet was mounted in place of the air filter on a blow-through carburetor. Since then TracoEngineering is the only other turbocharged Shark on the roadways. They have a similar setup with a custom exhaust manifold and blow-through carburetor.

You have to be really lucky to find one of the original exhaust manifolds cast by Air Research, and chances are more than four were cast for the production Sharks. Trouble is, where and how do you go about this monumental endeavor? Casting your own manifold is possible but expensive for a one-off copy; the other option is a custom-built header system, which is certainly more doable. The problem with that is the heat generated by the engine going through the pipes is detrimental to the underhood components. Exhaust temperatures tend to be higher under heavy loads when boost pressure is up and can approach 600 to 800 degrees. Coating, wrapping, and shielding the pipes can help control some of the heat if you really want to be a pioneer in the Shark turbocharging arena.

Callaway Turbochargers

In 1987, Callaway Cars turbocharged new Corvettes for General Motors, making them a true pioneer in turbocharger retrofitting. These turbocharged Corvettes (RPO code B2K) were covered under GM warranty-passed emissions testing and were available in all states except California. Their approach to turbocharging was well-thought-out and very reliable. They place a small turbocharger on each exhaust manifold beside the engine. Intercoolers were placed above the valve covers, then an air inlet connected the two turbo outlets to the tuned port intake. They used a custom-built exhaust manifold composed of stainless-steel tubing for the installation.

Now for the reality of it all: the option that added 105 hp was $20,000 for a base vehicle that cost approximately $30,000. This was thanks to the extensive engineering required to make the turbocharged Corvette a true street-driven powerhouse. Certainly it can be done for less money, but not for any driver who gets behind the wheel, which is a must when a manufacturer is building cars. If you put together something at home and end up on the side of the road, sure you'll complain, but

POWER ADDERS

it's easier to shrug it off than if you put out big money for it. The bottom line is, it takes time to think out and engineer each portion of the install, including numerous necessary heat shields. You must be concerned with any component within 2 to 3 inches of any exhaust component, including the turbocharger.

Turbocharger Installation

Once the turbocharger is mounted to the exhaust manifold(s) the plumbing begins, preferably to an intercooler then to the carburetor or throttle body. Summit Racing, Jegs, and Superchargersonline.com have many tubes and couplers available for the plumbing. Unfortunately, you have to use the trial-and-error method to find the plumbing pieces that fit your application.

A mandrel pipe bender for 3-inch-or-bigger pipe can help. One of my tricks is to use thin-wall PVC pipe (typically 3-inch) to fabricate the required tubing. Once I'm happy with the routing and fit, I have it as a sample for an aluminum fabrication shop's working drawing.

Another trick is to use poster board to make an air inlet, for example, and then cover it with fiberglass. When the fiberglass dries, the paper can be removed. The rough inlet is final-shaped and another two layers of fiberglass are added.

You need flexible coupling to connect the long runs of tubing to the air box or carburetor hat. No matter what tubing you are using, it is always a good idea to have a flex joint to allow some movement and isolate the heat if possible. At least on the turbocharger's outlet to the carburetor, you are working with somewhat simple-to-modify components. When it comes to connecting the exhaust out of the turbocharger, it takes some thought and a mandrel tube bender for the best performance.

Like a supercharger, a turbocharger requires an oil feed and drain-back line to lubricate the blower wheel bearings. Turbochargers can spin up to 20,000 rpm and must have clean oil at all times or major damage can result. The damage to the bearings is minimal if the rotor hits the housing and either component requires replacement.

Clean oil is mandatory and should be changed at a minimum 3,000 miles or pay the consequences. It is also very smart to let a turbocharged engine idle for 5 to 10 minutes after a long hard run to slow the turbo down and stabilize the engine temperatures. The hot oil cooks in the drain-back line and eventually clogs the line, limiting oil flow, and the result is major turbocharger damage. Timer systems are available to shut down the engine after a cool-down period. The ignition is shut off and the timer takes over monitoring the engine temperature and timing the event. When the required amount of time has passed, the engine is shut down automatically.

Intercoolers

Supercharged and turbocharged engines build heat from the air being pushed through the intake system, adding to the already hot intake air. Roots superchargers build as much heat as turbochargers. Centrifugal superchargers are the coolest-running but they too benefit from cooler air. To combat the inherent heat buildup and gain more horsepower, intercooling was devised, routing the pressurized air through a radiator device at the front of the vehicle to cool the air before it enters the engine. The benefits are twofold: better engine performance and less chance of pre-detonation that takes out pistons.

The problem is, where do you place this additional radiator? It did not have to be as big as the radiator in the Shark; it could be two units if twin turbocharging was used. One way of solving this problem was to lay the existing radiator down at a greater angle. The lower radiator accomplishes two things. It provides an area for the intercooler and a place to route the air inlet and outlet tubing.

This sounds easy on paper, but it means a custom-built radiator core support and most likely bumper support modifications. Intercoolers have been laid flat so that the hood can be sealed to them and an opening cut out for cool air to flow through them. Of course, once the intercooler is placed it must be plumbed, and that can be as difficult as the installation.

There are other ways to combat the heated air entering the engine with stand-alone injection systems. Some of the early designs used water and alcohol injection to cool the intake charge; others used windshield washer fluid. Adding the water and alcohol decreases cylinder temperatures and decreases the chance of pre-detonation.

Today's sophisticated systems use electronic controllers to handle water, alcohol, and methanol injection for precise injection flow at the requirements for the boost level. AEM, for example, has complete systems that are much easier to plumb into your boosted engine than it would be to design an intercooler.

The systems work, although they require a reservoir and filling on a regular basis. I have also found that the systems are fine if used regularly; if not, the injector nozzle can clog and limit or prohibit the much-needed flow of cylinder cooling fluid. Well-thought-out systems have warnings when the fluid is low or no flow has occurred. So there is an alternative to the ultimate intercooler setup for a pressurized Shark.

While it may sound cool to have a pressurized system on your Shark, it comes down to dollars and cents. Over the long run, this is a costly upgrade for the power gain.

CHAPTER 4

Performance Fuel Systems

General Motors equipped the C3 with a variety of carbs through its production run, and these Holley and Rochester carburetors can be optimized for performance and fuel economy. However, many aftermarket EFI systems can be installed on a C3 for improved performance, and it's a system that constantly adapts to changing conditions.

Carburetors and fuel-injection systems are fuel managers feeding your engine the required fuel load from idle to WOT and everything in between. Electronic fuel-injection systems precisely feed fuel while monitoring the engine's efficiency through various sensors, providing the best possible fuel control. Carburetors, on the other hand, are simple, easy to maintain, and have worked for many years with unquestionable results.

Carburetors

Fuel control through a carburetor is based on engine vacuum drawing the required fuel through a venturi, atomizing the fuel droplets into the incoming air, creating a homogenized mixture of fuel and air. Idle speed is controlled by the throttle blades' position, allowing just enough air into the engine to obtain the desired idle speed. Fuel flows through the idle mixture screws at the base of the carburetor to mix with the incoming idle speed air. To allow the fuel to flow through the idle mixture screws, a column of air is introduced into the circuit via emulsification tubes; this is often the problem with poor idle. Idle fuel flow rates are affected by the lack of available atmosphere (air) coming into the idle circuit.

Transition slots are placed above the throttle blades, typically within .050 inch of the blades at idle to draw fuel in as the throttle is tipped in (slight off-idle movement). These transition slots prevent hesitation as the throttle is applied until the power valve or piston takes over. A power valve or piston controls fuel flow rate through fixed orifices (jets) until WOT occurs, then the jets have maximum fuel flow. The power piston system uses a stepped needle that restricts fuel flow through the jets, while the power valve uses a single orifice to meter fuel to the jets. Both power enrichment systems use engine vacuum to control fuel flow rate: as engine vacuum decreases relative to throttle opening so does the fuel flow restriction. An accelerator pump is used to provide a shot of raw fuel as the throttle is opened quickly, avoiding hesitation during hard acceleration.

The carburetor's simplistic design is easy to work on and maintain, while

Holley carburetors are often installed because of their flexibility and ease of tuning procedures. The metering block (center) houses the metering jets and power valve, with the idle mixture screws in either side. It is very easy to remove the carburetor bowl and metering plate for a quick jet change, as opposed to changing the Quadrajet primary metering rod or spring. Holley uses center- or side-hung float assemblies to control fuel level. Center-hung floats work best for ultimate-performance Sharks. The power valves have two distinctively different spring rates for fuel enrichment. Engines that produce high vacuum require more spring tension to supply fuel as required under load. Using a high-tension spring with low engine vacuum results in a very rich-running engine. The best policy here is to pick up one of the many available books that cover the innermost workings of the Holley carburetor for the best results.

PERFORMANCE FUEL SYSTEMS

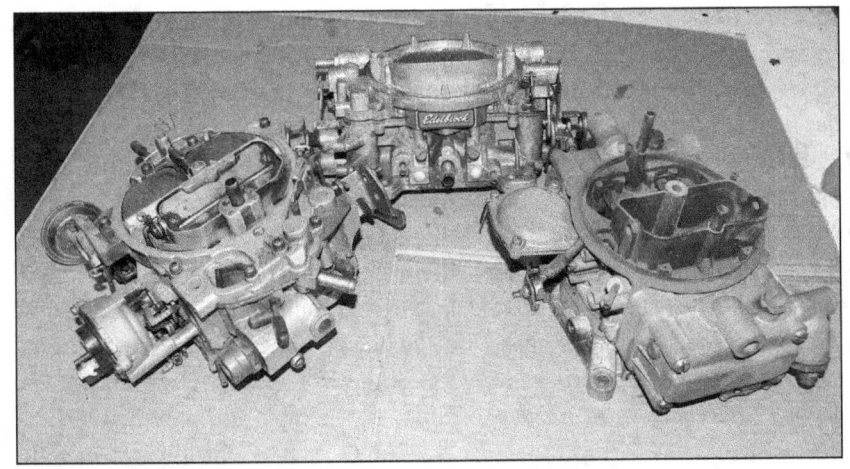

The Rochester Q-jet (left) was factory installed, making it the easiest to overhaul and install, but it has internal leakage problems, main body warpage issues, and is harder to power tune. Edelbrock's AFB-design carburetor (middle) requires major linkage, vacuum connection, and fuel line modifications to install. Once in place, though, it is easy to power tune. Holleys were on some of the special high-performance Sharks, making them easy to install. As with the Edelbrock, a carburetor base-plate adapter is required if you have a Rochester intake manifold. The Holleys (right) are the simplest by far to power tune of all of the offerings.

This is my favorite carb setup for the C3 when it is properly tuned. The progression from the center two barrels to the outer four barrels' opening is supercharger-like in feel. The round brass plugs behind the fuel inlets are there to check the fuel bowl level.

Remove the plugs while the engine is running; fuel should just barely dribble out as the engine is shaking around slightly. If the floats are set too high, a stream may flow out. Keep a cloth handy to absorb the fuel if necessary. To adjust float level, turn the brass screws with the 5/8-inch nuts on top of the fuel bowls. Loosen the screw and turn the nut clockwise to lower the fuel level; turn it counterclockwise to raise the level. Once you feel the fuel level is set, take the Shark for a ride and then check the nuts again. Sometimes it takes a couple of road tests to accurately set the float level.

Holley carburetors are notorious for loose idle-mixture screws that richen the idle mixture. A piece of 5-32 vacuum hose simply placed over the screw keeps it from turning. A factory-installed cork seal is inserted before the idle mix screw is installed, but over time it softens and the screw moves easily. The piece of hose stops that.

Another major issue is setting the carburetor too rich; these are Corvette engines, not Cadillacs. They idle a bit rough. The idle screw should only be out enough to smooth out the engine as much as possible without raising the idle speed. Too much fuel makes the engine lazy at the crack of the throttle as it tries to clear out the excess fuel.

providing your performance engine with the required fuel. The cost is less up front with less engineering to make the system work; fuel mileage can also be respectable when tuned correctly. There are some negatives, like anything in the mechanical world: constant tuning is required for ultimate power; cold starts and lower fuel mileage are the most annoying. The use of electric choke systems has lessened the cold hard-start woes, but they still have performance issues until the engine is fully warmed up. Carburetor jetting must be optimized for the prevailing weather conditions at the race track. The balance of full-throttle performance, cruising, and idle is difficult to obtain while providing ultimate fuel mileage.

Carb Sources

The 1968–1972 special high-performance Sharks had Holley carburetors factory installed. All others until 1981 had Rochester Quadrajet carburetors, then an archaic electronic fuel injection finished off the Shark's C3 generation for 1982.

CHAPTER 4

One backfire can ruin your afternoon if your pre-1992 Holley 4150, 4160, 4165, or 4175 does not have this power valve modification done to its base plate. To eliminate the possibility of this problem, Holley has a Power Valve Check Ball Kit (PN 125-500) for $15 with very detailed instructions on how to perform this simple fix. The port that supplies vacuum to the power valve is drilled out with the provided drill bit and stop; next, the ball is dropped into place followed by the spring. The provided washer captures the spring after peening the base plate. No more concerns about a flooded carburetor when the power valve diaphragm ruptures. All-new Holley carburetors have this check valve in place.

Holley carburetors could be found on the 1968–1969 big-blocks with more than 400 hp, but no small-blocks received them until the 1970 LT1 370-hp engine.

Oddly, the 1970 big-block engines all came with a Rochester Q-jet. Then, in 1971, the 425-hp 454-ci engine and 330-hp LT1 small-block had Holleys factory installed.

One Holley carburetor was used for 1972 on the last of the LT1 small-blocks for production Corvettes.

Holley Carburetors

Holley carburetors had the traditional square-bore (equal-size) throttle plates, primary and secondary. Holley also supplied the three deuce carburetors on the 427-ci high-performing engines for 1968 and 1969. The simplistic Holley-designed carburetors are the favorite of many racers, and it made sense to put them on the high-output engines from the factory. After all, many of these early Sharks were used in just that manner. The easily removed voluminous fuel bowls allow quick jet changes for ultimate track tuning.

The one drawback to the early Holley carburetors was the slightest backfire that pressurizes the intake would rupture the power valve's rubber diaphragm. The failed power valve would then allow maximum fuel flow at idle, causing extremely rich fuel mixtures unless you were at WOT. Holley has a fix for the early carburetors, and all new units have a check valve to prevent a backfire from ruining your day.

Although the Holley is by far the easiest to tune for performance use, you need to know a few things to prevent the necessity of constant tuning: Proper fuel bowl level and keeping the idle mixture screws from moving are the most important. Leaving your air cleaner off is a huge mistake because any debris sucked into the carburetor's air horn can cover up one or both of the idle bleed orifices, causing a no-idle condition. One backfire can ruin your day if you run around with the air cleaner off. Fiberglass burns quickly and is hard to put out immediately.

For many decades Holley has been known as the carburetor to have regarding performance. GM's Rochester carburetor division came up with a spread-bore design in 1968 for general use on all GM V-8 engines. The Rochester Q-jet carburetor has small primary throttle plates with huge secondary throttle plates. Holley decided to build its own spread-bore carburetor to replace the Q-jet.

This solved the problem of requiring the replacement of the intake manifold or an adapter for the traditional Holley square-bore carburetor. Hood clearance can come into play when the adapter is used for a square-bore Holley installation. One other note: Holley's Q-jet replacement flows 650 cfm, whereas the original Q-jets flowed 750 to 780 cfm.

If you are inclined to install a square-bore Holley in place of the Rochester Q-jet, it requires some extra pieces (including an intake manifold) to fit them together. There are also some ancillary items required because Q-jet throttle cable brackets do not work with the Holley. Summit and Jegs, for example, sell kits to fit the cable and provide WOT.

The Q-jet had a fitting cast into the throttle plate assembly for the power brakes; Holley does not provide a major vacuum connection port. Holley does provide the required large vacuum port for the PCV system; unfortunately, this port is also frequently used as a junction for the brake booster vacuum supply. The brake booster should have a dedicated vacuum supply without the PCV system's calibrated vacuum flow loss.

To make matters interesting, the Holley carburetor's elongated fuel bowls cover the intake manifold's only major vacuum supply port. Ironically, Edelbrock has a low-profile fitting available (PN 8096) to take care of the problem.

The use of a stock air cleaner can also be a problem, with the elongated fuel bowls hitting the dropped air cleaner base. Most opt for an aftermarket open element air filter and then place a breather in one of the valve covers.

Finally, if you want to have an operable choke Holley has either a manual or electric choke option; none fit the original Q-jet's divorced choke found on the 1968–1979 Sharks. The electric chokes work well, especially with headers and blocked exhaust crossover in the intake. They heat more quickly and the engine runs cleaner, faster. Those who opt for the Holley have parts readily available, making them the easiest overall to tune and repair and an excellent choice for frequent race track visits.

PERFORMANCE FUEL SYSTEMS

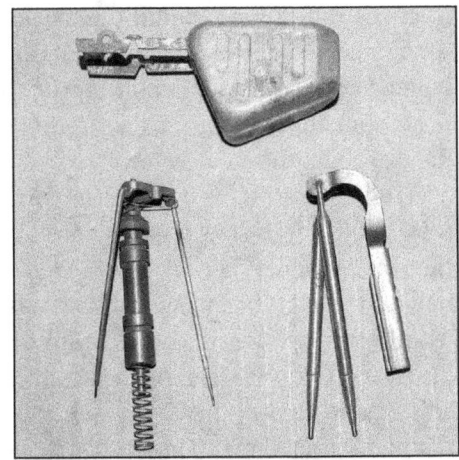

The Q-jet float assembly is made of phenolic plastic that eventually begins to soak up fuel, especially with ethanol blended fuel. Brass replacement floats are a must for proper fuel control no matter if you are easing around town or under full throttle. Metering rods are used for the primary and secondary fuel control.

Secondary fuel control metering rods (right) rely on the secondary air valve to pull them up and allow more fuel flow. The primary piston, spring, and metering rods (left) rely on engine vacuum to add fuel during enrichment. The primary piston spring is a crucial part of the line's performance. As vacuum decreases under load, the piston assembly rises, adding the necessary fuel. Rods are available with different tapers and diameters to make your engine feel just right under acceleration. The jets are also replaceable, making many combinations possible.

Rochester Quadrajet

When calibrated correctly, Rochester Q-jets operate beautifully and help produce respectable horsepower and fuel mileage. The small primary throttle plates were fuel savers, providing excellent low-speed torque. When the huge secondary throttle plates were fully opened the sensation was similar to a supercharger; the sound was awesome with a free-flowing air cleaner. Once tuned properly they worked reliably year after year with few issues.

A typical carburetor rebuild kit gives you a foam-rubber seal to stick in the secondary metering rod well area to seal if off. Lead plugs were used to seal off the area where the machine tools had to access the carburetor body; eventually all of these plugs leak. You'll know that is the case by a rich-running engine that cannot be leaned out.

Additionally, when you leave the car overnight, you have to crank the engine for extended periods of time until the carburetor bowl fills up. This hammer trick works better than relying on the foam seal that deteriorates quickly. A small ball-peen hammer is used to tap around the perimeter of the plug to tighten it in the housing. The other small plugs (white paint) also leak, and they are also lightly tapped to tighten them.

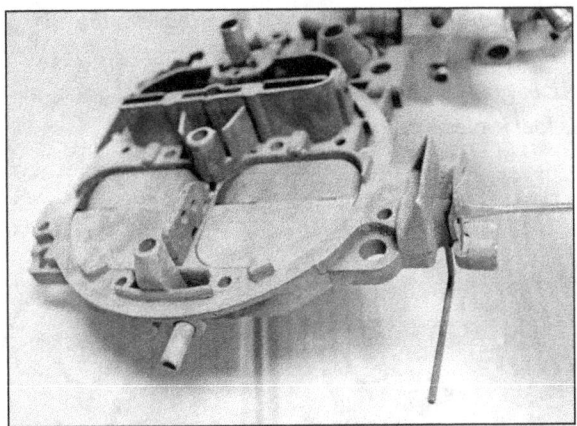

This is one of the most important adjustments on the Q-jet or, as it is often called, the Quadra-bog. The air valve over the top of a Q-jet controls the secondary tip-in air and fuel flow. Quite often the valve is set too loose; the valve opens immediately and the engine falls on its face. The carb top is removed for a better idea of how it works; the Allen wrench holds the adjuster spring screw. Loosen the Allen lock screw and tighten the adjuster screw clockwise for more spring tension.

The best way to set the air valve is too tight, where you barely feel or hear the secondary throttle plates open, and then loosen the adjustment in small increments. You can be very precise about how the transition takes place and tailor it to your preferences. This is fun: you get to open the throttle wide open, adjusting it until it feels just right.

There were some inherent problems, though. Main case leakage was number one and all leaked; it was just a matter of when. During the manufacturing process drills were used to machine the primary and secondary fuel passages; after the drills were used, lead plugs were installed to prevent fuel leakage. The plugs loosen and leak fuel into the engine, causing an overly rich fuel mixture. A common sign of loose plugs are long starting times after a prolonged time in the garage; the fuel bowl had to fill up before the engine fired.

Then there are the front mounting bolts that pass through the carburetor

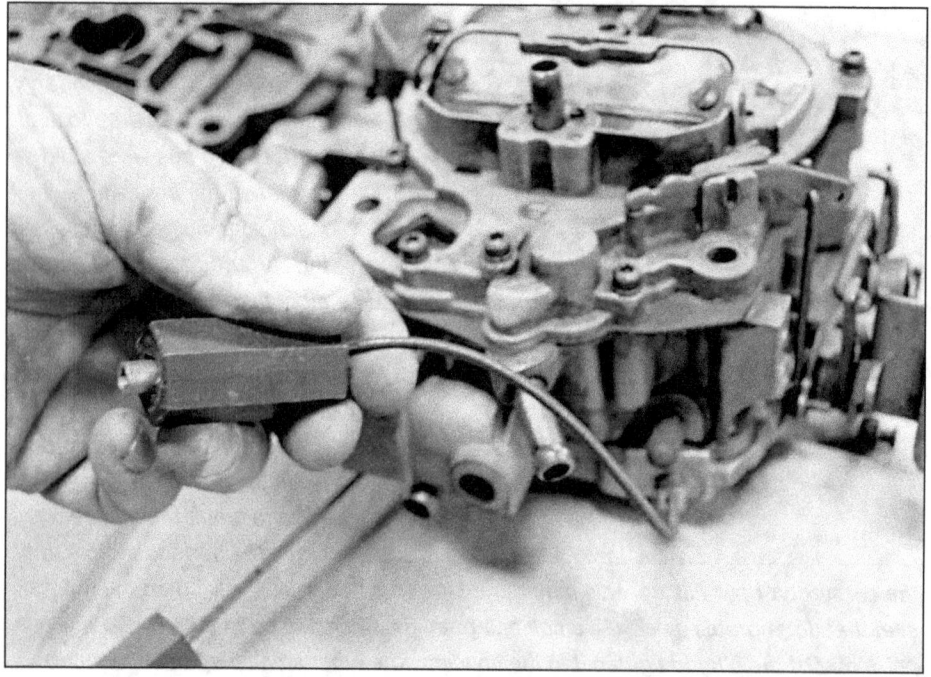

Quadrajets were introduced in 1968 and received many emissions control changes by the time the Shark ended up with fuel injection in 1982. By 1978 this special tool was required (in an attempt) to prevent do-it-yourselfers from tampering with the idle mixture. All of the factory-installed anti-tamper plugs covering the adjuster screws were removed by this time. As with the Holley carburetors, too much idle fuel is not good; the engine bogs down until the excess fuel is cleared.

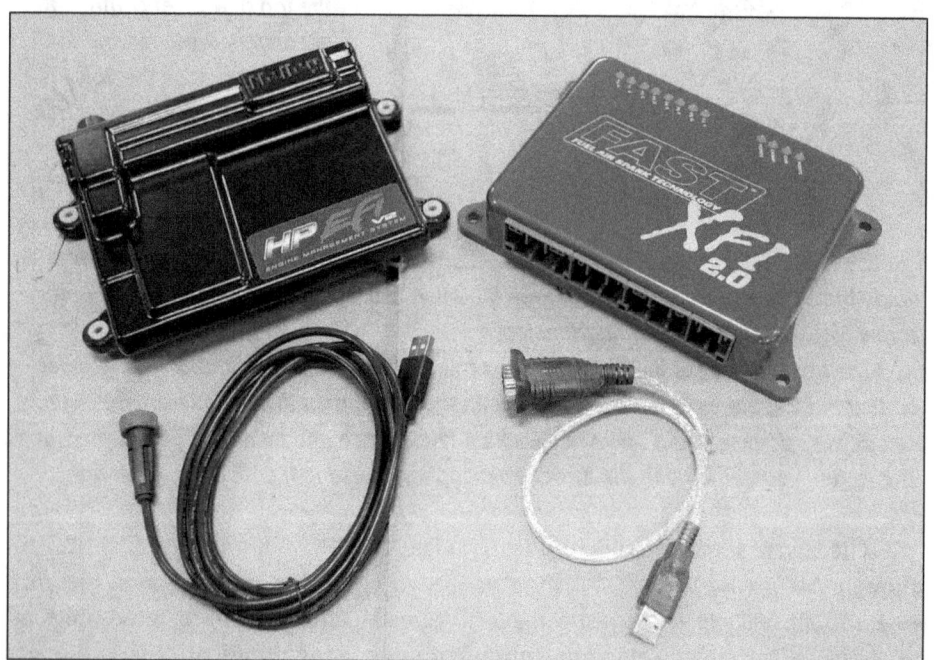

Both of these ECUs have very quick processing speeds with self-tuning capabilities, laptop setup, and fine tuning. Holley's HP ECU (left) handles fuel injection and coil-on-plug ignition systems, while the XFI requires an additional controller. The FAST ECU (right) allows several programs to be tuned and selected on the fly for the street-strip warrior.

from the top to the bottom; these bolts are often over-tightened on the main carburetor body. Q-jet's phenolic (plastic) floats sometimes absorbed fuel, causing flooded engines.

Tuning the Rochester idle mixture was simple and it stayed tuned, but setting the secondary air valve and choke pull-off could be tricky. An air valve was used to slowly let the secondary throttle plates transition in. The often-incorrect adjustment earned the Q-jet a reputation and the name "Quadra-bog." As the throttle was increased to wide open, the engine bogged and lost power until it could catch up to the massive amount of air ingested. Those who mastered the air valve setting made the transition seamless or gave you that wow factor as it tipped in.

Rochester stopped production of the Q-jet in the 1990s; Edelbrock took over for a number of years, manufacturing new exact replacements for the high-performance market. Today the only Q-jet source is a remanufactured unit or a long-forgotten new assembly in storage somewhere.

Regardless of who manufactured the carburetor, it wears most notably at the throttle shafts from the constant movement. As the wear increases, the throttle plates stick in their bores; when higher-tension return springs are installed, this exacerbates the wear even more. Poor idle and overall performance should be expected even after an overhaul with the typical carburetor kit available through the aftermarket sources.

Overhaul kits have gaskets, power valve (if used), needle, seat, and instructions on setting the float. The kits only work if you have a carburetor that has debris or contaminated fuel coursing through it. Since you are working with carburetors that can be at least 32 years old, replacement is the best policy. As you can imagine, over the course of so many years the wrong internal pieces can be installed because of lost or broken components.

Installing a new carburetor on a new engine should always be considered. All too often an engine is freshened up then topped with a worn-out carburetor; the result is a very distraught driver. The new engine runs okay, but unfortunately not at its potential due to the poorly performing carburetor. Replacement with a true remanufactured unit that has the throttle shaft bore wear issues resolved and all the correct internals installed (or a new unit) allows you to feel the full potential of that new engine.

Fuel Injection

Today's high-speed electronic fuel management systems have total control of all the most important engine functions, including ignition timing. Fuel and timing can be precisely set at every 400 rpm throughout the entire RPM range. Self-tuning systems such as the Holley HP Commander require some basic info, then you turn on the self-tune and drive your performance Shark while Holley tunes it for you.

What stands out most is the cold-to-hot drivability of electronic fuel-injection systems: jump in, fire up the engine, put it in gear, and go. This is where it can become aggravating for some first-time hot-rodders just getting out of their late-model fuel-injected vehicle. Depending on your camshaft and engine configuration, total fuel control is possible for optimum performance and fuel mileage under all operating conditions.

Radical long-duration camshafts can be used successfully with electronic fuel-injection systems. Most controllers have Alpha-N-based programs using throttle position and engine vacuum to distribute fuel. Alpha-N programming has no self-tuning for which the computer is constantly optimizing the fuel-air ratio. Basic fuel load is delivered using minimal engine sensors for the serious all-out performance enthusiast. This is typically used for purpose-built, track-driven race cars. Tuning this system is for the professional who has an engine dynamometer for the best results without engine damage.

One good reason to use EFI is the ignition control capabilities. High Energy Ignition (HEI) is good, but relying on centrifugal and vacuum timing advance for a serious performance engine makes little sense. EFI systems allow custom tailoring of the ignition timing to obtain the best power and drivability throughout the entire RPM band.

For instance, say you have a long-duration camshaft with close overlap, causing poor idle with a carburetor. The EFI allows additional fuel and spark timing in the particular cells where the camshaft needs it most for better idle. Like the fuel system, the ignition timing lead can be adjusted every 400 rpm throughout the engine's RPM range. My personal view: for the serious performance-minded Shark owner who wants the best of both worlds, EFI is the only way to go. The cost of EFI, however, is considerably higher than that of a carburetor, with additional fuel system support required.

An electric fuel pump and possibly a fuel return line back to the tank needs to be configured and installed. Some of the latest systems do not require a fuel return line; fuel pressure is modulated, with fuel pressure adjusted throughout the RPM range.

There are pros and cons here: dropping the fuel pressure by slowing down the fuel pump can be a good thing; pump wear is minimized and fuel is not warming up from inherent friction as it is forced through the lines. You have one more electronic device that may create problems down the road; however, the mechanical fuel pressure return system has proven to be foolproof.

Return Line Installation

1 Install Fuel Regulator

The majority of electronic fuel-injection systems require some sort of fuel regulator to keep the fuel pressure constant. This Holley regulator has infinite pressure control from 15 to 65 psi. The regulator has ports for two fuel inlet lines and one return-to-tank line. Engine vacuum is used to regulate fuel pressure, and when in boost the positive pressure increases fuel pressure above the zero-vacuum pressure setting. Carbureted engines sometimes require fuel pressure regulation to avoid a rich-running condition; unlike electronic fuel-injected engines, they rely on high flow, not pressure. Be sure you are using the regulator for your needs. EFI regulators do a poor job of controlling fuel pressure for a carbureted engine, and vice-versa for the carburetor-designed fuel regulator on an EFI engine.

2 Install Return Line

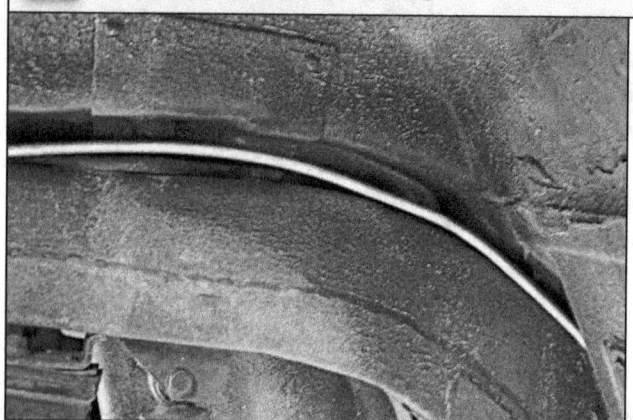

If you decide to use a fuel-injection system with a traditional early-style return line, you need to install a return line (it is the toughest part of the installation job). This 5/16-inch fuel line has been routed on top of the passenger-side frame rail kick-up, then it follows the portion of the frame rail at the floorpan. Unfortunately, there is no pretty way to force the line into place. I take the 5/16-inch line, cap it, and force it between the floorpan and the frame at the rear corner of the frame.

Two people can do a better job: as the person under the car pushes the line, the person in the fender well area pulls. As the line is pushed inward, the person under the car has to bend the line slightly upward. Bending the line upward places the line closer to the frame rail. Keep bending the line until enough line is in place to reach the fuel tank area. Once the return line is in place alongside the frame rail, rubber-coated clamps with self-tapping screws placed about every foot work best to keep the line in place.

Rubber hose is often used for this retrofit because it is easier; unfortunately, it does not last long and the potential for leaks is greater from debris thrown at it. Rubber hose deteriorates within a few years, requiring replacement. Also, the rubber hose keeps heat in the fuel, which is not good either.

Bend the fuel line with your hands to match the existing 3/8-inch fuel supply line before installing the original clamps. This line was pushed over the top of the frame rail kick-up. On the inside of the frame rail, use the existing clamps even though they are for 1/4-inch line. The 5/16-inch line fits in them. The trick is getting the 1/2-inch hex-head bolts out between the floorpan and frame rail. I use a modified wrench to remove them. The area where the box end attaches to the wrench has been ground down so it can go down over the bolt head. (The camera angle may make it look as if there is plenty of clearance but it is tight, especially as the bolt is backed out.)

EFI Manufacturer Options

The majority of systems require a laptop to access and tune the EFI unit. As time passes, each system has become easier to understand and tune. The best part is that the latest systems are very reliable long term; if you decide on a major performance upgrade simply tune as required for the new components.

Holley

Holley has some of the most powerful and fastest-processing EFI systems on the market, and they can be effectively integrated into your C3. If you decided to install a complete LS engine and electronically controlled transmission in your Shark, Holley's Dominator EFI electronic control unit (ECU) has complete control available in one box. If you want to build an all-out turbocharged nitrous-water-methanol-injected engine, this Dominator ECU properly handles the feeding of your beast. Coil-on-plug distributorless ignition system controls are integrated into the Dominator and HP ECUs, so you have tuning control over the entire operating powerband of the engine. Data acquisition is also included for proper tuning and fuel mapping. This is the ultimate controller in one that has all the requirements covered for street performance or all-out race Sharks.

Holley's HP ECU has plenty of power with engine fuel, ignition control, nitrous, boost (supercharger or turbocharger), and water methanol. There is no electronic transmission control with the HP, making it a perfect candidate for your manual transmission–equipped Shark. Their Avenger ECU is perfect for the first-time EFI user with some trepidation. The Avenger does not require laptop programming; this is a true self-learning system that has you ready to pound the pavement in record time.

Fuel Air Spark Technology

Fuel Air Spark Technology (FAST) also offers a high-performance system, the XFI. This ECU has total fuel and

PERFORMANCE FUEL SYSTEMS

This FAST electronic fuel control system can be purchased with an unterminated harness to make a neat job of the wiring once completed. The job is not difficult because FAST provides a complete wire harness diagram. I find it best to group the wires in their respective areas for connection to the sensors and grounds as required. Labeling the bundles helps make sure everything is where it should be before cutting and installing terminals.

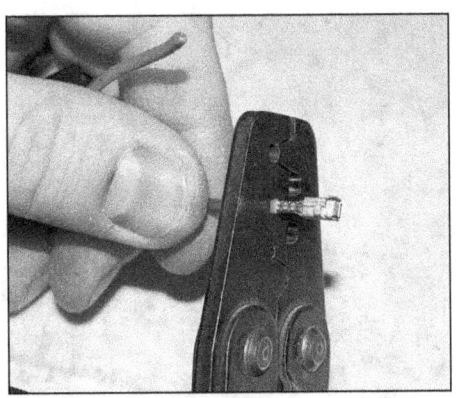

Holley and FAST provide the unterminated harness with electronic control unit terminals and connectors, which is the toughest part to do. The terminals found in the majority of aftermarket harnesses use this "W" crimp-style crimping tool. (NAPA is a good source). No matter how good the engine is (and the components connected to it), the wiring connections are critical for long-term reliable performance. Poor terminal crimps can cause many hours of heartache trying to find an intermittent loss of performance condition.

ignition control with fast processing speeds with boost and nitrous control. This system has multiple onboard tuning programs for on-the-fly changes from street to race mode with the flip of a switch. Distributorless and HEI ignition control are available for absolute engine control and performance. FAST also has a self-tuning ECU that requires minimal tuning knowledge for great results. Their EZ-EFI takes a different approach, with throttle body–mounted injectors allowing you to use the intake manifold of your choice. This stealth design has just a few items that might give away the fact that you have an EFI-equipped engine. Once a drop base air cleaner is installed, the majority of components are hidden.

ACCEL

ACCEL has an engine builder plug-and-play EFI kit that uses a dual-sync distributor for sequential fuel injection. Their kit comes with a special ignition module and E-core ignition coil. They also include their intake manifold with all the appropriate EFI hardware. One nice feature for those with trepidation about using nitrous for the first time is their configurable nitrous versus fuel requirements application. Simply input the required data into the tuning software, and the configuration takes place.

The Choice is Yours

All of the EFI systems mentioned above use wide-band oxygen sensors for extremely accurate fuel-to-air ratios measuring from 10:1 to 18:1 for optimum fuel control. These heated oxygen sensors begin sampling air-fuel ratios more quickly and more precisely for the serious tuner. Coupling the wide-band oxygen sensor with the self-tuning ECUs means a quick start-up and learning period for the novice user. These systems also have the capability to run sequential fuel injection, which is huge if you have a radical long-duration camshaft with 110 degrees of overlap or less.

Choosing the right system for your Shark depends on how serious the engine is. For example, you can fuel inject your Shark's original L-82 with a Holley Avenger throttle body injection system for around $2,000. Installing a FAST XFI or Holley multi-port EFI system would be neat to look at but not worth the cost or performance gain on the L-82.

If you want to build an engine with more than 400 hp, it makes sense to step up to FAST's XFI or Holley's HP multi-port system to gain the most performance.

Don't forget the importance of the sequential EFI if you decide on a radical camshaft with long duration and short overlap. You need a dual-sync distributor for the camshaft position so the injectors fire only when required.

The cold hard facts are, the better the fuel and spark are controlled, the better the performance. Engine life is also increased from less fuel in the oil from the precise fuel control.

Wiring

The required mechanical pieces are bolt on and easy to install. Wiring may seem straightforward, but you must carefully and methodically route and mount the wiring harnesses. Electrical noise is a major concern to avoid poor sensor information to the ECU. The ECU sensors operate on a regulated 5-volt current and provide consistent information

CHAPTER 4

The majority of aftermarket electronic fuel-injection systems use an oxygen sensor for precise fuel control. Early on, one-wire oxygen sensors were used; today high-tech heated wide-band sensors are the norm. This FAST system uses a heated wide-band oxygen sensor to start controlling fuel mixture very quickly. The best place to install the sensor is as close as possible to the down pipe or merge collector on a set of headers; this also aids in quick warm-up. Oxygen sensors do not begin their work until the exhaust gases reach approximately 600 degrees F. Be sure to consider the steering and suspension components as they move throughout their range of motion before cutting the hole and welding the sensor's bung into place.

Seems simple enough: bolt the throttle body on in place of the carburetor, which is true for the most part. As with a carburetor, it is critical to set the idle air volume. EFI units need this adjustment to be done per the manufacturer's recommendations to prevent stalling when the throttle is released suddenly. Idle air volume is controlled via an electronic valve, but a minimum amount of air must be entering the engine for the tuning to work properly. Setting up the linkage between the primary and secondary throttle valves is also crucial for proper transition. Some EFI units require the throttle position sensor reading to be input into the basic setup menu when the secondary throttle valves begin to open.

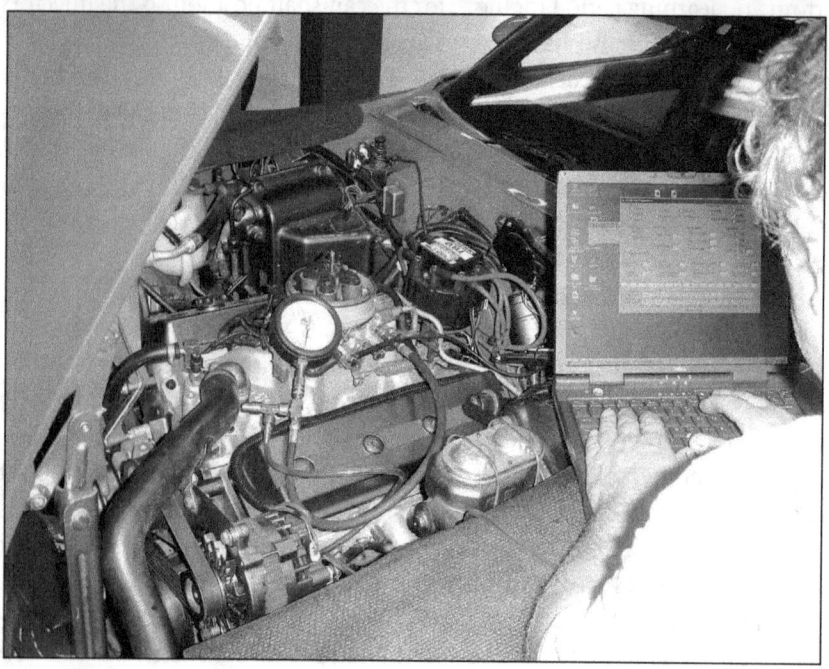

The performance industry has come a long way; you simply set up a few basic adjustments and the laptop does the rest. Checking the fuel pressure before tuning is a must. Holley has made the fuel pressure adjustable with a couple twists of a wrench. Many aftermarket EFI systems allow the use of multiple oxygen sensor manufacturers requiring specific input of the sensor into the initial programming. If incorrect data is supplied, costly oxygen sensor damage can result. Make sure you visit all the areas that the initial programming requests. This 375-hp 383-ci small-block has Holley's HP throttle body injection. Once the engine is running systems such as this, Holley HP tunes itself, so to speak.

back to the ECU. However, the charging system must remain at a 13.0 minimum charge rate so the ECU operates correctly and fuel supply is accurate.

Routing the alternator's power lead with the sensor wiring, for example, is not good; cross talk can occur from the alternator lead as load increases or decreases. Maintaining consistent and accurate voltage through the EFI is vital. Higher voltage or voltage spikes through the sensor wiring make the sensors send incorrect information to the ECU. If there is no way to avoid contacting the sensor wires, they should cross over at right angles, not run parallel to the high-voltage offenders.

You can use unterminated harnesses to avoid the mess of tangled-up wires that have to be rolled up and tied to keep them from being in the way. Correctly installing terminals takes some practice and is very important to prevent phantom problems resulting from poor connections. Most EFI systems come in terminated (ready-to-go) or build-it-yourself versions.

If you have concerns about how well you can properly install the terminals, you should use the custom-made, ready-to-go harness. Some extra wiring is required with the ready-to-go harness, and in most cases, it's easy enough to hide the harness from sight when installing it. You must accommodate for engine movement during installation and allow enough slack in the harness to avoid pulling on or stripping the harness when the engine is under full-load or WOT runs.

Although obvious, keep the wiring away from the exhaust and other heat sources to prevent insulation damage. If you install the ECU in the passenger compartment, always use a rubber grommet to keep the wire harness from chafing where it passes through the firewall.

Many manufacturers state that their EFI systems need to connect ground and power wires directly to the battery. The idea is to prevent ECU interference from other accessories, such as fan motors, that send multiple voltage spikes into the ECU's electrical system.

Another concern is placing multiple grounds at one position: crosstalk can occur as the grounded components seek ground on the other components in the ground wire stack. The best policy is to use multiple locations for the grounds, and give them adequate area to dissipate their required ground circuit as components are used. If a connector fits loose and comes off easily with minimal effort, beware: this is a future problem that could keep you on the side of the road.

Fuel System

Engine fuel consumption is configured using a brake specific fuel consumption (BSFC) algorithm. BSFC is a measurement of fuel used rather than horsepower produced, and it's typically calculated in pounds of fuel consumed

This is the fuel sender/pick-up tube assembly found on the 1968–1974 Shark; it is placed in the bottom of the fuel tank. Placing an electric fuel pump in this tank is difficult using the existing fuel sender/pick-up unit because the pump does not fit through the opening. Adding a fuel return line adds to the difficulty. On a positive note, if you use an external fuel pump, the sender configuration helps keep fuel at the pump to avoid pump cavitation. Installing a fuel filter in this location on carbureted cars protects the mechanical fuel pump from sucking debris into it before the carburetor.

This is the Rock Valley Antique Auto Parts fix for this original 1968–1974 fuel tank's electric in-tank fuel pump installation. They fill the tank with water for a period of time and vent it to the atmosphere to allow the fuel vapors to dissipate before doing any internal work. Then they cut the tank for the installation of the pump assembly. To prevent fuel starvation during cornering, the fuel pump is placed in a cylinder with holes at the base to allow fuel to flow in (but not out) quickly. Although this modification can be done at home, it makes sense to have a professional do it.

CHAPTER 4

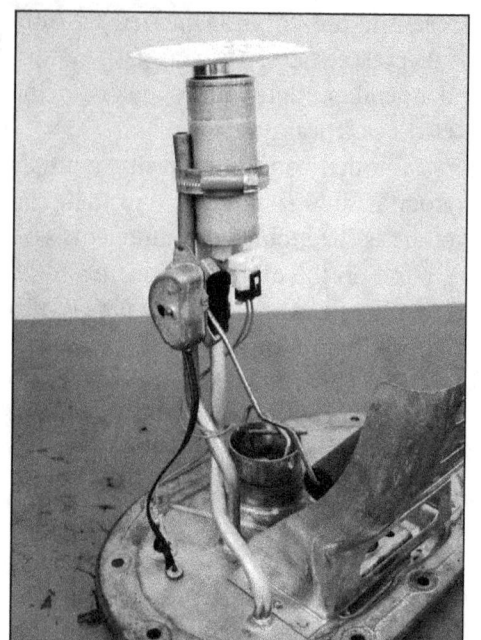

This fuel sender found in the 1975–1977 Shark is do-it-yourself friendly, although you must pull the fuel tank to access the sending unit assembly. Multiple screws hold the unit in the tank from the top. The original carburetor's 3/8-inch fuel supply tube is left in place and converted to the return line.

The sender's original 1/4-inch return line tube was removed and then the hole in the sender where the original line passed through was opened up with a tapered line-up bar. The tapered line-up bar forces the metal inward for a tighter fit of the new 3/8-inch tube, and more soldering surface is available.

Next, a 3/8-inch piece of steel tubing was formed as the new fuel-injection system supply tube and soldered in place. I had our local radiator repair shop silver solder the tube into the plate. The fuel pump is made for a 1982–1984 Corvette with throttle body injection at 10 to 12 psi. This works fine with a Holley TBI unit.

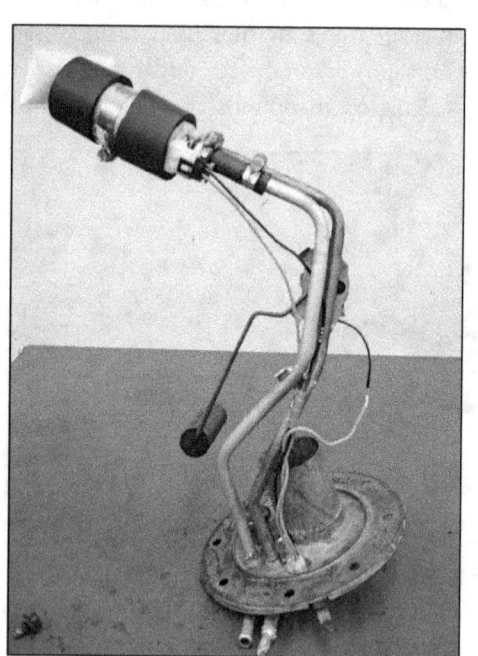

This fuel sender is for the 1978–1982 Shark, and it's easy to make the electronic in-tank pump conversion. One benefit to working on a later Shark is the fuel sender assembly can be removed from the tank after removing the fuel fill door. Once the screws holding the sender in place are removed, it must be rotated counterclockwise to pull it out past the tank opening and body. It takes some practice, but it does come out easily once you master the removal. Be patient.

You can use the same approach to install the pump. Note the fuel return line runs alongside the pump. The fuel returning to the tank should not drop more than 3 to 4 inches or static electricity could occur. You are risking an explosion if it does.

Another obstacle to overcome is the fuel pump wiring pass-through. This connector was scavenged from a junk later-model GM EFI fuel sender. Any GM EFI sender with a wiring pass-through works. The trick is getting the metal retainer ring off the pass-through fitting; work it back and forth a little at a time until it is finally off. Drill the sender so the pass-through connector is a tight fit as it passes through the sender. Install the connector and push on the original retainer ring (previously removed) with a socket while you hold the connector from the backside with your hand. This pump is a 1985–1996 Corvette EFI pump that produces 40 to 60 psi for multi-port injection.

per hour. This is a true measurement of the engine's efficiency, so the engine configured using the same components should have a similar BSFC regardless of the size or displacement of the engine.

On the other hand, internal engine component choices, fuel octane, and power enhancers can significantly affect the BSFC fuel requirements from one engine to another. This information concerning BSFC is a basic overview: it is highly suggested that you heed all engine builder, engine component, and fuel system manufacturer's recommendations.

The typical naturally aspirated (N/A) engine has a BSFC of .4 to .5 pounds x horsepower equals fuel consumed per hour. When a supercharger or turbocharger is added, the fuel requirements are expected to rise .6 to .75 pounds x horsepower of fuel consumed per hour. Nitrous-oxide-equipped engines' BSFC requirements are in approximately the middle for an N/A engine and super- or turbocharged engine. As an example, a 500-hp N/A engine requires .45 pounds of fuel x horsepower equaling 225 pounds of fuel consumed per hour. The same engine using a supercharger requires .7 pounds of fuel x the 500 hp, bumping the requirements to 350 pounds of fuel per hour. It is always better to use the higher number for safety's sake: for example, use .5 when working with an N/A engine or .75 for pressurized applications.

Determine Horsepower for Fuel Calculation

If you use Virtual Engine software during the engine build or have your engine dyno tested, you should have a clear idea of the fuel requirement. You can use an example of horsepower figures from another engine that has similar pieces. The idea is to get the fuel consumption on the high side (safe) rather than the low side. Remember, the fuel consumption numbers shown are guidelines, for typical engine combinations that have been proven over many years of research. Your engine may require a little more or less if it is tuned properly. The most important thing is providing adequate fuel to prevent starving your engine of fuel under load, extreme cylinder heat builds, damaging pistons, and possibly taking out cylinder walls along the way.

Too much fuel is not desirable either. Excessive fuel flow is detrimental to the fuel pump as the restricted flow heats up the fuel. It's not a good plan to use a pump capable of 600 to 800 pounds of fuel an hour at 50 psi on a 300-hp engine with a 3/8-inch fuel supply line. The pump works too hard trying to push the immense amount of fuel available through the system. Depending on the fuel control system in place, over-fueling could force raw fuel into the crankcase, which washes the cylinders of lubricant, causing premature wear on the rings and rotating assembly.

Flow Rates

Carbureted engines work under relatively low fuel pressures while requiring high-flow rates. A carbureted engine typically requires 5 to 7 pounds of fuel pressure to prevent the carburetor's needle valve from losing control of fuel flow. Higher pressures push uncontrolled fuel into the engine, causing rich fuel mixtures, if the engine runs at all. On the flip side, at WOT the carburetor's fuel flow rate is maxed out, giving the fuel pump a workout.

In an EFI system, the pump needs to maintain a fuel flow rate of 35 psi at idle, then jump up to 50 psi or more with adequate flow at WOT. Some of the later aftermarket fuel-injection systems and LS engines require 55 to 60 psi at all times while maintaining the required flow rate at WOT. What you have to remember is this simple rule: fuel flow rate drops off as fuel pressure increases. You have to select a fuel pump that flows the correct amount of fuel at the required pressure. The system should not be operating at full capacity every time the throttle is held wide open because a system operating at 100 percent capacity is under stress and more likely to fail.

This same principle applies to electronic fuel injectors and their flow rate. To prevent overheating the injectors during race conditions, their duty cycle must be considered. The preferred injector duty cycle is a maximum 80 percent at WOT to keep them cooler while allowing for any additional unexpected power increases. The calculation goes like this: The .45 x 500-hp engine requires 225 pounds of fuel an hour. Next, you divide 8 (number of injectors) by .80 (the duty cycle) to arrive at 6.4. Then you divide the 225 pounds of fuel per hour by 6.4 (indicating the use of 35-lb/hr injectors).

Aeromotive systems cover from 200 to 2,500 hp whether your engine is carbureted or fuel injected. These components have passed the test of time on the road and at many race events.

Fuel Supply System

Regardless of what power enhancement system you decide on, a reliable high-flow fuel supply is key to making power and preventing engine damage. It is also very important to properly install any and all components to avoid the resulting fire dangers from poorly constructed systems. Severe physical harm or death can occur from improperly assembled systems.

The original fuel system configurations of the 1968–1974 Sharks had separate fuel fillers and an under-tank-mounted fuel level sender/supply tube assembly. These original steel fuel tanks support up to 400 hp except under high-g loads from cornering or launches. The OEM fuel tank has no baffling to control fuel slosh, and this can be a particular problem when the fuel level decreases. The fuel sender pick-up tube placement is in a decent location for hard launches when the fuel tank is at least half full.

The 1975–1982 Sharks have a fuel level sender, filler neck, fuel supply tube, and return tube in one assembly. With this arrangement, it's much easier to modify the tank assembly and install an electric fuel pump for fuel injection; it could be installed on the factory assembly. By 1978, you could also remove the multi-use filler/sender assembly from the topside without disturbing the fuel tank. The 1982 Sharks filler/sender assembly was the first with an in-tank electric fuel pump for the Corvette's Cross-Fire fuel-injected engine.

All 1975–1982 C3 models' fuel tanks had bladders, similar to fuel cells, for some crash protection. With these models, General Motors used a rubber compound, and then a plastic liner eventually replaced the troublesome rubber liner. You must always inspect the fuel tank on every C3. Then you should flush the lines to ensure no debris or sediment is found in the tank. After a thorough inspection and flushing, you can confidently send fuel through your new fuel system.

To manage fuel line heat soak concerns, General Motors used a return line on all Sharks to help burp the fuel line, so to speak. The 1968–1969 small- and big-block engines had a provision for the return line in the fuel filter. In an effort to simplify the return system, a return line connector fitting was placed in the fuel pump from 1970 to 1981. A return line is used to route the vaporized fuel back to a separator and then into the fuel tank.

The return system relieves air pockets from vaporizing fuel through a restricted orifice in the pressure side of the system. This alleviated inherent vapor lock from tight engine compartments with high heat. This is a good system to keep in place, although many believe engine performance is limited due to the restricted bleed off of fuel pressure. This is not the case; the fuel pressure loss is negligible. If the fuel pump is weak, losing pressure to the return system could hurt performance slightly.

The OEM 1968–1981 fuel supply system is composed of 3/8-inch-diameter steel tubing and it provides enough fuel for a 500-hp-plus engine. In addition, the 1968–1981 C3s used a 1/4-inch return line, and the 1970–1982 had an additional 1/4-inch line for fuel vapor return to the fuel tank. Contrary to popular belief, the original 1/4-inch fuel return line is not adequate for an EFI conversion. The line needs to be upgraded to a high-pressure-line type and increased to 5/16-inch to prevent overly rich fuel mixtures at idle and mid-range engine operation. In an effort to limit hydrocarbon emissions fuel vapors could no longer be released to the atmosphere. The 1970-and-later fuel systems had to store fuel vapors and burn them off when the engine was in cruise mode/light throttle applications. An additional 1/4-inch steel line is on the driver's side of the chassis that handles fuel tank vapor recovery. In turn, a vapor storage canister is mounted below the brake master cylinder.

Fuel Filters

Clean fuel is essential for the entire system whether you have a carburetor or EFI system on your Shark. You should use a pre-filter before your mechanical or electric pump and one before the carburetor or fuel injectors. I have installed in-line fuel filters near the fuel tank on Sharks of many years. I install these filters where the supply line comes out of the tank to prevent fuel pump contamination. Mechanical fuel pumps use check valves to control fuel flow. One opens on the intake stroke and sucks fuel in while the other opens to let fuel out on the exhaust stroke. Any debris caught under a check valve renders the pump useless; the filter before the pump protects the pump and carburetor.

Fuel-injected engines need a high-flow filter in-line before the injectors to keep them from plugging up. They also need that pre-filter to keep a piece of debris from stopping the pump's rotor. Just one slight piece of debris can break a rotor vane, and the pump is junk. Be sure the filter you choose for the pressure side is rated for the typical EFI's 50 psi with a 20 percent safety margin factored in. Do not use glass or plastic bowl filters for any EFI installation. For that matter, do not use them for a carbureted version either. One simple hit and the filter can leak, causing a major fire danger.

Aftermarket Fuel Tanks

Often the most forgotten performance item, a correctly configured fuel system starts at the source. Fuel tank choices include custom-built fuel cells and purpose-built fuel tanks, and replacement OEM tanks.

Fuel Cells

True fuel cells are foam filled to prevent fuel slosh and reduce fuel from spraying out in the event of a collision that damages the fuel tank. They require custom installation; few if any are available as ready-to-install assemblies for any year Shark. This is the ultimate fuel tank for the ultimate fuel system in all respects. Just about any configuration of fuel pump and pick-up can be used. This is for the serious performance-minded Shark owner who plans on plenty of time at the racetracks, where sanctioning bodies expect to see total fuel control if the unthinkable happens. Considerable modifications are required to install the tank and have the fuel filler in the original opening. Fuel cells have a limited life span due to their construction materials, and they should have periodic inspections, which make them true race components.

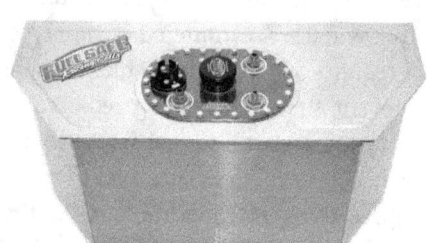

This lifetime fuel filter allows you to disassemble the housing and clean the internal screens. Pure Power manufactures this aluminum-bodied stainless-steel media filter for high-horsepower applications. It's universal use for up to -10 (5/8 inch) fuel lines. They also have specific applications with many connection possibilities. One major advantage of this filter is being able to periodically check your fuel quality for contamination. Another plus is that you don't have to locate a replacement fuel filter if you happen to fill up with bad fuel. You may have to clean the filter numerous times until the tank is cleaned but at least you are mobile.

Fuel Safe has been providing U.S.-made fuel cells in just about any configuration imaginable for high-horsepower applications for 30 years. Each fuel cell is engineered for the specific application, making the Shark installation more of a custom build. If you do sanctioned racing you can be assured that the fuel cells will pass the certification requirements of SFI and FIA. NASA and SCCA, along with a multitude of other race organizations, have approved them for use.

Fuel Cell Assembly

1 Install High-Flow Fuel Pump

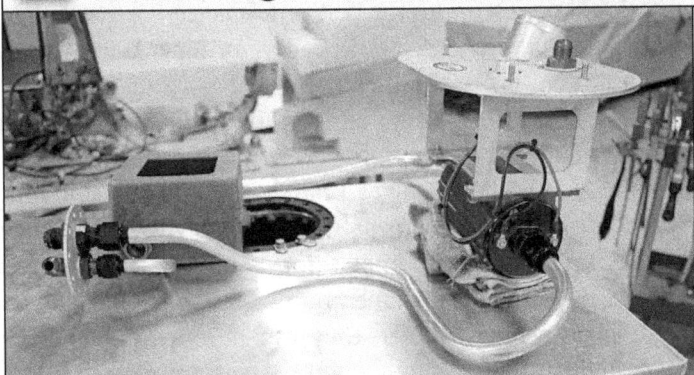

This EFI engine requires an Aeromotive 1000-series pump for the 700-plus-hp supercharged engine. I constructed a fuel pump mounting support, attaching it to the fuel filler plate of this true fuel cell. A 1/2-inch aluminum tube with AN flare fittings was used to supply the bulkhead fitting.

This takes careful thought about tube bending; long flowing radius bends promote high fuel flow rates. I use professional-quality tubing benders; Harbor Freight has a bender for about $40 that works well and does not crush the tubing.

As tubing diameters increase, so does the bend radius, often dictating the placement of the components. Stuffing the fuel pump, collector, and tubing into the tank with the foam in place is an interesting endeavor. I threaded four 1/4-inch bolts in from the underside of the bracket after tapping the holes for them. This allowed me to put the top plate on after all the pieces were stuffed inside. Fuel Safe recommends that the fuel cell be filled with water and vented to atmosphere to allow fuel vapors to dissipate before doing any internal work. That means anything that causes static electricity, including removing the foam, should not be done until the fuel cell has been rid of fuel vapors.

2 Assemble High-Tech Fuel Pump Pick-Up

This gray collector box makes sure the engine does not starve for fuel during cornering. To ensure the best possible fuel delivery, the collector is placed at the lowest part of the tank; rearward, for hard launches. This collector was configured on the horsepower and cornering requirements: the collector inlet size for proper fuel flow, whether they had check valves to keep fuel available at all times for this EFI engine, and placement of the inlets for cornering g-forces. (If I were drag racing, the collector would have multiple inlets at the side facing the front of the car for high-demand straight-line fuel requirements.) Fuel Safe supplied a pass-through connector with correct wiring insulation that is safe in fuel for the fuel pump power supply. The Fuel Safe connector (PN WH04M4) is an alternative if you cannot or do not want to use a salvage-yard connector in your Shark sending unit.

3 Assemble Fuel Cell

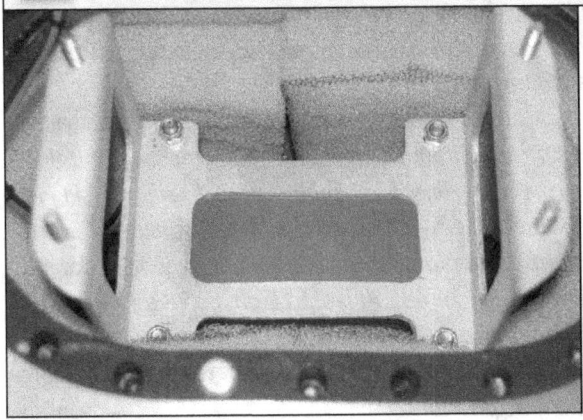

The pump, pick-up assembly, and bulkhead plate are installed in the fuel cell's foam. The sections of foam were carefully trimmed to fit the tubes and surround the components. Fuel Safe rubber O-rings were placed on the 1/4-inch studs and the filler plate was installed. This high-flow fuel system is for use in a road- or drag-race Shark where ultimate fuel safety is required. Remember, these fuel cells have a limited life span and require periodic maintenance, including bladder and foam replacement.

CHAPTER 4

Purpose-Built Fuel Tanks

Purpose-built fuel tanks are the most common performance tanks used for their ease of installation and long life. Stainless steel is the most common construction material with internal baffling to prevent fuel starvation and fuel slosh during high-g-force cornering. These tanks are set up with the appropriate supply pick-up assemblies and required return lines to support whatever horsepower you can throw at them. They also have correct sending units to work the original fuel level gauge. Stainless-steel tanks are much more durable than a factory tank if they are subjected to a crash. Some aluminum tanks are available but few are in use due to their issues with corrosion when subjected to water-laden fuels. The stainless does not corrode like aluminum can; the slight addition of weight is in the best possible place, making them the preferred material for long-term usage.

Over the past 10 years I have used Rick's Hot Rods (RHR) fuel tanks exclusively in my high-output Sharks. Just recently they put together a custom 18-gallon fuel tank for the 725-hp 1968 Shark Project. I required a tank that had 1/2-inch NPT fittings for a 5/8-inch fuel supply and 1/2-inch return lines. An Aeromotive 1000 series fuel pump was installed internally into a baffled compartment to keep the fuel around the pump's inlet under all the g-forces. The EFI 510 all-aluminum Donovan big-block performed as expected, with adequate fuel at WOT. The really nice part is this custom application was also a drop-in ready-to-go and it was not their first time feeding a high-horsepower application. Let them know your horsepower needs and fuel capacity, and they can put one together for you.

RHR fuel tanks also offer ready-to-go fuel tanks proven to support up to 600 hp. They are built on an assembly-line process. This approach has enabled RHR to put together a program to build tanks for the masses at affordable prices. The finely crafted stainless-steel tanks are set up for internal or external fuel pumps and whatever sending unit you may require for fuel level sensing. They are built to fit exactly in place of the factory tank, making this an easy swap in any year Shark. They also recommend using an Aeromotive Billet fuel pump speed controller to keep fuel delivery in constant control, depending on engine fuel requirements. The Aeromotive 1000 series pump is capable of flowing much more fuel than your engine requires at idle and low engine speeds. By slowing down the fuel pump, flow is lessened and so is the pressure on the system; in turn, the slower rate of flow keeps the fuel cooler. We all know cool fuel is good fuel for the best performance.

Rock Valley Antique Auto Parts is another national source of fuel tanks. They offer ready-to-go stainless-steel tanks for 1967 Corvettes and earlier. They can build a custom tank for your Shark if that is what you desire; they are known for modifying factory tanks for tuned port injection engines. If you prefer, they can modify your existing tank or build a tank from a sample or drawing with in-tank fuel pumps available per their website. The tanks are all baffled to prevent fuel starvation during cornering and are well built.

Purpose-Built Fuel Tank Installation

1 Install Stainless-Steel Fuel Tank

Rick's Hot Rods built this stainless-steel tank for the 1968 Shark application with an internal Aeromotive fuel pump for long highway road trips. They supply and install the correct stand-alone fuel sender for factory or aftermarket fuel gauges. You must consider the wire gauge requirements for the fuel pump power. We used a 12-gauge yellow power wire because of the almost 12-foot run of wire required from the engine compartment to the rear of the Shark. Depending on your application, you need either a 20-amp relay or, as in our case, a fuel pump speed controller that has a built-in relay.

Relays are used to control a high-amp circuit with a low-amp signal from a switch. This 1968's fuel pump is controlled by an Aeromotive billet fuel pump speed controller placed in the passenger-side rear compartment behind the seat. If you are using a relay it can be placed at the front of the vehicle, usually on the firewall above the starter. Make sure there is no voltage drop from the power source to the pump; it does not matter whether the relay is close to the fuel tank or not. At least 14-gauge wire (12-gauge is preferred) is required from the power source to the pump, with the relay in-line controlling the pump. The relay should have a fuse or fuse link as close to the power source as possible to protect as much wiring as possible.

PERFORMANCE FUEL SYSTEMS

1 Install Stainless-Steel Fuel Tank CONTINUED

The EFI ECU manufacturer provides a ground circuit to control the fuel pump relay. Once the ECU ground circuit control wire is connected, you need to wire a 12-volt ignition power source to the relay using 18- to 20-gauge wire, similar to what the ECU uses to control the relay. The recessed fuel supply and return fittings allowed maximum tank height. The straps and surfaces that the tank sits on are covered with the soft side of Velcro to keep the tank from rubbing on the steel pieces.

2 Install Custom Fuel Line

Note the rollbar frame mounting plate and the fuel supply and return line. The custom-fabricated fuel lines are stuffed into the frame at the front of the kick-up and come out for connection to the Mr. Gasket Shadow series AN fittings with stainless-steel flexible hoses. These are custom-built hose assemblies with removable or replaceable fittings that can be installed in your shop or garage. Stainless-steel or any high-pressure hose assembly requires the correct selection of fittings for the hose to be used: fittings are specific in their hose-retention methods.

I use a high-speed cutoff wheel to cut the hose; place tape around the hose so that the cut is in the center of the tape. This prevents the steel wire from fraying. The outer socket is then rotated counterclockwise onto the hose. After that a mark is placed at the end of the socket on the hose; this ensures that the hose has not pushed out of the socket too far. A manufacturer-approved lube is applied to the inner hose and threads, then the fitting is screwed into the socket.

Look at the previous mark. It should not move outward more than 1/8 inch. If it does, disassemble and try it again. I have found that keeping the hose back about 1/8 inch from the end of the socket prevents the hose from being forced out and is acceptable per the manufacturer's requirements.

Also note that the fuel lines are secured with rubber-coated strap clamps to prevent cracking from vibration as the Shark rolls down the highway.

3 Install Mounting Frame for Custom Fuel Tank

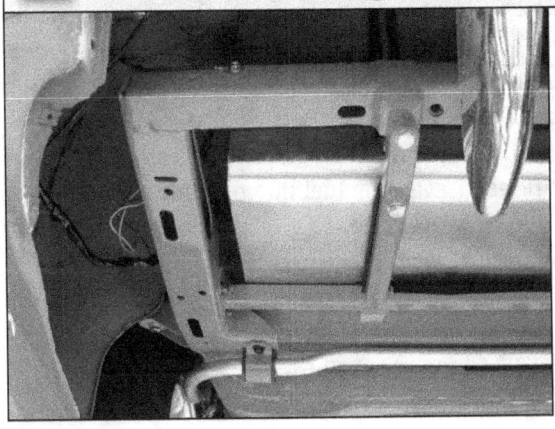

A custom fuel tank mounting frame was fabricated out of 1-inch, 20-gauge square tubing to drop the tank as far as possible. This allowed a taller fuel tank for longer stints on the Hot Rod Power Tour. Rick's Hot Rods built our tank from our drawings and a cardboard replica. That's right; a cardboard replica was assembled and then shipped to them to ensure a perfect fit. There is nothing like an exact replica to make sure everything fits.

Replacement OEM Tanks

If you are watching your dollars and EFI is in your plans, the 1975-and-newer Shark's factory fuel tank and sending unit simplifies the installation of an electric pump in the tank. The large sending unit/fuel filler assembly has plenty of room for the pump installation, much like a 1982 model's factory in-tank pump installation. The 1968–1974 Shark fuel tanks have a small-diameter fuel level sender/supply tube assembly that does not have enough room for the electric pump to pass into the tank's opening. In the past I have seen others modifying the tank with an access door for pump installation. This requires a fill-up with water to remove any fuel vapors before cutting

CHAPTER 4

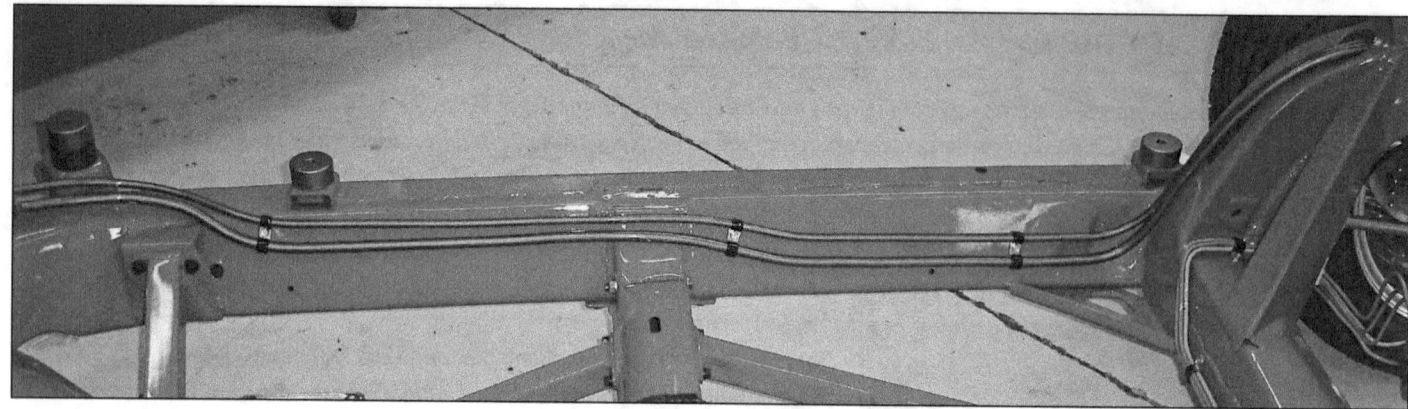

Bending tubing is an art, and it can be frustrating until you get the hang of where the bends end and begin. To acquire tube-bending skill, practice on some cheap or used tubing. This 725-hp 1968 Shark has 1/2-inch supply and 3/8-inch return lines installed with minimally sharp bends for maximum fuel flow. Proper support is essential for tube life and your safety: tubing that rubs on the chassis eventually wears. Using aluminum on long-haul projects is too risky unless frequent inspections are performed. Choosing the correct fittings is important to avoid flow restrictions.

There are a couple of alternatives to supply additional fuel if you plan to use nitrous for a power adder. This Y-block feeds the electronic fuel-injection system's fuel rails with two 1/2-inch lines. A 1/4-inch fuel feed line connects to the nitrous fuel solenoid for adequate fuel supply during a nitrous boost. On the bottom side, where the fuel supply is coming in, a 5/8-inch aluminum line feeds the Y-block with an Aeromotive 1000-series electric pump sending fuel to it. This feeds our 800-hp big-block 1975 Shark without any issues, even under nitrous boost. A 1/2-inch fuel return line is used to keep fuel heat buildup to a minimum under low-fuel-requirement loads.

or welding. At this point you should calculate the cost of the conversion. Then you can see how much sense it makes to go through all the trouble of modifying the tank, rather than purchasing the purpose-built tank.

Fuel Lines

Adequate fuel supply lines are required to get the fuel to the engine, if you plan on surpassing 500 hp or using nitrous, turbo, or supercharging power enhancers. Your fuel transport system must be designed to feed the additional fuel load.

Installing a high-flow and pressure fuel pump is only as good as the fuel it receives or pushes. Frequently incorrect internal diameter fuel lines are installed or the original lines are left in place, starving an engine of its much-needed fuel and robbing it of its performance potential.

For starters, I prefer to use as much steel or stainless-steel line as possible, avoiding long sections of rubber hose. Rubber hose deteriorates over time, eventually causing leaks that may lead to major underhood fires. Heat buildup is inevitable when fuel is pressurized. Long sections of rubber hose keep the heat in, acting as an insulator. Some say that is a good thing because it also keeps heat out of the fuel. It does, but once it gets to the surrounding areas' temperature, it takes a long time to dissipate the heat buildup. Steel or aluminum lines allow airflow to help the cooling process occur much quicker.

Always factor in the increase in fuel loads. Nitrous may require the addition of a stand-alone fuel line associated with the flow of nitrous. A correctly configured fuel system with an adequate single supply line can be used to avoid the use of the additional nitrous fuel supply line. However, the fuel line requires adequate flow to match the engine's horsepower output with the nitrous system fully engaged.

Here is an example: one of my projects required a fuel line change to handle the 700-hp supercharged nitrous-fed 427-ci engine. In some applications, such as an engine equipped with a supercharger and nitrous injection, a -8 fuel supply line and a standalone -4 fuel supply line are installed for a more than adequate capacity. The supply line was increased to -10 so the nitrous could be fed off the single supply line.

PERFORMANCE FUEL SYSTEMS

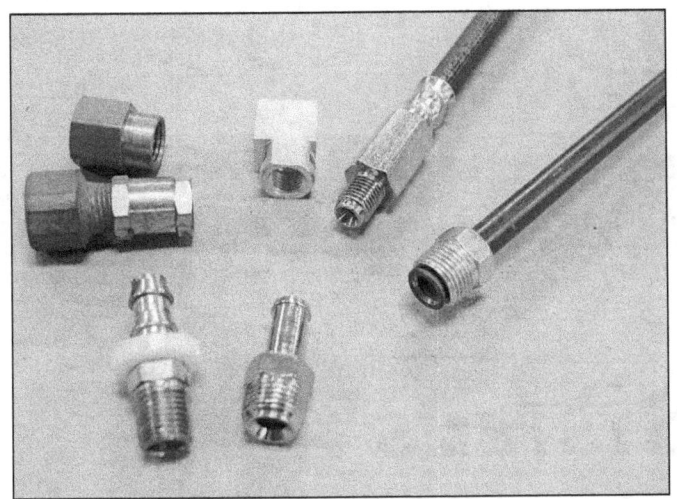

Your fittings must be compatible and complementary. If they are not, they restrict fuel flow and often leak, such as two NPT female fittings screwed together (left), with one fitting capable of doing the job (upper left). The tough part about automotive plumbing is the variety of fitting types; the two hose barb fittings (at the bottom) look similar, but the one to the right has a straight thread flare for direct installation into a carburetor fuel inlet. The fitting on the left is a tapered national pipe thread for multiple uses. The yellow plastic ring means it is a push-on hose fitting that does not require a clamp if the proper hose is used.

If a clamp is used it would cut into the hose and cause leaks. The steel line with tubing nut (far right) is commonly used for brake and fuel lines. The brake hose (upper right) uses the same straight-thread tapered-seat technology and should always be used on brake systems. The square block fitting (top right) used for the brakes has two different thread pitches.

If your fitting does not screw easily into the block, it's the wrong fitting. The rule is, if it requires wrenches to seat the fitting, something is wrong. Wrenches are for final tightening.

As engine horsepower output increases, the health of the fuel system becomes more important. Pipe bending for these high-output engines requires careful thought with long sweeping bends to avoid flow restriction at high RPM. Only a few tubing materials are used for plumbing performance fuel systems, such as carbon steel, stainless steel, and aluminum. Each tube type has its benefits and drawbacks.

Carbon steel is the auto manufacturer's choice because of its ease in bending and flaring. Carbon steel corrodes internally and externally, so most tubing manufacturers apply a coating to prevent external damage. The internal corrosion is a real problem today with some of the ethanol fuels, especially vehicles that are left in the garage long term.

Stainless steel is impervious to corrosion and can be polished for a really clean look. Bending and flaring stainless-steel tubing is difficult; aluminum tubing is easy to work with but it is also damaged by the slightest bump of a tool.

Aluminum tubing is typically used only in race cars to save weight and dissipate heat quickly. Proper tubing support and shielding practices are of the utmost importance to avoid fuel line damage. AN fittings are recommended for use with any aluminum tubing for proper tubing reinforcement. Keep in mind that race cars are disassembled on a regular basis, and each component is inspected for wear and damage. If you choose aluminum for your tubing needs, inspect it often for damage to the soft material. Bending the aluminum tubing may seem easy, but it also dents, dings, and crushes easily. I only use aluminum tubing for high-horsepower-application autocross and road race Corvettes.

Stainless-steel tubing is perfect for show cars and performance applications that require a maximum 3/8-inch-diameter tubing. Aluminum and stainless-steel tubing should be single flared for the best possible sealing under pressure. The same flare procedures can be used on any type of tube and over any compression fittings that have a tendency to leak, as the sleeves compress and loosen. Carbon steel tubing should be double flared to strengthen the connection if that is your choice. No matter how careful you are, the carbon steel tubing coating comes off and corrosion starts. Applying paint is recommended to keep the corrosion to a minimum.

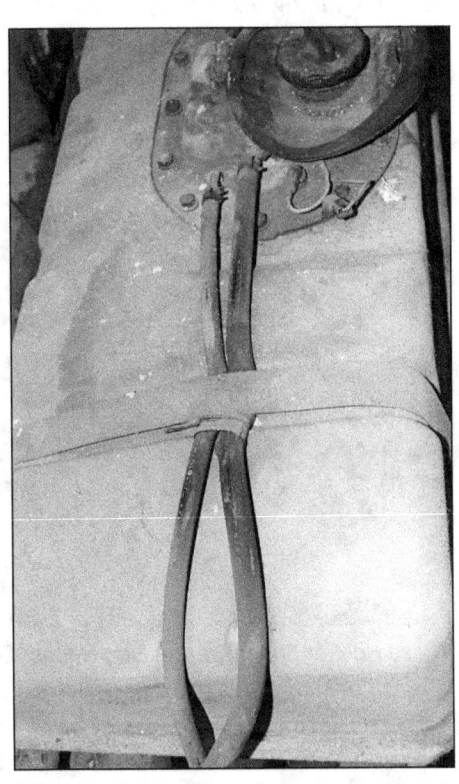

When the body of a customer's car lifted I found this absolute power limiter in place on the fuel hoses. From the looks of things it had been many years since the tank was out. This is not the first time I have seen crushed fuel supply and return hoses. I have also seen a 5/16-inch washer head screw caught between the fuel tank shield and the hoses; it crushed them.

CHAPTER 5

EXHAUST SYSTEMS

Many exhaust system installations are overkill or hurt performance due to design or tubing size. Catalytic converters are dumped because of the preconceived notion that all of them limit performance.

General Motors used cast-iron manifolds on the big- and small-block engines until 1980. Shark small-blocks were equipped with cast-iron "rams-horn" exhaust manifolds with 2-inch-diameter outlets until 1979. The 1968–1974 big-block engines had some hefty cast-iron manifolds with 2½-inch-diameter outlets. Although heavy, both the big- and small-block iron manifolds had decent flow for factory pieces. All went downhill in 1980 when General Motors dropped the rams-horn manifolds for a poorly assembled shorty-style replacement manifold. The tiny 1½-inch-diameter stainless-steel primary tubes had huge amounts of welding slag left behind. Those puny-tube, poorly welded, exhaust-choking shorty headers belong in the scrap heap.

These Hooker Super Competition smooth flowing side pipes have 1⅞-inch primary tubes and a 4-inch collector. They can be very noisy or quiet depending on the muffler insert. For many they are the way a Corvette should look and sound. Something else to remember is they are about 4 inches below the frame, reducing ground clearance and possibly scorching the grass if the engine is left running. They do well on the performance side, depending on the inserts. Hooker supplies the hardware to mount them onto the frame at the front and rear with carriage bolts and rubber isolators. The tricky part can be installing the lower valance once the side pipe is in place; that has to be done first to access the mounting nuts. Sometimes the lower valance requires trimming to get it off the side-pipe mounting brackets.

This high-flow 2½-inch Corvette Central exhaust system flows through Magnaflow modified mufflers and fits in the original location. The close-to-underbody fit is just what is required for the 1979 2-inch-lowered Shark. Random Technology catalytic converters for an emissions-legal retrofit (not for all states) were installed on this 1979 Shark. The front pipes were modified, and the rear pipes were just as they came out of the box. Although the front pipes were ready for the shorty headers, I had to cut out a section of pipe on each side for the catalytic converter installation. This system is a true out-of-the-box bolt-on when using shorty or stock exhaust manifolds without catalytic converters. The sound is unique, with a subtle idle that becomes more noticeable under hard throttle.

EXHAUST SYSTEMS

One trick to keeping that factory look while enhancing exhaust flow on the small-block is to use a pair of 1964–1965 Corvette rams-horn manifolds with 2½-inch-diameter outlets. These are the best-flowing factory manifolds and are sought after by circle-track racers restricted to factory pieces. The outer cylinder's exhaust gases flow into the center cylinders, acting as a scavenging system, and draw out the spent exhaust gases. Due to popular demand, General Motors and aftermarket reproductions of the 2½-inch small-block rams-horn manifold are available. Although the factory big-block exhaust manifolds had decent flow, they absolutely respond favorably to a set of well-designed headers because of the unavoidable manifold restrictions in a tight engine compartment.

Headers

Headers have been available for the small- and big-block Chevy engine for many years; by now the best designs have certainly been rethought many times. Shorty, equal length, long, Tri-Y, large, or small tube are the common header terms to contend with when on the hunt for headers.

Shorty headers are presently all the rage; many folks like the lower cost with the look of headers. The other positive is they can be easily connected to a stock exhaust system. Shortys promote slight gains in exhaust flow while looking better than the cast-iron rams-horn manifold, although they are not the best choice for serious power gains. Headers use primary tubes connecting each cylinder into a merge collector. Long, equal-length primary tube headers promote cylinder power balance and increase flow. This is where you also need to be careful: not all long-tube headers are equal length. Headers may be advertised as long-tube, but in reality the tube lengths are designed to work in a crowded engine compartment with the least hassle. Equal-length long-tube headers are difficult to design; the primary tubes have to twist their way through the engine compartment, passing by many obstacles. You also have to watch out for poor-fitting headers that can cause hot spots around fuel lines and coolant hoses. Sometimes you have to compromise for the ultimate power gain, dealing with tight-fitting tubes and other components that get in the way.

Choosing the Correct Headers

Many first-time performance engine builders want headers with primary and collector tube size diameters that are too large. The rule of thumb is to choose a header with a primary tube size 10 percent larger than the exhaust valve. Professionals start with that simple algorithm and then make minor modifications from there. For instance, a small-block cylinder head with 1.60-inch-diameter exhaust valves performs best with 1.75-inch-diameter primary tube headers.

Header tube size also affects torque versus high-RPM exhaust flow. Using a set of smaller 1.625-inch-diameter primary tube headers enhances low-speed engine torque on a 350-ci engines with a 1.60-inch exhaust valve diameter. This would be beneficial if your engine has lower compression (9.0) and a higher mechanical gearing (3.08:1) differential ratio as opposed to a 3.73:1 ratio. The 1.750-inch-diameter primary tubes would promote high-RPM breathing on the same 1.60-inch exhaust valve–equipped engine, while sacrificing low-RPM torque. The larger primary tubes would be applicable with the 3.73:1 differential gear ratio and 10.0 compression ratio.

The same rules apply to big-blocks to a lesser degree: the large-cubic-inch engine has more available torque. With large primary tubes, you often see higher-RPM horsepower and a reduction in lower-RPM torque. It makes sense to use a set of 1.750-inch-diameter primary tube big-block headers on a heavy truck application, not a Corvette. Whether you are working with rectangular-port cylinder heads with 1.88-inch-diameter exhaust valves or the oval port's 1.72-inch-diameter valves, 2.00-inch-diameter primary tube headers are above the 10 percent rule. Moving up to the 2.125-inch-diameter primary tubes is for an engine with aftermarket cylinder heads, a 10.5:1 compression, and 3.73:1 diff gear ratio.

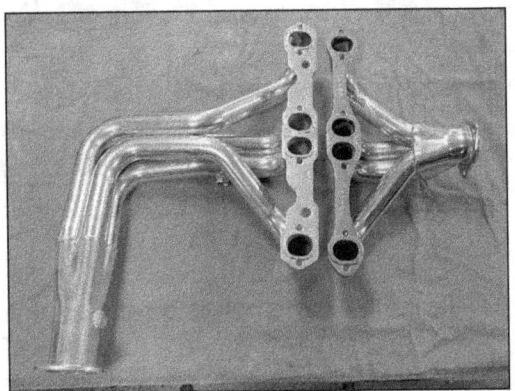

The long-tube set of Hooker Super Competition headers (left) gives you an idea of how the exhaust is tuned as it leaves the engine's cylinder head. The PerTronix shorty header (right) has similar tubing bends with close to equal-length tubes. Long-tube headers typically flow better at high RPM while the shortys provide more torque. Shortys are suitable for the street-driven Shark that occasionally goes to the track. They free up the stock manifold restrictions, especially the 1980–1982 factory stainless manifolds. If you want all-out high-RPM performance, the long tubes are for you. Engine compartment fit is similar with some additional tight spots on the long-tube set as they work their way around the starter. Gear reduction starters are recommended to get some clearance between the starter and the header tubes.

CHAPTER 5

Header Collector Configuration = Torque/Horsepower

Header collectors terminate the primary tubes into one large tube for the exhaust pipe connection. Contrary to what many think, larger collectors do not always mean more power. For example, take the primary tubes; torque can suffer if the collector diameter is too large. The general rule goes like this: small-block 1.625-inch-diameter primary tube headers work fine with 2.50-inch-diameter collectors, and 1.75-inch-diameter primary tubes benefit from 3.00-inch-diameter header collectors.

Big-block headers with oval-port cylinder heads, 1.750-inch-diameter primary tubes, and lower compression work best with 3.00-inch-diameter collectors. Rectangular-port cylinder heads with 2.00-inch-diameter primary tubes work best with 3.50-inch-diameter collectors. The science is in the collector length, which affects the taper. Shorter collectors have an abrupt taper, forcing the primary tubes down into the collector's exhaust connection. You need to look at the length of the collector: the longer the better, to an extent. As collector length increases so does low-RPM torque, while taking off some high-RPM-horsepower output. How the tubes are formed as they enter the collector also affects flow. This is the stuff that is out of your hands though, unless you plan on making your own headers.

Alternate Exhaust Flow Science

In an effort to enhance low-engine-speed airflow, Tri-Y header tubes were created. Tri-Y headers have two of the primary tubes merging into one large header tube; the larger tube then connects to the main collector. The concept is this: when two pairs of primary tubes are merged into two separate tubes, exhaust gases help draw exhaust flow out of the engine. The scavenging (or vacuum effect) promotes flow from idle to 5,500 rpm, making them more street friendly. The majority of Tri-Y collector headers are used for larger vehicles that require high-torque output to get them rolling.

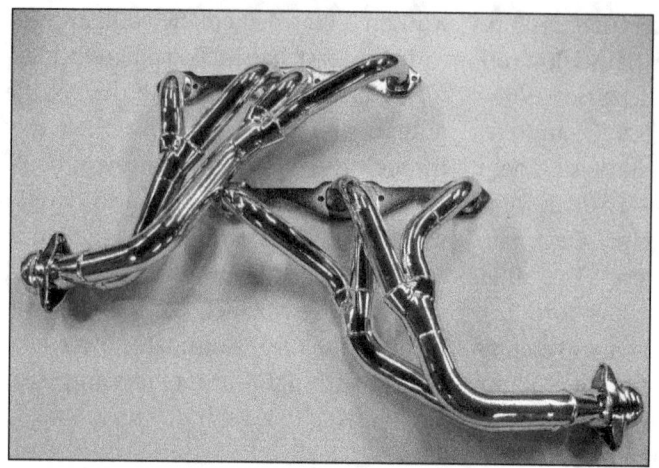

This Tri-Y set of Stan's Headers for a 1968–1982 Shark is a well-built set of headers that promotes exhaust flow at 5,500 and lower RPM. The exhaust pulses from one tube draw exhaust out of the other tube. If you want the most torque from idle to 5,500 rpm these are the headers for you; they are the majority of street/strip warriors. Another plus is the larger two-tube lower-tube set allows for more ground clearance, which is always a good thing. The 16-gauge tubing with 3/8-inch-thick flanges keeps the exhaust contained with the hydro-fused metal-core gaskets that come with each set of headers. The ball-type header flanges are not new technology but very smart for use on any exhaust system. The connecting exhaust pipes do not have to be perfectly straight to make a leak-free connection. If necessary the flanges can be disconnected without worrying about replacing a gasket.

Designing and building your own headers is something that you may consider. Today the best pieces are available, and high-tech welding equipment is also readily available. The tubes can be absolutely equal length and exact fit at the cylinder head exhaust ports and the optimum merge collector can be configured. The cons are you must be an accomplished welder or know one willing to work with you. Paying a professional to build a one-off set of headers is expensive and really not necessary with all the headers available out of the box. Finding and buying a ready-made set of headers is the smart money for the majority of performance builders. As cubic inches and horsepower increase, custom headers may be the option that works best for extracting that last bit of power.

A few final thoughts: smaller-diameter primary tubes and collectors enhance low- and mid-range torque. These smaller-tube headers are the best choice for smaller-cubic-inch engines with less drivetrain mechanical advantage. Large tube headers are for high-RPM use and more drivetrain mechanical advantage.

Preferred Headers

Stan's Headers has a set of Tri-Y headers for the 1968–1982 small-block Shark. Tri-Y headers are a welcome addition to the 1975–1982 Shark with a basically stock engine, boosting torque for an everyday driver. Those planning on major engine modifications expecting to extract maximum power should consider the long, equal-length primary tube headers. Hooker Super Competition headers are my favorite for out-of-the-box performance pieces for big- or small-block applications.

They have one set of small-block headers with 1.75-inch OD tubing and two sets of big-block headers with different-diameter collectors. They all fit well and are as close to the bottom side of the Shark chassis as possible, limiting the inevitable scraping of headers on the road surface. Additionally, there are no problems with fuel or brake lines being too close, causing more problems.

Side Exhaust

Don't forget that the GM factory installed side exhaust on 1968–1969 Sharks, making the installation possible on any Shark, albeit 1975 and up, catalytic converter models. Sharks of 1975 and later should have catalytic converters, creating a bit of an engineering feat to have the side pipes with the cats. Today catalytic converters are available that work if you really want to have side pipes, as long as you have a welder or muffler shop to do the install. The factory side pipes had a 2.00-inch diameter for the small-block and 2.50 diameter for the big-block. Although the connecting tubes were not mandrel bent, the long sweeping radius curves flowed well. There are no differences on the sound that factory-style side pipes emit; big-blocks sound throatier because as the fiberglass packing deteriorates the sound deepens.

Factory side exhaust pipes have a multitude of stampings that created openings in the tubes, allowing exhaust resonance sound waves to flow into an outer sealed tube. As mentioned, the area between the inner and outer tubes is filled with fiberglass cloth to aid in sound absorption. Although the sound deadening is somewhat effective, side pipes can be *loud*, especially when coupled with high-output engines with high compression.

This Shark-style chassis has a set of factory side pipes on a 300-hp engine. The smooth-flowing pipes have zero kinks or depressions because of their long, sweeping bends. These easy bends are more desirable than a larger inside pipe diameter. The muffler sections of the side pipes have dimples where the cutouts are deflecting the exhaust to help quell it. Unfortunately, it looks unrestrictive and it is. This factory setup costs about $2,600: it looks cool, but it's not the best for performance.

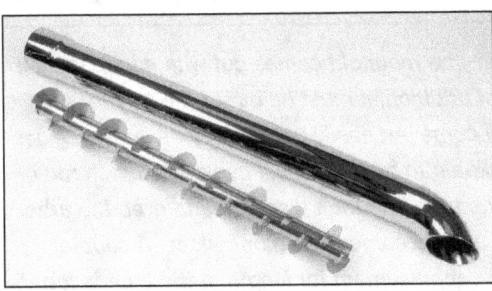

Spiral Turbo Specialties side-pipe inserts make a major difference in horsepower. Instead of the exhaust gases flowing forward as with the typical insert, this design allows the exhaust to exit the side pipe at the end of the pipe. As the exhaust flows straight out the pipe, noise canceling occurs as each of the spiral baffles absorb resonance. The sound is deep and has an authoritative rumble when in wide-open-throttle mode, but not like an unrestricted pipe.

The original side pipe covers had an aluminum and pot metal outer cover with fiberglass inner panels to lessen the exterior heat. Original reproduction side pipe covers are pricey, in the $2,500 range for the complete system minus manifolds. Aftermarket covers resembling the factory metal covers are available made of fiberglass, and these won't break the bank if you must have the side exhaust. In most cases the covers are painted car color to let them blend into the side of the Shark, concealing the fact that they are not the original, shiny, factory-style pieces.

Aftermarket Sidepipes

Hooker Headers has a complete sidepipe system that has everything from the cylinder head to the 4.00-inch-diameter exhaust-exiting sidepipes. They have both big- and small-block applications of the visceral-looking pipes in chrome or black coatings. These sidepipes make a statement even at idle. When the throttle is held wide open, everyone will be looking. The muffler part of the Hooker sidepipes uses fiberglass, forcing the sound waves into the outer area, similar to the factory pieces. Spiro Turbo Specialties is an alternative: they manufacture a baffle (muffler) for Hooker sidepipes. During dynamometer testing, horsepower loss was negligible whether they were in place or not. The noise level was higher than the Hooker sidepipe mufflers and certainly much more noticeable with no baffles in the sidepipes.

If you want the benefit of long-tube primary headers with factory sidepipes, Hedman Hedders has a set for big- and small-block engines that bolt directly up to factory side pipes. Couple those with the big-block 2.50-inch-diameter factory sidepipes and you have a free-flowing exhaust for Sharks with up to 500 hp.

CHAPTER 5

Header Buying Tips

Here are four things look for when buying headers for your Shark.

1. Flange thickness is an important factor for the best sealing at the cylinder head; 3/8-inch-thick flanges are the recommended minimum.
2. Check the header flange port configuration for proper fit: the header tube at the flange should be larger than the cylinder head port, never smaller.
3. Check the gaskets for proper fit; they too can block the header or cylinder head ports.
4. Use good-quality header gaskets or pay the price in aggravation by constantly tightening the bolts and listening to exhaust leaks.

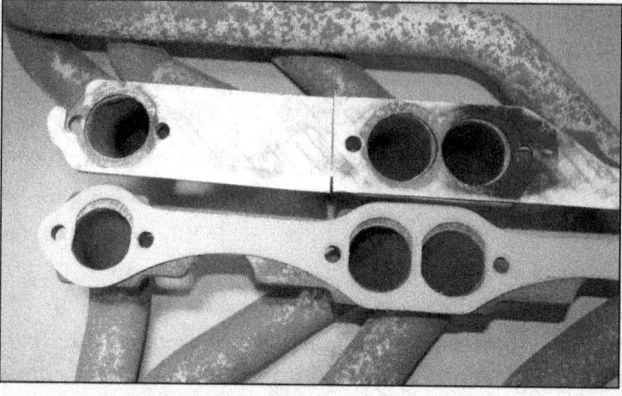

The original gaskets (top) supplied with the headers fit correctly on the inner portion of the tube. The lower header gasket fit okay on the bottom while the top of the gasket barely covered the tube. The gasket could easily slip off the tube and cause a major exhaust leak within a few hours of operation (if not immediately). The header flange has the tubes pushed through about .125 to allow the weld to be ground down after the welding process is complete leaving the tube protruding above the flange. Poor fitting gaskets can also cover the tube, which restricts flow. You may be surprised to find out that if the gaskets block exhaust flow it can take a very long time to burn away, if ever.

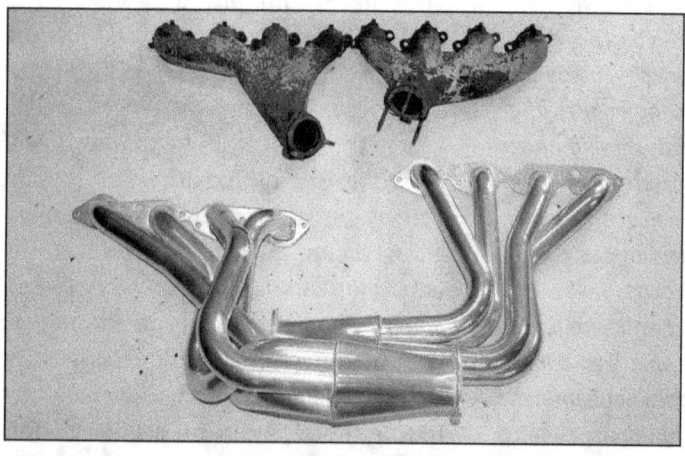

The factory 1969 427-ci exhaust manifolds (top) flow decently for low RPM. Somehow Hooker stuffed all those equal-length tubes into the chassis with this set of Super Competition headers (bottom). The 1⅞-inch-diameter primary tubes woke up the big-block on the top end.

Header Installation

1 Remove Oil Level Dipstick

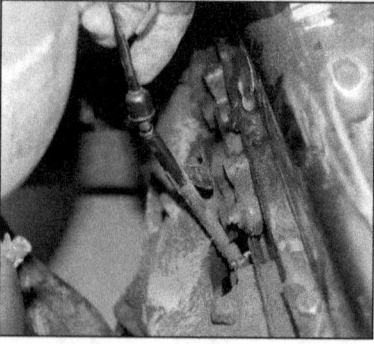

Remove the oil dipstick now, even though the cast-iron manifold comes out with it in place. All too often the tube is left in place and damaged. In addition, it must be out of the way for the headers flange. Big-block dipstick tubes typically come out easily unless they have been glued in place. Small-block dipstick tubes can be a real pain to break loose. I use a 5/16-inch rod or a number-two Phillips screwdriver inserted into the tube and then Vise-Grips to grab the tube. This prevents crushing it and, with care, the tube usually comes out in one piece. A couple words of caution: if the tube does break, check the replacement for length. If the tube is too short or too long the oil level will be incorrect, starving the crankshaft of oil or causing oil leaks. I also remove the spark plugs to gain more clearance to avoid breaking them off.

EXHAUST SYSTEMS

2 Remove Driver-Side Exhaust Manifold

Remove the spark plugs to make the exhaust manifold removal easier. You can either remove the coolant temperature sensor in the big-block driver-side cylinder head, or not. If you do, you have to drain the radiator. If you choose not to remove the sensor, take extra care to avoid the sensor when you lift the manifold up and out. The 1972-and-newer small-block Sharks have a coolant temperature sensor in the driver-side cylinder head between cylinders 1 and 3. These must be removed or they will likely break during this procedure.

Big-block engines have an oil line connected above the oil filter that can get in the way. The best policy is to remove the line and get it out of your way. Some small-blocks also have an oil pressure sender in the same location: be sure to remove it. I also take as many manifold bolts off as possible while the Shark is in the air.

3 Remove Passenger-Side Exhaust Manifold

The passenger-side exhaust manifold is very close to the starter and positive battery cable, so make sure the battery has been disconnected. You can also easily break the starter solenoid's plastic cover when you remove the exhaust manifold. From the bottom, I use a socket and ratchet to remove the 9/16-inch hex head nuts that retain the exhaust pipe flange to the manifold. In addition, remove all the 9/16-inch manifold hex head bolts.

Small-block engines may have a cooling fan control switch in the passenger-side cylinder head. You can remove the manifold from the bottom or top. On this project, I removed the manifold from the top after I took out the spark plugs.

When you install the headers, manifolds, or shorty headers, it is extremely important that you make sure the battery cable and starter wiring are located away from the new header tubes and secured so they do not come loose and burn on a hot tube.

4 Install Headers from the Bottom Side

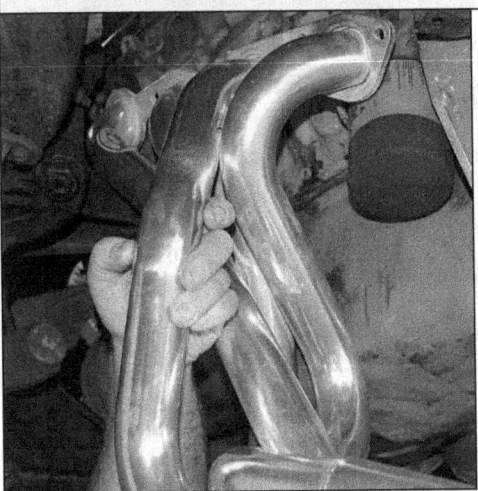

The Hooker Super Competition header slips into place from the underside. I thread one bolt loosely at the rear of the header to keep it in place until I get to the top side. Most header gaskets have slots at the front and rear. The gaskets can be slipped into place and then the rest of the bolts can be installed. I make this look easy with the 1969 Shark being on a lift; you need to be at least 2 to 3 feet off the ground to get the header installation angle right.

5 Install Header Gasket

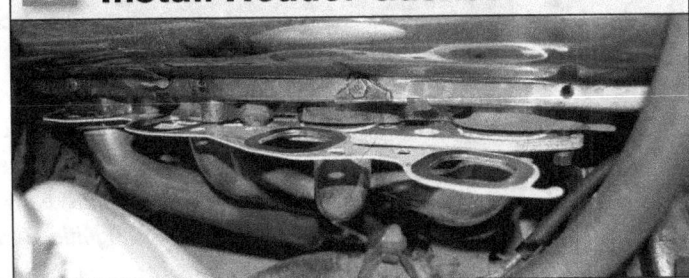

With the Shark on the ground, I install a header bolt into the front bolthole, and the Earl's exhaust header seals are slipped into place. These seals work long term; I have a Shark with 100,000 miles on one set of Earl's header seals. I've never had to even tighten the bolts after the initial installation. I do not use locking devices and have never had an exhaust leak. The key is to tighten the bolts again after the engine has run at least an hour; after that, leave them alone. You do have to be careful with these seals, though; the centers are soft and can be knocked out during installation. Once a few bolts are started, you have nothing to worry about.

6 Connect Headers to Exhaust System

This 1969 Shark had a new Corvette Central factory exhaust system already in place. The first step was cutting off the front pipe about a foot from the header flange so that there was room to fit the connecting exhaust tubing. I welded a couple of 45-degree mandrel-bent pieces of tubing together to attach the headers to the existing exhaust system. The tubing was securely tack-welded in place, then removed for final welding; fiberglass floors do not like welding heat. By 1975, General Motors replaced the fiberglass floors with steel to handle the catalytic converter's heat. I still would not weld the pipes close to the floor, whether they are steel or fiberglass: carpeting and padding burn quickly.

7 Inspect Header Installation

I drive and drag race this 1969 big-block Shark as often as possible. The Hooker Super Competition headers fit well and there are no road clearance issues. The equal-length tubes do not clang around in the engine compartment, either; even the starter has plenty of room to be removed if necessary. Another plus: these Hooker headers do not come as close to the starter as the factory manifolds, so no starter shield is required.

Sharks from 1968–1969 have deflection shields to prevent debris from entering the cockpit; both required trimming around the header tubes. Always check for possible pinch points or lines that may be lying against the header tubes. I have found that some headers are very close to the rear brake line on top of the driver-side frame rail. If so, either move the line or shield it. Have someone turning the steering wheel lock to lock and make sure there are no obstructions before the first road test.

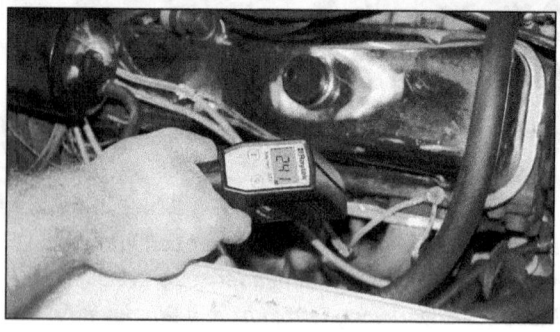

You can expect to see a heat gun display 300 to 500 degrees F at idle; if you see the tubes approaching 900 to 1,000 degrees F, shut the engine down and let the tubes cool. Most likely you have late ignition timing. Have your timing light ready for the next time you start the engine. Pay close attention to the ignition timing if the engine is running at fast idle due to the choke setting. The timing should advance to a minimum of 32 degrees at 1,500 rpm with no or light load. As engine speed and loading increases, temperatures can rise close to 1,000 degrees F. You're probably not under the hood during that workout; a long uphill grade is when the tubes get the ultimate heat buildup.

Header Coatings

Header coatings have come a long way since the days when you coated them with white or black high-temperature VHT spray paint. Although a coat of high-heat paint may seem smart if you are on a budget, long term it really is not. Painted headers rust and do so quickly, shortening their life. Ceramic coatings are more than a shiny finish to show off your headers. The ceramic thermal barrier helps thermal efficiency by keeping the heat in the header tube and promotes better engine performance. The engine also benefits from the heat barrier with cooler intake air as heat builds in the engine compartment. Hooker Headers offers a titanium ceramic coating for the ultimate thermal efficiency and long life.

EXHAUST SYSTEMS

The heat shield welded to this set of Hooker big-block side pipes is why I prefer to coat the headers after checking for any obstructions or possible hot spots that the header tubes may be creating. A Borgeson vibration isolator steering shaft connector was used to install the Flaming River steering column onto the rack-and-pinion steering. Leaving the isolator's rubber coupling unprotected from the big-block's header tube heat would certainly damage it. The shield was fabricated from .080-inch sheet steel, then welded to the pipe before coating. Check for header tube fit and pay particular attention to the boltholes at the header flanges to the cylinder heads. At times there may be an area that requires a small depression in the header tube to pass by the chassis, or the header bolts are difficult to install. A small dimple in the tube and the bolt is easy to access. You'll be glad you did when the time comes to install them for the final time.

This exhaust tubing is routed through the crossmember to gain clearance. The owner had larger tubing added to gain plenty of extra room for the exhaust. This type of modification works for most transmission versus exhaust system situations. The 700R4 overdrive transmission pans come very close to the crossmember. The welded exhaust system must be completely removed to remove the crossmember. Many Shark exhaust systems are completely welded to eliminate hanging exhaust clamps.

Now with that being said, an improperly tuned engine with late ignition timing melts the best ceramic coating quickly. Most header manufacturers recommend coating the headers after the engine is tuned or using a set of raw headers for tuning purposes only. When the header coating approaches 1,300 degrees, you can expect it to peel up and flake off. The titanium coating is rated for 1,600 degrees, which gives you a little more time to have the tune ready. The smart plan is to have an infrared heat gun handy to monitor the header tubes as the engine is running. This could save you the grief of replacing the headers or recoating them before you even get a chance to enjoy that first test drive.

My recommendation is to buy your headers uncoated, check for fit, break the engine in or tune the existing engine, then have a ceramic coating applied. I feel strongly about this. The Shark engine compartment is tight, and even the best-made set of high-dollar headers may require minor fitment changes. Often a small modification should be performed, such as a simple indentation at the header bolt area for wrench clearance. Once the coating is applied that is out of the question. Maybe you're going to go EFI and need an oxygen sensor bung or want a port for an air/fuel sensor in the header collector. Do that before the coating.

Exhaust System Obstacles

Exhaust systems have a few obstacles you may encounter, including ground clearance, backpressure, and tube bending.

Ground Clearance

The Shark has two limitations when it comes to the ultimate exhaust system: ground clearance and the transmission crossmember's 3½-inch-diameter pass-through sleeves. To gain ground clearance, General Motors used two sleeves in the transmission crossmember to keep the exhaust system as close as possible to the underside on the 1968–1979 Sharks. The crossmember's sleeve diameter does allow a 2½-inch-diameter exhaust pipe to pass through without clanging around over every bump. A larger-diameter pipe may go through the sleeve, but it will constantly rattle. Companies such as Keisler Automotive have purpose-built transmission crossmembers to alleviate this bottleneck; these crossmembers allow plenty of room for 3-inch-and-larger-diameter-exhaust tubing.

Backpressure

The statement that maximum power is obtained by zero pressure in the exhaust is only partially true. There should be absolutely no backpressure from the header collector rearward: the greatest efficiency for an exhaust system requires a minimum speed for good exhaust gas velocity. Overly large exhaust pipes lose the scavenging effect, negating the inherent pulses in the exhaust system's flowing gases. In simple terms, the larger-than-required tube exhaust system becomes a reservoir for the exhaust gases slowing down the flow. So tubing size does matter. Let's cover what is available.

Tube Bending

Another limitation is the factory-supplied exhaust tubing; it has ripples, kinks, and flat spots from the tubing bender as it pulls and pushes on the tubing during the bending process. From the exhaust manifold or header rearward, original-equipment exhaust tubing requires minimal bends to fit under

CHAPTER 5

This Bowtie Overdrive replacement transmission crossmember allows ample room for the clearance of just about any exhaust system tubing. You can bolt the replacement crossmember into the factory locations using the same hardware. You need to specify which transmission you're installing so you choose the correct crossmember. You may have to raise or lower the rear of the transmission for proper driveshaft angle. Keep that in mind if you are doing the crossmember swap only for the exhaust benefits.

the Shark, until it reaches the rear of the chassis.

Loss of tubing diameter and ground clearance becomes an issue as the pipes snake around the differential and rear spring before connecting to the muffler.

To maximize flow in smaller-diameter tubing, mandrel bending equipment is used, which leaves a smooth inner and outer tubing wall during the process. The smooth inner and outer wall throughout each bend promotes exhaust flow; this makes it the preferred choice for all high-output applications.

It costs more to mandrel-bend tubing for any vehicle, and your local muffler shop typically cannot justify the cost of the required equipment to do them on a daily basis. Specialty manufacturers are now building custom-fit mandrel-bent tubing systems for a limited number of vehicles. Luckily a few manufacturers have included the Shark Corvette in their mandrel-bent tubing lineup.

Few people want to believe that a properly configured 2.50-inch-diameter mandrel-bent exhaust system allows a 500-hp engine to breathe properly, but it's true. You don't need 4.00-inch-diameter pipes exiting the rear to avoid horsepower loss. More than 600 hp requires 3.00-inch-diameter mandrel-bent exhaust systems.

One key component of the properly configured system is an X- or H-pipe to enhance flow. Exhaust flow comes in pulses, not a steady flow. Like water leaving a hose, connecting the tubing allows each positive pulse to react with the slight backpressure occurring simultaneously in the other pipe. The positive pulses help draw the backpressure pulses out of the tubing, enhancing exhaust flow. H-pipes were used early on; now X-pipes are the most common. However it is accomplished, the most important thing is to merge the two pipes to enhance exhaust flow.

Catalytic Converters

Then there are those catalytic converters we all hate to deal with. If necessary, there are multiple catalytic converters available that have minimal impact on exhaust flow. Random Technologies Super High Flow SHF converters, for example, meet EPA and California ARB requirements with flow-enhancing construction minimizing restriction and allowing maximum horsepower.

Full-race catalytic converters are available for those who require them for their particular racing division; if you require them there is no reason to be dismayed.

Mufflers

Mufflers are the toughest decision for most of us: you want that perfect sound

Be sure your C3 has this important center support attaching the exhaust pipes to the transmission. I have seen many leaking exhaust systems that are missing this hanger. General Motors provided a center exhaust hanger for this very reason. When transmission swaps or larger-diameter pipes are installed, most of the time the hangers get tossed into the junk heap.

The pipes are attached to the engine/transmission assembly, so the pipes move with the transmission under load. It also helps to keep the pipes tight on the manifolds or header flanges. This 1979 Shark has a 700R4 transmission swap with a Bowtie Overdrive crossmember. To fabricate the exhaust hanger I used 3/4-inch tubing and a .125-inch-thick flat steel plate that is sandwiched between the transmission mount and the transmission case. To make it easy, two exhaust clamp saddles were welded to the 3/4-inch tubing. The exhaust tubing's close proximity to the transmission shifter cable and pan on the passenger's side was the reason for the header wrap installation. Quelling some of the rising heat from the exhaust tubing is also a good idea for more cockpit comfort.

EXHAUST SYSTEMS

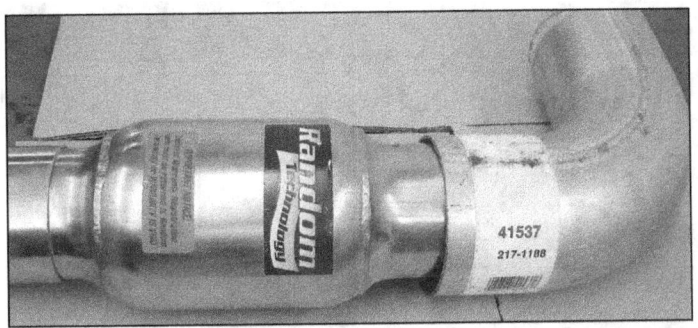

If you are required to use catalytic converters in your state, it won't be a big detriment to your performance build. These Random Technology monolithic-style catalytic converters keep the exhaust flowing with very little restriction. The stainless-steel bullet body keeps them alive for many years, and they come in a multitude of inlet and outlet sizes up to 4 inches. Some states do not require catalytic converters once your vehicle reaches a certain age, while others require the same factory-installed component. These Random Technology catalytic converters should out-perform any original-style converter from the Shark era in cleaning up the exhaust. All of the Sharks had flow-restricting bead-type converters. In reality, you would be helping by replacing the old-school, ineffective cats.

These Random Technology catalytic converters have been installed on this 1979 Corvette, dubbed "Shark Attack." To keep the floor cooler I fabricated heat shields out of 20-gauge steel, then MIG-welded them onto the catalytic converter's case. The cats were also placed as close as possible to the shorty headers so they would heat up quickly and begin their work of cleaning the exhaust. Wrapping the pipes front and rear prevented heat loss to the cats. I also placed the orange-colored heat shields on the speedometer cable and hydraulic clutch hose to ensure trouble-free, long-distance cruising.

or that sound your buddy's car has. The problem is, engine components and tune play into the sound emitted from any muffler. My preference is a throaty roar while under hard acceleration. Others like that ear-splitting noise from idle to WOT.

If you hear a particular vehicle and like the sound, ask about the engine components too, not just the mufflers used. Large-cubic-inch high-compression engines with long-duration camshafts sound deeper than a small-block with low compression, smooth idling, and low horsepower.

Kit Options

Kits are available in stainless-steel or aluminized tubing. Stainless-steel tubing should outlast the vehicle; you should be able to swap over to another before it has any major issues. However, stainless-steel tubing is even more difficult to properly fabricate and route. Stainless-steel tubing grows up to 1 inch in length or more as it heats up, making it more difficult to prevent the tubing from contacting the chassis. In some cases the stainless-steel tube expansion makes it difficult to find the sweet spot where it is not going to make noise when either cold or hot. Cost can be a factor too, if you are working with a tight budget.

The alternative is aluminized tubing, which could last 10 years or longer. If you go the fuel-injected route you could surpass 15 years or longer. Aluminized tubing and computerized engine controls have just about put the muffler shops out of business. Engines run leaner, eliminating the acids that ate up the old carbon steel tubing found on early vehicles. Back in the day you replaced the mufflers and rear exhaust tubing every couple of years.

Corvette Central

Today there are some great out-of-the-box options. These are complete kits that come with all the required pieces to make the install in one afternoon. For engines putting out 400 hp or less, companies such as Corvette Central have a true 2.50-inch-diameter dual-exhaust system for any year Shark. They use in-house original-type benders for proper fit under a Shark. During the writing of this book, Corvette Central added a new, state-of-the-art CNC pipe bender that eliminates many of the typical kinks and flat spots found when the old-school benders were used. That same 2.50-inch-diameter system comes to your shop or home ready to support up to 500 hp. The systems come in kit form, beginning with a set of shorty headers and ending with your choice of available mufflers. They also have available the correct exhaust tubing hangers for whatever system you choose. Correct-fit muffler choices are available from Magnaflow's deep throaty sound to the original stock sound for a custom-built system.

CHAPTER 5

Exhaust System Installation Tips

1 Install Muffler Hanger

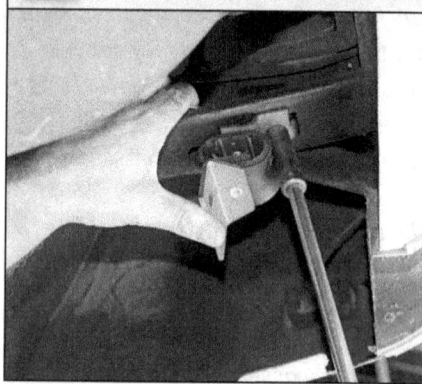

These Corvette Central hangers make installation much easier on the original Sharks chassis. There is not much leeway with the rear valance panel and exhaust mufflers tip, making it necessary for stock-type hangers to properly fit the tip in the opening. The mufflers also require strong, reliable hangers to prevent damaging the rear fenders. These original-style hangers have side-to-side adjustability at the frame and the muffler. You need good-quality hangers. After all, they are holding up the entire exhaust from the center of the Shark back. Keep everything loose (just tight enough to move around slightly); once all the pieces are in place begin tightening the muffler at the rear pipe, then adjust the hanger.

2 Install Mufflers

I chose Magnaflow mufflers for this 427-ci big-block to keep the noise down at highway speeds. Under throttle, they sound good with plenty of flow available for the big-inch engine. One problem with the Shark exhaust system is the lack of tailpipes, making them notorious for drone at constant highway speed. The stainless-steel case and internals mean you can just about have them for a lifetime. Another obstacle can be space with the mufflers tucked under the rear fenders. I do like the fact that Corvette Central had the correct bracket welded in place for the factory exhaust hanger.

3 Clamp Rear Exhaust Pipe to Muffler

This may seem simple enough: tighten the clamp and away you go. I place the ugly clamps upward for aesthetics and ground clearance. If the front pipes and rear pipes are placed correctly, the clamp should pass by the rear spring. If it is too close other areas hit the frame. With fiberglass springs, it is absolutely imperative that the clamp does not hit the spring as the exhaust moves. Any nicks in the spring can cause spring failure and loss of vehicle control.

The muffler can be moved up or down at this connection to make the exhaust tip look correct at the rear. I just snug this clamp up until all the pipes are in a happy place; once everything looks good they get a final tightening. If I'm happy with the sound of the exhaust I usually weld the connection to avoid the chance of them slipping: this way the clamp can be removed and there are no worries about the spring or ground clearance. I also add a spot weld (opposed to a full weld) if the owner decides to keep them clamped.

Hooker Headers

Hooker's approach is a kit that includes all the necessary mandrel-bent pipes for connection to their headers; you choose the mufflers. The aluminized mandrel-bent pipe kit is a sweet deal at under $200. Hooker Headers and Flowmaster offer mandrel-bent aluminized tubing in various bends for a custom welded system. This requires a lot of time and decent welding skills to make the system from scratch. The kit looks very enticing when you consider the work involved in fitting and welding up a custom system: they did all the hard work.

Pypes Exhaust Systems

If stainless steel is your mindset, Pypes Exhaust Systems offers a true bolt-on kit from the headers back to the muffler's mandrel-bent form. The Pypes system comes with an X-pipe and three possible sets of mufflers. There is a noticeable price difference over the aluminized kit, but they do supply mufflers. Be extra careful when it comes time to order either brand of kit, as transmission crossmembers, muffler outlet position, and muffler tips can be a concern on certain year Sharks.

CHAPTER 6

PERFORMANCE COOLING SYSTEM

Boosting horsepower and performance driving inherently creates additional heat in all of the underhood systems that require lubricants and coolant. Controlling drivetrain temperatures prolongs component life while maintaining the performance level you expect.

Understanding how a cooling system uses liquid to cool the engine's combustion process through convection is often misunderstood. The heat from the combustion chamber migrates into the surrounding engine components, and convection then draws the engine heat into the lower-temperature coolant. The water pump's job is to circulate the coolant through the radiator, where forced air once again uses convection to draw the heat out of the coolant. This endless cycle takes place thousands of times while the engine is running.

In many cases the original cooling systems are very close to the maximum heat load they can handle. Nothing is worse than having plenty of power and having to watch the temperature gauge the entire time you're on the road. As you approach a line of traffic your heart races, and you think "What do I do now?" You know that sitting in line is going to cause your temperature gauge to max out, and then the coolant will belch out onto the roadway. Having an adequate cooling system increases the life of your engine and the attached driveline components also allow you to extract all the available horsepower.

Cooling System Design

The C3's cooling system design was groundbreaking with its angled radiator canted back at the top for the lowest possible front-end height. The angled radiator core allowed a taller core to be used, although it created another issue: the radiator filler was below the top of the engine. General Motors went through a learning curve beginning with a remote reservoir located higher than the top of the engine to store and fill coolant. This made it much easier to keep air out of the cooling system, promoting better flow while keeping corrosion to a minimum. A remote reservoir (known by most Corvette owners as an expansion tank) was used depending on horsepower and engine cubic inches until 1972. By 1973, the expansion tank was gone, replaced by massive four-row copper tube radiators with side tank coolant fill for the high-performance applications.

An OEM radiator is designed to cool a stock engine. If your engine is producing far more horsepower (producing much more heat), you need a radiator with a higher cooling capacity. Using an aluminum replacement, such as this Griffin universal product, offers the best possible heat transfer at a cost savings. You have to do some measuring and fitment changes to the brackets; overall, this unit requires some thought but it's very doable for any year Shark.

C3 CORVETTE: HOW TO BUILD AND MODIFY 1968–1982

CHAPTER 6

Finally, in 1974, a brilliant idea came about: store coolant in a remote reservoir that kept the cooling system filled to the top with coolant at all engine temperatures. The coolant fill located in the radiator's side tank was used with a remote reservoir to store the heat-expanded coolant; as engine heat dissipated the coolant was drawn back into the radiator. A very simple valve was used in the radiator cap that allowed the expanding coolant to escape into the reservoir, until the coolant closed the valve, allowing system pressure to build. As the engine cooled off the valve dropped, and the inherent suction drew coolant out of the reservoir back to the radiator tank. When operating properly there are no air pockets in the cooling system, providing full saturation of the engine's component heat.

Although the Shark's radiator size is maximized by laying the radiator down, airflow is restricted with the small grille openings and is also somewhat blocked by the headlights when they are in the closed position. General Motors used openings in the lower valance panel below the grilles with an air dam to force air into the radiator area. One absolute Corvette cooling system fact: maximum airflow is critical for adequate engine cooling. To maximize airflow through the radiator, component sealing to the radiator core support is mandatory. GM sealed the radiator core to its support with foam strips, ensuring that any air in the radiator area went through it. Recognizing that every bit of air was precious, foam strips were also used to seal the radiator shroud to the radiator.

Shark core supports have multiple purposes, including holding the nose of the vehicle and radiator retention. The 1968 Sharks are much like the 1967 Corvette with a body makeover, and the core support is designed like the 1967 support. This is significant because the radiator core size is limited even though 427-ci engines were in the 1967 Corvette. Core supports in Sharks from 1969 and up equipped with A/C have the largest radiator openings. Radiator width is limited to the space between the inner fenders, and General Motors opened them up as much as possible later on. If you have a non-A/C car you can either change the core support or open it up with a cutting tool. Check it before doing any cutting, though; most core supports are in bad shape because of heavy corrosion.

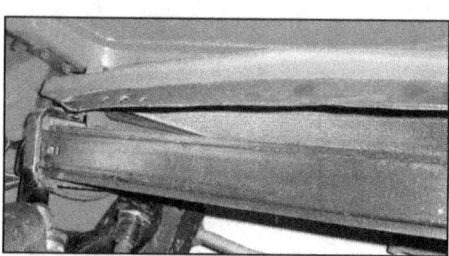

All too often the foam seals between the radiator and the core support are missing. Here I am checking for proper fit and placement. Once the fit is verified I install the shroud first, if the application has an engine-driven fan. The radiator is installed next, sandwiched between the shroud and core support. Companies such as Zip Products have complete kits to replace all radiator, shroud, and core support upper seals. Note the upper core support seal that seals the hood to the core support. All the available forced air must be funneled through the radiator and A/C condenser for maximum cooling efficiency.

If you plan to use an engine-driven cooling fan, this is one very important piece to keep your high-performing engine cool. General Motors placed foam seals around the exterior edges of the fan shroud to make sure every bit of air was sucked through the radiator, so this means the shroud is most important at low speeds and while idling.

Essential Airflow

When you think you have seen all the possible cooling system problems, a customer comes in and surprises you. The problem, like so many Sharks that come in, was overheating at highway speeds. As speed increased, so did the heat. Many shops had taken a stab at fixing the problem, replacing numerous pieces. My first look under the hood showed the typical concerns. It had no foam sealing strips but did have a flex fan for maximum airflow, new hoses, and a water pump. When I peered under the nose, something caught my eye immediately. The front portion of the inner fenders was missing. For some reason the inner fenders had been cut out, which left the front tires exposed as well as two large areas for any incoming air to bypass the radiator. I went to work cutting up some cardboard panels and used some 300-mph tape to seal up the new cardboard panels to the fenders. The results were immediate on the road test: the temperature held steady at 200 degrees. After fabricating some fiberglass inner fender panels the unfixable was fixed. It left an indelible mark on how important that maximum airflow is through the Shark's radiator. ■

PERFORMANCE COOLING SYSTEM

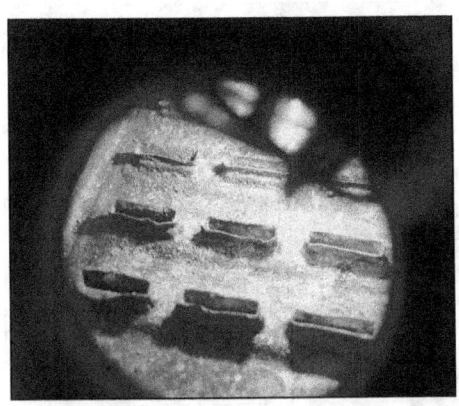

Small, heavy cooling tubes and corrosion buildup from acid-core solder are inevitable when using four-row copper radiators. Over time, the 1/2-inch tubes become rough internally from corrosion and scale buildup; consequently, any particles that might be in the coolant stream help to clog the tubes. This technology was good for the era, but today's aluminum radiator is lighter, easier to install, and lasts longer.

Radiator Choice

After many years of service, the original copper/brass radiators in your Shark often get plugged up, causing at least some restricted flow. In many cases, it has probably been a long time since the radiator in your Shark has been cleaned. The design of the copper/brass radiator lends itself to self-destruction because of the acid core solder used to sweat the side tanks to the radiator core. Solder has impurities; couple that with the acid core flux used to clean the pieces before soldering and the corrosive materials leached out, causing voids and eventual leaks. When copper/brass radiators were commonly used, true professionals disassembled the radiator and manually cleaned them, inserting rods into each tube to push out the crud. The first obstacle, if your radiator was adequate for the additional horsepower, was to find someone to clean it properly.

Another consideration is that radiator design has come a long way from the ultimate early-design four rows of tube radiators, typically found in performance applications. Early on it was thought that adding extra tubes would expose more coolant to the forced air entering the core for extra cooling. The resulting thicker radiator core actually resulted in decreased airflow through the multitude of tubes, and in many cases caused the engine to run at the same temperature or in some cases hotter than with a thinner radiator with three rows of tubes. If your budget dictates, it makes much more sense to chuck the heavy copper/brass radiator for a new aluminum radiator, which has better construction and heat convection.

Today the majority of automotive manufacturers use aluminum radiators. The plastic tanks are held on with aluminum tabs that are part of the radiator core's header. The upside is the late-model radiators can be serviced by just about anyone with a little patience and a pair of specialized pliers to crimp the tabs. Aftermarket performance radiator manufacturers do not use the plastic tanks due to the complexity of the process required to make specific tanks for each application. Performance radiators have fabricated aluminum tanks that are TIG-welded to the aluminum radiator core header.

Be Cool Radiators (in addition to their regular lineup of TIG-welded aluminum radiators) offers a stamped aluminum tank resembling the original factory tanks, making them hard to detect. The Be Cool stamped radiator tank option is the answer for someone who is concerned about the original look but also wants the best cooling system performance.

Aluminum is the answer. One-inch-wide tubes can be used without adding extra weight; more core area is exposed to airflow. Two rows of 1-inch-diameter aluminum tubes are also thinner than four rows of copper 1/2-inch-diameter tubes due to the required spacing between the

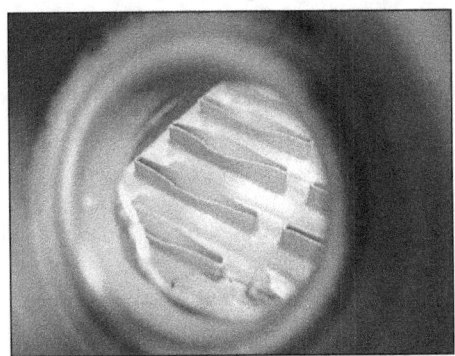

This 1-inch-tube aluminum radiator has more coolant flow capacity, and the exterior of the tube is exposed to more airflow. The aluminum radiator is thinner than the same copper replacement, with less chance of clogging thanks to the wider tubes. This is a high-quality aluminum radiator with furnace-brazed tubes. If you see evidence of epoxy sealing of the tubes to the header (where the tubes are placed through for tank installation), beware. Leaks usually begin early on.

tubes. The overall better airflow and heat absorption from cool air passing through an aluminum core makes them more efficient than any copper radiator.

The fins that reside between the wider aluminum tubes play an important part in how the heat is removed from the tubes. The finned area absorbs the heat and subsequently cools to the fluid passing through the tubes. Too much fin restricts airflow; not enough fin lets air pass through so quickly that the heat exchange does not occur. To sum it up: for most people lighter weight and better cooling justify the extra cost of an aluminum radiator. The TIG-welded tanks rarely have any leakage issues from contamination or expansion, making them very reliable over the long run.

Tube Requirements

Two rows of 1-inch-diameter tubes are adequate for performance Sharks up to 800 hp. At the 450–500 hp level, you

CHAPTER 6

Ground Factors

Corvette fiberglass bodies and electrical grounds have been a concern. As difficult as this may be to believe, the lack of a solid ground can affect the radiator's life. Corvette radiator core supports are grounded well to the chassis, while the radiator is held in place with rubber cushions. The lack of a proper ground means the coolant is the ground circuit from the engine to the radiator. As coolant ages and begins to pass the metal particles that typically occur from use, checking for excessive voltage is important. Aluminum radiators are more susceptible to damage from the voltage, because voltage attacks the softer metal. ∎

Electrolysis can occur in your Shark's cooling system, especially when ground straps/wires are omitted during assembly. General Motors placed ground wires on the radiator core support and the engine to combat this problem; frequently these grounds are left loose or become dirty, which causes this serious problem. You can check for excessive current in the cooling system by placing the multi-meter's positive probe into the coolant and the negative probe on the battery's negative post. Check on both AC and DC settings. Any more than .15 volts means corrosive damage is occurring to your engine and radiator.

This radiator shows no signs of electrolysis at the radiator fill cap area. As corrosion occurs, a black film covers the aluminum. If you find that the voltage is above .15, disconnect the battery and check the voltage again. If it is still high you have coolant that is becoming acidic and must be changed. At .5 volts, serious cast-iron and aluminum component damage results.

can find and purchase a direct fit radiator that works with minor installation modifications. Many aftermarket radiator manufacturers recommend electric cooling fans after 400 hp is reached for ultimate cooling. As horsepower rises into the 600-plus range, electric cooling fans and quite possibly a purpose-built radiator may be required. A 700-hp Shark driven on the street to the local cruise-in and occasional drag-strip use does not require the same radiator as a 700-hp road-raced Shark.

The most important item on the street-driven Shark is an adequate electric cooling fan setup for the low-speed, in-city driving. If your project exceeds 700 hp, expect to pay extra for a custom radiator and core support modifications to handle the additional heat load.

Shark radiator removal and installation is tough. There are some tricks that you need to know to accomplish the removal of the radiator and shroud.

Radiator Removal and Installation

1 Remove A/C Condenser Upper Screws

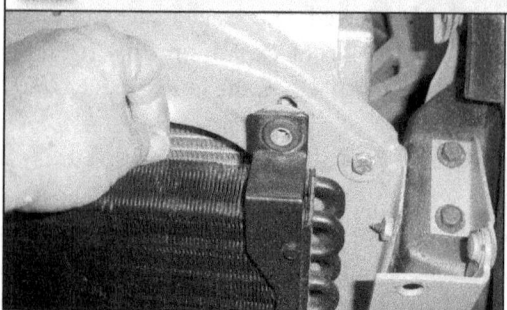

All 1968–1982 Corvettes use the same radiator and shroud retaining system when equipped with A/C. Non-A/C Sharks from 1968–1972 have a very simple one-piece retainer at the top of a tiny copper radiator that any respectable performance Shark would not use. The lower condenser retainers simply slide into the grommet and sleeve that looks similar to the upper condenser retainer. The condenser retainer through-bolt is also part of the radiator upper retainer. The bolt to the right (arrow) must also be removed. When it's time to reinstall the radiator, be extra careful of bolt length. Installing an incorrect bolt can pierce the radiator tank.

PERFORMANCE COOLING SYSTEM

2 Remove Core Support Screws

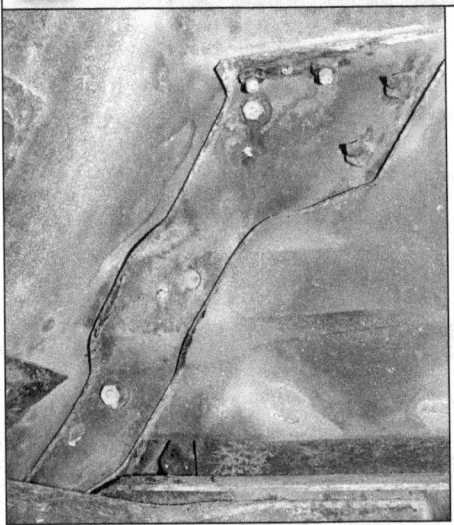

The 1/2-inch hex-head screws (with yellow paint) are the key to removing the radiator and fan shroud without damage. Remove the upper and center side screws after backing out the hood hinge screw to gain access to the side screws. The screws are found inside the inner fender; once removed they allow the core support to be moved enough to remove the radiator and shroud. In some cases the lower 5/8-inch hex-head bolts at the bottom of the core support require loosening to move the shroud enough.

3 Remove Radiator from Core Support

Once the core support is loose, the radiator can be removed (with a helper). The core support is pulled toward the front of the car while lifting the radiator out. Here the A/C condenser has been removed to avoid condenser fin damage on the headlight actuators. It is possible to remove the radiator without discharging the A/C. During A/C condenser removal, be very careful as you pull the support forward during radiator removal. Almost all the condensers have battle scars from radiator removal.

Coolant Flow Rate

The appropriate coolant flow rate is crucial for optimal cooling, moving at just the right flow rate, absorbing engine heat, and then releasing it to the atmosphere. Coolant flowing too rapidly can actually cause overheating because the coolant does not have enough time to absorb the engine's heat before its return trip to the radiator. Thermostats are typically dual-purpose, controlling coolant flow temperature and coolant flow rate. Removing one can actually cause overheating. Installing a high-flow water pump may not be beneficial from a flow-rate standpoint; they are beneficial for other reasons. Their efficient impellers raise flow rate while preventing cavitation or tiny bubbles in the coolant stream. Minimizing cavitation helps the coolant achieve full saturation on the engine's internal components, aiding in the cooling process. It does make sense to use a high-flow water pump for this reason; the thermostat regulates flow, slowing the coolant for optimum saturation.

The water pump on the left is a typical remanufactured part. The stock stamped-metal impeller at the back of the pump does a fair job of circulating water for a bone-stock engine with low horsepower. All of those pits are from cavitation. As the poorly performing impeller churns air into the coolant, the tiny bubbles pop and etch away at the internals of the water pump and engine. The Edelbrock aluminum case water pump on the right has a cast machined impeller that fits tightly into the precision casting bore. The efficiency is much greater with less turbulence, maxing the water flow potential.

Cooling Fans

All Sharks have engine-driven cooling fans. By 1979 electric fans were installed as a factory option on L-82 Sharks to aid the engine-driven fan when engine temperatures exceeded 230 degrees.

Mechanical

All engines had mechanical-driven thermally controlled clutch fans for the most effective and fuel-efficient engine cooling for the time period. The fan clutch uses a viscous fluid for cooling fan engagement, while a thermal spring operates valving controlling fluid flow and fan engagement. As engine heat drops, so does the fan's engagement to lower parasitic drag. As good as this fan clutch worked for the era, the fan only activated as fast as the engine RPM allowed. Many Shark owners removed the clutch,

C3 CORVETTE: HOW TO BUILD AND MODIFY 1968–1982

Coolant Flow Tip

During testing it has been found that the rear of the engine can have a considerable air pocket, and local hot spots occur. Both cylinder heads have water jackets at the rear that are closed off to coolant flow. A dome of hot air becomes trapped, causing the rear cylinders to have poor coolant flow. To combat this known problem I drill and tap the intake manifold at the rear, where the intake closes off the cylinder head coolant port. A 1/8-inch-diameter NPT pipe fitting is installed for a coolant bleed line that is tapped into the heater return hose; this is the hose that comes from the heater core to the water pump. The return heater hose is usually 3/4-inch diameter and the supply is 5/8-inch diameter. Some aftermarket A/C kits use 5/8-inch-diameter hoses for return and supply; always tee into the hose at the water pump. This ensures full coolant saturation at both rear cylinders and the best possible coolant flow. ■

This 1/8-inch NPT tap has been used to tap threads into the rear of the intake close to the distributor and the angled side of the intake. Placement depends on your particular intake but it's purpose is to alleviate a known steam pocket that occurs at the rear of the cylinder heads. From the bottom side of the intake you can see the area where the intake manifold gasket surrounds the rear water jacket port. The best place for the fitting is close to the top of the rear water jacket port as long as it does not interfere with any bolts or the distributor.

First, drill a hole with a 5/16-inch drill bit. Then use the 1/8-inch NPT tap and thread-tapping fluid. Run in the tap until you have about 3/16 inch of the tap thread showing then back it out, clean the area, and you're ready for the fitting. During the thread-tapping process run the tap in two rotations then back up the tap at least one-half rotation to clear the cutting threads until it's at the necessary depth.

This GM setup is used on the L-98 Corvette engine. The 45-degree inverted-flare fitting has the correct 1/8-inch NPT male pipe threads to screw into the block. The piece of 5/16-inch tubing has an inverted flare to seal tightly into the 45-degree fitting with a hose barb to keep the hose from slipping off the line. The hose is plumbed into the return side of the cooling system. This can be connected into the 3/4-inch heater hose with a three-way tee. The hose can also go forward and be connected to the radiator tank on the passenger's side, which is the return side of the cooling system. The fitting should not be any larger than 1/8 inch to avoid too much flow without radiator cooling. The coolant that leaves the rear of the engine is not routed to the inlet side of the radiator so it does not receive the benefit of cooling from the radiator. When filling the cooling system for the first time, leave this hose off to prevent any air pockets from forming; when coolant flows from the fitting you know the system is full.

When an LS engine is installed a coolant bleed line at the front of the engine must be plumbed into the radiator on the inlet side of the radiator. A 3/8 NPT female bung was TIG-welded into the aluminum tank to facilitate the installation of the bleed line. Do not omit this bleed line; poor cooling system operation results with possible engine damage.

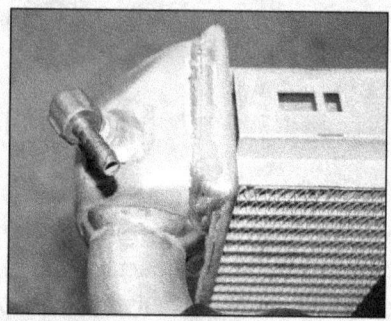

The LS engine does not have a traditional water outlet at the top. It comes out of the water pump. General Motors added the 1/4-inch rubber hose and crossover tube to bleed air out of the cylinder heads to avoid overheating. Sharks must have this hose connected to the water port that flows out of the engine to the radiator. The connection is made at the radiator. This is a bleed line only; it does not need high flow just enough to relieve steam pressure.

PERFORMANCE COOLING SYSTEM

This thermal fan clutch is easy to spot with the thermal coil spring at the front. Some thermal fan clutches have a thermal strip of metal in the same location; these also work well. The bi-metal spring heats up as hot air flows over it, directing the internal fluid for maximum fan engagement. Centrifugal fan clutches do not have any type of switching device on the front of the clutch assembly; they rely on engine RPM to engage, working at their peak efficiency when you need them the least. If you need a fan clutch eliminator and seven-blade fan to stay cool at speed, something else is wrong because of poor airflow through the radiator. Why use precious horsepower to turn a cooling fan if you do not have to?

installing eliminators or flex fans to help cool engines at idle. You could always tell when the eliminators were installed from the jet-like engine noise as the heavy metal fan blades spun up. Flex fans worked better, flattening out as engine RPM increased and lowering the inherent parasitic drag required to spin the fan.

Electric

Today few cars have engine-driven fans because electric cooling fans are much more efficient and effective. They make so much sense for many reasons, including less parasitic drag and maximum airflow through the radiator at idle while operating only when required.

I recommend the use of electric cooling fans. I set them up to come on at 200 to 205 degrees and then off at 190 degrees using a 180-degree thermostat. This setup works great with short fan-on times with a properly tuned engine.

Engine temperature hovers in the 190-degree range on the highway during cruising and is slightly elevated into the 200- to 205-degree range when driving under severe track conditions. Using a 195-degree thermostat causes an unbalanced hysteresis; the cooling fan stays on for long periods of time with the thermostat and fan-on temperatures being so close together. A manual switch on the dash is for cooling the engine after a long full-throttle run.

Many electric cooling fan are hastily installed and that is obviously not the way to go. You need to correctly install the fan to achieve the ultimate benefits from it.

I use the EFI controller to control the fans if that is the fuel control system chosen. If the fan system is to be used on a carbureted engine, you can use a very simple fan control switch. The switch is installed in the cylinder head, closing its internal contacts when the prescribed temperature is achieved. Two GM factory relays are used to supply current to the fan motors. This is a very simple, easy-to-install electric cooling fan system that is extremely reliable.

Some folks wire the fans to activate as the engine is started, saving the cost of switches and additional wiring. The thought may be the cooler the better, but then the fan has a constant parasitic drag on the engine, which requires more electrical current from the electrical system and the alternator. Your engine runs cooler but at an additional cost, and the cooling fan motor's life is shortened. None of the cooling fans available are built for continuous duty, so expect to replace the fan motors often if they run all the time. This practice is not recommended and is not beneficial in any way because performance, fuel mileage, and engine life are adversely affected.

Kits

Aftermarket cooling fans are available in kit form with multi-function controllers and fully adjustable temperature ranges. Most Shark kits come with two 12-inch electric fans, relays, and controller. If you choose to use an aftermarket electronic fuel-injection engine

This is the commonly found Shark aluminum radiator replacement with aftermarket cooling fans installed. As you can see, the entire radiator core is not covered by the fans, which is adequate for 350 to 400 hp in northern climates. The rubber flaps at top and bottom help at highway speeds, allowing maximum airflow through the radiator. The downside to using the aftermarket fan setup is finding replacement fan motors on a road trip.

CHAPTER 6

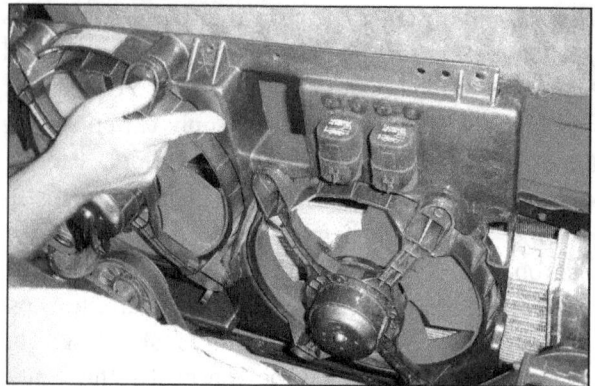

This is a Dewitt's factory-fit aluminum replacement radiator with a set of GM cooling fans from a 1990–1996 Corvette. When I install the 1990–1996 Corvette cooling fan assembly, it requires trimming the sides of the mounting shroud to fit the fan assembly closer to the radiator. The suspension's upper control arm is in close proximity to the outer portion of the fan assembly, requiring the thinnest possible mounting of the fans. The setup was installed in a 1979 Shark with a 375-hp 383 and A/C. The Project "Shark Attack" Corvette was driven on two Hot Rod Power Tours with no cooling issues whatsoever; it drag raced and sat for many hours in traffic. This setup works well with engines producing up to 500 hp. All GM cars from the mid-1980s onward use the same cooling fan motor.

My latest 1997–2004 Corvette fan assembly installation into the Shark consists of a very simple aluminum tab retaining the fan assembly at the bottom of the core support. The 20-gauge aluminum tab is placed into the original 1978–1982 fan shroud's installation cutout; once in place, a 3/16-inch aluminum rivet is used to keep it from coming out. The same procedure can be used on the 1968–1977 core supports. Place the tab on the outside of the support and use two rivets to hold it in place. The radiator cooling fan is captured between the core support and lower radiator core flange, which allows you to simply pull the radiator cooling fan assembly out without getting under the Shark.

When the 1997–2004 fifth-generation Corvette was introduced, this was the cooling fan General Motors used. I found that it works even better than the 1990–1996 Corvette fan assembly due to its thinner mounting shroud. The upper radiator cooling fan mount was fabricated from 20-gauge 1-inch aluminum angle stock, fitting it between the radiator tanks. The angle was attached to the radiator core's upper flange, and the cooling fans were then attached with 10 to 24 screws and Rivnuts placed into the fan assembly.

Removal and installation is simple, and the aluminum angle prevents any loss of critical airflow through the fans. Oh, yes, the same GM fan motors are used here for an easy fix on a road trip.

Here the 1997–2004 Corvette cooling fan is being set into place. Again, the radiator core support is being pulled forward to allow installation. This is a two-man job guiding the cooling fan assembly into place while trying to avoid A/C condenser core damage from the headlight door actuators. The headlight actuator doors have vacuum nipples that stick out. Removing the vacuum hoses gives a little more room for the radiator to move forward for the installation. I found it works best if the driver's side of the fan assembly is slightly lower to pass by the upper control arm as the assembly is lowered into place. Note the foam rubber seal at the top of the radiator between the core support.

PERFORMANCE COOLING SYSTEM

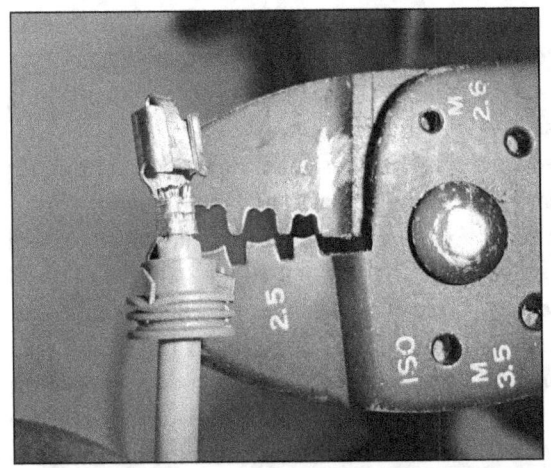

Electric cooling fans require 10 to 12 amps of current while in run mode. The amp requirements spike up to 15 to 20 at fan startup. That means you must have adequate wiring and good, clean, tight connections. GM-style Weather Pak connectors prevent corrosion and provide the best possible wiring connections.

These nifty W-crimp wire crimping pliers make a factory-style crimp to prevent any loss of current. NAPA, for example, offers pliers with five different-size W crimps for just about any wiring requirement. EFI Connection has the connectors, terminals, and seals for a professional installation for just about any electrical wiring project.

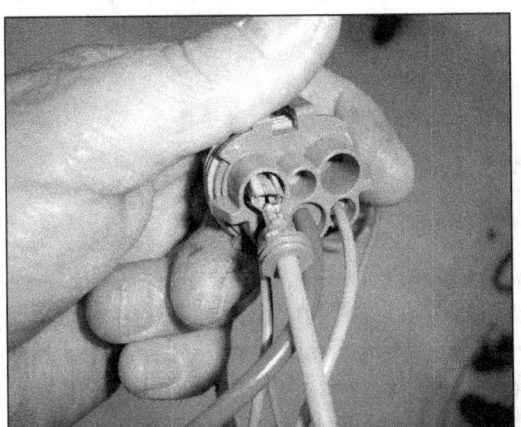

After the proper W-crimp is applied to all the wiring, the relays are inserted into this relay connector. General Motors used this first-generation weatherproof connector relay (PN 14089936 SPST) for numerous applications; it is readily available from Terminal Supply. Replacement relays have the wiring schematic printed on top of them, and the connectors have the same alpha designations.

Here, the light green 12-gauge wire that provides high-amperage 12-volt current to the fan is being inserted into relay connector position A. A 10-gauge red wire has been installed into relay position E, which has battery current coming directly from the starter's battery cable positive post. The lighter-gauge pink wire placed in relay connector position D is coming from an ignition source. The light blue wire in relay connector position F supplies the ground circuit, controlling the fan on and off.

controller, many control the cooling fans through their coolant temperature sensor. Spal makes a fancy controller for two electric fans that uses a pulse-width-modulated (PWM) controller for infinite temperature control. It uses a standalone sensor for input into the PWM controller that you adjust for optimum fan-on and fan-off temperatures.

Ancillary Cooling Systems

You may require other cooling systems to keep your engine oil, transmission, and power steering within acceptable range during performance driving.

The correct way to approach the ancillary cooling systems is to incorporate them into one plan. For instance, if you need an engine oil or transmission fluid cooler, where should you place it, and will it affect the engine's coolant temperature negatively? You know that placing any finned core in the front of the radiator impedes the airflow through the radiator to some degree.

Here you have a conundrum: oil coolers are a good investment for any performance Shark. Oil coolers come in oil-to-air and oil-to-coolant options. The typical oil-to-air coolers are finned radiators circulating liquids through tubing that is exposed to airflow. Oil-to-coolant coolers are placed in two possible areas,

This oil-to-coolant oil cooler is simply sandwiched between the oil filter and the engine block; it works extremely well. Engine coolant circulates through it from the bottom of the engine block and then out to the water pump's inlet side (lower radiator hose). You can expect a minimum 20-degree drop in engine oil temperature under heavy-load conditions. General Motors used these sandwich oil coolers on 1985–1991 Corvettes as an extra cooling package option. At Corvette swap meets, these well-built oil coolers are often found for less than $50. The aluminum tube that carries the coolant to the water pump can often be found lying next to the oil coolers, making the install relatively simple. The tube assembly works with the Shark suspension and steering without any modifications. The Pure Power reusable oil filter (shown) also helps keep your engine cooler with its heavy aluminum case drawing heat out of the oil into the air stream.

CHAPTER 6

Our 510-ci Donovan big-block benefitted from cooler oil when the 725-hp powerplant was put to the test. It made sense to use a radiator with an oil cooler built into the tank. Ron Davis put this special radiator together for me. The cooler was plumbed with 5/8 or -10 aluminum oil tubing from the engine. Using aluminum tubing is more difficult, but it looks cleaner and helps dissipate heat, whereas shiny braided hoses retain heat. High-pressure hoses connected the aluminum tubes at the bottom of the radiator to the engine's aluminum tubes. Any performance car benefits from an oil cooler because cooler oil means longer engine life.

sandwiched between the oil filter or in the radiator. Either one uses coolant flowing over the circulating oil-filled tubing to draw heat away.

The best all-around cooler choice for a street/strip Shark is oil-to-coolant. Your engine oil maintains enough heat to burn off any internal condensation in the oil and is hot enough to reduce engine parasitic drag. It's a known fact that a cold engine takes more horsepower to turn the oil pump. Race teams use heaters to make sure the engine oil is at the optimum temperature before their race car goes out onto the track.

The oil-to-air cooler removes more heat and makes sense for an all-out

Air-to-oil coolers are very efficient, sometimes too efficient. The oil should reach at least 200 to 220 degrees F for the best performance and long component life; lower temperatures allow condensation to build up in the component. At 200 degrees F condensation evaporates and oil viscosity is at the optimum level, causing less viscous drag. This cooler is being used for the power steering system; it would work equally well as an automatic transmission cooler. In fact, an air-to-oil cooler works best for transmission or steering system fluids because they tend to run hotter and get hot quickly.

A power steering cooler can be as simple as a piece of 3/8-inch tubing formed into an oval. This is the perfect location; the radiator cooling fans blow on the tubing and it is out of the cooling system's main airflow. The tubing is connected to the low-pressure return side of the system. As the heated fluid leaves the steering control valve it is routed through the tubing, then to the power steering pump's reservoir.

race Shark. If you plan on spending the majority of time at your local road course, choosing the oil-to-air cooler makes sense. During the warm-up laps your engine oil heats up and is at the optimum temperature for competition. Most of the oil-to-air coolers are installed between the radiator and A/C condenser. If so equipped, this raises the engine's coolant temperature slightly if the oil temperature is higher than normal.

Automatic transmission coolers are a must for hard-driven track Sharks to control torque converter temperatures. Torque converter temperatures can exceed 300-plus degrees under high-RPM heavy loading. The trick is placing the cooler in its own air stream away from the radiator; the restricted airflow in front of the radiator negates any possible effect. I disconnect the factory cooler in the radiator and place the air-to-fluid cooler under the Shark near the transmission with a scoop directing air into the cooler at speed. Using an air-to-fluid cooler is not recommended for a moderately driven street/strip Shark for the same reason as the engine oil cooler. The fluid and internals need to get hot enough to burn off any condensation.

Power steering system coolers can be very beneficial for road race or autocross Sharks. I install a power steering cooler on any performance-prepped Shark; it is mounted between the radiator core support and the front crossmember. Moderate airflow across the power steering cooler and the addition of extra power steering fluid all add up to less wear and better steering performance. This is why it makes sense to consider all the cooling system requirements before ordering any pieces.

Cooling System Tips

Poorly tuned engines can cause overheating. If your engine is overheating, you need to take a step-by-step approach to identify and resolve the core issue. First, verify that your ignition system is in good operating condition and the timing is properly set. Then make sure your fuel system or carb is properly jetted and operating correctly. If these systems are correct, then it is time to start examining the cooling system.

Always maintain a maximum of 50/50 coolant to distilled water or hotter engine temps can be expected. In warmer climates, 60/40 works best as long as freeze protection is taken care of. Use a 60-percent distilled water to 40-percent coolant ratio to cool your engine as heat dissipates from water quicker.

Engines that run too hot at idle typically have either poor airflow or inadequate coolant flow. Place a high-airflow stationary fan at the front of your Shark, directed at the radiator. Watch the coolant temp gauge. If the temperature drops, then airflow is your problem. You may need to replace the fan clutch or add an electric cooling fan if you are using an engine-driven fan.

Coolant flow may be too slow, not subjecting the hot coolant to airflow quick enough or too fast, not allowing the coolant to absorb the heat. To determine if this is the issue, raise the engine RPM to 1,200 and see if the coolant temperature decreases. If this is the case, then a high-flow water pump or smaller-diameter water pump pulley may be required. If all else fails, try slowing down the coolant flow. A flow restrictor from Moroso Products, for example, takes the place of the thermostat, and allows you to test for the best flow rate efficiency.

Hot engines at road speed can be due to poor airflow from a leaking radiator to core support seals. As difficult as this may be to believe, an improperly chosen electric cooling fan can block airflow at highway speeds. This is also where engine tuning is going to cause excessive engine heat, especially incorrect ignition timing advance and/or lean fuel mixtures. You may not have any overheating issues until you are on a long uphill grade, where a lean fuel mixture really drives engine temperatures skyward.

Many first-time performance builders do not understand that engine efficiency is better at 195 to 200 degrees of coolant temperature. Old-school thought was any temperature in the 160- to 170-degree range was going to enhance horsepower and keep engines alive much longer. NASCAR has proven that cold intake air with coolant temps in the 200-degree range are optimum for mileage and performance. I have seen this in real-time testing; my nephew dyno tests Sprint Cup engines and proves the theory.

Accessory Drive Systems

Shark Corvettes have old-school multiple V-belt-driven accessories with stamped steel or cast-iron supports and brackets. The original accessories have specific placement requirements because of engine compartment restraints. Alternators usually are on the driver's side outside the valve cover with the power steering pump below. Air-conditioning compressors are installed on the passenger's side, outside the valve cover. The alternator can be swapped from side to side with the A/C compressor. Most compressors are installed on the passenger side to ease A/C refrigerant hose routing. The accessories are outboard and as low as possible to fit them under the hood. Minimal clearance is available between the suspension's control arms and the engine, which prevents A/C compressors and alternators from fitting down low. General Motors used short water pumps on all Sharks; the short pump is easy to spot because of its close proximity to the timing cover. The radiator's angle (tipped back toward the engine) requires the use of the short water pump on all Sharks.

CHAPTER 6

Engineering the factory big-block accessory drive systems was quite a feat, fitting the components between the radiator and overall longer engine case. General Motors had to run the alternator off the power steering pump pulley because there was not enough room for three belts to rotate around the front of the engine. They also used an idler pulley with a belt that went around the water pump and crankshaft to make sure the power steering belt could handle the added load of the alternator. All the major Corvette suppliers have the pieces to make the original parts work in any year Shark.

Performance Accessory Drive Objectives

Performance vehicles are typically built for high-RPM use that requires careful accessory and pulley alignment to keep the belts in place when the rev limiter is bumped between shifts. Pulley diameter should also be considered to prevent over-revving the accessories at WOT. Alternator armatures do not like repeated 8,000-rpm blasts. Power steering, on the other hand, becomes sensitive as engine RPM increases above 6,500, causing poor high-speed vehicle control. Air-conditioning compressors come apart at high RPM. In this case there are two solutions: increase the pulley diameter or disengage the compressor clutch at WOT. If you plan on making long high-speed road trips, increasing the A/C compressor pulley diameter makes the most sense. Drag racing or infrequent full-throttle runs perform better with the compressor clutch disengagement at WOT.

Original Equipment

Using factory Shark accessory drive supports, brackets, and pulleys with original components is certainly a possibility on small-blocks. The same goes for the big-block components. The short run time and lower production numbers make it difficult to find many pieces lying around in junkyards. Fortunately, the majority of pieces for both big- and small-block engines have been reproduced, making them readily available at reasonable prices.

Brackets and pulleys from 1968–1977 early Sharks have decent alignment, keeping the old-school V-belts in place at high RPM. General Motors equipped the 1968–1972 Shark's special high-performance engines with deep groove pulleys, knowing that they spin upward of 6,500 rpm. The 1968–1972 Shark SHP engines were rated at 350 hp for the small-blocks and more than 400 hp for big-blocks. Pieces from 1978–1982 were not so good, especially the R4 A/C compressor itself; it did not like high RPM.

Here's one trick to keep the belts in place: use a 3/8-inch-wide belt for the A/C compressor drive instead of a typical 1/2-inch-wide belt. Using special high-performance deep-grooved pulleys also helps keep the belt on at high RPM. Moroso Performance has a multitude of V-belt pulleys to slow down your accessories and keep them in place at high RPM.

Underdrive Pulleys

Using underdrive pulleys is a common way to reduce parasitic drag and increase horsepower due to less engine loading at high RPM. Although this is an inexpensive way to free up some wasted ponies, it can bite you if the pulleys are too small (crankshaft) or too big (alternator, A/C compressor, or power-steering pump). You could be constantly chasing a weak or dead battery problem. The Shark factory-equipped power steering system is actually a power assist to allow more road feel; smaller pulley diameter can make it feel like the steering is way too sensitive. In addition, you cannot install a larger-diameter pulley; chassis restrictions won't let you.

One thing to watch for is the volt gauge reading at idle. If you find that the volt gauge reads below 12.6 the majority of the time, a dead battery is in your future. This pertains to those who might be idling the engine for long periods of time. To prevent a dead battery, the alternator must maintain at least 12.6 volts at idle to keep the battery alive. If necessary, decrease the size of the alternator pulley to speed up the alternator at idle.

Another tip: Watch the alternator fan on the early Delco alternators that are found on all Sharks. They have a propensity to bow outward at high RPM, which damages the belt. My first drag car kept cutting the belt, and I finally realized that the alternator's fan was bowing outward at 8,000 rpm from centrifugal force, cutting into the belt.

Warning: Do not place your body in harm's way. Looking over the front of the

This underdrive pulley is being removed to make way for a serpentine-belt accessory drive system. The 6-inch-diameter crankshaft pulley was used to slow the alternator on this early Shark. The typical Shark crankshaft pulley is 8 inches in diameter except for the special high-performance engine options. If you are constantly revving your engine above 5,000 rpm smaller-diameter pulleys make sense to avoid accessory damage.

PERFORMANCE COOLING SYSTEM

This is the alternator and power steering pump side of the 1988–1991 Corvette accessory supports and brackets. Note the large-diameter pulley for better road feel at high RPM. I made a custom A.I.R. pump eliminator pulley support and braces so I could use them on this 1979 Shark. A Dayco (PN 89009) serpentine-belt idler pulley was used to eliminate the A.I.R. pump.

engine while the throttle is blipped at high RPM can be very dangerous; a belt could be thrown off and slap you, causing severe injury.

Serpentine Belts

Other alternatives are available to bring your accessories "up to speed," and eliminate the inherent issues with the old-school V-belts. Serpentine accessory drive systems are used today on every engine configuration you can imagine.

These flat, multi-ribbed belts provide more traction surface area than the V-belt. The belt construction uses a much stiffer weave material, controlling the serpentine belt's overall length long term, while the V-belt is continually stretching until it finally breaks. One very important piece in the serpentine belt system is the belt tensioner, which keeps consistent pressure on the belt. When a belt tensioner is correctly engineered into the system, it applies greater pressure on the belt as engine RPM rises. You can expect maximum accessory traction with a properly designed serpentine belt tensioner.

I am pushing hard on the tensioner facts to make sure you understand the importance of the tensioner's configuration. Whether you are choosing the correct system or building a properly operating drive system, you need to understand the mechanics of the tensioner. The rule of thumb is that the belt tensioner must apply pressure and take up inherent belt slack as RPM increases. This can be seen as the belt tensioner moves inward toward the center of the engine as the throttle is blipped. There are systems available that do not have the correct tensioner engineering, causing squealing and belt slippage.

General Motors upgraded the 1984–1991 C4 Corvettes to use a serpentine belt system with a short water pump, although the 1988–1991 Corvette system is preferred. Corvettes from 1984 to 1987 used the R4 air-conditioning compressor, making them usable if no other option is out there. This factory accessory drive component system can rev past 7,000 rpm repeatedly without ever flipping off the serpentine belt.

The problem is that it usually takes a complete engine to find all the pieces to cannibalize for the swap. No one with a complete engine wants to sell separate pieces, unless the engine has catastrophic major damage.

I have installed a few of the 1988–1991 serpentine systems on Sharks when I can find them at a reasonable price. A reasonable price is in the $250 to $300 range for all the pieces, including the nuts, bolts, and studs. I mentioned the studs because of their unique design, which is difficult to duplicate or find lying around. The price may seem low for all those pieces; you are buying the supports, brackets, and hardware. If the A/C compressor comes in the deal that is one bright spot: they are reliable and work for many miles, which may be one piece that you could use without overhauling.

V-Belts

General Motors never mated serpentine big-block accessory supports and brackets with short water pumps. Late-model truck applications are the only possibility, and they are very tight with the long water pump. The work required to cobble something together makes no sense. If you're trying to save a few bucks, use V-belts.

This 1988–1991 Corvette A/C compressor support works fine in the Shark engine bay on any small-block. The Corvette's Nippondenso A/C compressor bolts to the support and is a very reliable assembly under high-RPM use. If these components can be found the price ($250 to $350) is a huge savings over aftermarket serpentine systems, plus they are easy to install.

Aftermarket Kits

Some excellent aftermarket options are available if you choose to deep-six the original archaic V-belt accessory drive components for a serpentine system. Here are a few things to look out for.

Avoid accessory supports comprised of multiple pieces supporting one component: they can be difficult to align and stay tight, especially under high-RPM use. For example, some aftermarket alternator supports are in two major pieces so they can be aligned, compensating for an ill-fitting assembly. The multiple pieces make them weaker and more vulnerable to breakage.

Many early aftermarket accessory drive kits used Heim joint rod ends, with adjustable sleeves instead of a belt tensioner; these are troublesome, requiring frequent belt adjustment. Then there are the systems with Heim joint rod ends and tensioners. The rattling rod ends wear, typically preventing the tensioner from taking up enough belt slack. A properly installed belt tensioner automatically takes care of the inherent long-term belt stretching.

Flashy chrome accessory drive components are fine for show cars; fit and function are what you are after. After long road tours with high-horsepower engines under the hood, I can attest to how important finding and installing a dependable accessory drive system is.

Beware of poorly fitting supports, brackets, and components during the installation of any accessory drive kit.

Always watch for raised surfaces that may keep the supports from sitting flat and square on the mounting surfaces. Water pumps, for instance, sometimes have a machined area for the bolt and washer. When your new bracket is sitting on the machined area, it may throw off the alignment of the accessory. If the supports are hanging on an edge, you may get lucky and just throw a belt from misalignment or, worst case, crack the support.

Make sure you know the required water pump rotation for your accessory drive system; most serpentine belt conversions require a reverse rotation pump. If you just changed the accessory drive system and the engine began overheating, check for the correct water pump rotation. You may be surprised how few people put this together and spend many hours trying to solve the problem.

Vintage Air has an accessory drive system that is well engineered with compact dependable components for the aftermarket. The accessory support architecture is as close to the center of the engine as possible while using a short water pump. Their use of one main support structure saves weight and ensures correct alignment after every installation.

Vintage Air has built vehicles for Bonneville Salt Flats (cooling a 200-mph-plus car); they know what it takes to save horsepower and keep you running at high speeds. Yes, their belt tensioner does work properly and is easy to handle during belt installation. They have Gen I small- and big-block versions that fit into a Shark. Vintage Air also has an LS application for a conversion, making the swap as easy as possible.

If you're concerned about the aesthetics multiple coatings are available for that show look or visceral I-want-to-play look. I like the raw aluminum look for ease of cleaning and maintenance. This is a performance car, right?

This complete Vintage Air accessory drive system is one of the easiest to install and it really works. If you want shiny, they have it. There is much more to the system than beauty: the single beam–type alternator and A/C compressor support allows the most engine compartment room without the typical vibration and drone of aftermarket setups. The power steering pump costs extra and has different options for any particular application requirement.

PERFORMANCE COOLING SYSTEM

Vintage Air Kit Installation

1. Install Accessory Drive Studs

Vintage Air supplies stainless-steel studs for their Front Runner accessory drive system. Sealer should be applied to the threads; I use Permatex Ariation Form-A-Gasket sealant. I also apply this sealant to the water pump and block surfaces to ensure a tight seal. Note the position of the supplied heater hose inlet tube. Incorrect rotation positioning can create interference between the tube and the main accessory mounting support. Each Front Runner kit comes with a Stewart high-flow reverse-rotation water pump for the best cooling system performance.

2. Install Power Steering Bracket

Once the water pump is in place, the lower brace or power steering pump support is installed over one stud, and two bolts hold it at the bottom of the block. Vintage Air has machined and recessed areas in the brace or a power steering pump mounting bracket to center the spacers. Make sure the spacers are seated into the bracket. All hardware going into the block should get a light coating of Never-Seez on the threads.

3. Install Main Support

This hefty main support is installed next, with the appropriate spacers. The A/C compressor and alternator were installed on the main support at the bench, and then the assembly is slipped over the studs. Take a look at the water pump's heater inlet fitting; check for any clearance issues before proceeding, and if necessary rotate the fitting out of the way. The trick here is to position the parts, start the bolts, and tighten all the fasteners.

4. Install Tensioner

The idler assembly uses a brace similar to that found on the power steering side of the system. The brace/tensioner was preassembled on the bench after checking and positioning the tensioner per the instruction sheet for A/C-equipped engines. Two supplied aluminum spacers are used at the bottom, mimicking the pump side with 12-point fasteners.

5. Install Mount Plate

This Vintage Air Front Runner big-block application with a front engine mount plate worked out well with our crank trigger ignition. The engine mount plate was made from the same-thickness material as the trigger wheel to keep the system in alignment. A ground strap should be installed at either of the alternator through-bolts. The surface conditioning of the components prevents a good ground, and possible charging system issues can occur.

CHAPTER 7

Transmissions and Driveline

If your C3 engine produces much more horsepower than stock, you need a transmission, driveshaft, and differential to match its performance. Many high-performance manual and automatic transmissions with overdrive gears are available. These efficient transmissions not only increase performance but they also increase fuel economy.

Manual Transmission Technology

Manual transmission technology in general has grown tremendously from the early Muncie and BorgWarner gearboxes that were available in the Shark era of Corvette production.

General Motors offered multiple gearbox ratios in the Muncie M20, M21, and M22 for Sharks until 1974. From 1975 to 1979, BorgWarner supplied wide- and close-ratio T-10 transmissions in C3s. Sharks built from 1980 to 1981 had either a wide-ratio manual gearbox or automatic. The last year of Shark production coupled GM's 700R4 overdrive automatic to the first electronic fuel-injected engine as the only available drivetrain.

The Muncie 4-speeds are good gearboxes that had a few known problems. Durability is the first major problem. When torque loads approach 400 ft-lbs, the internals cannot handle the loads and failure often results. Owners often applied high-torque loads as well as installing wide sticky-compound tires to replace the narrow bias-ply tires. The transmissions couldn't handle the extra load and failure was inevitable.

The aluminum cases take a beating at the countershaft bores, loosening the shaft the countershaft rides on. The loose-fitting countershaft support shaft moves the countershaft away from the main shaft gear set, causing wear and noise; eventually internal damage occurs, along with a gear oil leak.

BorgWarner T-10 4-speed gearboxes were more durable from my perspective: I drove many Chevrolet vehicles (including Corvettes) very aggressively in my

This early Shark is receiving a modified T-5 but most modern manual and AOD transmissions can be swapped into the C3. It is a tight fit with the non-removable transmission crossmember. Use a transmission jack to lift the transmission at an angle. After the bellhousing and clutch are hung on the transmission input shaft, raise the front of the unit. Another issue is the shifter location; placing the shifter stick in the center of the tunnel requires either a custom console or no console.

I consider this a fuel mileage benefit replacement. By the time you find a re-buildable unit and buy all the upgrade transmission internals (mainshaft and countershaft gears) to help it handle some real torque, you can buy a ready-to-go unit that handles the pressure.

TRANSMISSIONS AND DRIVELINE

early years. These gearboxes took hard drag-race launches better than the Muncie gearboxes. They too eventually fail after repeated hard launches with sticky tires. It just takes a little longer.

Because you are concerned with performance issues, the emphasis is on replacement gearboxes with the latest technology. The majority of performance car builders know that you want versatile vehicles that can get your heart rate up and still cruise the interstates. The following information covers the serious race options and the street performer build concept.

Today's purpose-built streetable units can handle up to 700 ft-lbs of torque with ease. The latest transmissions have geartrain tolerances that are much tighter than the OEM transmissions on the C3s. Many have roller bearings supporting the components. The tight clearances and better bearings require lighter-viscosity fluids in many of the latest manual gearboxes. The smelly high-viscosity gear oil of old also slows gear changes in the heat of battle. Those early loose gearboxes required the high-viscosity oils to fill the bearing and gear voids. Using 75W90 gear oil in a late-model gearbox makes shifting very difficult, especially at cold temperatures.

Old-school transmissions used tapered brass synchronizer rings on steel cones to slow down the gears during shifting. The brass synchronizer rings dragged on the cones, acting like brakes to aid in gear shifts. The synchronizer was forced onto the cone's taper, and this slowed down the gear for a smooth shift. That is, until they wore or broke, causing that inevitable gear grinding.

Today synchronizer blocker rings are lined with fibrous materials so they act as true friction braking components. Automatic transmission–type friction materials in the latest synchronizers help slow down the gears much better for smoother shifting at high RPM. In fact, many late-model manual transmissions use Dexron fluid, which complements the friction materials used on the synchronizer blocker rings. Bearing clearances are also much closer for precise shifting at high RPM.

One of the best innovations is the internal rail shifter most late-model gearboxes use. Having the shifter mechanisms internally lubricated keeps the shifting process smooth for many years with minimal service. The shifter rails are supported well internally, and this further enhances shift control.

In the early days of the C3, the Hurst aftermarket shifter was a common and welcome replacement for the Muncie-supplied sloppy factory shifters and light-duty shift linkage. The internal shifter is one step above the superior Hurst shifter, which has changed the shifter marketing plan for the aftermarket suppliers forever. No more adjusting shift linkages as they wore or if transmission servicing was performed. Shifter mechanisms, shift knobs, and sticks are about the only items available for the latest transmissions.

Transmission Gearing

When someone says they have a higher numerical first-gear ratio, they have a better mechanical advantage. As the ratio numbers get higher, less effort is required to get the wheels rolling. Conversely, lower-number gear ratios require more torque to get the same effect as the higher number.

Torque multiplication of the transmission and differential gearing aid in vehicle launch. Here you have to be more concerned with mechanical torque multiplication factors, without having an automatic transmission's torque converter aiding in vehicle launch. To achieve the automatic transmission's 2:5.1 torque converter multiplier effect, you need a steeper or higher numerical first gear in your manual transmission to help get the Shark rolling at the same velocity.

Here's the Math

To arrive at the gearing torque multiplier number when figuring total mechanical advantage, multiply the first-gear ratio by the differential ratio. For example, have a manual transmission with a 3.06:1 first-gear ratio and a differential ratio of 3.08:1. The torque multiplication is 9.42 (3.06 x 3.08 = 9.42).

Now let's factor in the engine torque output factor. Let's say your engine develops 200 ft-lbs of torque. You multiply the torque by the torque multiplication figure (9.42) to get the output factor. In this case it's 1,884 (9.42 x 200 = 1,884). When your clutch fully engages, your rear tires should have 1,884 ft-lbs of torque applied to them.

That may seem like plenty of applied torque at the time of clutch engagement lock-up, but remember the typical Shark Corvette weighs 3,500 pounds or more. About 400 ft-lbs of torque sure sounds better in theory with 9.42 x 400 = 3,768 ft-lbs of torque applied at launch.

Let's take this a step further. If your 327-ci engine develops torque at higher RPM or your engine is down on torque, you need to use a higher first-gear ratio to help your Shark get moving. Your 327-ci engine may have 3,768 ft-lbs or more of torque available. However, your camshaft does not provide peak torque until 3,000 rpm, so this limits your available torque unless you do a full-throttle launch.

Many do not want to drive a Shark that way, and it's not feasible if you drive on city streets. Either you increase the transmission first-gear ratio or you replace the differential gear set with higher numerical pieces to get your Shark rolling.

CHAPTER 7

Determine Differential Gear Ratio

For many years, you had to experiment to find the right combination. Today we have proven practices and theories that can save plenty of extra work and dollars. It's easy to make the wrong gear-ratio choice, and here's a common example.

A customer brings in his 1979 Corvette with a freshly installed 5-speed mated to a mild 350-ci engine with 405 hp, with 385 ft-lbs of torque at 2,400 rpm. The customer felt that first gear was not necessary to get the vehicle rolling. When they ran the engine to redline in first gear, it was short-lived and ready for second gear almost immediately. After some checking, I found the differential had a 3.73:1 gear set and the 5-speed had a 3.27:1 first gear that provided a 12.19:1combined first gear ratio. This 1979 Shark was ready to climb a vertical wall with the 385 ft-lbs of torque.

If the engine had a longer-duration camshaft, the torque curve changed to 3,000 to 7,500 rpm and the 12.19:1 final ratio was required. Instead, this car needed a 3.23:1 differential gear ratio: the car didn't go to redline immediately in first and it performed to the owner's expectations. The customer had the use of first gear and fuel mileage increased, so he was satisfied. Don't forget about the overdrive gear ratio that must also complement the differential gear set. As an example, having an overdrive ratio of .68:1 with a 2.73:1 differential gear set rarely required you to put the transmission in overdrive, due to engine lugging. Couple that combo with a camshaft power band in the 3,000 to 7,000 range and you had one sluggish Shark.

Now, once you got rolling on a long road course above 100 mph, the gearing was to your advantage. Always consider the engine's torque output (and when it comes in) while configuring your transmission gear choices. Torque gets the vehicle rolling, while horsepower moves it quicker after the initial launch.

Here is an example of a well-planned drivetrain, from the engine's torque output to the differential's final-drive gear ratio. The 383-ci 473-hp engine develops 400 ft-lbs of torque at 2,500 rpm, peaking 455 ft-lbs at 4,500 rpm. I chose a transmission with a 2.66:1 first-gear ratio and 3.73:1 differential gear set. Using the earlier figures, I have a 9.92 mechanical advantage applying 3,968 ft-lbs of torque at 2,500 rpm. A .68:1 overdrive gear utilizes the 400 ft-lbs of torque wisely, cruising 77 mph at 2,500 rpm. This combination provides excellent throttle response while maximizing fuel mileage.

Not only is this combination fun to drive, drivetrain wear is minimized and you can expect long clutch life. Fuel efficiency is also maximized regardless of your engine configuration. That may not be much of an improvement, but every drop saved is beneficial. Keep in mind any long-term engine plans too. You may have to compromise performance a bit upfront. No one wants two or three transmissions sitting around until that perfect one is found. A combined first-gear ratio in the 9.5 to 10.5:1 area in the 2,250- to 3,000-rpm range is a good rule of thumb. Larger-cubic-inch engines allow you to use lower combined first-gear ratios. ■

On the other end of the spectrum, a 427-ci Shark with plenty of low-end torque works better with a lower numerical first gear. Here it makes sense to use a 2.87:1 transmission first gear with a 3.23:1 differential gear set: 2.87 x 3.23 = 9.27:1 combined ratio.

Transmission Options

The original Muncie 4-speed and Turbo-Hydramatic 350 are antiquated by today's standards. There are many high-performance transmission options for the Shark today whether you feel like shifting manually or letting the transmission select gears for itself.

Tremec T5

Let's begin with GM units that are available for a Shark. Tremec (formerly BorgWarner) T5 5-speeds were found in S-10 pickups and 1985–1992 Camaros.

The 1983–1987 T5 versions are dubbed non-world-class and only capable of handling a wimpy 265 ft-lbs of torque. The 1988–1992 models are world-class and have better main shaft support, so the torque rating is 300 ft-lbs. Parts are available and some specialists are upgrading them to handle some serious torque in excess of 600 ft-lbs. That is questionable, though: the cases are not that tough and the gear designs do not withstand the elevated torque even with superior materials.

If you decide to go the T5 route upgrade, parts are available from places such as Medatronics Corporation and D&D Performance. Each supplier has its own opinion as to what is best for a high-load T5, which means you have to do some serious investigating to make this decision. Because of the lower cost of this unit compared to other Tremec

TRANSMISSIONS AND DRIVELINE

and Richmond offerings, it makes sense to buy a complete assembly. The ready-to-go box is a safer bet unless you are well versed in the innermost workings of this gearbox.

Camaros equipped with V-8s and T5s had two first-gear ratios available. The Throttle Body Injected (TBI) engine had a first-gear ratio of 2.95:1, while the Tuned Port Injected (TPI) engines had a ratio of 2.75. Both had a 1.94 second, 1.34 third gear, and two possible overdrive ratios. The TBI engines had a .63 ratio and the TPI used a .74 final-drive ratio. T5s were also used with 4- and 6-cylinder engines with first-gear ratios as low as 4.03, but be careful not buy one of these for your Shark. They are too fragile to withstand 200 ft-lbs of torque.

One consideration is that the T5 is lighter and fits easily in the tunnel with less overall installation work. They have smooth-shifting internal rail shifters for consistent shifts. The 2.95 TBI first gear and .63 overdrive gear make them a smart decision for a lower-torque-output long-distance cruiser, not a high-performance Shark with torque loads in excess of 350 ft-lbs.

Tremec T56

General Motors used a Tremec T56 6-speed in a number of vehicles between 1993 and 2004. This transmission is a popular swap for any Shark with those who want two overdrive ratios.

General Motors engineers specified a 2.66 first gear, 1.78 second, 1.30 third, 1.00 fourth, .74 fifth, and a high torque requiring .50 final gear for the 1993–1997 Camaros. Due to demand, Tremec offered an aftermarket T56 application that has a 2.97 first gear, 2.07 second, 1.43 third, 1.00 fourth, .80 fifth, and .62 sixth gear.

As discussed earlier, the 1993–1997 Camaro gear ratios require a steep differential gear set (4.10:1) or a high-torque engine to use the transmission effectively. The aftermarket T56's gear ratios are middle of the road for an engine that produces its torque at higher RPM.

The Camaro/Firebird and aftermarket T56 transmissions have a center-located shifter and the shifter location is farther back than the Shark's original offset shifter. So, the factory console requires a custom console plate with a modified shifter opening in the original tunnel.

The Tremec 6-speed is a world-class gearbox that is capable of withstanding 450 to 500 ft-lbs of torque on a daily basis. They use the latest synchronizer gear technology, and fibrous materials replace the old-school Muncie brass blocker rings. Dexron automatic transmission fluid lubricates the internals for minimum internal resistance, saving a few ponies while rotating the shafts. Used T-56 transmission availability is also pretty good. The T-56 in a Shark chassis has a removable crossmember. Physically the transmission is a tight fit in the transmission tunnel, without any modifications to the transmission or tunnel. The toughest part of the installation is the transmission crossmember-mount conversion.

Lengthwise, the 1993–2002 Camaro/Firebird and aftermarket applications place the shifter close to the original shifter access opening at the center of the tunnel. I use a sheet-metal plate to cover the existing shifter opening and mount the new shift boot after transmission tunnel modifications. An adapter plate is required to mate the 1993–1997 Camaro T56 to the original Shark bellhousing.

The Tremec GM aftermarket T56 comes with the adapter plate, allowing the use of your original bellhousing. The 1998–2002 LS engine–equipped Camaros with T56s are also compatible when an adapter plate is used. They also require the installation of a 1993–1997 T56 input shaft due to the LS engine bellhousing's shorter length. Either application works with the original Shark or a Lakewood blow-proof bellhousing.

Aftermarket T56 6-speeds are equipped with a mechanical speedometer drive provision, while the stock T56 transmission on Camaro/Firebird OEMs are not equipped with this provision. These stock F-Body transmissions use an electronic vehicle speed sensor (VSS) that communicates with the speedometer.

Shift Works has a housing that drives an electronic VSS and mechanical speedometer cable. It's $1,000, but it does solve the dilemma. An electronic fuel-injected engine that requires the VSS has both areas covered as it can still drive your factory speedometer cable.

In addition, you can have Bowler Performance Transmissions machine your T56 extension housing to accept a mechanical speedometer drive for $550.

You have a few other options to resolve the speedometer issue. These options include replacing the factory mechanical speedo with an aftermarket electronic unit or using a CableX speedometer drive system. The CableX uses the VSS input to run an electrical motor that drives the mechanical speedometer cable.

The only downside is the CableX takes a moment to get the speedo cable moving and catch up to the vehicle's speed; the cost is less at $300.

Heavy-duty, high-performance manual transmissions are available for engines that produce up to 700 ft-lbs of torque. Tremec manufactures the 6-speed gearbox for late-model Corvettes, which produce in excess of 600 ft-lbs of torque. The TR-6060 is the ultimate high-torque manual transmission, and it has the best components for ultimate torque and smooth shifting capabilities.

These specially built gearboxes use larger shafts, gears, and synchronizers. One major issue with the TR-6060 was fitment into the place of the T-56. Overall, the transmission is longer and the input shaft is larger diameter.

It took a little while, but similar components have been stuffed into a T-56 case, making the Magnum T-56 capable of withstanding 700 ft-lbs of torque. There is one issue, though: the Magnum T-56 requires an LS bellhousing and clutch assembly. As mentioned earlier, the LS bellhousing is shorter than the early small- and big-block bellhousings. Tremec has a direct-install Magnum T-56 that allows the use of your original bellhousing and clutch assembly.

Tremec TKO 500-600 5-Speed

Several aftermarket companies offer versions of Tremec TKO 500 and 600 5-speed transmissions. These are modified for direct installation into the Shark chassis with correct shifter placement. The TKO-500 has a steep 3.27 first, 1.97 second, 1.34 third, 1.00 fourth, and a .68 overdrive gears.

This is a great box for that low-torque-output-engine-equipped Shark that wants to cruise at highway speeds. The TKO-600 has a 2.87 first, 1.89 second, 1.28 third, 1.00 fourth, and .64 overdrive gears. Larger-cubic-inch or high-torque output engines work well with this unit.

For road racers, Tremec also offers a TKO-600 with a .82:1 overdrive gear to keep the engine RPM up on long straightaways.

Keisler RS Series 5-Speed

Keisler offers multiple manual transmission kits for a Shark. The company uses Tremec TKO 500 and 600 gearboxes and then modifies the internal rail shifter to fit in the Shark's original external shifter location.

They also have a Tremec RS series with a rounded top case, allowing a wider range of applications without modifying the transmission tunnel. Keisler is able to offer the RS at lower cost because it starts as a used assembly. Ninety percent of the internals are tossed out for new pieces, then the case is cleaned, inspected, and prepped for assembly. Choosing a used

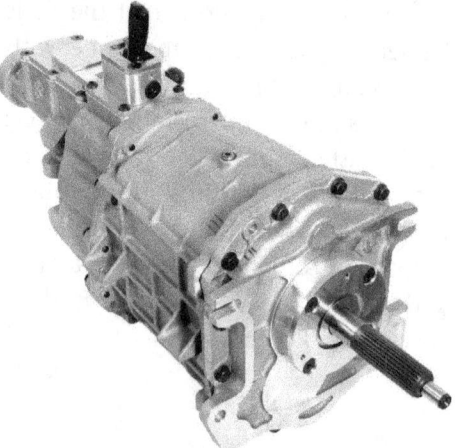

Keisler has resolved the problems with the Tremec TR45 5-speed overdrive transmissions; they shift smoothly and consistently. Three high-torque RallyeSport transmissions are available in three ratings: 400-, 500-, and 600-ft-lb versions. Another plus is that the RS transmission fits nicely in a Shark with less chance of any rub points, even with worn body cushions. They also have a custom shifter mount, placing the shifter in the original location. They require engine removal or at least moving it forward to get this transmission in the chassis unless the crossmember is modified for removal.

The TKO 500 and 600 5-speed gearboxes were built for late-model high-performance cars. The top-mounted shift mechanism (similar to the Ford Toploader transmission) makes the TKO box a tight fit in the Shark's tunnel; they do fit, though, and it's well worth the required work to install them. They fit a bit tighter in the 1968–1973 Sharks with worn body-mount cushions. The sagging body gets closer to the frame; consequently, so does the transmission. One very nice aspect is these Keisler components come as complete kits with all the required pieces in one box for installation ease. If the time you spend locating and testing parts fit is a concern, complete kits are the best choice for a quick, easy installation.

core unit for the RS buildup allows a substantial savings.

Keisler SS 5-Speed

Keisler's latest SS 5-speed gearbox is from a clean sheet of paper with plenty of torque-handling capabilities. The case height is lower, fitting in the Shark's transmission tunnel with ease, plus the 700 ft-lb torque rating means these units are available for a high-performance engine. Multiple mounting fitments make this bolt directly to the original GM small- or big-block bellhousing.

Gear ratios are 2.66 first, 1.78 second, 1.30 third, 1.00 fourth, and .68 or .80 overdrive ratio. They have a 2.97 first gear ratio gear set in the works.

Richmond Gear

Richmond is another alternative to the original 4-speed transmission in your Shark. The company offers 5- and 6-speed transmissions for direct installation. One approach to the fuel-mileage dilemma is unique with its 5-speed offering. A five-forward gear set is used with a 3.28 first, 2.13 second, 1.57 third, 1.24 fourth, and 1.00 fifth gear, rather than the traditional four-forward gear choices with an additional overdriven high gear.

The Richmond 6-speed gearbox is similar to the 5-speed box, including its torque-handling capabilities. The shifter is a high-quality Long unit with high-strength shifter rods and swivel rod ends for minimal deflection under heavy stress loads, but it is subjected to the elements, making them prone to wear as they deal with whatever the roadway throws at them. The use of an external shifter helps in a race environment though; when the transmission is serviced between rounds at the track it is easily removed and set up. Proper shift linkage setup and shifter gate alignment are key to quick, clean shifting. I prefer to do the linkage adjustment out of the chassis for the best results. Long supplies an alignment rod that is inserted into the shifter, then the shift rod length is adjusted. It's best if you hold on to the rod end, keeping it centered as the lock-nuts are tightened to prevent the outer portion of the rod end from rubbing on the shift levers.

Off-the-line launches are better because a low numerical gear ratio differential can be used, say a 2:73.1, for lower-RPM cruising. The five forward gears without overdrive make the gear change transitions smoother with less RPM drop between shifts.

Richmond also has a Super Street version of its 5-speed gearbox with an overdriven fifth gear. The three gear ratio selections offered for first gear are 3.33, 3.06, and 2.89. The ratios for the other gears are a 1.85 second, 1.31 third, 1.00 fourth, and .77 overdrive. This gearbox is rated for 600 ft-lbs for more robust applications. All of the Richmond Gear transmissions are designed for direct bolt-up installation on a small- or big-block bellhousing.

Richmond's 6-speed transmission has overdrive gearing available. Similar to the road race gearbox, the 6-speed has eight first-gear ratio options, starting with a 2.08:1 and ending with a 4.41:1 first gear. Two selections are available for the second through fifth gears, with two overdrive gears, .80:1 and .84:1, respectively. This makes it easier to match your engine's torque curve without major compromises.

Richmond Gear's approach leans to the race-orientated Corvette owner; their aluminum main housing case splits

Finally, here is a 5-speed transmission built to fit early vehicles including the Shark Corvette. The Keisler low-profile internal rail-shifted high-torque-capable transmission fits with the least amount of effort in a Shark and is capable of withstanding up to 700 ft-lbs of torque. An old-school speedometer drive and VSS is part of the new design to allow retrofitting with just about any engine combination. Shifter placement is right where it needs to be. As with other Keisler offerings, no console modifications are required.

CHAPTER 7

Prepping for the Install

You need to check the following before installing one of the new-style transmission gearboxes to prevent vibration. Each transmission install should receive the same checks for a long, trouble-free life.

Bellhousing concentricity to the crankshaft's pilot is very important for long bearing and main shaft life. Many of the old gearboxes have .015 to .030 concentricity run-out due to engine line boring over the years. I have found very few bellhousing transmission pilot holes that are close to the recommended .005 maximum run-out.

These new transmissions do not like the strain that the excessive run-out puts on the gear train. The gearboxes vibrate and wear, causing eventual excessive noise until major bearing failure occurs. I spend the required time to check and adjust the concentricity on every install for the transmission's sake. Offset bellhousing dowel pins are available to make the necessary adjustments to maintain the prescribed .005-inch maximum run-out.

The new transmission technology does not allow the old sloppy tolerances. The dial indicator is centered and held in place by the stout magnet, then the flywheel is rotated and the run-out readings recorded on the bellhousing. Because it is difficult to perfectly center the dial indicator, any reading should be divided by two to compensate for the off-center reading. The first check was with just a few bellhousing bolts hand tightened, leaving a .035-inch off-center reading. The bellhousing was removed and the surfaces cleaned, then all the bolts were torqued to 45 ft-lbs. The next check dropped the reading to .025. At .025 we have a true .0125 run-out, well above the .004 maximum that should be maintained. Offset dowel pins are required to make the readings bearable; I use .007 to get us in the correct range.

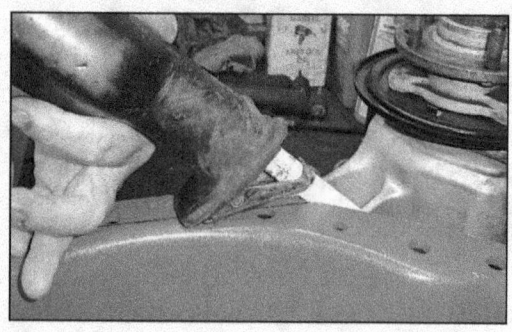

The SFI foundation has set up guidelines for minimum racing safety standards. I cut off the very bottom lip of this Lakewood bellhousing to afford more ground clearance. In the grand scheme of things, I would rather have the clutch assembly blow out at the bottom of the bellhousing in the area where the two engine-to-plate bolts are missing. When installed, the large-diameter bellhousing sits well below the engine oil pan and any other chassis component. If you were to hit something at speed with the lower edge of the bellhousing as the bellhousing comes out of the box, catastrophic engine damage or loss of vehicle control could occur.

in half for easy servicing or quick gear changes. Once the gear housing is split, the main and counter shaft assemblies come out quickly. During frequent race events, the transmission could be disassembled numerous times for inspection and repaired trackside if necessary.

Richmond recommends using its synthetic 75W140 gear oil in all of their gearboxes. I feel that Richmond's transmission offerings lean toward the true racer, who uses the Shark primarily for drag or road racing.

Clutches

Many clutches are available for your Shark. The Shark uses a specific clutch fork, and that's the only significant difference for the Gen I small-block and Mark IV big-block engines. The new LS engines use hydraulic actuation systems. The clutch assembly works by clamping a disc connected to the transmission's input shaft between the flywheel and a pressure plate to control application. Clutch designs vary from a simple one-disc to multiple discs and different compound materials.

Like the brake friction materials, as the clutch horsepower requirements grow so does clutch aggressiveness. Multiple-disc clutches are used to gain friction surface area. In many cases, this helps alleviate some of the required pedal effort to disengage the clutch. Determining how much clutch you need is the first part of the equation. Installing a clutch for a 700-hp engine on a 350-hp engine means a lot of wasted effort on your left leg in traffic. High-horsepower clutches also tend to chatter due to their aggressive nature.

Clutch pressure plates come in two designs: diaphragm and lever. Diaphragm clutch pressure plates are used by General Motors in all of their manual transmission applications. Lever-type pressure plates require more effort to disengage the clutch, while diaphragm pressure plates apply more force on the clutch disc as engine RPM increases. That means diaphragm pressure plates apply more pressure while requiring less pedal effort. Who doesn't like that?

There is a minor problem with the diaphragm design, which causes the clutch pedal to stick on the floor, disengaged at high RPM. The same centrifugal forces that increase the pressure plate's clamping power tend to keep the multiple pressure plate fingers from releasing. However, the correct clutch diaphragm finger positioning at WOT can prevent this problem.

Two methods are used to prevent the clutch pedal from sticking to the floor. One is to fabricate a stop under the clutch pedal to shorten the travel on hydraulic clutch systems, or you can add free-play to the clutch linkage. You need just enough clutch pedal travel to release the clutch. The adjustment takes some trial and error before you find the sweet spot.

Spec Clutches has five different clutch stages, for the everyday driver to the all-out race vehicle. This carbon semi-metallic Stage 3 clutch assembly is aggressive but still drivable to and from work. High-torque springs in the clutch disc center hub help to smooth out off-the-line engagement while still providing an aggressive launch.

Clutch Installation

1 Install Clutch Disc

This high-torque, large-cubic-inch big-block has an aluminum flywheel for quick revving. It's not a good choice with a small-inch engine and radical camshaft. Installation begins with a new roller bearing pilot assembly with a proper socket that fits the outer diameter of the pilot bearing. Hammering close to the center of the pilot bearing can damage the seal and cause the transmission input shaft to fit tightly, and gear clash results during shifting.

Thoroughly clean the flywheel clutch disc friction surface with an alcohol-based cleaner.

The line-up tool should fit easily into the bearing; if it is tight, you need to replace the bearing or get used to gear grinding when shifting. Always check the manufacturer's install note on the clutch disc before installing the line-up tool into the clutch disc and the pilot-bearing.

Carbon semi-metallic clutch discs such as this Spec Stage 3+ hold well and are aggressive on flywheel and clutch pressure-plate surfaces. All that grip and a manageable clutch engagement is what this disc is about. You can expect smooth clutch operation even when plying the city streets.

CHAPTER 7

2 Install Pressure Plate

Centerforce clutches are another option that work well for the occasional road-racer who drives on city streets. The weighted diaphragm clutch fingers allow for less left-leg fatigue in traffic while applying extra pressure from the centrifugal force as RPM increases. These can be tricky to balance due to the weights moving around at low engine speeds. All in all, the Centerforce weighted diaphragm clutch finger design is proven and a good choice for someone using a Shark for a daily driver or as a weekend warrior.

Make sure whatever clutch you use survives. Like the flywheel, the pressure plate surfaces should be cleaned with an alcohol-based cleaner to remove any oil or grease preservatives. Once the bolts are all finger tight, start tightening them in a crisscross fashion, a couple of turns at a time, to evenly seat the pressure plate and disc on the flywheel. Torque the bolts at least twice starting at 20 ft-lbs to seat the pressure plate, then finish with the manufacturer's recommended torque (typically 45 ft-lbs). A good practice is to mark where the pressure plate is on the flywheel. If you did not have the assembly balanced you can install the pressure plate in the same position, if there was no vibration. Chances are if you're having fun you will revisit the clutch assembly multiple times as you learn your Shark's weaknesses.

This clutch has Kevlar pucks instead of one continuous layer of friction material. The idea is for the individual pieces of friction material to retain less heat if the clutch assembly is worked often in autocross or short road-course events. Following is the way the clutch assembly is installed if you choose not to modify the crossmember for removal on a 5-speed manual transmission–upgraded Shark.

The bellhousing and clutch pieces are loaded on the input shaft, then the transmission is raised into position. Once the loose assembly (transmission, bellhousing, and clutch assembly) is close to the correct position, someone carefully installs the clutch pressure plate to flywheel bolts loosely. Then a modified line-up shaft is inserted into the clutch disc and pilot bearing. The shaft (with a piece of mechanic's wire) must be removed after the pressure plate bolts are tightened. The bellhousing is then installed, and if you were able to properly line up the clutch disc, the transmission slides into place.

This does not make sense for anyone building a modified Shark. Chances are you will revisit this at some point and will regret that you did not remove the crossmember.

TRANSMISSIONS AND DRIVELINE

Clutch Actuation Options

All 1968–1981 Corvettes use mechanical clutch linkage to actuate the clutch. These work effectively, so why be concerned about it? For many applications, there's no need to modify or change what already performs well. Hydraulic clutch systems were installed on Corvettes in the mid-1980s and have become the standard all manufacturers use today. Flexibility is the key, requiring one flexible hose to connect the clutch master to the slave cylinder.

Another factor is clutch pedal effort. By simply moving the pivot point to the clutch actuator rod location, clutch effort can be highly modified. If you plan to use a clutch assembly that requires high effort, hydraulic clutch actuation should be considered.

Another reason to use the hydraulic system is a conversion from automatic to manual transmission. Welding the clutch equalizer support to an automatic transmission–equipped frame can be difficult unless major components are removed.

Automatic Transmissions

The 1968–1982 Corvette production run included four different automatic transmissions: Turbo-Hydramatic 400, Turbo-Hydramatic 350, modified Turbo-Hydramatic 350, and 700R4 overdrive. All of them have good track records for durability, except for the first-run overdrive unit found in the 1982 Shark.

The Turbo-Hydramatic 400 started the Shark era, then a lighter-duty Turbo-Hydramatic 350 series took over for a number of years. In 1980, General Motors tried a modified Turbo-Hydramatic 350 with a lock-up clutch torque converter to increase fuel mileage and eliminate inherent torque converter slippage. The final year of the Shark production ended with a 700R4 automatic overdrive with a lock-up torque converter as the only available transmission.

The TH400 transmission is a stout and durable transmission for a big-block. Unfortunately, they were also heavy and required extra horsepower to make the hefty internal components rotate.

Turbo 350s were a great advancement, and these lighter-weight units were still tough and easily rebuilt. Big-block engines appeared in a few early C3s from 1968–1974, so if you have one of

An aftermarket Wilwood hydraulic clutch master cylinder is fitted to a 1972 Shark before the body is installed. Converting from automatic transmission to manual transmission was the reason for this installation. American Powertrain has a complete ready-to-go kit that bolts in the same fashion as this assembly. The trick was getting the correct push point on the clutch pedal for the clutch pedal feel but American Powertrain has that figured out. The mounting plate fits in the original clutch boot's area without any modification. The original clutch linkage through the firewall boot is removed, then the hydraulic clutch master cylinder is installed using the original screw holes as guides. The port at the end of the cylinder receives the clutch flex hose to the hydraulic slave cylinder. The port in the center is for the fluid from the reservoir; it uses a flexible rubber hose that is impervious to brake fluid.

The back side of this clutch master cylinder uses an additional reinforcement plate to stiffen the firewall. The reinforcement has the same configuration as the master cylinder, so the bolts go through the firewall, cylinder, and plate. You need someone to hold the cylinder and the bolts in place while the plate is installed with the nuts. The clutch cylinder pushrod slides over the original clutch pedal linkage pin and uses a supplied retainer to hold it in place.

Some kits require you to remove the clutch pedal assembly and push out the existing linkage pin. That sounds easy enough until you try to remove the pedal. Due to design, the dash cluster must come out first, then the clutch/brake pedal support is removed, starting under the hood. Four 1/2-inch hex-head bolts retain the support and can be found in the driver-side wiper pivot area (usually covered with undercoating concealing them).

The master cylinder (or brake booster if power-brake equipped) is removed. Manual brake cars have two more 9/16-inch hex-head bolts to remove from the firewall above the master cylinder. Finally, two more 1/2-inch hex-head bolts are removed from the support under the dash, and it can be wrestled out. The linkage pin requires grinding and then hammering out. If a press is available, it is much easier to push out. While the pedal support is out, I usually replace the pivot bushings.

CHAPTER 7

Torque Converter Mechanics

Torque converters multiply torque through the use of a stator that directs fluid flow for the best possible liquid coupling. They typically have torque multiplier ratios of 2.0:1 to 2.5:1.

As an example, if a torque converter's stall speed is 3,000 rpm with a 2.5:1 multiplication ratio coupled to an engine with 200 ft-lbs of torque, an additional 500 ft-lbs of torque is produced at the moment stall speed is achieved (2.5:1 x 200 = 500).

Stall speed occurs when maximum torque converter fluid coupling is achieved. To achieve torque converter stall put the transmission in gear, apply the brakes, and then accelerate the engine until you can no longer hold back the vehicle. While this is not the most accurate way to check stall speed, it gives you a good approximation. Stall speed is affected by engine torque, vehicle weight, and roll resistance. Torque converter choice is more important than the transmission itself concerning overall performance.

Words of caution: Do not repeatedly stall the converter, as extreme heats builds, cooking the fluid. After a couple of stall speed checks, put the transmission in park and let the engine idle. Let the transmission fluid cool for at least five minutes before attempting another test. ∎

Choosing the correct torque converter stall speed for your Shark begins with the camshaft specification card. Your cam card has the engine's powerband noted. If you have a camshaft with a powerband in the 2,500 to 6,500 range a 3,000-rpm stall converter is the best choice. Having a higher stall speed than required is better than choosing a stall speed that is too low if you might be thinking about changing the transmission and converter before the camshaft. Using a higher stall-speed converter than the power band can handle flattens the top-end performance. The trick is compromising to use the off-the-line performance gained.

---

these rare Sharks, you are probably going to keep the original equipment because it is so valuable. The low-compression 350s produced anywhere from 165 net hp to 235 net hp and didn't require a heavy-duty transmission.

The 1980–1981 two-year lock-up turbo 350 transmission experiment coupled a fine-working transmission with a clutch-equipped torque converter, eliminating torque converter slippage and upping fuel mileage a minuscule 2 percent. When the torque converter clutch (TCC) was applied, engine speed dropped approximately 200 rpm. One nagging issue plagued the first-design TCC operation: a vacuum switch–controlled clutch operation locking the torque converter in at 28 mph in high gear. The engine immediately bogged down when the TCC came in; the majority of owners disabled TCC operation.

The installation of the 700R4 overdrive into the 1982 Shark allowed Chevrolet to use their latest transmission creation as a test bed for the rest of GM's lineup. The groundbreaking transmission had an overdrive gear and a TCC torque converter. An ECM engine control module controlled the TCC application, making them more desirable than their first attempt at a fuel-conscious transmission.

Like the turbo 350 lock-up units, TCC came in very early to conserve fuel, making the already anemic crossfire fuel-injected engine even more so. In the shop you modify the prom chip to have TCC come in at 50 mph, and the immediate thought is you added 50 hp.

Modify or Swap?

Your first option is to modify the original transmission. If you plan to keep close to home and ply your local streets

B&M has an easy-to-install shift improver kit that provides firmer automatic transmissions shift changes. The kit can be installed in a day. Installing a shift kit also increases the life of your transmission especially as horsepower increases.

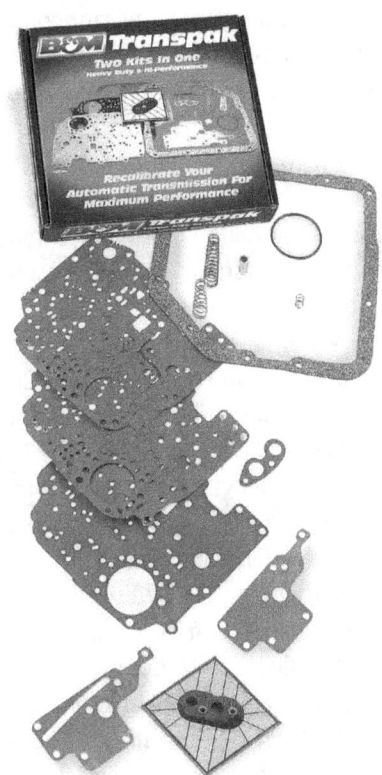

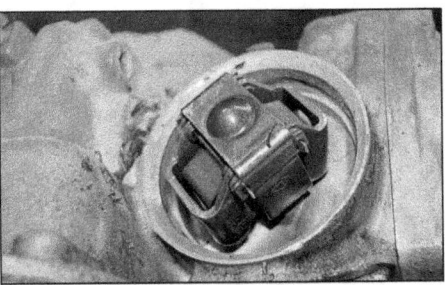

This B&M Transpak kit is available for the Turbo 350, 400, or 700R4 if you choose to upgrade to an overdrive. While the Shift Improver firms up the shifts, the Transpak provides driver manual control while improving shift quality. You can hold the transmission in any gear without the factory predetermined upshift as RPM increases. You do have to be cautious until you learn how the transmission reacts to downshifting at any speed. You can overrev the engine and lock up the wheels. Selecting a gear upon command gives you ultimate control.

Once the pan and filter have been removed, valve body removal is next to access the separator plate. The separator plate has two gaskets, one for the case and one for the valve body. They must be removed for proper sealing. Carefully clean the gaskets. Watch for steel check balls as the valve body and plate are removed; they must be put back in the same location. Some shift kit separator plates omit some of the check balls. Be sure to read the instructions carefully before beginning the install. Go easy on the valve body bolts; 110 in-lbs (or 20 ft-lbs) is the maximum torque.

This is what the automatic transmission governor looks like when the cover is removed. The Turbo-Hydramatic 350 transmission (shown) has a round bell-type cover that presses on with a metal bail to keep the cover in place. The 350 governor is on the driver's side of the transmission above the pan rail close to the extension housing. The turbo-hydramatic 400 has a similar governor placed in a similar location on the passenger's side of the transmission with a cover that is held in place with four 1/2-inch hex-head screws. Turbo 350 and 400 governors cannot be interchanged because of their placement: one rotates counterclockwise and the other clockwise while driving in forward gears. Try to prevent dirt from entering; if it does remove as much as possible before covering things up.

and drag strip, modifying your original transmission makes sense. Before you start, take a long test drive on city streets to really work the transmission, shifting through the gears. Use the torque converter and run it up to stall speed to get the fluid heated up. If the transmission still has decent shifts without slipping, it is a candidate for modifying. If there is any slipping during shifts, do not expect a shift modification kit to fix the problem.

Shift kits are available for the turbo 400, 350, and 350 with TCC. Turbo Action has one that precisely and reliably shifts the C3. The easy-to-install kit replaces the separator plate between the transmission case and valve body. The company's Positive Action for Corvettes kit requires no spring replacements or modifications. A few check balls are deleted from the original count and you are ready to go. However, other intricate kits require spring and valve modifications. It's best to install these during the overhaul of a transmission. Tweaking the governor weights and/or springs is one method to optimize the shift timing. The governor uses fly weights to apply pressure to the shift speed control pressure valving, which regulates shift timing.

Shift kit installation is one of those Saturday-afternoon projects that require a clean work area without sand and debris blowing around. After the transmission has been assembled, the results are immediate. You experience a firm shift under moderate throttle to barking tires at WOT.

Another mod for an original transmission is a full manual control valve body so that the driver has full control over all up and down shifts. Early automatic transmission shift technology was fair with sketchy control of shift timing. As an example, when downshifting from high gear, anticipating a second gear shift and engine braking, the transmission downshifts into first gear, causing the tires to chatter or over-rev the engine. The full manual control valve body is suited for competition and aggressive driving, so it can be used for road racing, autocrossing, or gymkhana events.

CHAPTER 7

Manual control valve bodies operate similarly to a manual transmission because they give you full control of shifting. You must select the gear you want regardless of engine RPM. The task is similar to the separator plate replacement. The replacement valve body bolts in place of the original with a few adjustments and you are ready to go. Manual valve bodies are available for the 350, 400, and 700R4.

The price is not too stiff at $200, considering the cost of performance pieces today.

Your second option is to swap in a different transmission. Although extremely durable, the TH350 and 400 are not the best high-performance automatic transmissions for your Shark. These transmissions have higher mechanical first-gear ratios (turbo 400 2.48:1 and the 350's 2.52:1), and therefore they are a detriment to your off-the-line launch when using a small-block engine. In addition, these transmissions do not have an overdrive gear, so they do not provide fuel economy for long-distance driving.

The 200R4 was installed in various Buick, Oldsmobile, and Pontiac models and used with various engines. Most notably, the 2004R4 was fitted to the 3.8-liter turbo V-6 in the Buick Grand National. General Motors did configure some 200R4 cases in universal form for use behind the Chevrolet small-block engine. A 2004R has a similar length to the TH350 in the 1977–1981 Sharks, so the retrofit to a C3 is much easier with this transmission than many others. In addition, the original Shark driveshaft is compatible with 700R4 for most applications.

Currently, the 700R4 or 4L60E, which is a 700R4 with electronic shift control, is the most common automatic transmission swap into a C3. Very few 2004R transmissions were found behind small-block Chevy engines, but the 700R4 transmissions were factory installed in hundreds of thousands of GM vehicles. This makes the 700R4 the most popular choice because of the massive quantities of available units and performance pieces marketed for them.

An overdrive transmission provides the best balance of performance and economy for street driving. In fact, they deliver the benefits for all-around performance driving in long haulers. Also, the engine RPM reduction quiets down the drivetrain, has less heat buildup, and provides a comfortable long highway cruise. The 2004R gear ratios are 2.74 first, 1.57 second, 1.00 third, and .67 overdrive. The 700R4 gear ratios are 3.06 first, 1.62 second, 1.00 third, and .070 for overdrive. This makes the 2004R more desirable for a higher-torque engine that has a lower-RPM redline. The 700R4 is more suited for a long-duration camshaft that produces less torque at lower RPM.

Here the governor is disassembled for cleaning before any modifications are performed. Note the "apple-cored" driven gear. If the transmission is eating itself up from a major component failure metal tends to tighten the governor in the bore; eventually the gear fails from the added torque load. Once the gear is off, the valve (at the bottom) can be removed, it should fall out if the governor weights are moved away from the valve. If the valve sticks (and you have to bang the end of the governor on the workbench to move it) and the gear is worn, you need to rethink the plan because the transmission is in catastrophic failure mode. If the gear is simply worn it can be replaced. After driving out the pin (shown below the gear), the gear can be pulled out by hand. The new gear is not drilled for the pin; it must be drilled to 1/8 inch after fully seating the gear in the governor. Then the pin is inserted.

This B&M governor recalibration kit is ready to be installed on the governor. The kit comes with different-tension springs and weights to make the shift occur earlier or later. Governor fluid pressure acts with the valve-body fluid pressure moving shift valves to control shift timing. Governors spin at output shaft speed trying to force the centrifugal weights outward as speed increases. Heavier weights make the centrifugal event happen sooner; in turn, the shift point is lower. Lighter weights require increased output shaft speed; consequently, the transmission shifts later.

If your engine performance work raised the torque curve you want the shift points to occur later to utilize the torque curve benefits of the new camshaft. The governor controls the shift points after approximately half throttle. You can still ease through parking lots if you modify the shift points without the fear of the engine revving to 5,500 just to move from one parking space to the other. The beauty of this modification is you can tailor the shift speeds to your liking without having to deal with a pan full of hot transmission fluid each time you make a change. A small amount (a tablespoonfull at most) of fluid comes out when the cover is removed.

The overwhelming popularity of the 700R4 has made it a hot commodity, with many suppliers providing ready-to-install units. The pieces for the conversion are readily available for a seamless install; your Shark can look like it always had an overdrive unit in place.

Supplier Search

Choosing a supplier can be frustrating because of market saturation. There are a few things to consider when narrowing down possibilities. First, it costs extra for good workmanship and quality parts, so expect to pay for it. You need a strong, reliable, and efficient transmission, and these cost a fair market price. If you buy a cheap unit, some costs have been cut and, typically, inferior parts have been used. Consider the warranty, such as on the internals. Longer warranty coverage periods cost more while short warranty coverage means that lower-quality pieces were used and life expectancy is less.

You can also find plenty of rebuildable units on Craigslist, eBay, and at your local swap meets. Try to avoid using original 700R4 units from 1982 through 1986 if possible. The hardware was adequate, but the parts improved from 1987 and on. General Motors used a 245-mm input shaft with 27 splines that was replaced with a 298-mm 30-spline shaft in 1987 for all V-8 units. The rear planetary gear assembly had improved thrust washers with an oil weir to control oil flow to the gear set. A wide sprag unit replaced the thin, wimpy, low-reverse assembly. Most important, the forward sprag assembly was modified to hold torque much better. Quite often the forward sprag fails before the smaller 245-mm input shaft does. As with any mechanical component, improvements are made as time passes.

Summit Racing, for example, has a neat kit with all the pieces in one box to make any 700R4 like new again.

When rebuilding any automatic transmission, you need to maintain a clean work space and pay close attention to clearances, as shown in the overhaul manual, which you acquired before the work began, right?

Once the unit is overhauled, or before the new one arrives, consider the torque converter. Many suppliers give just a little better discount if you purchase the entire assembly at one time.

This is the transmission for those who want the best possible shifts and shift timing. The Keisler 4L65E Shark retrofit automatic transmission connects to their proprietary controller via a harness (shown) with a couple of other required electrical connections: ignition-fused power through the supplied fuse holder, vehicle speed sensor, and throttle position sensor. The harness is routed inside to connect to the controller and access the data through a laptop connection for troubleshooting and tuning.

The Ultimate Swap: A 4L60E

The ultimate overdrive automatic swap is a 4L60E, the electronic version of the 700-R4. This transmission contains top-quality components, and it has been developed to deliver superb performance. The early 700R4 problems have been resolved, and complete electronic control makes them an easy install and tune.

That's right, I said tune. You use your laptop and adjust shift feel and speeds. If you want a bit more aggressive shift, dial it in. Want the shift speeds to be earlier or later? No problem. This requires a software program (such as HP Tuners or EFI Live) to link up and modify the GM controller that is used for the 4L60E.

Another option is using a Compushift II standalone controller from a source such as HGM Automotive Electronics if you are not using a GM controller from a late-model engine/transmission swap. The Compushift II controller does not even require a laptop; the display allows you to go in and tune the unit. HGM provides a program to get started, and you can tweak the settings for that perfect shift feel and timing.

The 4L60E shift control is superior because it eliminates the poor shift feel and timing controls that plagued the 700R4. The 700R4 uses a cable connecting the throttle valve (TV) actuator in the valve body to the engine's throttle shaft lever. The more pedal you need to put into the throttle, the later the transmission shifts, and it also affects the crispness of the shift. The 700R4 TV has also been known to stick in the transmission's valve body, and shifting becomes erratic.

The 4L60E does not experience this problem because it's electronically controlled. In addition, it is easier to install than the 700R4, but it does require some extra work to install a throttle position switch, which is required for shift timing. Installing this switch is easier than

CHAPTER 7

Paddle Shifter for C3 Corvette

I was lucky enough to test-drive a Keisler prototype paddle shifter setup in a 1978 Shark Pace car through the Tennessee hills. The engine braking option was awesome as I flipped the shifter paddles, downshifting the transmission through the gears. Applying throttle, I made another quick flip on the paddle and it immediately upshifted as I powered through a slight uphill grade. As I approached a steep upcoming grade, the paddle shifter coupled to the 4L60E transmission's electronic valve body quickly downshifted, and supplied plenty of power for the climb.

This was the real deal. The 4L60E automatic shifted crisply at the touch of a paddle, and my hands never left the steering wheel as I enjoyed the curvy uphill and downhill grades.

This is a simple afternoon project: no wiring is required in the steering column. You just need a Phillips-head screwdriver. The original horn wiring is used as a serial data link to operate the transmission and horn simultaneously if required.

The horn button is popped off with a plastic blade, preferably, to avoid scratching the wheel and button. Three Phillips-head screws hold the horn contact switch through the steering wheel to the hub. Then the steering wheel's six machine screws holding the wheel to the hub are removed. The paddle shifter is placed

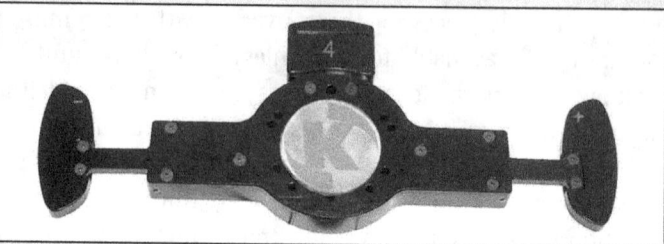

Keisler's paddle shifter is sandwiched between a custom or original steering wheel. Paddles are at 3 and 9 o'clock and rotate with the steering wheel. A digital display above the horn pad tells you what gear you have selected.

between the original wheel and the hub (be sure to use the supplied screws or longer screws if you want something different holding the wheel on).

The paddle shifter and electronic automatic transmission use CAN-bus technology requiring only one wire for all the functions including the original horn.

Keisler supplies a connector to interface the original horn's black wire that connects to the electronic transmission control module. Plug in the supplied harness to the controller and it's time for a road test. ■

---

installing a mechanical cable and the correct ratio TV actuator lever onto the engine's throttle shaft.

If you choose to use a 4L60E, you also have the option of upgrading to a steering wheel–mounted paddle shifter. The factory shifter can be used for daily driving, with the addition of the paddle shifter: a couple of clicks and full manual control of the transmission is possible. Overall, the 4L60E installation is costlier than a typical 700R4 install, although the benefits are noteworthy. The paddle shifter adds cost for the ultimate package, which is certainly worth considering before you take the plunge. This is for the Shark owner who really wants to drive long distances and enjoy performance driving at multiple events and varied courses.

The 4L65E transmission fits in place of the Shark's original Turbo-Hydramatic 400 with one minor modification. A Shiftworks modified transmission extension housing was required to drive the electronic speed sensor and the 1973's mechanical speedometer cable. The PCM uses an electronic VSS to control idle speed, and it's a must for an automatic transmission to shift the electronic transmission. Manual transmission–equipped projects do not absolutely require the electronic speed sensor, although it is recommended for the best idle control.

Transmission Installation

Your first obstacle is the transmission crossmember, regardless of whether you put together your own performance setup or use a kit in a box; the transmission crossmember most likely requires modification or replacement.

The 1968–1979 factory-equipped manual transmission Sharks have non-removable transmission crossmembers, making it very difficult to install the longer 5- and 6-speed gearboxes. All automatic transmission–equipped Sharks have removable crossmembers. The majority of aftermarket manual transmissions can be installed without cutting or modifying the transmission crossmember. However, in order to install the transmission, the engine must be removed or you need to unbolt it from the motor mounts and move it forward on the frame so you have adequate room to install the transmission.

If you decide to leave the transmission crossmember welded in place, you will have difficulty servicing the clutch because there is not much clearance between the clutch and the crossmember. The smart way is to remove the crossmember; it makes the install and future servicing easier. This is one thing that I have done numerous times over the years: removing the crossmember and making it look like a factory removable automatic transmission–equipped frame.

Installation Tips

Installing a modern manual or automatic overdrive transmission typically requires some modification and fabrication of the crossmember. The following tips explain how to fit various modern transmissions to the C3 so your car can realize increased performance and better fuel economy. ■

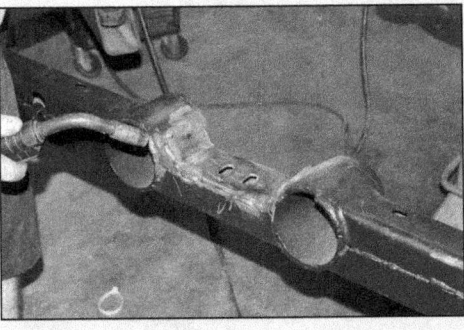

The 1968–1979 Shark crossmembers must be modified for the automatic overdrive transmission mount to fit on top. Cut out the top section of the crossmember at the split line. I used a piece of .125-inch-thick steel bending it to fit into the lower section. I used a 7/16-inch bit to drill two holes next to each other. Next I used a die grinder to open them up leaving the oval adjustable transmission mount bolt holes. You must use the existing removable mounting plate as a guide for the oval holes. The Weld the plate in place ready for the transmission installation. Be sure to maintain the same height as shown at the split line for proper driveline alignment.

The TKO 600 trial-fitted into this 1968 Shark shows just how close the top of the transmission is to the tunnel. All Sharks use a 1/4-inch-thick heat shield in the tunnel, which often gets torn up when the TKO 500 or 600 is placed at the proper driveline angle height. The 1973-and-up Sharks have slightly more clearance with their rubber body cushions. Replacing 1968–1982 body-mount cushions with urethane cushions ensures that the transmission-to-transmission tunnel clearance will remain constant. This American Powertrain transmission has been modified for an original transmission mount. The switch, with two studs about mid-main case, controls the reverse lights. Push-on terminals with pigtails are provided for connection to the original Shark external mechanical reverse light switch (pink and light green wiring).

Custom transmission crossmember brackets can easily be made to fit just about any transmission in a Shark, such as this T5 installation. Some .125-inch sheet steel was used to craft an adapter mount. Always remember that driveline angle is critical for transmission output shaft and driveshaft U-joint life. Placement height of the transmission must be considered once the final welded bracket is installed; placing the bracket too low is better than too high.

Case in point: this T5 is using a Ford Mustang transmission mount for the transplant; a shim plate can be used between the mount and the transmission, if necessary, to tweak the driveline angle. Manual transmission Sharks use the removable bracket to allow transmission removal. Even with this bracket gone, Muncie transmission removal and installation is difficult. Note the speedometer cable port above the transmission mount. The cable clears the tunnel but comes close to the exhaust as the radius flows forward. If necessary, a heat shield can be applied to the cable for safety. This Tremec transmission uses a Ford-type speedometer cable and gear, which Keisler supplies as a hybrid: GM at the speedometer and Ford at the transmission.

Here a 4L65E automatic overdrive is installed in a 1973 LS-engine Shark that began life with a Turbo 400 and removable crossmember. This versatile Bowtie Overdrive replacement crossmember works with TH350, 400, 2004R, 700R4, and 4L65E installations. The same crossmember allows the use of any of the manual transmissions previously discussed. The Shiftworks extension housing and adapter allow the use of the VSS on the passenger's side of the transmission, and the mechanical speedometer cable and gear can be utilized on the driver's side of the housing.

This 4L65E is installed in a 1978 Shark with an original 350-ci small-block L-82 engine. The Keisler kit has a slightly different approach to the mechanical speedometer concern: they machined the original housing to accomplish the task. The kit also comes with the replacement crossmember and correct-length driveshaft to ease the installation. Be aware of the close proximity of the parking brake pulley and the driveshaft yoke during any modifications to an existing crossmember. On a positive note: you unpack the boxes and start the installation. The only trip you need to make to the parts store is for fluid.

This throttle position sensor and wiring replaces the 700R4's mechanical throttle valve cable and connector, controlling shift speed and firmness. The Keisler throttle position switch comes with the correct mounting plate and all hardware for installation. However, you have to know what intake manifold you have or plan to use. Once installed, you must check and adjust the switch according to Keisler's instruction sheets. Depending on your application, you may have to install a lever on your existing carburetor's throttle shaft to operate the switch.

Transmission Fluid Tips

Frequent fluid changes and minimum annual checks are recommended if you are a street/strip warrior. Always check the pan for any clutch material that shows up as flakes of what appears to be paper. Placing a magnet in the pan also gives you an idea if any needle bearings are coming out of a planet before catastrophic damage occurs. Check the magnet carefully at least annually for large metal pieces.

The pan and internal transmission pieces are eventually coated with a black film, which is normal; do not be alarmed unless the color turns brown and the film is not easily removed. The discoloration is telling you that the fluid is burning, clutch plates are slipping, or the cooler is not adequate. When the clutch plates are failing you usually find other debris in the pan (clutch plate material).

Always use top-quality fluid designed for your application. Some transmission parts suppliers recommend a certain designation, but the majority recommend Dexron IV. Never overfill the unit because the fluid becomes aerated. Aerated fluid causes pressure fluctuations and clutch damage. Installing an additional transmission fluid cooler is also an excellent idea.

Do not use old cooler lines that have been sitting around open unless they can be thoroughly cleaned. Cleaning the internals of any steel line is tough in most cases; the smart money is on using new lines. Rinse out the new lines and then blow them out, making sure no debris has found its way into the lines.

 **700 R4 Automatic Transmission TV Adjustment**

This is by far the most critical adjustment for any 700R4 that can affect the life of the transmission's internal components. Improper adjustment can cause slipping clutches under WOT conditions.

TV positioning at WOT may seem such a simple task. The problem is, many aftermarket carburetors and even factory-supplied Quadrajet carburetors do not have the correct leverage. It's all about how far away the pin is that the TV cable connects to from the throttle shaft. The TV cable travels farther as the connecting pin distance is increased from the throttle shaft. Ideally, the TV cable should have full travel from idle to WOT. I have found that the best option is to remove the transmission pan during the initial TV cable setup. What may appear to be the correct setting can be too much, causing an upshift, quick downshift, then upshift event going into third gear. Worse yet, the TV cable or linkage may be hanging on something, giving the appearance that the cable is pulling to the WOT position. WOT shifts are then lacking the fluid pressure increase they need for long clutch life. ∎

CHAPTER 8

DRIVELINE

Eaton cast-iron differential housings were installed on 1968–1979 Sharks. A Dana aluminum differential housing and mounting structure was installed on the 1980–1982 Sharks.

A unique stationary crossmember mounting system suspended the cast-iron housings, and a rubber-bushed mount was used at the front to prevent differential rotation. In the 1980–1982 Shark differential, the major difference was the integral differential cover and support structure. The rear aluminum cover and differential crossmember casting assembly removed a few pounds at the rear.

Both early and late differentials were a key component of the rear suspension for propelling and maintaining alignment of the rear wheels. The axleshafts pressed against the differential's carrier pinion gear shaft, creating a pivot point for the rear suspension. You need to determine the application of your C3 in order to decide which differential is best for it. High-performance street Sharks that infrequently enjoy a weekend at autocross events are not going to be an issue if you are using 8- to 10-inch-wide tires and you have less than 600 hp. As horsepower and traction increase, so does the differential's load, making it a weak point for more than 500 hp and wide sticky tires.

One thing to consider is that road course and autocross events don't start out with smoky burnouts: the majority of load occurs as you exit a corner. Smooth driving with good accelerator control gets you around the road course faster and your differential is able to handle the load much easier. One definite note on the differential: Regardless of how easy you are, road racing eventually takes out a high-mileage factory Eaton or Dana differential.

All OEM Shark differentials have difficulty withstanding the loads in drag racing. Original Shark tires were rated at about 400 hp or more and were a maximum 8 inches wide. They were not nearly as good as modern tires and provided only a modicum of traction. Today we have sticky wide tires with traction compound on most drag strips. You can be assured differential obliteration is imminent if you have more than 500 hp under the hood. When you surpass 500 hp with sticky tires, the strap-type axle yokes that connect the differential to the axleshafts on your Shark can fail.

This informative Shark differential photo shows some of the things that Corvette specialists Mid America Motorworks in Effingham, Illinois, can do for you. The 1968–1979 Eaton differential carrier is easily seen through the differential's cutaway housing. The right side of the differential has all factory low-horsepower components and strap-type universal joint yoke retainers. On the left, high-strength universal caps are installed with a performance camber control strut rod. (Photo Courtesy Mid America Motorworks)

C3 CORVETTE: HOW TO BUILD AND MODIFY 1968–1982

CHAPTER 8

These heavy-duty steel caps are the preferred method to hold the U-joints to the axleshaft yokes. The ARP reduced-head stainless-steel bolts make it much easier to service these high-strength caps. Always use Never-Seez on stainless-steel bolt threads to prevent thread galling. Beware of trying to rotate the rear wheels when the rear spring and suspension are unloaded (the wheels hanging free); these caps tend to get close to the axleshafts and can cause binding. The possibility of binding U-joints is not a concern during road racing or autocrossing, and certainly not while drag racing. If you plan to jump cars you need to be concerned, and that is not a subject I will be covering.

These Van Steel 31-spline axles are a must for high-torque and drag race Sharks. They handle more than 400 ft-lbs of torque with sticky tires. The high-strength spindles are hardened with a higher spline count for a stronger mechanical connection to the universal joint hub. You have a choice of the standard 7/16-20 or beefy 1/2-20 studs 3 inches long for adequate wheel retention and to keep the tech guys smiling. If you feel that you need more torque-handling capabilities HD 1480 series universal joint flanges are available. They assemble like the originals and can be installed in your original spindle bearing supports.

General Motors used a cap-type U-joint axleshaft on the special high-performance small-block and all big-block Sharks to add some extra strength to the driveline (none of the Dana axleshaft yokes were available with cap-type U-joint retainers). You can expect to safely handle more than 500 hp with the original-equipment cap-style axle yokes and Grade-8 bolts.

Duntov Motor Company's Super Duty axleshafts, for example, are made to handle more than 600 hp, and certainly high-horsepower C3 drag cars need to be equipped with these. However, the rear axle spindles continue to be a weak spot in the rear suspension and can fail under high enough loads. When a spindle breaks, the only mechanical part holding things together is the brake caliper, and that does not do much. This is a potentially dangerous situation.

Regardless of what you do to the differential, the rear axle spindle should be replaced with high-quality performance components. Corvette Central, for example, has aircraft-quality drop forged heat-treated steel rear axle spindles (PN 582078). This will be the smartest money you spend for road or drag racing.

The rear axle and universal joints are two more crucial alignment driveline/suspension components. Unlike a solid axle, when a U-joint fails in the Shark's independent rear suspension, vehicle stability can be compromised and you can easily lose control of the car. In addition, an axleshaft flailing around the fiberglass rear floor is very dangerous as well.

When an axleshaft gets loose, wheel alignment can change dramatically. There is no longer a solid centering point for the rear suspension components. The rear axle spindles, axleshafts, and U-joints are critical to maintain control of the car, your safety, and the safety of those around you.

Differential

You can build a differential that's virtually indestructible for your application. Choosing the right parts is essential. A few aftermarket manufacturers have spent time developing performance Shark differential parts because the unique independent suspension driveline is not as strong as many solid-axle arrangements.

Eaton originally manufactured the early Shark's Posi-Traction carrier, and the company has a version of race-bred

DRIVELINE

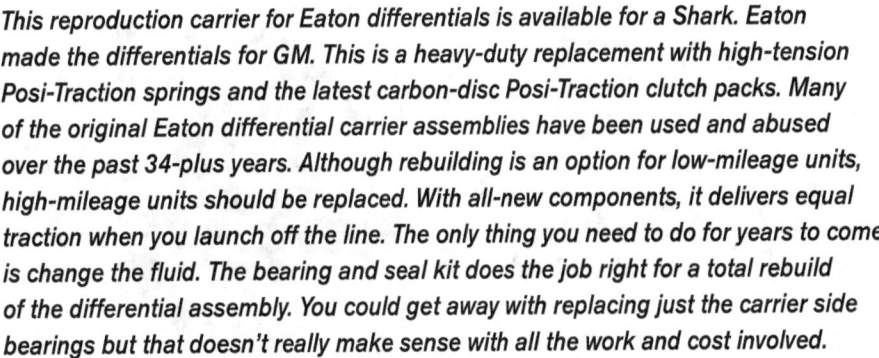

This reproduction carrier for Eaton differentials is available for a Shark. Eaton made the differentials for GM. This is a heavy-duty replacement with high-tension Posi-Traction springs and the latest carbon-disc Posi-Traction clutch packs. Many of the original Eaton differential carrier assemblies have been used and abused over the past 34-plus years. Although rebuilding is an option for low-mileage units, high-mileage units should be replaced. With all-new components, it delivers equal traction when you launch off the line. The only thing you need to do for years to come is change the fluid. The bearing and seal kit does the job right for a total rebuild of the differential assembly. You could get away with replacing just the carrier side bearings but that doesn't really make sense with all the work and cost involved.

This is a typical Posi-Traction clutch plate from an Eaton carrier. They don't last forever; as you can see, this one has broken up. The only sure way to know the clutch plate condition is to remove it and inspect it. I replace all clutch plates for all performance builds to ensure even traction under load. Later designs do not have the reliefs cut into them for more friction surface, and they tend to cause noise during cornering when the fluid requires servicing.

carbon friction discs. The all-new carrier assembly (right out of the box) has the best parts and tight clearances to allow the most reliability in the design parameters.

Companies, such as Duntov Motor Company, have taken these well-built Eaton assemblies and added spring pressure to the Posi-Traction clutch pack for extreme conditions. Couple the new Eaton carrier with Duntov Motor Company's Super Duty axle yokes for a dependable 600-hp road race Shark.

The 1980–1982 Dana differential is another story; not quite as many pieces are available for the 500-hp-and-up applications. No new differential ring gear carriers are available unless you find a new old stock piece lying around somewhere. The 1980–1982 C3s produced only about 175 net horsepower or so, and therefore there's no need to replace the axleshaft straps on the yokes with caps.

If you are road racing, the stock axleshaft yokes are good for about 500 hp. You can find the Posi-Traction clutch packs, but they are designed without the Eaton-style coil spring pressure system. Adding extra torque loading to the clutch pack is not easy and is limited because of the convex pressure spring used.

The quoted horsepower handling numbers are subjected to the road course driver's style: abrupt starts and high wheel spin with immediate traction can kill the best equipment.

Ring-and-pinion gear sets are getting tougher to find, requiring multiple vendors to supply the available eight ratios from 3.08:1 to 4.56:1 for the Eaton carrier. With that being said, if you want a particular ratio, it may be a Richmond, Yukon, or US Gear assembly. Luckily, all of them are well made.

On a positive note, 10 gear ratios are available from 3.07:1 to 5.13:1 for just about any race application for the Dana parts. The trick to long life in a road-race environment is treating the gear set with a process that minimizes the flaws in the gear teeth surfaces. Duntov Motor Company has extensive background with road-racing Sharks that use the REM treatment to finely polish the ring-and-pinion gears' contact surfaces.

If you decide to purchase your new ring-and-pinion from Duntov Motor Company, the treatment is available as part of the performance differential parts line.

On true road-race applications, you should install a differential oil cooler to achieve long gear life. Duntov Motor Company has a modified cover with the required fittings to plumb a gear oil pump and cooler to your differential. They also have that option available for their complete race car application differential assembly.

Building a drag race–worthy differential for a serious high-output engine requires a specially constructed assembly. Duntov Motor Company has the track time and capabilities to build a differential to handle up to 700 hp. I highly recommend that you listen very carefully to the builder's suggestions or parts requirements if you build it yourself. The horsepower ratings that the components tolerate are approximate. Each driver is an individual who can be easy or very hard on the best equipment available.

Every time the driveline receives harsh engagement, whether it is from the clutch pedal being side-stepped or a high-RPM wheel spin with an abrupt engagement on traction compound, things break.

I know of one 1969 Corvette owner who has put the effort into making a bulletproof differential for the 1,000-plus hp under his hood. His differential assembly bolts into the original position, allowing him to use all the required Shark independent suspension pieces. The one-off differential build started life with a Strange Ultra center section 9-inch differential assembly. A Strange Engineering steel bare 9-inch housing was used, then short sleeves were welded into the housing that was fitted so the original Shark axle yokes could connect to the existing axles. The trick was retaining the axle yokes in the housing, which required a fabricated collar to hold the now-pressed-on bearings on the axle yokes. A mounting plate was welded to the top of the housing to bolt it to the factory Shark crossmember. A front differential mount was constructed of .125 steel and attached to the differential housing at the pinion carrier area.

This radical differential was built a few years ago, and as we all know, products are always changing.

Currently Dutchman Motorsports has a 9-inch differential housing assembly with axle yokes similar to the Shark Corvette. There is an area to mount the differential to the Shark crossmember. The challenge is mounting the rear spring and strut rod center mount to the bottom of the housing. It can be done and is much easier than engineering the axle yokes as they were in the first attempt.

At $1,250, the high-strength housing machined for the axle yokes will save a lot of extra work and dollars on experimental pieces. Additionally, they have axle yokes available that are CNC machined from high-quality 4340 chrome-moly material.

Assembly

Differential service can be intimidating for the beginner. All those gears and bearings whirl around in that confined space. You need to make sure that the gears mesh properly and have correct contact on the teeth.

Noise is a concern, but in some cases improperly set-up gear sets can destroy the gears quickly. If the gear contact is

Correct bearing removal and installation is critical for any differential service. This Mac Tools remover grabs the bearing under the bearing's inner race. The other half of the bearing puller is installed to grab the bearing around its circumference. If the goal is to reuse the bearing it must be pulled from the race, not the rollers, as it bends the roller cage, misplacing the bearing rollers. These tapered roller bearings, like all bearings, are composed of very hard, brittle metal; when they break, they often shatter. Using punches and hammers can get the bearings off, but this tool makes the job much easier and less costly if you don't install the correct shim.

Another very real concern is collateral damage that can occur if the punch misses and strikes the ring or, in this case, the pinion. The ultra-hard metal can chip or break a significant piece of a gear tooth.

This Mac Tools remover is ready to remove the inner pinion bearing. The outer band keeps the puller halves in place to ensure the bearing puller cups stay in place under the bearing during removal. Once the outer band is tightened with a wrench (not finger tight), the 1 1/8-inch forcing screw is rotated counterclockwise in turn, pulling the bearing off the pinion's shaft. In most cases, you can reuse the bearing if necessary during the pinion depth setup procedure. Having the bearing encased like this is also much safer: if the bearing breaks apart, it is contained. Using a punch can shatter the bearing when the piece is broken off at high speed. It is like shrapnel, capable of embedding itself in you.

off, gear strength is compromised from the minimal contact surfaces.

The next concern is removing the bearings from the carrier and pinion gear, and this requires special tools. Some choose to remove the bearings with heat, which can be harmful to the component if they are overheated. The 1968–1979 differential carrier uses shims outboard of the bearing races to control ring-and-pinion backlash. Once the old bearings have been removed, the replacements can stay in place during the shim selection process.

The 1980–1982 Dana differential carrier has a different approach to shim for ring-and-pinion gear backlash. Their shims go under the bearings, and if you don't pick the correct shims on the first try, the bearings must come off. That can be costly unless you invest in the correct bearing removal tools or make a lot of trips to the machine shop.

Keep in mind that not every machine shop has the tools to remove the carrier bearings for reuse. They can safely remove them, but they are junk.

In a cruel twist, the 1968–1979 Eaton pinion bearing has the pinion depth shim under the inner pinion bearing, and it requires a special puller to safely remove the bearing.

The 1980–1982 Dana pinion depth is set with a shim under the inner pinion bearing race; it is much easier to remove from the differential housing without damage.

Either way, the replacement of bearings and setting up the ring-and-pinion are not for everyone.

Differential Service

1 Check Ring Gear to Pinion Backlash

I have a magnetic base dial indicator setup checking the ring gear backlash on this finished project. Correct ring gear backlash is critical, especially for a performance ring-and-pinion. Too much allows additional shock loading, which shortens the gear set's life. I make a habit of always checking the backlash before and after if the gear set is to be reused. If the backlash changes during the service, there is a reason and it must be corrected. This is usually due to a change in bearing stack-up, whether at the pinion or carrier-side bearings, even when the same shims are reused. When I am sure that I will be reusing the ring-and-pinion, I measure the new pinion inner bearing stack height versus the original's. This is important for pinion depth. Chances are very good that the ring-and-pinion will howl due to a different pinion depth setup. If the pinion depth is correct, the carrier shims can be changed to compensate for bearing stack differences without the chance of ring-and-pinion noise.

2 Remove the Axleshaft Yoke Snap Rings

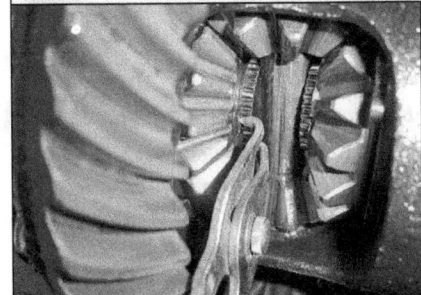

Axleshaft yokes are a critical part of alignment. This gives you an idea of how the axleshafts are centered on the pinion gears in the carrier. The snap rings hold the axleshaft yokes in place and are also a part of the alignment as the suspension is unloaded. A dip in the road causes the wheel to momentarily unload; the rear suspension's pivot point consequently changes, negatively affecting the camber and toe alignment.

You'll know if the yokes are worn when you jack up the car at the frame with the suspension hanging free. As the wheel assembly begins to leave the ground, the top of the wheel drops away as the clearance between the pinion shaft pin and axleshaft yoke is opened up. At that point, having someone pick up the wheel shows the axleshaft yoke going in and out. The axleshaft yoke (left) has minimal noticeable wear because of sharp edge on the splines. Frequently the wear is so severe that the yoke has mushroomed over, knocking the snap ring off completely. This creates a significant change in alignment, so much so that camber cannot be adjusted properly.

When severe mushrooming occurs, the pinion shaft pin has to be removed. A long drift punch is used to drive the yoke out of the differential from the opposite side if the other yoke comes out. If not, it takes a slide hammer attached to the yoke from the outside to slap it out. There is no way to totally eliminate wear on the axleshaft yoke ends; they spin with significant pressure on the pinion gear shaft during cornering.

3 Prep for Differential Carrier Removal

On this later Dana differential you can see two holes in a vertical pattern below the threaded cover retaining hole. They are used for a differential spreader tool that has two pins on each side of the carrier. The tool goes into the pins and then a forcing screw is used to spread the case for easy carrier removal. I always mark the cap and carrier to denote their location as you would with an engine main or rod bearing. The yellow dots assure me that the cap is right side up and on the correct side. Bearing saddles are machined with the caps in place; placement is critical for a true round bearing bore. Changing positions can cause the bearing bores to be off-center from the inside to the outside.

CHAPTER 8

4 Remove Pinion Yoke

Many differentials are damaged from the lack of proper tools; a two-jaw puller such as this should be used to remove the pinion yoke. I prefer a tight-fitting yoke on the pinion splines for performance applications. If the yoke just pulls off by hand, you can have trouble later. Leaks occur and spline wear is enhanced from the constant loading, and eventually the yoke can become loose. I have seen many hammers used to beat the yoke off of the pinion and then beat the pinion out of the differential case. That's fine if you plan to throw away the pinion gear. In spite of how hard the pinion is, the threads can become damaged. The two-jaw puller forces the yoke off the pinion, exposing the pinion shaft. Once the yoke is off, a brass drift punch and hammer can be used to knock the pinion out of the bearings.

5 Obtain Correct Pinion Bearing Preload

This Dana pinion gear has a shim pack between the inner and outer bearings to set bearing preload. The bearings should have zero end play after the bearings have been worn in. The shims allow the pinion gear flange to be tightened and torqued as required, while maintaining the correct pinion gear bearing preload. When set up properly, an inch-pound torque wrench is used to measure the rotating torque load of the pinion gear assembly. I set mine at 20 in-lbs for all performance applications. By the way, this differential received a new pinion yoke because of the rusty paste between the bearing and yoke splines. The rust denotes a yoke that became loose.

6 Adjust Pinion Depth

This Eaton pinion gear has the pinion depth washer exposed; Dana has this shim under the bearing race in the differential housing. This is the most critical adjustment of all; correct pinion depth can make or break the installation. Read your ring-and-pinion manufacturer's recommendations before doing any portion of the installation. They often have a recommendation for a starting point for the pinion shim selection; if not, I start with .028 inch on Eaton and Dana assemblies.

7 Install Inner Pinion Bearing

I use a hammer as infrequently as possible, because hammering or forcing a component often creates damage. This installation sleeve is a piece of tubing cut to size for pinion bearing installation. Beware: the inner diameter of the tubing can become stuck on the pinion shaft. I had to grind out the inner diameter just enough to allow the tube to slide over the shaft and then a hydraulic press was used to push the bearing on. Hammering this bearing on with a chisel or punch can be dangerous, and can damage the bearing. Extra-tight-fitting bearings are heated with a shop heat gun to ease installation, never with a torch.

DRIVELINE

8 Install Pinion Bearing Crush Sleeve

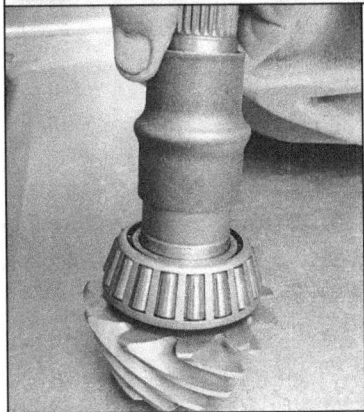

Eaton uses this "crush sleeve" rather than pinion bearing preload shims. The differential needs the same torque loading that can be achieved as this sleeve is reduced in height. Therefore, you do not have to remove the outer bearing each time to change a pinion bearing preload shim. If you go too tight on the preload, however, you have to remove the outer bearing and replace the crush sleeve.

Another issue arises when a pinion seal is replaced. Each time the pinion nut is backed off, the crush sleeve should be replaced to ensure that the preload is correct and will be maintained. This is essential for a performance differential. If the pinion seal is leaking the crush sleeve should be replaced, or you could end up with catastrophic damage. I have seen firsthand what happens when the pinion nut backs off and the pinion gear crashes into the carrier. Often the entire assembly is reduced to just a few salvageable pieces, if any.

9 Install Posi-Traction Clutch Plate Assembly

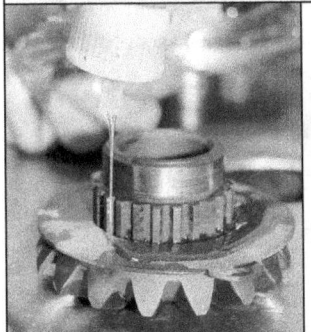

Moving on to the carrier assembly, start off by lubricating the Posi-Traction clutch plates as you alternately stack the plates. Do not miss this crucial step: getting lubricant between the tight-fitting plates is difficult even when the differential is full and the carrier is submerged in lube. The outer tab plates start the stack, with an inner splined plate next, and alternating the plates until you end with a tabbed plate.

10 Install Posi-Traction Clutch Plates in Ring Gear Carrier

The stacked assembly is placed in the carrier with the tab retainers and shims in place. I never reuse the outer tab retainers: I often find the broken tab retainers in the bottom of the differential housing. The shims are used to take up the slack when the axleshaft yoke snap ring is installed. If you use new Posi-Traction clutch plates and the yokes are in good condition, the original shim stack can usually be used. Once the differential clutch packs, pinion gears, and springs are in place, the snap ring fit tells you if you need to go back and add or remove shims. You do not need to fully assemble the differential to do the check.

11 Place Pinion Gear Washers in Ring Gear Carrier

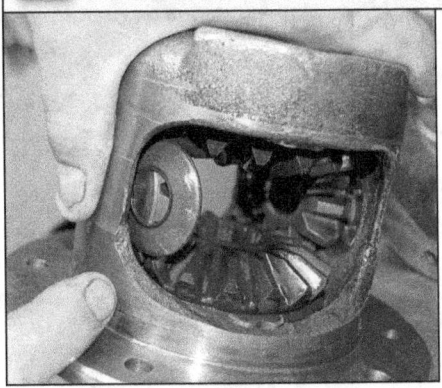

Now the tricky part begins. If you have new Posi-Traction plates, coaxing these pinion gear washers into place can be challenging. First, when the pinion gear and clutch packs are installed, make sure the gears are sitting flat on the plates at the gear side; especially the top gear and Posi-Traction plate assembly. It is easy to have an outer plate become out of place, holding the gear away from the plate. If you are having trouble installing the smaller pinion gears, check to see if there is a gap between the larger pinion gear and the Posi-Traction plates. If so, move the larger pinion gear around until it seats on the plate.

The smaller pinion gears are then meshed into the side gears and then rotated into place one at a time. Once the first gear is installed, rotate the smaller gear until it is to the back of the carrier, then the final small gear is placed into the side gears directly across from the already installed small gear. If everything is stacked correctly, the washers should just fit between the gear and housing. You can work the gears back and forth to slide the washer into place. I avoid using a screwdriver or punch to force the washers in place; the washers can become damaged, and you may never see it until major damage results.

C3 CORVETTE: HOW TO BUILD AND MODIFY 1968–1982

CHAPTER 8

12 Align Pinion Gear in Ring Gear Carrier

Next, the smaller gears are rotated until they are in the vicinity of the pinion shaft pin hole. If you lined up the gears, they are ready for the pinion shaft pin to be installed into the carrier. If not, rotate them back until one can be removed and try again to place the gear directly across from the other gear. It may take a couple of attempts. Once the small pinion gears are in place, I work the washers into place by putting the carrier on the axleshaft yoke so that the carrier can be rotated. It takes some patience to line up the parts; lifting the carrier off the axleshaft just slightly to alleviate pressure helps rotate the gears. The bolt placed in the ring gear mounting flange allows me to use a long screwdriver to rotate the housing (if necessary) to align the pinion gears.

13 Install Posi-Traction Clutch Tension Plates and Springs

I safety wire the Posi-Traction spring plates together so they stay organized for installation into the carrier. Place the plate assembly into a vise, then tighten the vise until the springs are coil bound. Safety wire is then tightly twisted until no slack is in the wire. Once the plate assembly is installed the wire is cut and pulled out. I always replace these critical springs and check the plates carefully for wear.

14 Install Pinion Gear Shaft

Make sure the pinion shaft fits snugly into the carrier pinion shaft pin's bore. It should require some force to install; if it is loose the retainer bolt/pin that holds the shaft in place is broken. In most cases the shaft is not why it's loose; the carrier itself is worn and requires replacement.

With all the carrier internals installed, the pinion shaft is installed in the carrier and retained with the 7/16-inch hex-head retainer pin. Torque the retainer pin to 120 in-lbs. The best policy now is to check the axleshaft yoke–to–pinion shaft pin clearance. The yokes should sit flat on the pinion shaft and the snap rings should fit tightly in the groove. If you have excessive clearance or the snap rings do not seat in their groove, the carrier requires disassembly to add or subtract shims. A feeler gauge can be placed between the pinion shaft pin and axleshaft yoke to determine the excess clearance and the required shim. After doing numerous differential builds, I have always found too much clearance, never too little.

15 Prep Ring Gear Carrier

Performance work requires extra-careful preparation, such as using a whetstone on the ring gear surfaces to ensure they are flat and the ring gear is running true. Work the stone around the surface, removing any nicks or high spots before installing the ring gear. Note the lack of pinion shaft retainer hex-head bolt. Dana uses two snap rings on the inside of the carrier to keep the shaft in place.

16 Install Ring Gear

Now the ring gear is installed with new bolts: ARP bolts are preferred for performance applications. Torque the bolts to 20 ft-lbs for the first pass, then to the manufacturer's specifications. This allows the ring gear to be pulled flat against the flange before the final torque is achieved. Red Loctite is recommended after the bolts and boltholes are washed with brake cleaner or an alcohol-based cleaner.

17 Install Differential Case Bearing Race

This Dana aluminum housing has the pinion depth shims under the inner bearing race. The bearing installer is used to ensure that the bearing race goes in the housing squarely. It may seem that all you do is set the bearing in place and hammer away, but that can get you in trouble. The bearing race must go into the bore squarely, or a piece of aluminum can become dislodged and be trapped between the bearing race and the housing. Place the bearing in the housing and then place the bearing installer (a tapered aluminum plug) into the bearing. Take a look at the bearing installers' shaft: it should be sitting straight up from the bearing race. Begin tapping the bearing race in with a medium-size ball-peen hammer.

Frequently check to see if the bearing installer shaft is still straight; as you deviate from straight, it becomes more difficult to hammer the bearing in place. If this occurs, stop and check to see which side is higher, that is, what caused the race to become wedged and tighter than it should be. If you are at the halfway point or further, move the installer to the high side and tap in that area until the race becomes level. Once the race is level, center the installer and begin tapping the race again until it is seated. If you just got the race started and it is cocked, stop, knock it out, and try it again.

18 Coax Ring Gear Carrier Side Bearing Shims into Place

When lightly tapping in the ring gear carrier bearing preload and backlash adjustment shim, you have to be gentle: too much pressure and the original shims can shatter. Replacement shims are made of more malleable material and can be tapped into place without breaking.

A differential housing spreader tool fits into the large round holes on each side of the housing to aid in carrier bearing shim installation. If you do not have this tool it is difficult (but not impossible) to start the shims into the housing. As long as the bearing races are tight against the bearings, most often the carrier can be pushed into the housing with the shims. If it takes more pressure than that, chances are the shims are incorrect.

Words of caution: when you install the bearing caps check to make sure there is some ring-and-pinion backlash to avoid damaging the ring gear as you tighten the caps fully.

19 Confirm Ring Gear Pattern

Reading the gear pattern correctly can be tough. To begin with, the marking compound that comes with almost every ring-and-pinion installation kit is brushed onto the ring gear for a pattern check. They even provide a small brush to apply the compound sparingly to the teeth, just enough to cover them lightly, with no big globs. Once the compound is applied, the ring gear is rotated until the painted teeth mesh with the pinion gear. I apply some drag to the pinion yoke while rotating the ring gear back and forth through the painted teeth to make sure the teeth are meshed tightly together to obtain a readable pattern.

You are looking at the coast side of the ring gear: the pattern is centered in the tooth, which is a great start. If the pinion depth were incorrect, the pattern would be at either end of the tooth and it would certainly be noisy during coasting. The pattern also goes almost to the very inside of the gear, which denotes the backlash is correct. If the pattern were only on the edge of the tooth, you would have too much backlash.

The drive side of this Dana ring gear needs to be centered, and you need to pay particular attention to it. In a performance application noise may not be a major concern, but tooth deflection is. Having the pattern centered and deep into the tooth ensures good long-term wear patterns and long gear life. As on the coast side, if the pattern were too low or high, quick wear could result. With that being said, keep in mind that if the pattern were closer to the toe (inside center of the gear), it would be preferable to being closer to the heel (outer diameter of the gear). The closer-to-toe pattern allows for inherent ring gear deflection and provides more gear tooth engagement with high-torque applications.

20 Crush Pinion Bearing Crush Sleeve

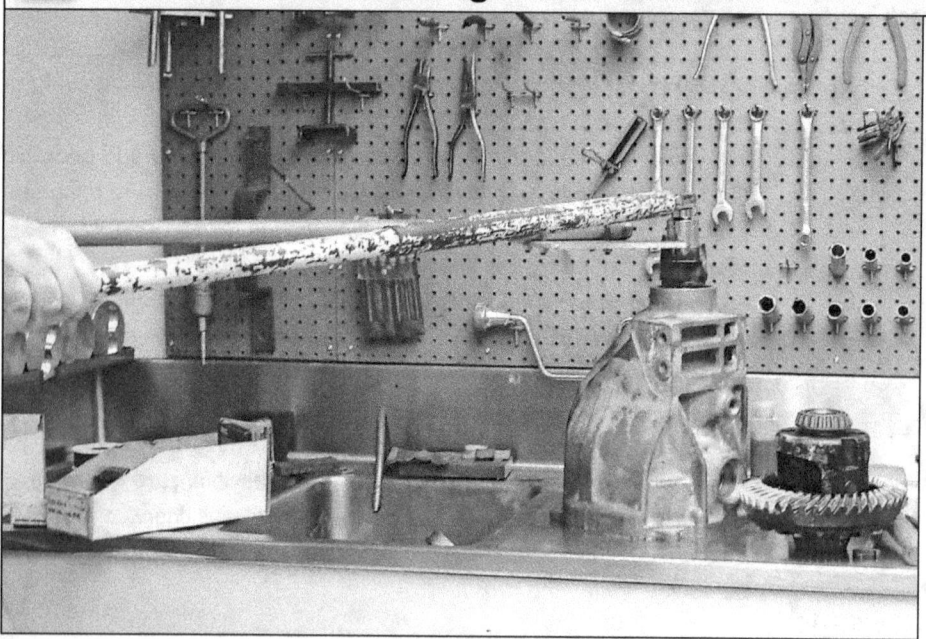

This is a later Dana out of a 1996 Corvette, but the process is the same for early Eaton differentials. The long bars are the only way to crush the sleeve unless you can put some high torque on a pull bar. Beware: aftermarket crush sleeves are available that can be crushed easily. Unfortunately, that also makes them come loose easily, losing their correct torque, and the bearings are loose. I do not recommend them for any performance application, although they are really easy to use. Another thing to remember is to check frequently during the crush process. It only takes a small rotation for the pinion preload to end up too tight.

DRIVELINE

Axle and Driveshaft

The Shark independent rear axle is unlike the typical late-model independent rear suspension. The late-model axleshafts allow the fixed wheel spindle assembly to move up and down while changing the overall length of the axle. This means that the Shark axleshafts multi-task, transmitting power and also aligning the rear wheels. Open-type universal joints are used for the connection of the axleshafts to the differential and rear wheel spindles.

Axleshaft and driveshaft tube diameter has some limitations for clearing the transmission tunnel, driveline, and suspension components. Up to 3-inch-diameter tubing clears without any issue. Increased-diameter tubing may require some modifications to the rear compartment vertical surfaces. Another possibility for an ultra-high-horsepower application is to increase the axleshaft or driveshaft tube's wall thickness for just about any horsepower you can inflict on them.

Aluminum replacement axles and driveshafts are often the best option. However, they too can have increased tube wall thickness to handle high-horsepower applications. The aluminum-tube axleshafts

Van Steel offers 3-inch diameter axleshafts with increased tubing wall thickness. They handle almost any torque you may be trying to apply to the ground. The all-new axleshafts are built with non-greaseable universal joints for maximum torque loading.

help to absorb the inherent harmonics that occur when twisting pressure is applied to power-transmitting components. Vibrations and harmonics kill rotating components. Anytime you can alleviate any amount, all the components live longer and your backside appreciates the smoother ride.

Denny's Driveshafts routinely builds custom drive and axleshafts for drag- and road-race Corvettes. They have Shark Corvette parts available for any power application ready to be shipped, including the difficult-to-find Spicer outer axle flange yokes. Summit Racing also has a good selection of axle and driveshafts from Inland Empire Driveline and Strange Engineering.

Your main concern is finding a driveline specialty shop that understands the requirements of your engine power output and traction capabilities. You need components that are rated at 25 percent greater than your application. Read the supplier's recommendations and use the best attaching components.

Universal Joints

Universal joints come in three versions. Workhorse universal joints found in everyday use have drilled passages to allow greasing during maintenance. The drilled universal joints last longer until they are used in high-torque-load applications. To provide the most possible torque-handling high-strength universal joints, do not have the drilled grease passages; the drilling weakens the shaft. The third version is used in aluminum shafts. They receive a coating that is applied to the cups to keep them from corroding and causing galvanic reactions from the aluminum versus steel yokes. These are rarely shown in catalogs but should be considered if you decide to move up to the aluminum shafts for long yoke life.

Today, most performance specialty driveline companies are well aware of the aluminum driveshaft requirements, and stock the coated U-joint cups.

Any rotating shaft, driveshaft, or axleshaft can suffer misalignment, bends or damage, or become out of balance, and this can create catastrophic vibration. Axleshafts turn more slowly than the driveshaft, for example, when you have a 3:73.1 rear axle ratio. Regardless of the transmission's operating gear, the driveshaft spins 3.73 times for every one revolution of the axleshaft. Therefore, driveshafts that are out of balance or installed at the wrong angle can produce significant vibrations.

In addition, axleshafts rotate at a slower rate and as a result, produce vibrations only at very high speed. Because of this, many people never suspect an axleshaft balance problem. On the other hand, driveshafts often cause a drone or vibration. You notice the drone as a rhythmic throbbing noise or a feeling that usually starts at about 45 mph. In most cases the drone goes away as your speed increases above 60 mph and then comes in again at higher speeds.

Driveline misalignment or an incorrect driveshaft angle typically causes a constant vibration that usually comes in at around 35 to 40 mph and does not go away until you slow down. Driveline angle vibrations occur when the transmission output shaft and/or differential yoke are in perfect alignment, making both assemblies one long shaft from beginning to end. The one long shaft prevents the universal joints from doing their job, resulting in vibration as the driveshaft whips around, much like a jump rope pulled tight and then rotated. To combat this phenomenon, transmission output shafts and differential yokes are set at different angles to separate the assemblies into three segments, allowing the universal joints to work.

CHAPTER 8

If you plan to use the original axle or driveshafts, take a couple minutes to clean the bores before installing the U-joints. I know the old-school, whack-'em-in with a big hammer is the way they are usually installed. That, unfortunately, damages the trunnions and cap bearing rollers. Tight U-joints are also a source of vibration and ultimately, driveline failure, which happens more quickly in a performance application. By the way, be easy with the sanding flap wheel. You just want to knock the rust and high spots down; too much cleaning ends up with loose U-joint cups.

This is the most important step in any U-joint installation and is often done haphazardly. Poorly seated retaining rings can cause big trouble. In my early years in the business, I remember replacing the U-joints in our family car. In my haste to impress my dad I left one ring not quite seated. The road test was quite an event as the driveshaft came loose at highway speed. I have also observed that if you use too much force the ring is distorted and can easily pop out. Make sure it is fully seated around its entire circumference.

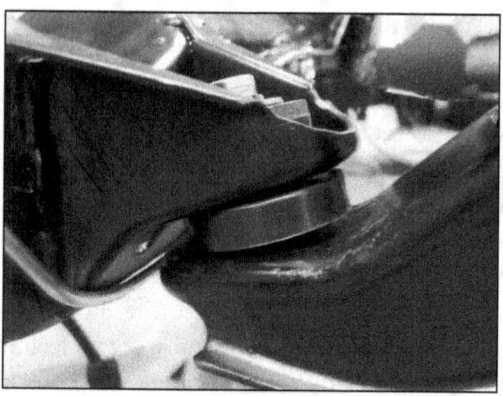

This dense, round, urethane bushing is used in place of the original soft-rubber pinion snubber, or in the case of the Shark Corvette, a front differential mount. As the rubber cushions aged they became soft or brittle, allowing the differential pinion to move around, changing the driveline angle under heavy torque loading. I prefer urethane because it does have some isolating properties and eases some of the inherent vibrations in the drivetrain. Unlike a solid axle suspension, the Shark differential holds a constant driveline angle under high-torque loads. Drag racing is another thing though; high loads are put on this front differential mount and some serious racers opt for an aluminum puck to replace the urethane cushion.

Universal joints must "work" to keep the driveshaft rotating in a true circle. The work part means the universal joint must roll slightly on the cups. The cups or trunnions house needle bearings. These bearings absorb the torque loading while rotating slightly as the shaft spins.

Upgrading or changing the gearbox can change the mounting height of the tailshaft yoke and therefore change the driveshaft angle; many new gearboxes are longer and therefore you need a shorter driveshaft. If you find that you have driveline vibration and require frequent universal joint replacements, chances are there is a misalignment issue.

The ideal driveline angle is 3 degrees maximum at both ends. Therefore, it should be 3 degrees down on the front and 3 degrees up at the rear. The angles can be opposed 3 degrees up at the front and 3 degrees down at the rear. The other rule is to keep the angles within 1 degree of each other: for example, 3 at the rear and 1 at the front is not good.

The C3's fixed differential mounting has benefits and drawbacks. Not much flexibility in the up and down movement limits the driveline angle changes that are available. On the other hand, the angles don't change much as the differential is torque loaded. Securely mounting the front of the differential is possible, and many chose to use less resilient urethane mounting cushions. Solid mounting is easily accomplished for a true race application. Urethane mounting makes the most sense, though, to resolve any inherent minor vibrations.

Shimming the differential at the front mount changes driveline angles, and this is certainly an option. Raising or lowering the transmission to accommodate a driveshaft angle change is another option. The transmission can only be raised and lowered small amounts, particularly when an aftermarket transmission is installed because of its taller case. It usually requires working with the differential and the transmission to get the numbers right.

CHAPTER 9

AFTERMARKET CHASSIS INSTALLATION

A purpose-built chassis built with stronger tubing or a full frame provides far greater torsional rigidity than the factory-supplied welded half-frame rails. The automotive aftermarket now has manufacturing equipment that only OEM companies used to possess. This technology allows these companies to research, develop, and manufacture complete chassis.

Equipment for water-jet steel cutting, CNC machining, and mandrel tubing bending is available for companies to build new purpose-built chassis. They can build these chassis on CAD/Cam machines and do it repeatedly. These are desirable chassis with the latest engine, transmission, and drivelines, allowing for late-model Corvette performance.

Do You Need One?

A full aftermarket chassis is desirable for high-performance applications and racing. This is certainly an option for a restorable C3 with a rusted bird cage, if you plan to complete a ground-up restoration with some aftermarket parts. An aftermarket frame and all the required trimmings is certainly a sizable investment, and with many C3s, it may not be worth the investment. Of course, that's a personal decision. But keep in mind that an original chassis is a solid performance platform, and for most street-going Corvettes the factory chassis provides more than adequate performance.

You have to ask yourself if you possess the skill to drive a stock C3 beyond the limits of its chassis. If you do, you probably need a chassis with the late-model components to match your skill level. On the other hand, if you do not possess the skill, do not expect the chassis to make you a better driver.

As far as cost, a bare purpose-built chassis is not that much more than buying a new original-equipment chassis. If you are careful about finding a donor car you could save considerable money. Then you can also offset the costs by selling some of the take-off parts from your original chassis.

Street Shop has become the leader in 1963–1982 Corvette chassis fabrication, using mandrel-bent rectangular tubing for rigidity. Realizing that the later Corvette chassis components would soon become hard to find, they began designing and building their own components. This chassis uses 1997–2004 Corvette suspension components and is covered with a 1981 Corvette body.

CHAPTER 9

Each chassis supplier developed and built a chassis that resolves the inherent shortcomings of the original chassis, and each has a different interpretation. You need to consider this aspect and determine what you want from the chassis. You may want a different wheel offset, but the builder does not offer that. In many cases, they do not make a major change in chassis width to accommodate your wishes. Think about the finished product so you can address all the details before you start on the project.

A few important suspension and steering upgrades occur with the aftermarket chassis. Rack-and-pinion steering is way up there and is much better engineered in an aftermarket chassis than the available bolt-on to the C3 chassis.

Suspension geometry with the increased positive caster is also important for high-speed handling. Depending on which generation of Corvette suspension you choose, you could also have true independent rear suspension with upper control arms for the best possible rear-end stability. The first designs were almost all for the C4 Corvette, which has a differential and rear suspension very similar to the Shark. Now many are available with C5 Corvette suspension for that ultimate handling and braking experience. C4 brakes can be upgraded, but the C5 brakes are better from the start so you can save a few bucks there too.

Three Project Examples

I have been a part of a few of the chassis builds and built a few from scratch and have found that compromises have to be made. My very first build was a 1961 with an SRIII chassis, then a Paul Newman 1968 chassis, and to date, a 1981 Corvette with a Street Shops chassis with C5 Corvette driveline.

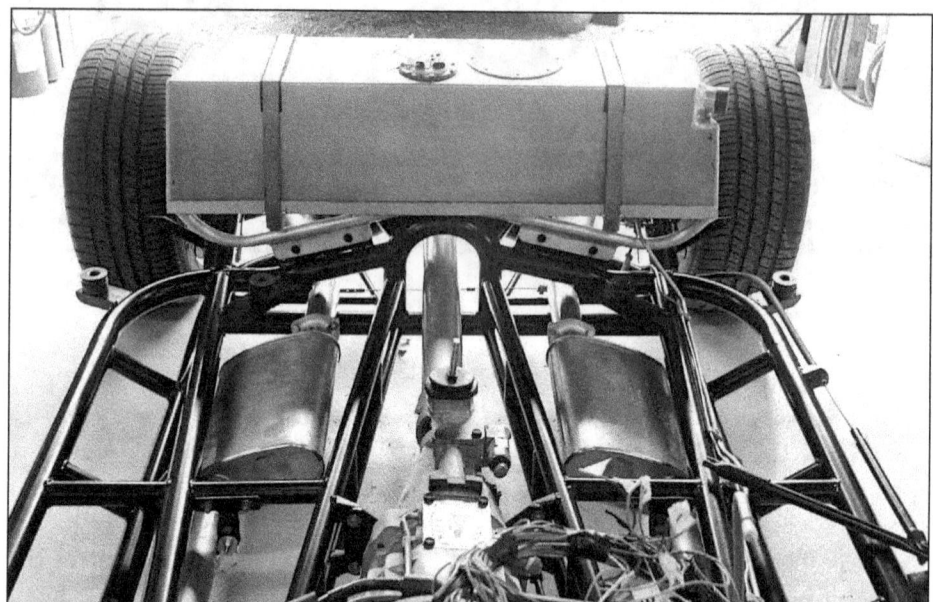

SRIII Motorsports uses 2-inch-diameter tubing for their chassis builds, triangulating the tubing for the main frame rail. The concept is sound and works well with only a few minor annoyances. The multiple tubes make it difficult to fit components in the tight spaces. They build a chassis to your driveline specifications; this project received an LS engine, Tremec T-56 6-speed, and all C4 Corvette suspension. SRIII uses a C4 rack-and-pinion with modified tie-rod ends, which are becoming difficult to find. In most cases the original rack-and-pinion must be rebuilt because of the lack of available cores.

The Paul Newman chassis began life as a GM factory frame modified for C4 Corvette suspension components. The front half of the frame is a fabricated piece welded onto the original GM frame. I added the stiffening pieces to minimize chassis flex under the 750-hp and high-torque loading it would receive. The plan was for an aluminum oil pan, and the stiffening pieces to also provide some much-needed protection from road obstacles. Many hours were spent fitting the big-block and Hooker side-pipe headers in the chassis frame rails.

AFTERMARKET CHASSIS INSTALLATION

1961 SRIII

When building a custom chassis, as I did for the 1961 SRIII, the level of planning and engineering is similar to building a car from scratch, although I had a completed bare chassis. I was one of the first few to buy a chassis from their first chassis design. As with any business, as the company evolves so does the product. Of course the 1961 chassis is different from the Shark, but the concept is the same, especially the work involved in engineering the entire package.

Many systems had to be customized and built, such as the fuel tank design and plumbing. Bumpers and safety equipment must be planned into the build. When building a project car, this is a critical job; it's your responsibility and your life depends on it. Many want to personalize their project, not build an exact replica of their prototype. Designing a one-off car is no small feat, and it takes a lot of time, energy, and resources to complete a fabricated car with a custom chassis.

1968 Convertible

The Paul Newman chassis was even more difficult because they had not completed a Shark chassis yet. So, I started the project with a prototype chassis. Remember way back in the first chapters when I said that the 1968 was a 1967 in a Shark body? Well, this was the case here. The 1968 body was set on a Paul Newman chassis built for a 1967. Many things were not considered, which required hundreds of man-hours to come up with solutions to make the chassis work.

When I went to the shop to pick up the 1968 convertible project (that had been at two other shops), it was apparent that I had a monumental project to sort out. The freshly painted body was sitting on the aftermarket chassis with no bolts to hold it down. The pieces were gathered and off to the shop I went. During the initial inspection it was clear that no one had thought about how the C4 Corvette differential's torque arm affects the 1968's floor and transmission tunnel. With the torque arm installed, the entire side of the transmission tunnel and part of the passenger's side floor had to be cut out to fit it in place. The customer wanted a full seat, not a jump seat, so I had to fabricate a differential mount that eliminated the torque arm.

Before I started that project I contacted the customer about wheel and tire choices to make sure the wheel and tire had that perfect spacing between the tire and wheel well lip. Good thing I did that, because the car sat like a 4x4 truck, requiring chassis modifications to lower it and raise the differential to get the driveline angles correct.

To make things even more interesting, when the Donovan aluminum big-block with ZL-1 intake was set into place it sat 2 inches higher than it should, which prevented the raised hood from closing. I juggled things around, lowering the engine as much as possible with a Stef's custom aluminum oil pan and raised the body 1 inch on the chassis to make it all fit. One other major problem was that no one had considered how the front bumper crash pieces or supports would be installed. They all required many hours of thought and hand fabrication to make sure there was crash protection and something holding the front end up.

The problems that arose from this project were not all the chassis supplier's fault. Communication was the problem. These items should have been discussed long before the chassis assembly began. When the project had been successfully completed, it was one of my proudest moments. During the project, I went through many trials and tribulations. I asked myself, "Why did I inflict this much pain on myself?" Fast-forward to 2007: I have a Street Shops chassis to build for a 1981. This is one fine chassis made from rectangular mandrel-bent tubing with multiple suspension configurations available.

C5 Corvette

Street Shops has C4, C5, or C6 suspension mounting points chassis; I went for the C5 fully independent rear suspension chassis. This company has developed expertise from building many chassis. When they set out to make their chassis, wheel and tire width was a major player in how wide the track would be. To keep the Shark look, wheel width is limited to fitting under the original wheel wells using the same offset as the original Shark. This uniformity is the key to making them affordable and is what the builder had in mind from the very first chassis. In addition, Street Shops has fabricated brake and fuel lines for its chassis.

You can also buy a rolling chassis that allows you to lift the body off your original chassis and roll the new purpose-built chassis in place, ready to go with few delays. To make a project such as this affordable, you need to find a good deal on the donor car and then make the pieces come together for a personal touch. I found a running, driving 25,000-mile 2004 Corvette that had rollover damage. Many parts can be used, while others can be sold to make up for some of the cost.

One thing to consider is that you can build the entire chassis before ever touching your Shark if you are driving it presently. If you plan to sell the engine and transmission or, for that matter, the entire drivetrain, including the frame, potential buyers can test-drive the pieces before the disassembly, which makes them easier to sell. That can add up to a considerable chunk of change, offsetting the project cost dramatically.

CHAPTER 9

Prep for Body Removal

You need to know that changing a chassis is a major event, and it involves a lot of tough work to get the body off the original chassis. The front, rear bumpers, and all the supporting structure must be removed. In addition, any cables, electrical, and parking brake hoses must be removed. The toughest of all requires the removal of the body mount cushions. In most cases, these have never been removed, or they have been in place for many years. Corrosion works on the body-mount bolt nuts. The idea was good when the cars were assembled, and as they age the nuts become one with the bolt.

Body Removal Prep

1 Remove Rocker Panel

The rocker panels must come off to remove the front splash shields. This may seem simple enough: take out a few Phillips-head screws and the panel drops off. These screws can be difficult to remove since corrosion eats at them. It is difficult to get rust penetrant onto the threads: drilling the head off is sometimes the smartest plan. With the head off and the panel out of the way, rust penetrant can be applied and the remaining screw shank gripped with pliers for removal.

2 Remove Bumpers

Chances are your Shark has rubber bumpers. I found that running a thread die on the bumper stud before attempting to remove the nut saves heartache down the road. These 10- to 24-thread studs are often broken from hasty removal, and it's costly to replace as the stud comes secured in a reinforcement strip.

3 Disassemble Bumpers

The front and rear bumper must be removed to lift the body. All of the bumper supports require removal. Here, the honeycomb crash absorber (to which the bumper supports bolt) has been removed. This is a major undertaking and much more than a chassis replacement is going to occur. Many issues with the body may be found, such as rust and corrosion damage to the steel fiberglass support structures.

4 Remove all Grounds

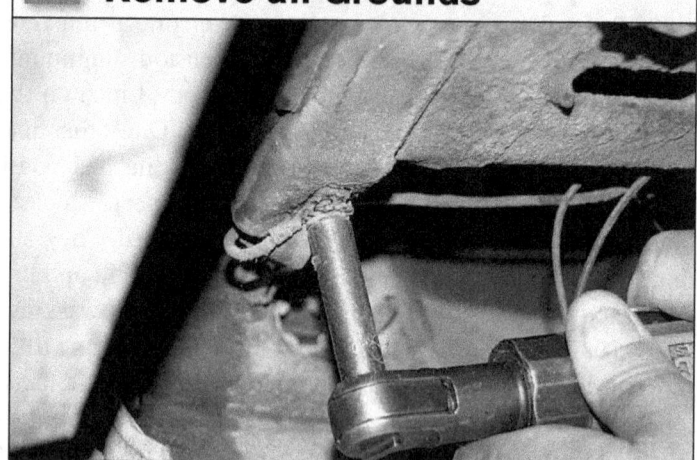

Sharks, like all Corvettes, have numerous grounds at the front and rear of the chassis. Removing them is one thing; making sure they are all put back on is another. One missing ground wire can keep you busy for days chasing a phantom electrical problem. Make sure you note where the grounds are and put them back with adequate wire and fasteners after a thorough cleaning of the terminal and mounting area.

AFTERMARKET CHASSIS INSTALLATION

5 Remove Cables and Wiring

Throttle cables and tachometer (pre-1974 Sharks) cables must be removed before the body lift. The engine harness requires removal before the lift, and the alternator power output lead must be removed. Take your time here; leaving a cable or wiring connected usually does more damage than just to the connected piece. I have seen serious component damage as the wiring is being pulled.

6 Remove Steering Column

You can either pull the steering column or remove the steering coupler nuts as seen here. As the body is lifted, the coupling separates. I usually remove the steering column completely to make this as easy as possible. During the body installation it is best to have the steering column out of the way; aligning the coupling during the body drop is difficult.

7 Remove Parking Brake Cable

If this step is missed it could be disastrous; the parking brake cable goes around this pulley wheel, which must be removed. The parking brake cable must also be disconnected at the rear cable that goes to each trailing arm. I cut the old exhaust pipes off at the crossmember to remove the entire rear section of the exhaust. The mufflers get in the way of the rear fenders during body removal.

8 Remove Radiator Core Support

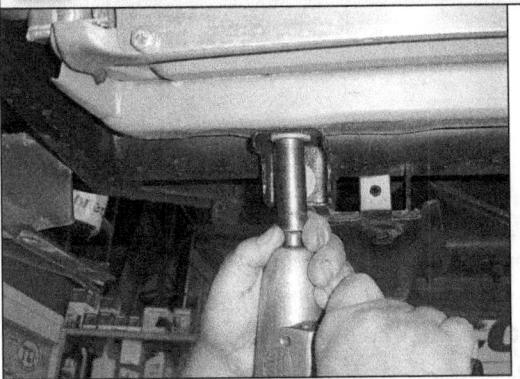

The Shark radiator core support sits on top of the bumper support. I usually leave the radiator core support bolted to the inner fenders and remove the two 5/8-inch hex-head bolts holding the radiator support to the frame. Sharks from 1968–1972 have the radiator core support held in differently than this 1979, but the concept is the same. Make sure you remove the proper bolts. Loosening these bolts helps when it comes time to remove the radiator so that the core support tilts forward with less effort.

CHAPTER 9

Water with all kinds of road minerals is thrown onto the body cushion bolts, requiring careful work to avoid major body damage. Using a torch around fiberglass is not recommended. Many people do and the burnt fiberglass shows. Rust penetrant works, but you need to think it out and begin dousing the bolts and nuts for weeks before you remove the body cushions. Sometimes you get lucky and the bolts break off, but most often they just spin and you must cut the head off the bolt. The body cushion bolts behind the rear wheels are always the worst. Fortunately, they can be cut off with a reciprocating saw.

Body Cushion Removal

Once the body is up and off the chassis, you need to inspect the C-channels that run under the sill plates. The C-channels are a crucial part of the birdcage structure supporting the Shark-body passenger compartment. If you find any rotted areas, they need to be properly repaired even though they are not visible. If required, you weld patch panels into the C-channels, especially around the body mount cushions. The areas around the body cushions often have the worst corrosion damage. Then you need to apply some primer and paint.

You should also make note of the body cushion shims. You have to put them back where they came from so the doors open and close properly. I often find that it takes some additional or sometimes fewer shims to get the door gaps uniform after a major project like this. This is a trial-and-error procedure unless you have shimmed a body a few times.

For instance, if the rear door gap is open too much at the top you need to add shims to number-4 body mount in the wheel well behind the rear tire. Always check the body gaps and shim with the tires on the ground, with no jack supporting any portion of the vehicle.

Body Cushion Removal

1 Remove Number-4 Body Bolt

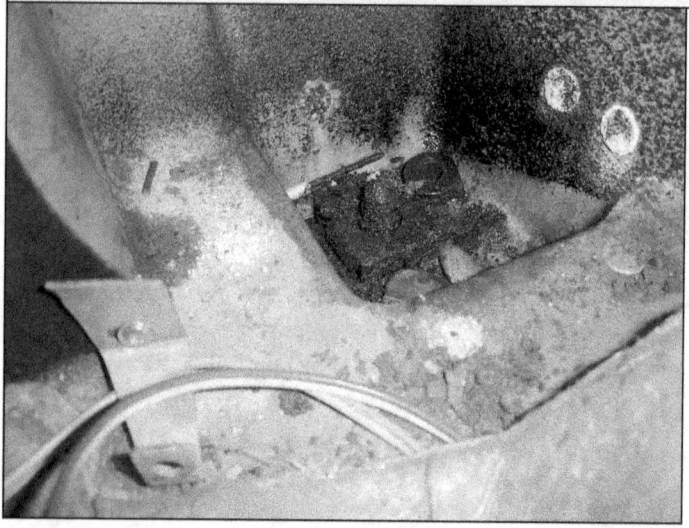

This is a common sight: a very rusty bolt sticking through the number-4 body mount retaining nut. The rear speakers are removed from this 1979 to gain access to this caged nut. Convertible Sharks have these nuts behind the rear deck supports, making them very difficult to access. A thin steel cage riveted to the fiberglass floorpan was used to prevent the nut from spinning, which breaks immediately because of corrosion. I soaked these nuts for days before trying to remove them. A crescent wrench can sometimes be used to hold on to the nut while someone turns the bolt from the bottom. Using an impact wrench helps immensely to hammer at the nut during removal as opposed to trying with all of your strength to pull on a ratchet and socket setup. Using to use the impact on a low setting, letting it slug on the bolt and knocking the rust loose.

This is often the alternative to removing a rusty bolt that does not cooperate; a reciprocating saw does a decent job of cutting the bolt. The problem is that the bolt begins to spin from all the force the saw places on it and then the bolt must be held from inside while the saw cuts the bolt. The bolts are also pretty tough, so the cut takes a while.

AFTERMARKET CHASSIS INSTALLATION

2 Remove Number-1 Body Bolt

This is by far the easiest body bolt and nut to remove: the nut and bolt are both accessible after the lower splash shields are removed. If you're lucky the bolt may break; if not, plenty of rust penetrant helps. I have found that loosening the bolt some and reapplying penetrant helps, then reverse the impact and tighten the bolt and apply more penetrant. The back-and-forth action along with the penetrant helps the removal process immensely.

3 Remove Number-2 Body Bolt

The use of an impact wrench can save many hours of aggravation removing the number-1 and -2 body mount bolts. The hammering effect of the impact wrench helps break the rust and corrosion from the threads, saving valuable time and possibly more work. Number-2 body mount bolts are behind both kick-panels. This 1979 Shark had clean, almost rust-free number-2 body mounts. Many of these body mount bolts are rotted away.

This special tool was made from a piece of bar stock. I found that by forcing it into the space between the body mount nut and frame pocket, it usually stops the nut from spinning. The tool is hammered tightly into the space. I have used this tool countless times with excellent results. Size does matter; take a little off at a time, making it end up with a square section about 2 inches long at the end to be inserted.

Lifting the Body

Our project required more work because it used the C5 Corvette differential assembly. The entire back section of the floor had to be removed to fit the body. Once the body was mounted to the chassis, a modified rear floor section was constructed to make the plan work.

This project used a late-model drivetrain, and that produced excellent fuel mileage. In addition, there were many other benefits to the project. Even a factory original engine exceeds 300 hp, and then there are the bigger brakes. These components on a purpose-built chassis are important on a road course or at autocross events.

CHAPTER 9

Lifting the Body

1 Use Cherry Picker or Two-Post Lift

I used a tow strap to lift this 1981 Shark body off the original chassis. The door bars were made from fence posts, then bolted into the door hinges and striker; they made excellent lift points for the strap. I used another strap from the front to the cherry picker to stabilize the body during the lift. The front strap is also holding on to the radiator core support, which is the only place with enough strength to avoid body damage.

If at all possible, use a two-post lift. You can slowly raise the body without it swaying, or hoping that you have the body weight balanced. Keep a watchful eye as the body passes by the number-4 body mount behind the rear tire. The body comes very close at this area on all Sharks; using the cherry picker can cause some body damage if you are not extra careful during the lift.

2 Prep for Body Drop

The Camaro Tremec T-56 6-speed transmission requires a new opening in the floor for the new shifter placement. I cut the smallest opening possible for the initial body drop, hoping to avoid adding material once the body is fitted. Depending on your drivetrain and particular year Shark, this opening requires modification to make the shifter work.

3 Remove Floor Section

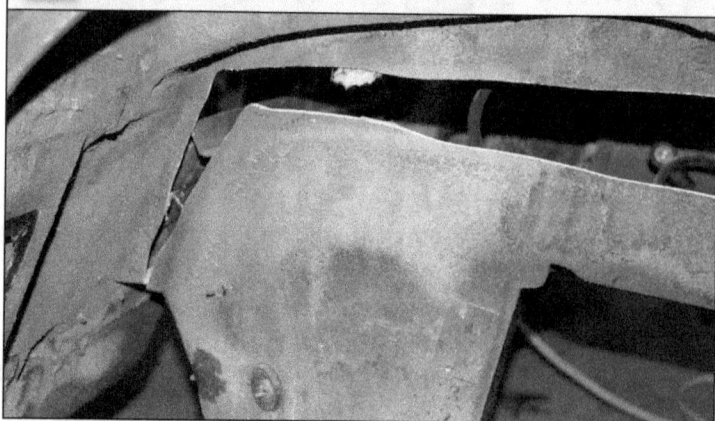

Our ambitious project was to use C5 1997–2004 Corvette suspension/driveline components on the Street Shop chassis. Because of this, we had to remove a major section of the rear compartment floor to fit the chassis. I do not recommend this for the novice or first-time builder; serious fabricating skills are required to build any floor section from scratch. The preliminary cut was done with a small, handheld air-powered reciprocating saw, leaving enough material to do a final cut.

AFTERMARKET CHASSIS INSTALLATION

4 Build New Floor Section

As you can see, the entire rear floor section is removed for the trial fitting of the body on the chassis. I do not spend a lot of time cleaning or prepping anything until the pieces are close to their final form. My policy when doing any project like this is to make everything work, then take it apart and make it pretty if you are inclined to do so. You can expect to have the body on and off numerous times until all of the areas are worked out. That is why I say this is for experienced builders. Street Shop does have a C4 suspension and driveline package for their chassis that does not require this much surgery. You should consider this for your first major build if a purpose-built chassis is for you.

5 Build Floorpan

I use 22-gauge aluminum panels to make a "buck" fiberglass mold for the modified floorpan. Three separate pieces are formed using hand tools for the preliminary buck. Each panel is fitted carefully with one thought in mind: always remember that the thickness of the fiberglass has to be added to computations. This is where careful fitting is important for the least aggravation.

6 Make Fiberglass Panel

The inner surface of the aluminum buck is covered with PVA, a release agent for the fiberglass panel to come off the buck. You may want to put your fiberglass on the outside of your buck; it all depends on which side you want to be smooth. The smooth side is always against the PVA. PVA can be found at most paint and body suppliers or marinas. The side pieces are glassed first, then the center is added for a final fiberglass mat application to make it one piece. Although you may not do a major C5 suspension/driveline purpose-built chassis, most performance vehicles get some fiberglass modifications. The same techniques can be used for any fiberglass addition.

7 Install Engine

The 1968 Shark Paul Newman chassis required a unique fix to our large-cubic-inch big-block engine installation. The injected big-block required a special hood to fit over all the components; the raised hood was not going to work. The solution was to raise the body 1¼ inches with the aluminum spacers shown. The engine was set as low as we dared allow it for the already lowered chassis. The lower you can get the center of gravity, the better. The conundrum was that the 18- and 19-inch wheels required the suspension to be raised anyway; this fix solved both issues. The wheel/tire combination fit in the wheel wells and the hood was not an issue. No one was aware of the solution. This is what it takes sometimes to make all of the things you want to come together.

CHAPTER 9

Suspension and Drivetrain Installation

1 Install Suspension Components

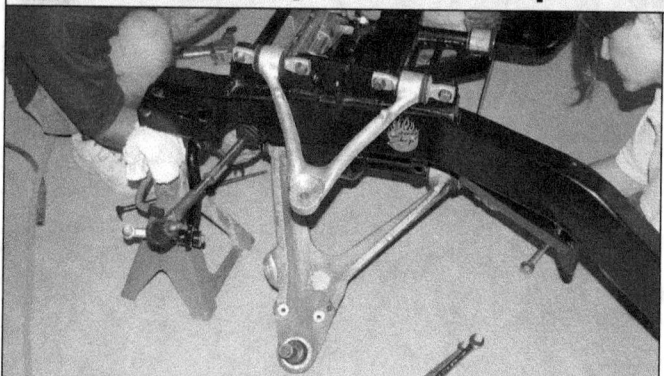

C5 Corvette suspension components are installed on this Street Shop chassis. The assembly is simple due to the use of factory components. The mandrel-bent frame rails make it a very strong chassis with minimal flex. Coil-over shocks are used on all four corners for the best handling and adjustability. Corvette 2004 OEM upper and lower control arms are being installed onto the frame from our donor car. The plan is to assemble the entire project, making sure the driveline and suspension perform to expectation. After that, the entire project will be disassembled. Then, the pieces will be cleaned properly and refinished.

2 Install Brakes

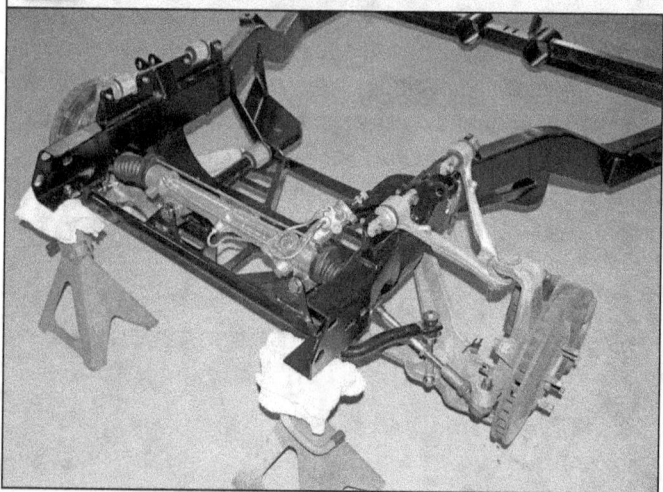

All of the 2004 C5 front suspension components have been transferred to the new chassis except the power steering rack. After the upper and lower control arms were installed, the complete spindle assembly (with brakes) was installed on the upper and lower ball joints. Street Shop provides a modified rack-and-pinion steering to accommodate the Shark's track, which is narrower than the C5. This steering rack, complete with outer tie-rod ends and urethane mounting bushings, bolts in place with the hardware provided.

Street Shop includes a power or non-power steering rack in the chassis package. They also provide a modified front anti-roll bar and links for simple installation. This well-thought-out chassis has the frame rails in the same place as the factory rails, so the original bumper supports work without a hitch.

3 Install Control Arms

This is where the C5 shines: it has upper control arms to positively position the rear spindle assemblies. The lower control arms are part of the rear crossmember and cradle assembly. Street Shop modifies the factory cradle to fit the C5 suspension components into the original Shark's narrower tire track width. For the first time, constant-velocity axleshafts were used on a Corvette C5 chassis to handle the suspension geometry changes as the wheel travels throughout its up-and-down range. The upper control arms are being installed onto the frame after the supplied U-brackets were installed on the control arms. At this point there is no need to tighten everything fully. Snug is fine; wait until all the pieces are together for the final torquing.

You can use a factory C5 service manual for the torque specifications, including the U-brackets for the upper control arms; General Motors provides torque specs for the appropriate bolt diameters. Having a bolt and nut thread gauge handy during chassis assembly is always a good idea with metric fasteners. It gives you millimeter thread and bolt diameters quickly.

4 Install Rear Suspension

Once the rear suspension is assembled, you can see that even at the highest point of suspension travel the rear wheel camber is close to zero. This is why the C5 Corvette handles better than its predecessors, maintaining the wheel alignment throughout the suspension travel. All factory torque specifications are used for the suspension assembly. I had a dilemma since I chose the C5 suspension and driveline system with rear-mounted transmission that uses a torque tube to connect the engine to the transmission. The C5 differential has no yoke to connect the torque tube to the differential. 21st Century Street Machines provided a rare conversion kit (no longer in production) that uses a Ford 9-inch conversion plate to front bearing assembly.

Street Shop has a couple of other options to make the C5 rear suspension work with a Dana differential. One is a Viper style and the other is their proprietary assembly design. Regardless of the differential you choose, Street Shop has the mounting brackets and supports ready to go for a simple bolt-in.

5 Install Engine

The crate LS6 bolts directly into the chassis with an LS Camaro T-56 6-speed transmission for propulsion. All of the driveline angles have been determined by Street Shop and set appropriately, making this a simple drop-in of components. Unlike the LS transplant in Chapter 2, this chassis allows the use of a complete C5 Corvette engine without an oil pan change. The C5 engine mounts can be left on the engine and simply bolted into the chassis. Modifications are the same as with the LS engine transplant, including the cooling system, heater hose, and accessory installation. For that matter, due to the Shark body and chassis constraints, there is no difference to the engine install whether it is in this purpose-built frame or the factory frame. The major differences are the suspension and rear driveline component configuration.

6 Install SRIII Chassis LS Ancillary Components

SRIII Motorsports made enough room in the chassis for the C5 Corvette accessory drive system, placing the A/C compressor low and out of sight on the passenger's side. While this is a clean setup, placing the A/C compressor down low can be troublesome to service in the future because of tight fitment of the compressor and limited access. However, a complete take-out used C5 Corvette engine assembly can be used with all factory pieces. This is something to consider if you are a long-hauler; parts availability is much simpler if you are looking for factory parts over custom pieces. The heater hose connections are also tight because of the inner fender once the body is in place. Street Shop chassis require the use of aftermarket accessory drive supports to fit their frame. Although such small things may seem insignificant, the cost adds up. Fabrication skills are high on the list for hoses, supports, and all sorts of required ancillary components.

7 Install Wiring Harness

A set of 2001 Camaro LS exhaust manifolds were used for the engine installation because they fit close to the engine, clearing the frame rails. This GM LS crate-engine harness was routed onto the engine before the body installation to check fitment while it was easy to access the engine. You need to integrate the engine harness with the Shark's original harness. This comes down to preference: you are embarking on a custom path that requires you to work with all of the Shark's existing and add-on wiring systems. Very few of these projects are similar in the builder's choice of accessories or aftermarket components, including the engine's control system. The best possible solution for the novice is to use an engineered wiring system from a company such as Painless Performance, which has intimate knowledge of the LS engine requirements and the Shark body you are using.

8 Install Coil-Over

SRIII Motorsports incorporates coil-over shocks in all of their chassis builds (see Chapter 10). Depending on the chassis you choose, coil-over shock installation is quite easy: place a bolt, washer, and nut in the mounting points. Make sure you torque the bolts to the chassis supplier's specs, or use the thread fastener gauge to determine the bolt size for the proper torque spec.

SRIII supplies the rear toe link that bolts to a modified differential cover. You have to modify your cover per their instructions and then clean up the cut-off areas with a coarse grinding disc. C4 Corvette factory-style camber rods are used at the bottom of the differential; this aftermarket performance set with urethane bushings is from Vette Brakes and Products for simple rear camber adjustment with minimal deflection.

They can recommend the correct spring rates for the best overall handling. Keep in mind that they have built plenty of these assemblies and have driven them to prove what works. This C4 suspended chassis uses all the original components, which is important if you plan on really driving your project. Nothing is worse than having a part failure and hearing that you can't get them for two weeks or more on a road trip.

9 Inspect Assembled Chassis

The Street Shop chassis is a "roller," ready for body installation. I tried a set of C5 Corvette headers hoping that they might fit; unfortunately, they come too close to the transmission. Street Shop has pre-bent fuel and brake lines to make a very tough part of the project much easier. I prefer to make my own because I have all the required tools; this can be pricey for one-time use. The chassis can be put in the corner until your Shark is ready for the transformation.

CHAPTER 10

Chassis Modifications

Having high horsepower available at the touch of the throttle pedal is a major rush. But you need to be able to use it exiting a corner. As such, you need to upgrade the chassis components to make the most of the drivetrain performance.

General Motors used a perimeter frame with very similar suspension components for the 1963 to 1982 Corvettes. Although the 1968 Shark body was a fresh new design, the chassis was a modified 1967.

From the beginning, some minor suspension component changes were made during the 1963–1964 years. From 1968 until 1979, all of the components remained the same. The 1980 Shark Corvettes had rear suspension changes and an all-new-design aluminum differential housing by Dana. For the 1980–1982 model years, fiberglass mono springs replaced the heavier steel multi-leaf springs.

The 1968 was the last year for small-diameter spindle bearings; by 1969 a beefier large-diameter bearing was introduced and remained until 1982. If you plan to build a 1968 Shark, spindle replacement is a good idea and easily done. All the parts are interchangeable and (for the most part) available. Take a good look at your spindles: they wear quite a bit on the bottom side and can cause a wheel balance problem that is very difficult to detect. What do you do to the control arms, shocks, springs, and reinforcing the chassis to get better performance?

General Motors offered power steering assist for the Sharks, not a true power steering that was found on the rest of their lineup. The idea was to provide some help turning the steering wheel but to maintain road feel. The drag link–mounted assist cylinder received its information from the control valve to boost pressure during turning. This reduced the effort to turn the steering wheel, especially on a big-block engine. This is important information to remember as you strive for the best possible handling and steering feel.

The Shark's front suspension uses unequal-length upper and lower control arms, and these are durable components. They too have a limiting factor concerning alignment specifications for the ultimate-handling Shark.

The Shark's rear suspension is quite an amazing system that provides effective

The final few pieces are being installed on this factory-style frame before the body is installed. The Shark's original chassis was so severely corroded that it was replaced with an Impact Restorations complete frame assembly. A complete Van Steel coil-over kit with their tubular control arms was installed up front. Stainless Steel Brakes Corp (SSBC) calipers and rotors were used at all four corners.

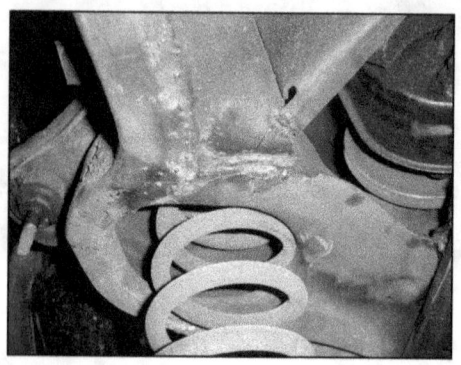

Look closely in the spring pocket area that has been cleaned off for cracking. Make sure that this suspension is sound before you order any suspension parts or start any front-suspension assembly. The cracks emanate from the multiple welds over time and must be ground out and welded at short bursts. If you re-weld these areas, be sure to manage heat application and not warp the arm. Do not weld for long periods of time without quenching the work area with air or water. The area around the steering box is also prone to cracking from the flexing it endures over long periods of time. If you find multiple cracks throughout the frame have someone well versed in material structure check it out before just welding the cracks. The material can become brittle and continue to crack, especially if put under race conditions.

The C3 is at least 30 years old, so over the course of time the frames often rust. On this 1968 C3, you can see corrosion at the lift arm at the rear corner, and it's a serious structural problem for the car. The entire rear kick-up may be substantially weakened and it could potentially fail, particularly after a couple of hard launches. While this is severe corrosion, it does happen to quite a few Sharks. Inspect this area thoroughly before proceeding. Usually, when the rear is this bad, the entire frame is close to being sent to the scrap metal heap.

control and traction, yet it is simplistic in design. There are no upper control arms to maintain the rear suspension's geometry. Each axleshaft pivots off the differential as the centering point. The design worked so well that General Motors used it on the Corvettes until 1997.

Now there are limitations here, also. As the strut rods maintaining camber go through the suspension's travel, they change length and camber. If you were to go over a pothole deeply enough the suspension can cause axleshaft bind, as the universal joints come to the end of their travel. One obstacle is the use of a trailing arm to support the rear suspension, limiting wheel width.

Damage Inspection

A thorough chassis inspection is required before you order any parts. Sharks are known for cracking around the steering box mounting area on the frame. If you have a buddy turn the steering wheel from lock to lock, you see why the cracking occurs. The steering box moves around noticeably, twisting the frame rail as pressure is applied to it. Sometimes the cracks are small and difficult to detect; other times very noticeable spiderweb cracking is apparent.

Another common rust or corrosion area is at the rear frame kick-ups. Dirt accumulates, then water keeps the area ripe for corrosion. Add any road salts and there you go: major corrosion concerns. You certainly do not want to be supplying additional power to an already weakened frame. Today many parts are available to repair this common area of corrosion, so take some time to carefully check out the integrity before buying pieces.

The rear frame kick-ups are the weakest point of the chassis. The welded upright sections of the frame are known to flex in the same area; the installation of a minimum four-point rollbar helps stiffen this section of the frame.

Front Suspension and Steering

For many years Sharks have had performance enthusiasts enhancing the chassis components; so many bolt-on pieces are readily available. For example, you can now have more than 7 degrees of positive caster while steering easily through any parking lot. You need the total package, though, to be able to use the increased positive caster. As positive caster increases, so does the steering effort required for low-speed maneuvering. Non-power-steering Sharks with more than 3 degrees of positive caster are very difficult to maneuver in tight parking lots.

With that being said, aftermarket rack-and-pinion steering kits and upgrade integral power steering boxes are available for simple bolt-on installation. I am not an advocate of aftermarket rack-and-pinion steering systems because they change the steering linkage–to–steering arm location. Possible bump steer can occur, plus the use of Heim joint rod ends without any safety device if the rod end fails does not make me feel comfortable installing them. The rod ends are also not protected from dirt and debris that will eventually wear them if you really drive your car. The Shark chassis was not set up for rack-and-pinion and it shows when the kit is installed. Performance is

CHASSIS MODIFICATIONS

poor and requires plenty of work to try to make everything align properly.

These rack-and-pinion systems are installed below the front chassis crossmember, limiting road clearance. The steering coupling must be removed, and it is replaced with an input shaft that has two universal joints and a support bearing. Getting the shaft and bearing to rotate without binding is difficult, especially considering that the frame does flex in that area over road surfaces. What may seem good when static is not on the roadway during the input shaft's adjustment setup.

When I installed a rack-and-pinion system in a customer's Corvette, a peculiar issue plagued the alignment shop. During the road test, the steering wheel eventually moved off-center after making a few turns. The shop re-centered the steering wheel, and it maintained its correction orientation until the steering wheel was turned enough for a 90-degree turn. After a few attempts they found that depending on whether they made a right turn or left turn last, it affected

Front Suspension Adjustment

You need to be familiar with caster, camber, and toe as you adjust the front suspension for optimal handling. Caster has a huge effect on handling, especially as speed increases. It also affects how well a vehicle returns to the straight-ahead position after exiting a turn. Camber also affects handling at speed and can be adjusted to help control during cornering. Unlike caster, which can be set at the high end of the specification, camber adjustments must be limited to avoid extreme tire wear for a street/track Shark. Toe-in or -out adjustments are critical for handling, more so to avoid extreme tire wear.

Caster

This is an adjustment that positions the weight of the vehicle on the front spindle. If you were to draw a line from the lower ball joint stud upward to the upper ball joint stud you would find that the upper ball joint is back toward the rear of the chassis. This places more vehicle weight rearward on the spindle, referred to as positive caster, and requires more effort to turn the steering wheel in parking-lot maneuvers. All Sharks originally had minimal positive caster, 2 to 3 degrees maximum to allow the steering wheel to be turned with less effort. Caster alignment specifications play heavily into the power steering systems role, as mentioned earlier, limiting positive caster unless you upgrade the power steering system. You can still use the old-school power steering assist pieces. Steering effort is considerably higher and the old steering box requires more turns lock to lock.

Caster can be set at a higher number on one side for vehicles racing on oval tracks; this is called cross-caster. These purpose-built race cars actually require you to work harder at maintaining the straight-ahead motion than cornering.

Camber

Camber is about the wheel assembly leaning in or out. If the top of the tire is in more at the top it is considered to have negative camber. As negative camber increases so does handling during cornering. The factory setting usually limits the negative camber to 1/8–1/4 degree for the best overall handling and tire wear. Corvettes set up for road-course events may go as high as 1½ degrees negative or more if the track has few long, high-speed straightaways. Using the big negative camber numbers with 7 to 9 degrees positive caster allows faster corner entry and exit.

Toe

Toe adjustment concerns how the tires are pointed going down the road: either slightly inward at the front or rear. Toe is rarely set at zero because of the inherent stretch of steering and suspension components. Setting the toe at 1/4 toe-in, for example, allows the suspension and steering components to move around and maintain close to zero toe for the least rolling resistance. The other factor is suspension component movement during road variations. The unequal-length control arms are used to maintain suspension geometry within reason. In other words, it is impossible to have the same alignment specifications at ride height, when the front end is lifted hard under acceleration, or on the lower bump stops during braking. That's why it does not work to lower your Shark to the ground without considering where the control arms are at, especially at ride height.

Bump Steer

Another couple of concerns to discuss: bump steer and rear strut rod positioning. As the chassis gets lower, steering component angles change. If you look at a factory set-up steering linkage, the tie-rods are not perfectly straight from side to side. While this may seem beneficial if done that way, the straight-across linkage cannot use the tie-rods' inherent flex to absorb road variations.

The slightest road bump can cause the steering linkage to move unexpectedly, transmitting up to the steering wheel. At the rear of the Shark, camber struts are used to keep the rear wheel assembly aligned. The inner mounting point of the strut rod is placed higher on the inside than it should have been for maximum road feel at speed.

CHAPTER 10

You have some options when it's time to upgrade steering linkages. Some folks opt for the Heim joint ends in place of the traditional tie-rod ends (shown). Speedway Motors has adjustable tie-rod adapter studs that allow the use of a Heim joint rod end as the tie-rod end. These are not recommended for street use because of contamination from road grit and grime. Seals-It has a Heim joint seal to keep the joints clean and it is highly recommended if you go that route. The majority of street Sharks use DOM tubing (at the bottom here) for steering linkages with traditional tie-rod ends. Lock nuts are used to keep the tie-rod ends tight on the DOM tubing sleeves for the obvious reason of maintaining the alignment specification. Another good reason is to prevent wear, as the loose nut allows the tie-rod's threaded stud to wear in the DOM tubing threads until part failure occurs. The DOM tubing sleeves should have the lock nuts checked for tightness at every oil change or race event.

the steering centering. I watched the rack-and-pinion assembly while turning the steering wheel. I found that the rack moved on the mounts that were provided in the kit, and I couldn't easily correct the condition by improving the mounting of the rack. There were no through bolt–type mounting points for the aftermarket rack.

By customer request, I removed the rack-and-pinion system. I found a much better alternative that is a bolt-on replacement for the stock steering box: a quick-steering-ratio Borgeson power steering gear. It has a much quicker 12.7:1 ratio that replaces the original 16.0:1 ratio gearbox. This integral power steering gearbox kit bolts in to replace the original manual steering box and maintains the original steering geometry. You eliminate the original power steering control valve, hydraulic cylinder, and two additional hoses, which are all potential leak points. Long-time Shark owners know that they will replace multiple cylinders and control valves because of leaks and poor performance.

To retain the original pieces, you need to spend about $300 for remanufactured parts, hydraulic cylinder, control valve, and hoses. If you do retain these pieces, you will experience slow, loose steering feel and be concerned about when the

I think the Borgeson integral power steering box is the best steering upgrade for your high-performance Shark. While many prefer a rack-and-pinion steering system, kits use multiple pieces to make the rack-and-pinion fit where it really does not belong. The steering box bolts in the factory location keeping the original GM geometry. Modifications are required to the steering column for the connection. The steering rod is in a straight line from the box to the column, eliminating any binding of the steering shaft. The 1969–1982 Sharks have a collapsible steering column for crash protection. When the Borgeson box is installed, the shaft is tapped inward approximately 1½ inches for the connection. This does not compromise the steering columns safety factor in any way. The 1968 Shark requires cutting the steering shaft 1½ inches for it to work. New steering column shafts are available for the 1968 Shark, which is good to replace because of spline wear.

CHASSIS MODIFICATIONS

Borgeson provides a new steering coupling that fits their replacement steering box and a Shark's steering column. Once the Borgeson steering box is installed the steering shaft must be collapsed approximately 2½ inches for the box to connect to an original style 1968–1982 steering coupling. I used a large hammer to lightly tap the shaft back the required distance to make the connection. By 1969 federal requirements mandated a collapsible steering column to prevent severe bodily injury in frontal crashes. It does not take a lot of force to get the shaft moving and the 2 to 3 inches that the shaft is shortened does not affect performance negatively or create any safety concerns. It makes sense to start at 2 inches and then try the column fit; the steering column has two slots for the mounting bolts for centering.

You can install Borgeson power steering conversion box a few different ways. This application uses a non-power-steering drag link. Two heavy-duty springs push against pivot ball seats that capture the pivot ball stud. The outer screw is turned in and it applies pressure to the springs and the cotter pins, so it doesn't back out. If you have power steering already, Borgeson has an adapter that replaces the existing power steering control valve. Although the adapter works fine, I prefer to use the non-power-steering drag link for performance applications because there are fewer mechanical connections. The Vette Brakes and Products tie-rod sleeve is visible in front of the drag link end. The heavy wall tubing resists deflection and is highly recommended for performance driving.

Heim Joints

Some manufacturers use Heim joint ends for tie-rod end replacement as high-performance replacements, but you need to periodically inspect them for wear. The unprotected rod ends are subjected to water and dirt and who knows what can be thrown at them, causing them to fail prematurely.

Be sure to install heavy, large-diameter washers at the top and bottom of the Heim joints to prevent total steering loss if a joint fails. ∎

next leak will occur. The Borgeson gearbox kit retails for $799 with all the necessary pieces for the install, and no more worries about leaks and sluggish steering. It seems well worth the additional $500 investment over the long term.

Old-school tie-rod sleeve tubes have a machined slot that allows the tube end to flex and tighten onto the tie-rod end. Circular clamps are used to squeeze the tube sleeve and capture the tie-rod end. While these function fine for common street driving, they are not suited for performance cornering and should be replaced with high-strength tubing with jam nuts. Drawn-over mandrel (DOM) tubing is preferred for steering and suspension uses. Unlike pipe that is designed to hold fluids, it is produced for structural applications. Vette Brake and Products, for example, has high-strength tie-rod sleeves with lock nuts in kit form.

Many new aftermarket suspension components use jam nuts to secure the alignment settings. While jam nuts typically make assembly/disassembly work easier, they do come loose if not tightened properly. Under the typical suspension movement and vibration that occurs you can expect the loose nuts to cause damage to the steering or suspension components threads, as the loose rod end works in the threaded portion of the tubing. I make it a practice to always go over all the suspension hardware after an alignment and before any play time.

Control Arms

With an integral steering box you can set positive caster at optimal settings without sacrificing a tight turning radius or requiring a lot of steering effort. Today the use of up to 6 degrees of positive caster is possible for stable high-speed driving. At the low end, you should install aftermarket upper control arms, but if you can afford it, I recommend complete upper and lower control arm kits. This will pay off whether you decide on drag racing, autocrossing, or road racing.

All aftermarket control arm manufacturers use urethane bushings at the pivot points. It makes no sense to optimize handling and have rubber causing deflection during hard cornering. Urethane bushings squeak at times; damp or humid days, for example, may get them going. This is a small price to pay for the best possible handling.

The main focus is on upper control arm replacement to gain positive caster and improve negative camber adjustability.

Speed Direct offers an aluminum set of upper control arms, dropping 8 pounds in an advantageous area while providing increased positive caster up to 6 degrees and negative camber. I do like the large-diameter urethane bushings and the stout castings.

Van Steel has a different approach with tubular steel upper and lower control arms; basically the same changes are in place. Caster and camber is enhanced with more rigid control arms to minimize flex. There are a couple of kits too, one with upper control arms, and one with upper and lower control arms for use with stock springs. My only concern is the small-diameter urethane bushings and how well they stand up to road abuse. Van Steel stands behind their product with a limited lifetime warranty.

An ultimate pair of upper control arms is available for the serious road racer or autocross enthusiast. SPC upper control arms allow up to 10 degrees of positive caster with very easy-to-adjust links. The adjustment links can also provide some serious negative camber for those wanting to go around turns at higher speeds. These upper control arms are tough too, and have Clevite bushings for a smooth yet controlled ride.

The majority of upper control arms require ball joints except Van Steel's offering. They have a set that comes with them already in place, ready to be bolted in. Speed Direct offers performance ball joints for an additional camber gain. All of the products mentioned work well and do what they are intended to do; you should have a good idea of their attributes.

Bushings

Increased caster/camber control arms are an important handling upgrade for your C3. If you cannot afford new control arms, you should install urethane bushings in the front and rear suspension. Urethane bushings are not just denser than rubber; they act like a bearing instead of the rubber bushings' shearing action as it travels through suspension travel. The free-moving urethane bushing promotes quicker suspension reaction, but the service life can be shorter and therefore they require replacement as the bushing material wears on the shaft steel sleeve.

Many people think they last forever and they forget that they should periodically check the bushings for looseness at the pivot points. On a positive note, once the bushings are switched to urethane, replacing the bushings themselves can be easily accomplished.

Energy Suspension has front and rear urethane bushing kits available for Shark Corvettes. I prefer to use all of their products, with the exception of the rear trailing arm bushings (that will be explained soon). A front bushing kit (PN 3.3108) from Energy Suspension costs around $65.

Control Arm Bushing Installation

1 Install Urethane Control Arm Bushings

Upper line denotes control arm shaft true centerline.
Lower line denotes control arm shaft offset.

Centerline denotes control arm true center

This line is the ball joint positive caster offset.

This is one of the first aftermarket upper control arms, available from Vette Brake and Products. These beefy upper control arms are a very good street upgrade and use stock type urethane bushings to pivot on. You can increase positive caster up to 5 degrees with these ready-to-go upper control arms. Here, the offset upper control arm shaft is in the position that decreases negative camber; rotating the shaft 180 degrees increases negative camber and enhances cornering stability. The upper control arm shaft positioning is determined during alignment and is rotated for the maximum negative camber unless the frame has accident damage. The accident damage to the frame should be rectified first but in a pinch the shaft can be rotated to gain the correct alignment. Something else to remember is that any deviation from the factory-set ride height affects camber.

1. Install Urethane Control Arm Bushings CONTINUED

Follow this procedure to install control arm bushings: The outer bushing shell houses the urethane bushing, which is a slightly snug fit in the shell. The steel sleeve is also a snug fit, and is pushed out of the urethane bushing. Then you can easily remove the bushing from the shell. The shell is inserted into the control arm and the hydraulic press pushes the shell until the outer ring is tight against the control arm. Note the piece of tubing that runs alongside the vertical control arm shaft to prevent control arm distortion while the bushing sleeve is pushed into position. You can use a piece of 2-inch-diameter tubing cutting in half lengthways to make the control arm support fixture. Some choose to set the control arm in vise jaws that are open enough for the bushing shell to fit. Use a large hammer to beat in the bushing shells. Be careful that the bushing shell goes in straight to avoid a tight bushing from a collapsed shell.

2. Install Urethane into Bushing

First apply a liberal coating of silicone grease to the bushings inner circumference where the sleeve slides into it. Avoid applying any grease to the bushings outer circumference to prevent it from rotating in the shell. You should be able to push the bushing into the shell with your hand, there should be light resistance required to seat it against the shells outer lip. Do not use a hammer to install the bushing; if you need a hammer, there is a problem with the shell. If the shell is distorted badly enough the bushing does not seat and keeps pushing out; this requires the installation of a new shell. Jamming the bushing into a distorted shell causes excessive squeaking and premature bushing wear. Worse yet your suspension will have a tight spot affecting handling.

3. Torque Control Arm Retaining Washers

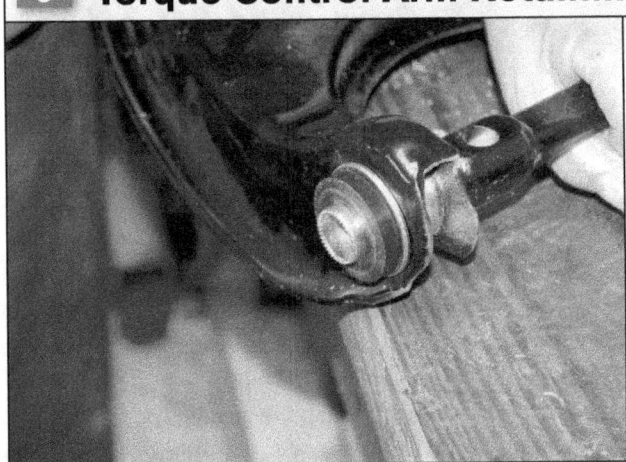

Now the sleeve has been inserted and an ample coating of silicone grease has been applied to keep the bushing quiet and rotating freely. If the shell and control arm are not distorted, the sleeve should press in with some resistance, but it should not require a hammer. If it does not press in, then the shell and control arm may be distorted. Use a small block of wood to push against the sleeve during installation. Once the sleeve has been inserted, apply silicone grease to the outer surface of the bushing where the retaining washer rides on the bushing.

CHAPTER 10

4 Torque Control Arm Retaining Bolts

Unlike rubber bushings the control arm bushing retainer bolts and washers can be torqued at any time. The urethane bushings stiffen the suspension mounting points and they rotate with minimal drag so the springs and shocks work at their very best. Apply red Loc-tite to the retainer bolts and check them for torque after any competition to make sure these bolts do not come loose. One loose bolt that backs its way out can allow the control arm to come off the control arm shaft and a catastrophic accident could occur.

5 Install Upper Control Arm Bushing

This set of Van Steel upper control arms allow up to 6 degrees of positive caster and increased negative camber. The original control arms were maxed out at 2 or 3 degrees of positive caster; for that time they were fine. The more positive caster the better. Highway stability pays off while it takes more effort to steer due to increased caster. These Van Steel upper control arms use a special urethane bushing, which is an all-new approach to the aftermarket upper control arm. Factory-style upper ball joints are used with grade-eight bolts for the installation.

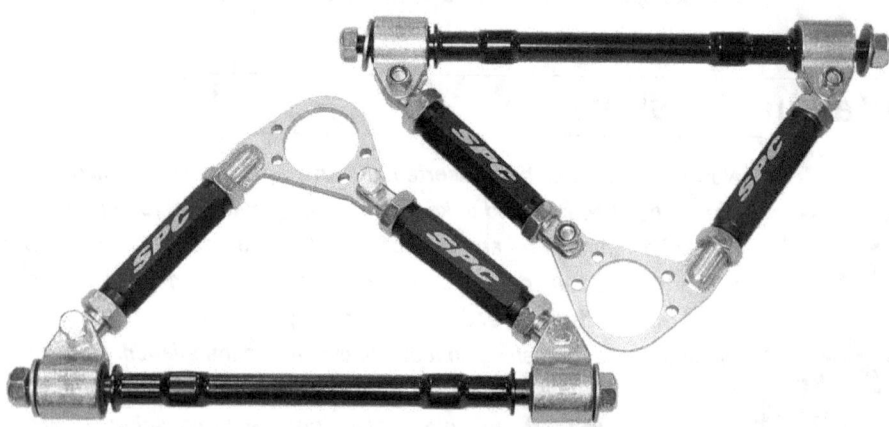

SPC has fully adjustable upper control arms that can be easily adjusted for maximum positive caster up to 10.5 degrees. The control arm pivot shafts are fixed: no fiddling with shims that can come loose in a race environment. The hex adjusting sleeves and lock nuts make the changes quick and simple. Lock nuts are used on the sleeve ends and should be checked regularly for proper 45 ft-lbs of torque.

This street control arm (PN 94630) has OEM-style Clevite rubber bushings to minimize suspension shock loading. That means when the arms are installed, do not tighten the pivot shaft nuts until the Shark is sitting on the ground at ride height. Once the suspension has settled, the pivot shaft nuts are torqued to 72 ft-lbs.

The race control arm (PN 92740) has greaseable custom pivots for the upper control arm shaft with minimal deflection. The greaseable pivot points are smooth and do not cause any friction during road variations but is tough on an daily driver Shark.

CHASSIS MODIFICATIONS

6 Install Upper Control Arms

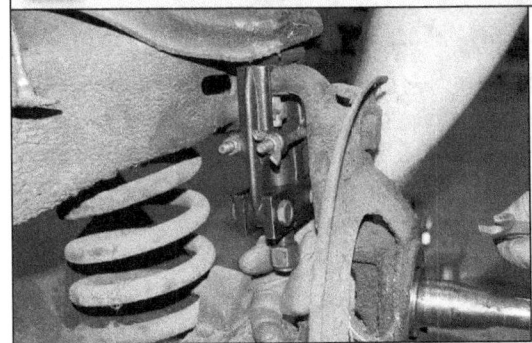

There are almost always a multitude of ways to accomplish tasks; this ball joint separation is no different. I prefer to do this tough job the easy way with a puller. This double-duty puller was designed for pitman arm removal and it works fine for ball joint stud release. Suspension components use tapered bores to securely attach themselves to prevent loose couplings. The puller-forcing screw provides enough pressure to pop the stud loose from the bore. Here's some advice from my trial-and-error younger days: Don't use a big hammer.

Radiator Fan Shroud

Removing the upper control arms is difficult, because you must remove other parts before you can access the upper control arms. In fact, you must remove the radiator fan shroud because it covers the front upper control arm shafts. To remove the fan shroud, you must remove the radiator first. Frequently, mechanics lose patience and do not remove the radiator or the fan shroud, so the shroud is cut up or broken up to get the control arms out. At $200 or more for a replacement fan shroud it makes sense to remove it properly even if you plan on installing electric fans without the shroud. Someone at a swap meet is looking for a genuine fan shroud and will usually pay good money for one.

Radiator and fan shroud removal is covered in Chapter 6. With this information, you should plan your modifications before any disassembly takes place. In the shop I recommend radiator servicing and front suspension work at the same time to save the customer a few bucks. Installing an electric cooling fan is also good for future servicing of the upper control arms.

Front Springs

To accomplish lower control arm bushing replacement, you must remove the front springs. This is often required because the power steering pump leaks fluid on the driver-side rear bushing. The steady drip of power steering fluid eats away at the rubber, which is another good reason to use urethane bushings: the fluid does not attack the urethane. Once the front spring is unloaded and removed, the lower control arms come out for bushing installation.

Front Suspension Disassembly

1 Remove Front Spring

This is where you can hurt yourself or someone nearby if the front spring comes loose. Place the floor jack as close as possible to the outer portion of the lower control for the best leverage. Once the ball stud is loose raise the jack to take tension off the nut. Remove the nut and then lower the jack to release spring pressure.

Original Shark springs are very tall and still have some spring pressure with the lower control arm completely lowered. Ease the spring out of the lower control arm spring pocket with a long bar. Thankfully the replacement springs are shorter and easy to install into the spring pocket Then raise the lower control arm into position.

2 Adjust Spring Height

When I was assembling my 1979 Project Shark Attack Corvette I wanted the front end to be down about 1½ inches in the front. To do this inexpensively I cut off one full coil using a high-speed grinder and cut-off wheel. This wheel does not make the spring too hot, which would change the tempering and cause the spring to lose tension. It's extra work to remove one coil at a time until you get the ride height you want but it stays there (unlike with a torch).

Lowering the front end more than 2 inches is not recommended because changes occur to the suspension and steering geometry that affect high-speed handling. Plus you'll be scraping the frame. There are no drop spindles available to safely go lower. Control arm modifications to offset the drop and anti-bump steer tie-rod assemblies are required if you want to go that low.

3 Install Front Spring

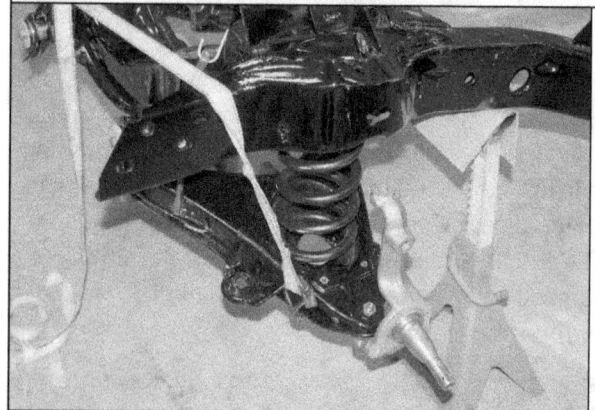

Replacement springs are shorter and easier to install if you are using OEM springs. Cutting off one coil makes it even easier. Although this may look unorthodox it works when it comes time to install the spring into the lower control arm and the upper control arm ball joint to the spindle. The strap is placed on the other side of the frame and rides on the smooth section of frame rail as it is tightened, pulling up the control arm and spring. The strap technique also works for holding it all together until the jack is placed under the control arm. If the engine is installed in the chassis, a jack can be placed under the control arm in the same manner as it was for removal of the spring.

One thing to check before connecting the upper control arm to the ball joint is proper spring placement in the upper spring pocket. The spring has a tendency to push outward and must be pushed in as the lower control arm is raised. You can use a piece of 1 x 2 wood, placing it between the spring and frame, to keep the spring in place until the ball joint connection is made.

All the right pieces are installed on this 1979 Shark's rear suspension and differential. The differential axleshafts with non-greasable universal joints are secured with high-torque-load supporting caps, not straps. A TRW 315-pound rear fiberglass spring softens the ride while keeping the tires planted on the roadway. Vette Brakes and Products' rear Smart Strut is used for the best possible camber control throughout the suspension travel. Finally a set of Bilstein sport shocks handle the wheel control over the roadway. This is the best setup for all-around Shark street performance use without breaking the bank.

CHASSIS MODIFICATIONS

Rear Suspension

The original trailing arms are two halves of stamped steel welded together every couple of inches pivoting on two rubber bushings. The trailing arm, which has tapered bearings, supports the rear wheels. The tapered bearings have an interference fit on the wheel spindle hub requiring special tools to service them.

Simply removing the spindle nut is just the beginning: a special push tool assembly forces the spindle out of the inner wheel bearing. Use of a spindle bearing setup tool is required to check bearing play before assembly so you arrive at the correct specification. Then you avoid multiple disassembly of the components until the correct shim is found.

The rubber trailing arm bushings also require a special tool to stake them in place. Urethane replacements have a simple tool included to do the staking process with the modified product. Because of the cost of required special tools (or unless you plan to do multiple trailing arm rebuilds) it makes sense to have the bearing services performed by a professional.

Vette Brake and Products offers this all-new offset trailing arm ready to go for the widest possible wheel under the rear of a Shark.

Trailing Arms

An aftermarket trailing arm available from Van Steel is made of heavier gauge steel with better welding to produce a stronger arm. The stronger offset arm can withstand a much higher load and resist flexing far better than flex in the original stamped steel arms. The bushing ends are also beefed up for the best possible hold on alignment specifications. These Van Steel trailing arms come with Johnny Joints instead of the traditional trailing arm bushings with greasable fittings. The Johnny Joints reduce friction while maintaining accurate alignment specifications.

Aftermarket offset trailing arms are also available from Vette Brake and Products; they allow for wider wheels with an additional 2 inches offset inside. These offset trailing arms are fabricated from heavier gauge steel than the original GM arm to beef up the offset area, preventing flex. The idea is to allow additional tire clearance inside the fender well: they require rear spring modifications if you go the maximum 2-inch additional offset.

Tire contact patch is paramount to handling: this is something to consider if you have a high-torque and high-horsepower engine under the hood.

Trailing Arm Removal

1 Remove Strut Rod/Shock Mounts

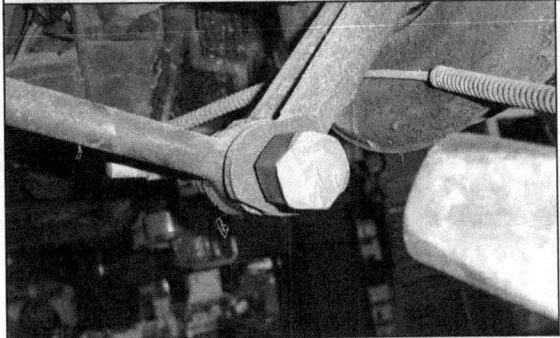

However you decide to handle the rear suspension components, you have to remove the lower shock mounts. Zip Products, a major Corvette parts supplier, has this nifty tool available to break the shock mount loose. In an effort to prevent rotation of the shaft, General Motors serrated the shock mount stud where it goes into the spindle bearing support. This means that even when you are doing a Shark that has been out of the elements, this shock mount can be stubborn to remove. Be sure to tighten the tool securely before giving it a beating. If it does not come loose after a number of good hard blows, check to make sure the tool is still tight.

2 Disassemble Trailing Arms

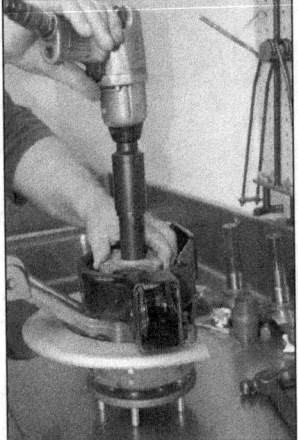

This fixture is required to service the rear spindle bearings; it requires great pressure to force the spindle out of the bearings. If you plan to road race the trick is to have the spindles machined to allow bearing installation with a very slight interference fit. Your local machine shop can remove enough material from the spindle bearing surfaces allowing you to easily remove the bearings. The cost of the tools for servicing the bearings one time just doesn't make sense.

3 Set Up Trailing Arm Bearing Clearance

This is the spindle bearing stack-up with the spacer and shim to the left side of the bearings. The tool allows bearing clearance setup without assembling the spindle and all the seals. This is a must-have if you plan on setting up your own bearings. Bearing end-play clearance should be 0 to .0015 inch maximum for the best overall braking. Loose rear spindle bearings affect brake calipers by pushing the pistons back, especially during hard cornering. No one wants to discover a low brake pedal at the end of a straightway.

4 Service Parking Brake at Trailing Arms

These parking brake assemblies are hidden behind the disc brake rotors. Yes, you can remove the shoes and hardware when the rotor is in place, especially if you were good with the game "Operation." Once assembled, a couple of 1/2-inch holes access the springs and adjuster. You may think that you can just put the entire assembly in the trash; better check with your race tech guys first. I certainly like having the parking/emergency brake on manual transmission cars.

5 Assemble Trailing Arm Spindles

Another reason to machine the spindles: this tool pulls the spindle into the bearings. You can certainly use a large hammer, but it is rough on the bearings from the constant shock loading. You may find yourself at the track with a wheel-bearing concern. Hammering there is not an option with a trailing arm hung off the bushing: more damage could occur. The new high-strength spindle has new studs, which are a must for any performance application.

6 Install Trailing Arm Bushings

These Vette Brake and Products urethane trailing arm bushings replace the soft-rubber factory bushings. Use this C-clamp to push the sleeve into the bushings after they are coated with silicone grease to keep them moving freely. After the C-clamp, use the bolt and flaring nut to capture the shaft and bushings. They can be shimmed to make sure they fit tightly into the sleeve. The bushing's job is to pivot the trailing arm and maintain rear toe alignment, which is huge when high-speed handling is considered; even minor toe changes cause rear steer and a scary feeling at speed.

CHASSIS MODIFICATIONS

Trailing Arm Bushings

You should upgrade the trailing arm bushings to achieve the best rear suspension performance. Urethane bushings are an important control and safety upgrade over the OEM rubber bushings. When a trailing arm with OEM bushings fails, rear control is compromised, sometimes to a dangerous degree. When these bushings fail, the rear tires can toe out so far that you lose control of the vehicle. In fact, the rear toe-out can be so extreme that the car responds as if it has rear-wheel steering. When accelerating, the trailing arms move in a certain direction; when decelerating, the wheels move in the opposite direction. The result is a dangerous loss of control. Urethane bushings are the best possible replacement for these very important control bushings. Always make sure you use trailing arm shims with a cotter pin to hold them in place and ensure that the pivot bolt is tight.

I find that Vette Brakes and Suspension products has the best urethane trailing arm bushings available. Vette Brake and Products rear trailing arm

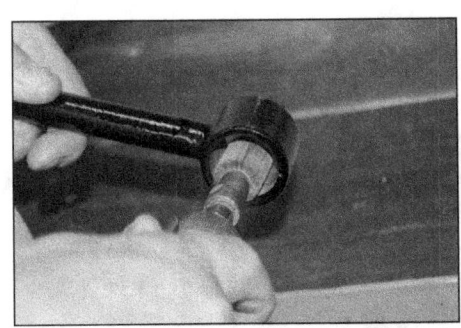

If your budget dictates, the use of original strut rods are greatly enhanced with the installation of urethane bushings. Before you replace the bushings you should make sure that you have the late-design strut rod. Factory strut rods from 1975–1982 have 1 3/8-inch-diameter bushings: they handle load better and last longer than the thinner bushed 1 3/16-inch-diameter 1968–1974 strut rods. Imperfections in the rod end of this original strut rod can make the installation of the urethane bushing difficult. This important step is often left out in the haste of finishing quickly: your new urethane bushings need to have some tension on the inner sleeves to prevent alignment changes, not so much that they restrict free movement of the rod.

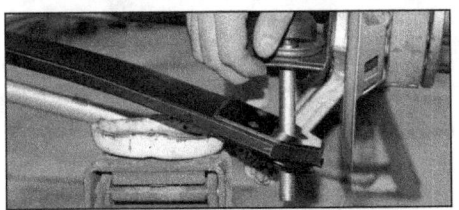

Note that the jack's cup is on the metal portion of the spring end to compress it for spring bolt installation. Do not place the metal cup directly on the fiberglass portion of the spring. These composite fiberglass springs are really tough until they are gouged, then they can shatter without notice. If the plan is to use one in your performance application, inspect the front edge for damage from debris that often gets kicked up. Deep nicks eventually crack.

Like the urethane control arm bushings, these urethane strut rod bushings are lubricated well at the inner sleeve area, and the sleeve is pushed in. It takes more effort to push the sleeves in once the bushings are placed in the rod end. They should push smoothly into the bushing with a slight resistance. The bushing is too tight if you need to use a cheater handle on the vise.

This could be due to a buildup of corrosion or damage from improper bushing removal. Your best option is to take the bushing out and check for any raised areas in the bushing bore. Make sure that the sleeve is slightly longer than the bushings, so the bushings are not scrubbing in the sides of the mounting bracket. We want the suspension components to travel freely with a slight drag, not bound up.

Vette Brakes and Products' Smart Strut assembly is very innovative. General Motors placed the original strut rod mounting points closer to the axleshafts, which allowed the camber to change significantly under hard acceleration. The original GM bracket is turned over compared to this VB&P Smart Strut bracket. Vette Brakes and Products placement of the strut rods limits the camber change under hard acceleration. The heavy-wall strut rod tubes make the camber adjustment easy and limits deflection. Another great feature is you can use the adjustment cams to optimize the position of the strut rods depending on your final ride height. The latest innovation is a set of forged rod ends for ultimate control and durability.

CHAPTER 10

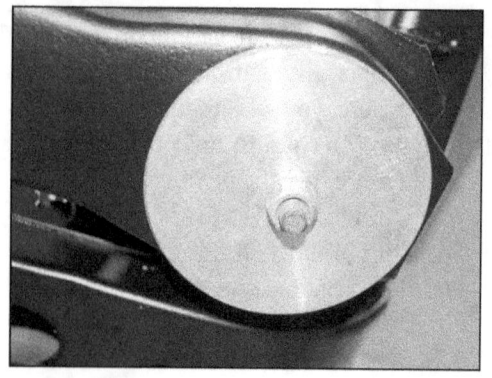

This round aluminum disc is used for differential crossmember reinforcement on 1968–1979 Sharks. The reinforcement prevents the differential from breaking the rubber cushions; if that happens, the disc prevents the crossmember from coming loose. A set of studs are provided to allow the use of a washer and nut to retain the crossmember cushion to the chassis. Then the disc is held with an additional nut and washer. These are a must have for a serious race application; more so with drag and road racing than autocrossing.

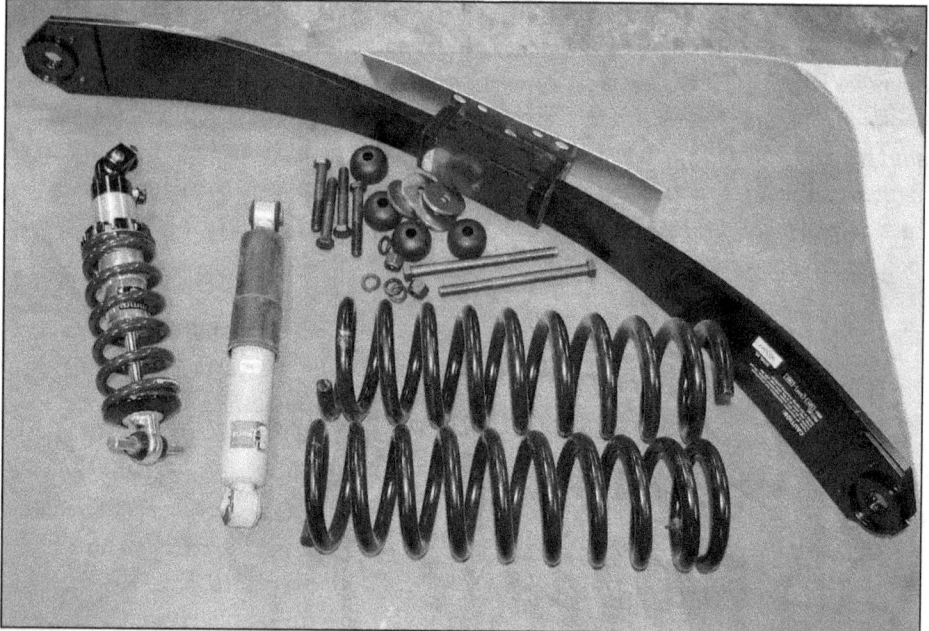

These are the choices for your performance Shark suspension: Moog standard-rate 315-pound front coil springs, Bilstein shocks, and TRW rear fiberglass springs rated at 330 pounds. The TRW spring is easily distinguishable by the increased outer diameter at the spring ends. TRW provides rubber cushions for the spring bolts, which I prefer for a street Shark that makes an occasional visit to the race track. Urethane spring cushions are available for minimal compression but not necessary unless you really are pushing the envelope all the time. The ride suffers for an everyday cruiser and over time the cushions do compress somewhat anyway minimizing compression.

The single coil-over replaces all the other components. For that reason alone it makes sense to use the compact lightweight coil-over assembly. Ride height, shock compression, and rebound rate are easily adjustable at each corner. Changing the springs can be done within minutes; conventional pieces take hours. Of course that comes at a substantial price; the coil-overs are approximately $3,500 for the front and rear set. The conventional pieces are in the $1,000 range.

This 1979 Shark has a large 1¼-inch-diameter Addco anti-roll bar kit. Use plenty of silicone lubricant to keep the bushings quiet and allow the forces to be transmitted side to side without binding. Equally important are the anti-roll bar's mounting brackets and the frame area. The rolled edges stiffen the bracket and keep the anti-roll bar firmly in place. Making sure that the anti-roll bar is securely mounted is vital. Loose bolts or distorted brackets negate the effect on the anti-roll properties if the bar can move around.

CHASSIS MODIFICATIONS

bushing kit (PN 41043) costs $63.99 but is well worth it. This is the only urethane bushing supplier for the trailing arm that assembles the bushing in the same fashion that General Motors did. The company used a sleeve to couple the inner and outer bushing into the trailing arm. The sleeve was then swaged to tighten the bushing and keep it under load at all times. All of the other urethane bushing suppliers use loose bushings that can be a pain during alignment; it's also difficult to make sure they are tight in the sleeves.

Smart Struts

The simple rear suspension has had no groundbreaking components available, with the exception of a set of Smart Struts used to control the rear suspension camber. Smart Struts are a big deal for the best possible rear wheel control over uneven road surfaces. As the original rear suspension traversed rough roads, major camber changes took place.

In an effort to maintain as much ground clearance as possible, General Motors placed the strut rod mounting bracket even with the lowest point of the differential. Lowering the bracket optimized the strut placement and minimized camber changes throughout the full rear suspension travel. Maintaining camber at optimum settings is important for high-speed handling, so the Smart Strut kit is a must-have.

Springs

Many different shock and spring combinations have been tried and tested on the Shark. For a high-performance Corvette, your plan should be to keep the tire on the road surface with as much weight as possible for optimum traction.

There are two ways to think about this: Use a stiff spring to force the tire down onto the roadway, or use a moderate spring rate to avoid chassis flex as the tire is forced onto the road surface. If the spring is so stiff that the chassis takes the deflection, not the spring, you are not accomplishing the goal.

The Shark chassis has flex front to rear and side to side. Put one on a twin post lift and watch the gap between the front of the doors and fenders grow as the vehicle is lifted. The objective here is to determine up front how important it is for you to eliminate chassis flex and use high spring rates, or be conservative and use lighter spring rates with the inherent chassis flex.

No Shark chassis-stiffening kits are available for retrofitting to an existing chassis. Old-school Shark racers welded the sections of the chassis where General Motors did not to tighten it up. I have added chassis-stiffening components on high-horsepower Shark builds in my shop. The truth is, most of us cannot use the chassis that is under the Shark to its limits. You are better off spending the chassis reinforcement money at a driving school to get more out of the build. If you feel that you must reinforce the chassis, it is best done with a 10-point roll cage to tighten it up at all points. It is important to make the decision before ordering any springs or shocks.

A few traditional front coil springs and rear transverse leaf spring choices are available. I recommend out-of-the-box aftermarket big- or small-block front springs for everyday driving. The best part is that almost every major Corvette Supplier such as Zip Products, Ecklers, and Corvette Central have them in stock. Mid America Motorworks also has these springs readily available. The best all-around choice without chassis stiffening is front springs rated at 460 pounds for small-blocks with or without A/C. The higher 550-pound-rate springs are suitable for the big-block applications. At the highest spring rate the tires can end up chattering over the road surface as they bounce over road irregularities.

The rear transverse spring links both rear tires so they react to loads and road conditions together. The spring also functions as an anti-rollbar or sway bar. When one tire goes into a low spot it lessens the spring load on the opposite side, leveling the rear of the vehicle.

General Motors used a rear steel transverse spring until 1980. In 1981, it used a fiberglass mono spring to shed a few pounds. While saving weight is important, this is not the best area to do it.

However, there are a couple of attributes of the fiberglass spring that makes it a viable option for a project car. Reaction time is quicker to road variations and the spring rate never changes until replacement is required. I prefer to use the 330-pound TRW-manufactured spring available from Zip Products unless a race-only Shark owner wants the 360-pound version, which is also available from Zip Products. Super-aggressive 420-pound rear springs are available for race-only versions but these springs are for accomplished drivers.

Shocks

A variety of shocks are offered for the C3, and a majority of them are monotube oil and gas charged. With shocks, as with many other parts, you get what you pay for. Cheap shocks tend to provide poor spring damping and control, shock bodies are of inferior material, pistons are not precisely manufactured, and overall piston and rod diameters are smaller. Not surprisingly, the ride and handling has a marshmallowy feel.

There are also good-quality shocks with large-diameter piston rods and larger bodies for more fluid reservoir capacity. At the other end of the spectrum are

CHAPTER 10

bone-rattling heavy-duty shocks for ultimate control. The trick is matching them to the springs for the best overall control.

You need shocks that dampen the action of the springs and don't fade under your application and driving style. The shocks need to effectively modulate and control the suspension, but they cannot be so stiff that they flex the frame on rough road surfaces. Fiberglass rear springs require different shocks to control the quicker-reacting composite material than the traditional steel rear springs. With suspension, you usually have to decide what you want: a firm ride and aggressive handling or a softer ride with less agile handling. Although you arrive at a compromise setup, this is something that requires research for the particular car and driver.

The combinations are nearly limitless and I cannot cover all the options in this book. However, a general suggestion is to use Monroe Monro-matic plus low-end shocks from a major auto parts retailer for the smoothest possible ride with a steel rear spring. For a hard-driven daily-driver Shark, install a set of KYB Gas-a-Just shocks all around with a 330-pound fiberglass rear spring. A Shark setup for street and occasional autocrossing benefits from a 360-pound fiberglass spring and Bilstein B8-SP shocks all around.

If you are seeking ultimate road feel and can really push your Shark to the limit, you should have double-adjustable coil-over shocks. This is a truly tunable system. Spring rates can be changed and the shocks allow bounce and rebound adjustments for almost any road conditions.

Coil-Over Kits

Years ago, coil-over shock/spring combinations were equipment specific to race cars and not viable options for street cars. Today they are readily available for the Shark Corvette. The first kit available was for the front only, installing the assembly in place of the traditional spring and shock. The lower portion of the spring sat in the lower control arm while the upper portion was captured on the coil-over shock. Today kits are available that use a common coil-over shock/spring assembly with modified mounting hardware for the front.

Van Steel is the pioneer in Shark suspension, and they offer the coil-over kits in semi and full-blown setups. Their semi coil-over uses a modified coil-over shock that captures the front spring at the top, and the lower portion of the spring sits in the original stock coil spring location. This is a great alternative to the factory setup because many spring rates are available for the serious cornering fanatic and the shocks are adjustable. The cost is reasonable for the springs, shocks, and attaching hardware at $649.

Van Steel's complete front coil-over kit comes with springs, shocks, single or double adjustable, all hardware, and upper and lower control arms. This $2,166.99 complete kit is by far the best bang for the buck for the serious cornering enthusiast who wants simple spring and shock changes at the track.

Rear bolt-on coil-over shock/spring kits are also available that place the assembly in the area of the original shock. Van Steel has also perfected the rear coil-over setup for the Shark. The only question is whether you want single- or double-adjustable shocks. Of course the springs are easily changed, and many spring rates are offered. You can visit a QA1 dealer to select the correct shocks for your car and driving style.

An engineered set of rear coil-over shock/spring assemblies similar to those found on F-1 race cars are also an option

These lightweight Van Steele upper and lower control arms shed the pounds in an opportune area for vehicle handling. The lower control arm uses the specialized mounting brackets and provides a mount for the coil-over spring/shock assembly. This setup is perfect for someone who is a regular at the track and wants to fine-tune the Shark for the ultimate hot lap. The coil-over shock assembly is easily removed for spring changes, and the shock adjustment can be done in minutes. This set of coil-over shocks has a single adjustable rebound control knob. QA1's latest shocks have a single knob for rebound and compression adjustment. Original factory-configured lower and upper ball joints are used in the arms.

CHASSIS MODIFICATIONS

A set of Van Steel rear coil-overs is installed on this 1973 Shark. First they must be installed on a set of trailing arms, which are provided in the Van Steel kit. Back off the coil-over shocks spring off to its lowest point and then jack up the trailing arm so it's easier to install the mounting bolts. This setup uses a long bolt in the place of the traditional shock mount with a flat spot machined into it to allow it to pass through the spindle mount. Once the long bolt is inserted into the coil-over lower mounting support, it must proceed through the strut rod and then the spindle mount. Move the jack up or down to make it a straight shot through all the pieces for the easiest installation. Be sure that the Van Steel–supplied strut rod bolt's flat side is facing downward.

from Speed Direct. These place the coil-overs in a horizontal position.

Although this is a very expensive option, it does place the rear spring closer to the stock location, which is important when you are working with suspension components. Placing the coil-over assembly in front of the axleshaft (as with the Van Steel product) changes the spring rate, because the trailing arm is now loading the spring in the center of the arm.

Speed Direct's answer is to use a cantilever system that places the coil-over in the same factory location. The real question is, will the typical driver know that? Most likely not. There is one distinct advantage when going the coil-over route: being able to adjust ride height at each corner is a good thing.

None of the suppliers of coil-over kits tell you that you need a lot more driving prowess to be able to benefit from a coil-over swap. In reality, the best product is a high-speed driving instructional course to reap the rewards of any of these exotic suspension systems. The increased caster control arms and Smart Struts do more for the typical driver than the coil-overs. Of course it is neat to have all the available adjustments at your fingertips, and the eye candy makes many owners happy too.

Anti-Roll Bars

Anti-roll bars actually prevent or minimize body roll during cornering. The anti-roll bar uses links to make the connection to each suspension component. Anti-roll bar diameter and arm end length are the adjustability factors: larger-diameter bars provide more anti-roll control. High speed and vehicle weight force the mass off-center during cornering; to counteract the forces, the anti-rollbar connects the sides of the suspension together. Anti-roll bar science involves many factors for the best possible selection, including tire choices.

The bars come solid or tubelike, depending on how much body roll you are trying to alleviate. Most often the largest-diameter, solid-material anti-roll bar is chosen in the belief that it will provide the most possible control. This is true to some extent. The problem is that you are better off if the bar is smaller than you need as opposed to the largest possible one that fits on the chassis. An oversized bar can transmit road anomalies from one side to the other, causing poor handling at just about any speed.

Let's say, for instance, that you are entering a turn and find a significant bump in the road. The stiff bar could make both tires lose road surface contact momentarily. You want the bar to be heavy enough to limit roll without losing traction from one side to the other. If anything, a smaller bar is better than an overly aggressive large-diameter bar. If you make a change to the anti-roll bar diameter, always take your Shark out and drive it in a safe place to make sure you know the limitations. Rear anti-roll bars are always smaller diameter to compensate for the lighter back end of the vehicle.

The typical choice for the front anti-roll bar is a 1.125-inch-diameter solid bar for an occasional autocrossing with 360-pound rear fiberglass spring and Bilstein shocks all around. The rear gets the .750 rear solid anti-roll bar. All other hard-street-driven Sharks use a 1.00-inch-diameter bar. Serious road race setups get a 1.250-inch-diameter front bar, coil-overs, and double adjustable shocks. At that point you are at a crossroads. You need to spend more time learning how the springs and shocks affect handling to really custom tailor a system to work for your project. Serious chassis stiffening is required to make the aggressive components work as well as possible.

Chassis Stiffening and Bracing

Reinforcing, bracketing, and gusseting the chassis can deliver exceptional handling and ride benefits. But before I discuss those options, you need to be aware that applying heat to any chassis component can be detrimental. Chassis bracing components for C3s on the market today are not ready for immediate installation. In other words, welding is required for almost any non-factory chassis work performed, so extra care must be taken.

Sharks built for road racing used frame rails that were welded the entire length of the rail, rather than the GM production method of stitch-welding the rails. You can do this yourself, but you need to be sure to quench the welds with air or water and take your time, so the rails are not overheated and the welds do not become brittle. This is a lot of work for minimal return. At this point, go for a purpose-built chassis with mandrel-bent tube rails.

The next option is to fabricate bracing to triangulate the suspension points, which can be done with welding or bolt-in pieces. The inherent frame flex is where the major problem lies, and six- or eight-point rollbar installation is the best plan to eliminate that. Adding a rollbar is always an excellent idea for any performance car for the obvious safety factor and frame stiffening. You have to consider just how hard you plan to drive your performance Shark before the project begins.

The absolute weakest section of the frame is at the rear where the rear frame rails attach to the main frame rails. Rear frame stiffening braces can be made that help the flex and can be attached under the car.

Alignment

Alignment is the most important part of the entire performance suspension project. No matter how well the pieces are installed, they must point the tires in the optimum position. Dealing with most alignment shops today can be very frustrating. Modern alignment machines tell the tech exactly what to do: input the make, year, and model to be aligned. The machine tells the tech when

This smaller 1-inch-diameter anti-roll bar uses a urethane bushed non-adjustable set of end links connecting the bar. All of the connecting link kits have a partially threaded bolt that, in theory, sets the bushing's tension. There are variables here, and the idea is to achieve a tight-fitting set of bushings without collapsing them. You should always use a lock nut on top of the bolt after the correct tightness has been attained. You can get end link kits with a spring between the bushings and washers instead of the spacer. Adjustable types allow you to compensate for lowering the car, which typically requires shorter end links.

This 1968 modified chassis has stiffening tubes to tighten the convertible's frame. The body does little to aid in frame stiffening, which can be seen when lifting any Shark on a two-post lift. The door gaps widen as the wheels leave the ground. There are no off-the-shelf pieces out there: I used 1½-inch-diameter square tubing to fabricate the bracing and add the driveshaft safety loop. Each section is bolted into place with 3/8-16 Grade-8 bolts for rigidity after plates were welded to the original frame pieces.

CHASSIS MODIFICATIONS

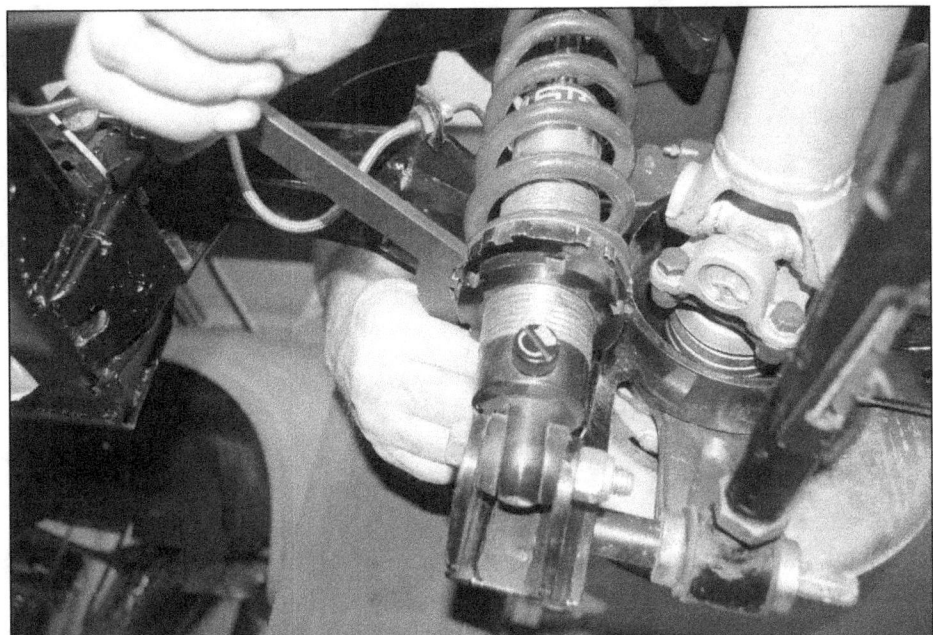

If your budget allows, getting coil-overs is the first step in any alignment process. Each corner of the Shark must be adjusted for height. QA1 has specific wrenches available but be careful: it can be difficult to turn them. One slip and injury can occur quickly. QA1 has Torrington needle roller bearings that are highly recommended; they can be placed between the spring and adjuster to ease the process.

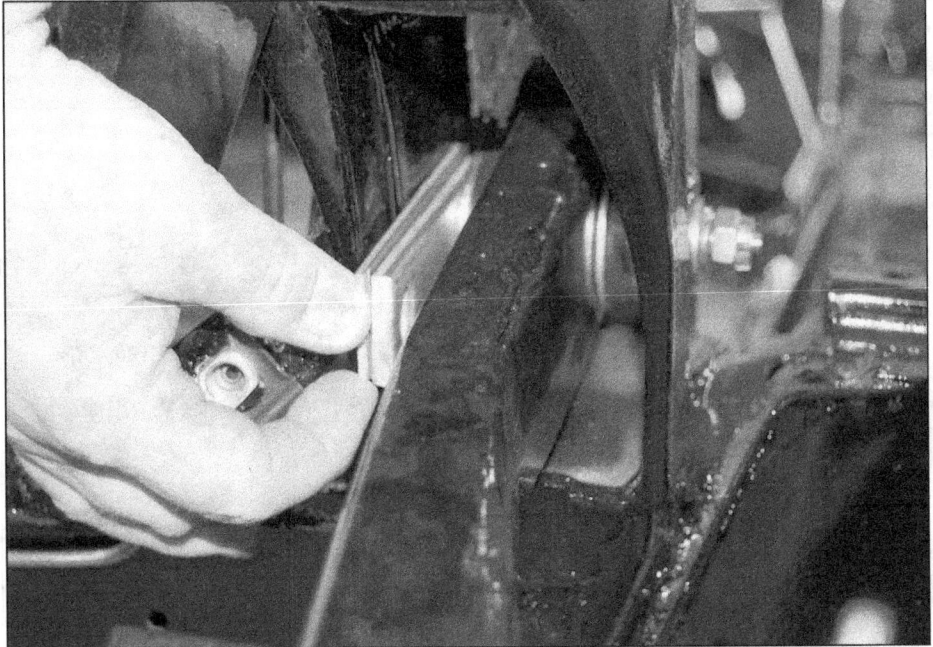

Rear trailing arm "toe alignment" is controlled by these shims on either side of the trailing arm pivot bushings. It is imperative that these shims fit tight and the pivot bolts are tight: any movement is immediately felt during high-speed driving. These shims must also be retained with a large cotter pin at the bottom of the trailing arm that goes through the chassis. As the trailing arms move up and down, the shims can work their way out even when tightened properly.

the factory alignment parameter is met. That's fine for an everyday driver. Accommodating custom settings takes extra time and the absolute knowledge of how alignment settings affect handling.

Today you can buy some really good precision alignment tools for at-home use. If you go this route, be sure you understand alignment terminology. Remember, chassis problems may make it difficult to obtain the preferred settings.

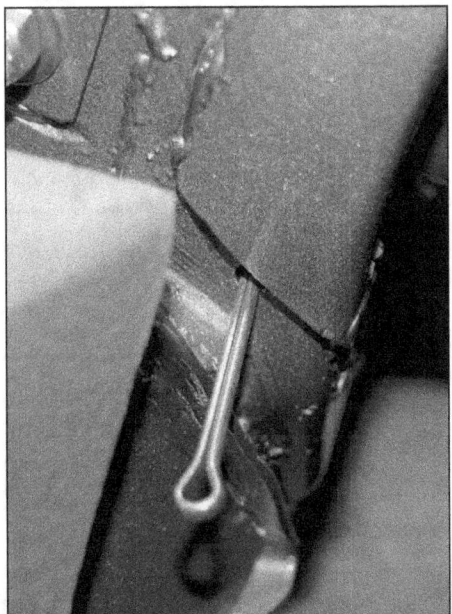

The 1968–1970 Corvettes use a non-slotted rear toe shim, which alignment shops really dislike because of the extra work needed to remove the trailing arm pivot bolt when swapping shims. I always drill out the frame on the outside and inside to install a long cotter pin to keep the shims in place once the conversion to slotted shims is made. Slotted shims were used on 1971–1982 Sharks that required simply loosening the trailing arm pivot bolt. Omitting the cotter pins can lead to poor (or even loss of) vehicle control when a shim(s) comes out. They positively do come out regardless of how well you tighten the pivot bolt; they work themselves up and out as the trailing arm follows pavement variations.

CHAPTER 11

BRAKE UPGRADES

General Motors equipped the Shark with high-performance brakes. In fact, General Motors used a cutting-edge-design "disc brake system" beginning in 1965 on the Corvette at the front end with disc brakes available on the rear. The 1966 Corvette received disc brakes all around, and that began the four-wheel disc brake system as standard equipment on the Corvette. There were minor differences as the years progressed, but for the most part the system remained unchanged through the 1966–1982 Corvette production run.

General Motors used four disc pad application caliper pistons, two on each side of the fixed caliper housings to clamp the disc pads. Larger-diameter caliper pistons were used up front to utilize the Shark's additional front-end weight for increased stopping power.

Race cars today use a similar system to apply brakes on road courses. The one drawback was that these were much higher-maintenance components than the standard disc brake systems on today's production vehicles. By 1969 General Motors phased out the four-piston fixed-caliper disc brake systems, except for the Corvette application.

At one point the Big Three auto manufacturers used a similar system on their performance cars from 1965–1968; they too phased them out in favor of floating caliper disc brake systems. The floating caliper systems required little maintenance and proved to be reliable for the masses. The idea was for the caliper to move as the disc pads wore, and this movement allowed the caliper to compensate for rotor anomalies. Any rotor lateral run-out creates major problems with the fixed caliper brake systems.

Up front on a Shark you have a race-bred system for excellent braking power that requires extra care during service. The fixed four-piston calipers have tremendous clamping force on both sides of the rotor, front and rear.

Wilwood makes this direct bolt-on aluminum-bodied caliper for the front and rear of a Shark. The Corvette Central drilled rotors complement the aftermarket calipers, but the drilled holes on the discs eventually crack.

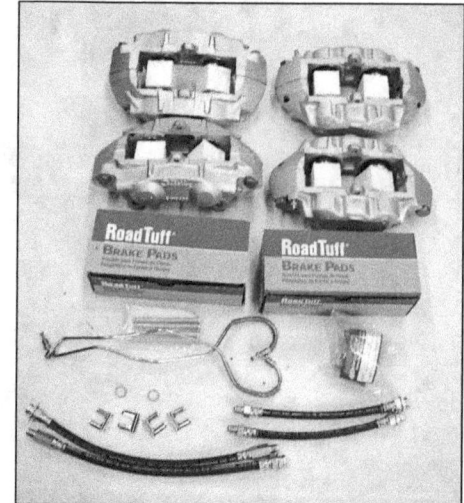

This is a fine set of calipers for a Shark that occasionally gets to play on the weekends. It includes the O-ring-modified calipers with all the attaching pieces that are commonly replaced. The rubber hoses can be substituted for stainless-steel braid, which is highly recommended.

BRAKE UPGRADES

One important thing to know about the original caliper design is that the cast-iron piston seal bore, which is susceptible to corrosion damage even when the brake fluid is changed often. As the caliper piston seals ride on the corrosion-damaged caliper bores they become torn, and cause leaks. A whole industry was born to repair this known problem by installing stainless-steel sleeves in each piston bore to remedy the corrosion issues for good.

Once that problem was dealt with, another one became apparent. Any rotor lateral run-out works the caliper pistons like little engines, causing even the stainless steel to wear. The resulting caliper piston pulsation drew air in at the caliper, and caused a low brake pedal. The longer you drove, the lower the brake pedal got, until it was on the floor.

This Mid America Motorworks cutaway caliper shows the early caliper's shortcomings. The original-style caliper pistons with lip-type seals (bottom) are shown sealed against the caliper housing. The upper caliper pistons are the preferred O-ring style because they seal better and keep the caliper piston in control when there is rotor run-out. Stainless-steel sleeves were installed in the upper and left lower caliper piston bores to provide a corrosion-free surface. The cutaway also shows that the weight of the beefy iron castings makes the aluminum replacement caliper a smart move to shed a few pounds in an opportune place.

Calipers

A number of choices are available today concerning calipers, including modified factory cast-iron calipers. One major upgrade to the factory caliper was when square-cut O-rings replaced the original lip seals. The square-cut seals held on to the pistons better and allowed minor rotor run-out issues without causing air intrusion in the system. You still need to maintain rotor run-out, but you could get away with .010 inch and not lose a brake pedal because of air intrusion.

The square-cut seals also reduced brake pad friction without losing pedal feel as the pads got knocked back slightly during driving.

The remaining drawback was added weight from the cast-iron caliper housings. Reducing unsprung weight at each wheel is always a good thing, and the latest aftermarket replacement calipers do that with alloy castings. They have the best of the best: lightweight, square-cut caliper piston seals and they look great with open-spoke wheels.

The available kits are bolt-on, and ready to go out of the box with the attaching stainless-steel braided hoses included. One thing to consider is the brake pad; each aftermarket caliper manufacturer uses its own disc pad. Ordering a set of replacement pads is a good idea so that you aren't waiting a week to get going after a race weekend. That is another point to consider: what disc pads are available for their exclusive design? Preferably a softer compound for the everyday driver and more aggressive race pads for a race weekend.

Caliper Installation

1 Clean Caliper Threads

I always clean the threads with a 7/16-20 tap to make sure my 65 ft-lb-torque reading is attained. At the rear axle, the caliper mounting bolt goes through the caliper and then into the mount. At the front, the caliper itself has threads and they are often worse than the threaded rear caliper mounting plates for corrosion and rust. When a Shark owner complains of a knocking sound during hard braking, these threaded holes are often the cause. The caliper is loose even though the bolts are tightened to their correct torque specification.

CHAPTER 11

2 Install Bolts

It seems simple enough: grab some bolts and install the caliper, right? General Motors used four 1-inch-long bolts to mount the front calipers and four 1⅛-inch-long bolts for the rear calipers. Using the incorrect bolt length can cause you to scar the rotors where the bolts dig into the rotor's surface. I use 1¼-inch-long Grade-8 bolts with a thick flat lock washer, front and rear.

3 Prep Caliper Before Install

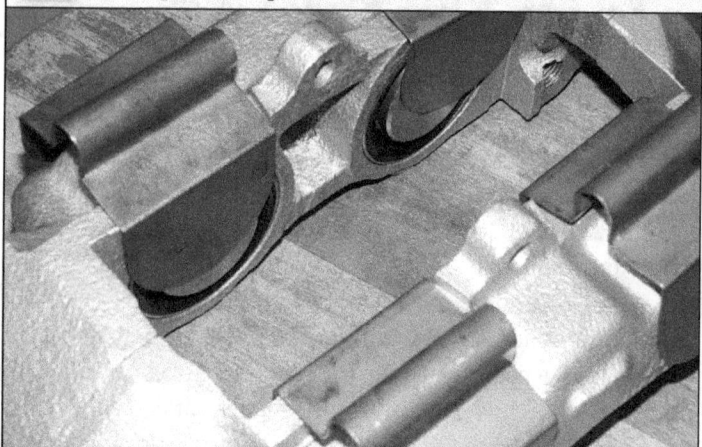

I am preparing to install a set of Vette Brake and Products square-cut O-ring calipers. I prefer their calipers because the square-cut O-ring–equipped cylinder bores help stabilize the caliper pistons, lessening the chance of air intrusion from rotor run-out. The caliper retention clips are provided in a complete caliper, disc pad, and hose kit to keep the pistons back until the disc pads are installed. I find it easiest to install them at the bench before installing the calipers.

4 Install Disc Pads

These hefty large-friction-area disc pads are one of the reasons the Shark has such good brakes from the factory. I am wearing the gloves to prevent any contamination from ending up on the disc pads, which would find its way onto the rotor surfaces. Never ever use any anti-squeak coating on the back of Shark disc brake pads: the adhesive-like substance sticks the pads onto the caliper pistons, causing caliper wear as the pads follow the rotors forcing the pistons in and out. I use a light coating of high-temperature silicone grease to keep the pads from sticking to the caliper pistons. The FF-coded pads work well during the warm-up and when under high-heat loading.

5 Install Calipers

This square-cut O-ringed and stainless-steel-sleeved caliper has been painted, installed, and is ready for action. These calipers are plenty adequate for a street-performance Shark, even one that may venture out onto a gymkhana track or autocross course. The trick to long, dependable braking is frequent brake fluid exchanges, especially after a race event–filled weekend. Note the outer bleeder screw. Both rear calipers have them; they must be bled, or you have a low brake pedal forever.

Disc Pads

Ceramic, organic, metallic, or a combination of friction materials are available for the Shark brake system. Sintered metal or metallic disc pads are typically the most aggressive and they affect the disc rotors in a big way, causing them to wear quickly. Metallic pads also require heat buildup to begin doing their job efficiently, although pedal feel is maintained after numerous high-speed stops. You have to apply more pedal pressure when the rotors and pads are cold. Combine that with an engine on high idle, and parking-lot maneuvering can become quite interesting.

Organic disc pads are usually the least expensive and wear quickly; heat fade can be a major concern after just a few high-speed stops. Ceramic is a good choice for an all-around performance pad with minimal dusting on your expensive shiny wheels.

Driving Styles

Disc pads have alpha coding to give you an idea of how well they work and at what temperatures. Full race pads typically do not use this DOT or FMVSS coding because their products operate at higher temperatures than the street/performance disc pads. Codes are found on the edge of the pads (usually in the center of the coding): you might find FF, meaning they have a friction coefficient of 0.35 to 0.45 in the 200- to 600-degree temperature range. Preferably you want the alphas to be close to each other; avoid major changes in braking performance as you go from no heat to full heat.

The bottom line is, you will need to do some testing and recording to find the best disc pad for your driving style. I suggest that you start with the FF and go to a higher alpha if need be.

An important part of disc pad life is how they begin life: bedding or burnishing is required by most performance brake pad manufacturers. The idea is to bring them up to their optimal operating temperature in a series of stops and then let them cool down. This allows the pads to transfer a layer of material to the rotor's surface for the best possible braking. Each stop increases in severity until the process is complete; refer to the pad supplier's instructions on the particular pads bedding procedure.

Pre-bedded or burnished pads are available, but they come with rotors. If you plan to do any serious racing it is good to have a set of rotors and pre-burnished pads on hand for a change at the track if necessary.

Disc Brake Rotors

Before you choose a disc brake rotor, you need to know that new rotors out of the box can end up with excessive run-out. The rotors themselves are not always the problem. Wheel bearing hub run-out can cause excessive rotor run-out. Minor wheel hub variations can add up to a major run-out issue. The fix is maintaining the brake rotor run-out at a maximum .004 inch at the far outside edge of the rotor's diameter.

You also have to be cognizant of the wheel bearing condition at all times. Loose wheel bearings mimic rotor run-out and allows the caliper pistons to be knocked back into the bores; excessive brake pedal travel results.

Wheel Hub Refurbishment

1 Inspect Disc Brake Rotors

You need to determine that your C3's brake system is safe and reliable. There are two very important disc brake rotor checks to make rotor thickness and run-out. If your rotor measures less than 1.215 inches thick, they should be replaced, General Motors says the rotors should not be machined if they are 1.230 or less inches thick. If your rotors are above that limit and you decide to have them machined, the rotors must be measured after the machining process to ensure minimum thickness has been maintained. If your rotors pass the thickness test the next objective is to maintain less than .004 inch of maximum rotor run-out to avoid a soft brake pedal from air intrusion. After the bearing hubs have been serviced and the rotors are installed, you should perform run-out checks.

CHAPTER 11

2 Service Bearing

The first step in maintaining the rotors' run-out integrity is to service the tapered roller bearings. Unless you know that the bearings and races have been recently replaced, I recommend replacing them while everything is apart. Two machined areas in the bearing race seat area allow use of a punch to remove them. Alternately, tap on the race so that the race comes out evenly to avoid distorting the machined surfaces. Keep the punch as upright as possible to avoid gouging the surfaces.

3 Remove Rotor Hub

General Motors used rivets to fasten the hubs to the rotors. Drill out the rivets to separate the hub from the rotor. The 1/4-inch rivet shank requires a 1/4-inch drill bit to cut off the rivet head. First, use a punch and hit center punch of the rivet head to get as close to it as possible. Center the drill on the head of the rivet and that often pops the head off the rivet's shank. Then use a 3/8-inch drill bit for the head removal if center punching did not take it off. Chances are you won't be using the rotor you are drilling.

4 Remove Rivets

Over the years, I have seen many Sharks with low brake pedals and found that new rotors were installed on poorly prepared hubs with the remnants of the rivets left in place. I use an air hammer and pin punch to knock them out. A large hammer works, but it takes more effort and time. But if you're careful and do not allow the punches to increase outer diameter they don't become jammed into the hub. The punch raises the surface around the rivet hole and causes rotor run-out issues. Once the rivet is punched out, clean the surfaces with a small sanding disc to knock down any raised areas.

5 Replace Studs

I install new wheels and studs on every brake system during the restoring of a C3. Rusty and damaged threads are also commonly found at this point. It is very easy and inexpensive to replace the studs. If you plan to change wheels or adding a spacer for wheel offset, you should install longer studs to accommodate the changes and ensure your safety. Most race sanctioning bodies want the wheel stud to be flush or protrude through the lug nut for any competing class.

This Lisle stud installation tool works well for stud replacement. The high-strength bearing that comes with the tool limits friction as the stud is pulled back into place. I feel for the serrations of the stud until they fit into the serrations left from the previous stud to get the best fit. Once the stud is seated into the serrations, the tightening begins. Yes, you can press the studs in with a hydraulic press. Unfortunately, it is very easy to have them pushed in at an angle.

BRAKE UPGRADES

6 Fix Loose Bearing Races

Over time, the bearing races wear from common or aggressive use. They get beat around or overheated and they can spin in the hub. The bearing race should have an interference fit into the hub. This helps locate a piece. Use a pin punch to raise the metal and tighten the bearing race. Apply bearing-mount Loctite or Threadlocker to ensure that the race stays in place. The green bearing-mount formula makes it difficult to remove the race in the future. Once the race spins in the hub, it continues to wear into the hub until the wheel is really wobbling around, which affects the brake performance.

7 Install Bearing Race

A bearing race installer is preferred for the race installation to prevent damaging the outer edges of the race. The trick is getting the race started and then driving it in straight to avoid race or hub damage. If you find the race is pushing down too much on one side, it is better to turn the hub over and back it out slightly to straighten it before proceeding. You can find these installers in kit form (with many different sizes of installer cones) at many car show swap meet areas for approximately $30.

8 Pack Bearings with Grease

Packing wheel bearings is never fun, but it is necessary. An inexpensive packer requires a downward push to pack the Valvoline synthetic bearing grease in between the rollers and inner bearing cones. Smearing grease on the outside of the bearing is not sufficient. If this is what you do, bearing failure occurs because grease must be packed thoroughly into the bearing. This nifty bearing packer has a cover that should be kept on when not in use. Never leave the packer in an area where grinding or dirt can find its way into the grease.

Tap the inner seal carefully into place. Use care to avoid distorting the metal outer portion of the seal. I often find the seals dinged up and disfigured, which allows grease to leak out of the hub and possibly attribute to early bearing failure. Another concern I see is the lack of new seal lubrication; this causes them to burn the rubber seal material because of high temperatures. Always wipe some fresh grease on the seal surfaces before installing. Drag racers use 90-140W rear gear oil for lubrication to lessen friction. That means the seals must be perfectly installed to keep the gear oil where it belongs.

CHAPTER 11

8 Pack Bearings with Grease CONTINUED

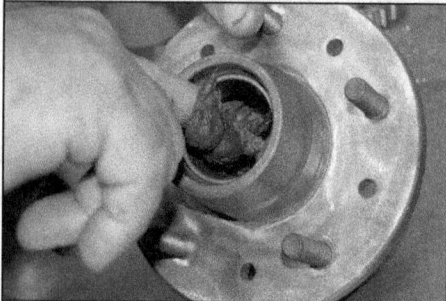

The chassis/bearing grease heats up enough on long trips to semi-liquefy. Apply a couple of tablespoons into the hub before installation to ensure enough lubricant at both bearings on long road trips. Never fill the hubs completely with grease because they need room for expansion as the hubs heat up. If you pack too much grease in the hubs, it squeezes out and you have a mess to clean up. Using the correct amount of grease gives you a performance edge without having to worry about early bearing failure.

9 Adjust Front Wheel Bearings

Proper bearing adjustment is the final step and key to long bearing life and the best possible brake performance. Rotate the hub as the adjusting nut is tightened. When the nut is bottomed out and requires effort with the pliers to turn, stop. Then, loosen the nut and do it once more; you want zero to .002-inch maximum clearance between the bearing rollers and races. When you reach zero clearance back the nut off to the closest cotter pin hole (two are provided). If you can feel play in the hub as you pull on it at the top and bottom, it is too loose. The hub should spin freely but if it takes effort to rotate it, the hub is too tight.

When properly maintained, the 1968–1982 Shark factory disc brake rotor is very good. The original rotors have stout, ventilated, 1-inch-thick disc pad surfaces on an 11-inch overall diameter surface. Cheap rotors are made of lighter-weight material and are more susceptible to run-out issues from thermal cycling. For the occasional hard-driven street Shark, a good-quality set of name-brand rotors (Wagner or Raybestos, for example) are sufficient.

Aftermarket rotors come in five forms: drilled, slotted, ball milled, drilled, and slotted, and ball milled and slotted. The idea behind drilling, slotting, and ball milling is to allow the brake pad gases and heat to be expelled quickly.

This is proven technology, with some drawbacks. Drilling a rotor causes checking (minute cracking) around each drilled hole from thermal cycling; there is no way to combat this; it will happen.

Slotting a rotor allows the release of heat without the inherent checking from the drilled holes, making it a better choice for a hard-driven street Shark.

Drilling and slotting a rotor is for ultimate heat control for true race cars that get frequent inspections, and the owners expect to hear that the rotors require replacement. Of course you can use the drilled rotors on street-driven Sharks. The idea is to keep an eye on the rotor surfaces for checking if you really use them for what they are capable of. If you only occasionally use the brakes hard they last a lifetime.

Brake Rotor Truing

1 Prep Rotor

This is another important step to ensure a true parallel rotating rotor. The high-speed right-angle grinder has a maroon Scotch-Brite cleaning disc to remove all the rust and corrosion that accumulates between the rotor and hub. Number 40- or 60-grit sanding discs are available, and sometimes they are required if the inner surfaces have been beaten up from rivet removal. I always wash the rotor surfaces with a degreaser such as Purple Power after any machining (or if they happen to be new) before installation. Many people use brake cleaner in spray cans to clean the rotors, but it does not flush out the metallic particles like soap and running water.

2 Check Rotor for Run-Out

This ball-milled and slotted rotor needs to be rechecked for run-out to make sure it is under the maximum .004 inch to avoid a low brake pedal. Because of the rotor design I had to check the readings on the inside diameter, which is not preferred because it is greater at the outer circumference. The ball milling and slotted rotors help hot gases escape quicker under hard braking. I prefer this style of rotors for street/strip use because they do not crack as easily around the milled areas.

3 Rectify Rotor Run-Out

You may be thinking that if the rotors are on the hubs when they are machined, they should be perfectly true. On the rear of a Shark the only way to machine the rotors on the hub is to do it on the car with the rotor on the drive hub. To easily rectify the problem I use a piece of .005-inch brass shim stock to make a shim and then install it at the low spot. Finding the true low spot can be tricky; sometimes I have to move the shim to the stud to the right or left to get the rotor run-out to be less than .004 inch. Always use at least three lug nuts in a triangular pattern and tighten them to at least 65 ft-lbs during the dial indicator rotor run-out testing. You may have to pull the rotor off numerous times until you get the run-out where it needs to be.

Brake Bias

You need to be concerned with the brake bias for even front-to-rear braking. Locking up the front or rear brakes entering a corner can be disastrous. Front brakes usually do more stopping because of the vehicle's balance, with 60 percent of the typical Shark's weight up front. Wider rear tires and suspension modifications can aid in the balance, but not as effectively as moving the actual weight.

General Motors did a good job with the original brake caliper design, using smaller caliper pistons on the rear to aid in brake balance. A combination valve was used to shut off one side of the hydraulic system in the event of a fluid leak or major loss. Combo valves have the functions of warning of a major fluid loss and regulating fluid pressure to aid in brake balance. Brake pressure was modified to the rear brakes with smaller fluid orifices in the combo valve to lessen rear brake application.

The best plan is to install an adjustable brake proportioning valve to fine-tune the brake balance. Track surfaces, tire sizes, and weight changes can be tuned for the ultimate brake application. The installation is simple and makes sense for a true performance Shark.

Brake Boosters

Boosting the brake system pressure is something that I never considered in the old days. That stuff added weight and required extra engine effort; I could be tough and live without it. Boy, that was not too smart. Today I want all the help I can get to keep the brakes under my performance cars boosted. Vacuum brake boosters have been a staple for factory-equipped Sharks and they work pretty well. Your camshaft selection may make that vacuum booster tough to handle. Low engine vacuum is not going to make a vacuum booster happy, and you certainly will not be, either.

Another consideration is the brake pads used today; aggressive pads are composed of denser materials that require more pedal pressure. This is especially a concern until the brakes heat up. Cold disc pads can make you wonder if you can hold back your performance vehicle during the first couple of brake applications. Your overall brake system choices dictate the best brake boost system for your performance Shark. As caliper piston sizes increase, so does the required brake pressure. You can go with manual brakes with a master cylinder piston size to aid in brake pedal effort; it just doesn't make sense if you plan to drive on twisty roads that require frequent braking.

Hydroboost System

Many performance builders have switched to hydroboost brake amplification systems to have dependable repeatable braking. The power steering pump does double duty by pressurizing the brake booster system while providing

CHAPTER 11

Plumbing Your New Brake System

Having all new brake components is a great thing, but leaving worn-out hoses and corroded brake lines negates any benefits. The original rubber brake hoses are fine for an everyday-driver Shark that sees little, if any, hard driving. The inner fluid casing is 3/16 inch in diameter: all that extra hose material is there to keep the hose from ballooning as pressure is applied. Stainless-steel braided hoses have a nylon inner casing that has less chance of ballooning as heat and pressure increase.

It really does not matter whether you choose stainless or carbon steel brake lines. The main concern is clean tubing without any kinks or crushed areas. Double-flared carbon steel or single-flared stainless steel is the preferred tubing and connection process to use. I have seen compression fittings used to repair damaged lines; they are not recommended as over time they loosen and allow fluid leakage.

Copper or aluminum should never be used for the high-pressure braking system. Always be aware of where the brake lines are routed. For example, it is not a good idea to have a brake line running under the harmonic balancer where a rotating component could hit the line and sever it or close it off. Many race sanctioning bodies frown on having brake lines close to the transmission bellhousing area, where an exploding clutch could sever the lines. If there is no alternative to where the brake line must be routed, the use of shielding is recommended to take the brunt of the blow before the line does.

Although this tube nut is in terrible shape, it can be removed to avoid replacing the line. The hose must be cut off before any heating takes place. As the hose heats up, the inner liner swells and closes. Soon afterward a mini-explosion occurs very close to where you are holding the torch. As long as the hose is cut within a few inches of the fitting to be heated there will be no problem and you can save the tube nut. Heat the tube nut after the line is out of the hose, to make sure it spins on the tube. Most of the time when corrosion has taken over, the nut does not spin. If you are not watching the nut during the removal, you might twist the end of the line off with the nut.

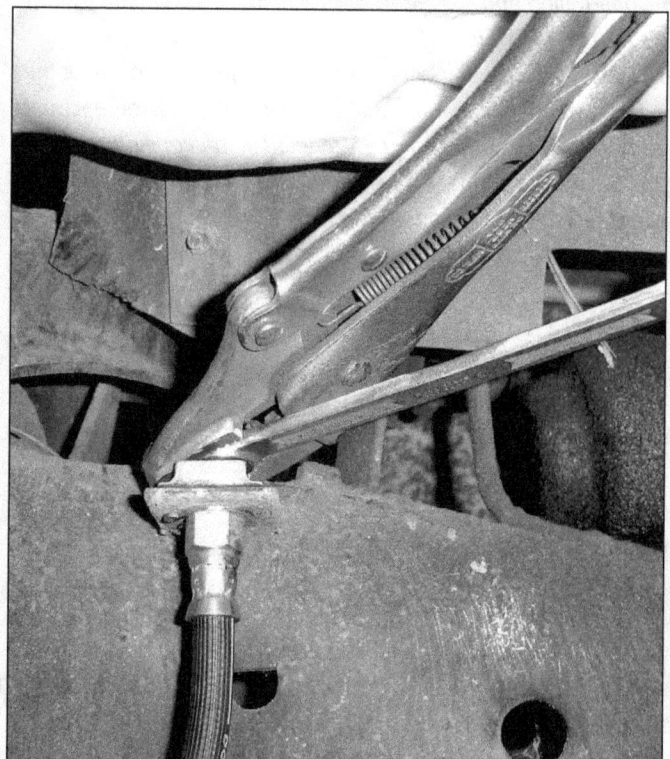

Sometimes it takes just a little extra help to get a stubborn tube nut loose or tight. If the tube nut is beginning to lose it shape, this trick works: place Vise-Grips on the end of a line wrench. In many cases, with the pressure of the Vise-Grips applied the end of the wrench closes just enough to prevent slipping. Of course changing the line is an option, but in most cases it's quite a bit of work. You should check the end of the line before putting things back together and see if any buildup of corrosion is present. If so, you have to replace the line. Chances are the lines are in the same condition and you end up pumping nasty fluid and rust particles through the system.

steering assist. Power steering pumps have plenty of capacity for a hydroboost addition. Hydroboost systems don't care what camshaft you choose; they work even at low engine vacuum. Other alternatives include using a stand-alone vacuum reservoir that stores vacuum for better brake boost at low engine speeds such as in parking-lot maneuvers.

The vacuum reservoir is a great inexpensive alternative, but you must remember that it will also be depleted of vacuum if multiple applications of the brake pedal are required. Hydroboost systems require some extra plumbing for the install, which takes up some room in the engine compartment, but the booster unit is smaller. Of course there is a chance of leaks, and when the engine stalls you lose steering and the brake boost pressure drops off within three applications of the brakes. All in all, for a long-duration-camshaft-equipped engine that is driven hard, the hydroboost makes the most sense. As long as the engine is running, you have brake boost.

The installation of a hydroboost system is a medium on the difficulty level due to access to the four nuts on the inside of the firewall. Ready-to-install kits have hoses already plumbed for a quick installation. Any custom power steering pump or steering system may require custom fabricated hoses. For a true performance Shark that is driven frequently, the hydroboost system makes good sense, and you can have your favorite long-duration camshaft too.

Vacuum Brake Booster

Vacuum brake booster systems rely on a steady vacuum supply. The idea is that on those long deceleration runs engine vacuum builds up in the booster and is stored for maximum braking effect. There are a couple of simple tests for the booster: start the engine, let it idle for a few minutes, shut off the engine, and apply the brakes.

The brakes should have some assist for a minimum of three brake pedal applications. Each push on the pedal gets harder as vacuum is depleted. If the pedal has no assist immediately you have a vacuum leak or bad vacuum check valve. The vacuum check valve should allow vacuum to draw through it from the hose side, not from the booster side.

Another test is to remove the check valve after the engine is shut off; you should hear vacuum escaping as the valve moves around. The final test is to turn off the engine, apply the brake pedal until vacuum is depleted, and then hold your foot on the brake pedal while you start the engine. You should feel the brake pedal drop as the engine vacuum assists after the engine starts. If the pedal does not have any boost once the engine starts, the booster is leaking.

Conversion

Using a GM vacuum brake booster can get you into trouble if you are making a conversion. From 1968–1982, Shark brake boosters look similar, with one major difference occurring in 1977 that was carried over until 1982; the master cylinder pushrod is shorter from 1977 on.

If you install a 1968–1976 brake master cylinder on the 1977-and-up booster, you have a low or non-existent brake pedal. It takes a lot of work to make the 1977–1982 master cylinder work on the pre-1977 brake booster.

Collapsed or incorrect vacuum supply hoses can render your booster inoperable. Fuel hose installed as the vacuum supply hose is a huge problem. It tightens or collapses under deceleration when vacuum draw is at its greatest. Finding original-equipment vacuum hose can be difficult but important. I use Aeroquip FC332-06 low-pressure hose in the shortest possible amount to ensure a constant vacuum supply. For this 1979 Shark, I had to tap a hole in the Edelbrock intake manifold for a separate brake booster vacuum supply. You may find that someone has tapped into the PCV valve's vacuum hose to supply the brake booster, limiting the brake booster vacuum supply. A dedicated vacuum supply is necessary for correct brake booster operation. Always make sure the 3/8-inch steel tubing is supported close to the end of the line to avoid broken tubing.

In an effort to get the brake pedal at its highest point the pushrod can be adjusted to keep the brakes applied lightly. As the brake fluid heats up and expands the problem is exacerbated until you can smell burning brake friction material and a distinct drag on the vehicle as you attempt to leave a stoplight. You can assess the problem by loosening the master cylinder nuts just enough to release the brakes. If that helps, you need to shorten the master cylinder pushrod.

Some brake boosters have an adjustable master cylinder pushrod that can get you into trouble. A low pedal is one problem; a locked-up brake system can have you stranded until you figure out why the brakes don't release.

Brake Fluid

If you are planning a track day or spending the weekend at a road course with long straightaways and low-speed corners, you may need to change the pads during or after the event. Once the disc pads are glazed, which is evident by extra pedal effort for any stopping chores, they require replacement.

Track days are also hard on brake fluid, causing it to come close to boiling or to actually boil after repeated high-speed stops. Any moisture in the system lowers the boiling point, which causes pockets of air to form in the brake calipers and/or lines. The age-old question for any Shark owner has been what brake fluid should I use, silicone or glycol?

Many experts have weighed in on this with mixed input. The facts are, silicone is more viscous and has more of a lubricating feel. Some say that the silicone fluid expands so much that brake lock-up is possible. An interesting fact is the military uses DOT 5 silicone in all of its vehicles, including the ones used in the desert. If silicone expands so much more than glycol fluids when heated, how do they get away with it? We all know that fluid expands when heated; so does glycol-based brake fluid. Silicone is perfect for Sharks that are driven infrequently because it does not absorb water.

Glycol brake fluids are hygroscopic, pulling water out of the atmosphere anytime the brake fluid system is opened. For a serious performance Shark, DOT 4 low-moisture activity brake fluid is going to be the best choice, that and changing it regularly. If your brake pedal comes close to the floor after some aggressive stopping maneuvers, you can rest assured you either have excessive disc brake rotor runout or overheated brake fluid. The best plan is to flush the brake hydraulic system if you know that the rotors are fine.

Do not keep opened cans of brake fluid for more than a month; they are already drawing water into the can. Do not leave the cap off the fluid reservoir for any amount of time (longer than necessary to top it off). Do not fill the reservoir to the absolute top: all fluids require room for expansion. Make sure the reservoir cap seal is working well; the rubber bellows allows the fluid to change level in the reservoir without exposing the fluid to the atmosphere.

Brake Bleeding

Bleeding the brakes on any Shark can be unnerving. Some say they gravity bleed the system, but that can take many days. Having a helper pump the pedal is an alternative, but even that can be difficult if the reservoir runs dry during a bleeding phase. Vacuum systems are available that connect to your brake bleeders and you draw the fluid out. They work, but the loose bleeder screw allows air to be drawn in around the screw threads. Of course this is not into the system, but it takes additional time.

One of the best-working simple bleeders is the Speed Bleeder, which replaces your existing bleeder screw. When the bleeder screw is loosened, an internal check valve in the Speed Bleeder allows fluid to be released, while preventing air from being drawn in when the brake pedal is released. Speed Bleeders have a sealer around the threads that prevents air intrusion. When the sealer deteriorates from multiple bleeding events, they allow air to enter the brake system.

I prefer to use a pressure bleeder that has a reservoir of clean fluid connecting it directly to the master cylinder. If your plan is to frequent race venues, this is the best option for quick, simple, one-person brake fluid flushing and bleeding. If you got caught up in a hot lap incident that required extra braking, you might find a need for a quick brake fluid exchange; this is the tool for you.

Performance Brake Kits

Buying brake kits can save you money and a lot of hassle by replacing the known troublesome pieces in one job. Before you decide on a kit, always consider the wheel-to-caliper clearance. Give yourself 1/4 to 1/2 inch at the tightest point of the caliper to the wheel. If at all possible, try to avoid wheel spacers, unless they are your only alternative.

Brake kits come in many forms: calipers only, calipers and disc pads, and high-end kits with all the pieces.

Baer Brakes

Baer Brakes has the ultimate Shark brake setup with up to 14-inch drilled rotors and forged mono-block six-piston calipers that costs approximately $7,200. This is the ultimate Extreme Plus brake system with two-piece drilled and slotted rotors, and hubs loaded with bearings to convert your spindle to work with their hub. CNC machined adapters are included to easily make the conversion to this system.

Baer has a Pro Plus system that shaves off about $2,000 with one-piece rotors and two-piece calipers with six pistons.

All Baer calipers are aluminum to save weight and they use banjo-style fittings to connect their supplied stainless-steel hose assemblies. To prevent corrosion, all of the calipers are powder coated in three options or a custom color you choose. Baer has fitment templates to help fit the monster rotors and calipers on a Shark; you need an aftermarket or later Corvette wheel to make that happen.

Aftermarket Caliper Installation

1 Install Caliper Shims

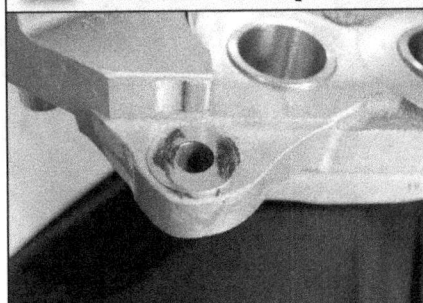

SSBC's aftermarket calipers are lightweight aluminum castings that are ready to bolt on to your stock Shark suspension components. SSBC provides this shim with the 3M adhesive on it to hold it in place until the caliper is installed. This centers the caliper pad surfaces between the rotor surfaces. Their calipers are beefier in turn, making them come closer to the rotors than the OEM cast-iron calipers. Make sure you have the rotor in place with at least three lug nuts during this checking procedure. After the calipers are torqued to 65 ft-lbs, make sure the rotor spins freely without any hint of the rotor touching the caliper. As heat builds, things grow, and can become a clearance issue.

2 Install Caliper Pads

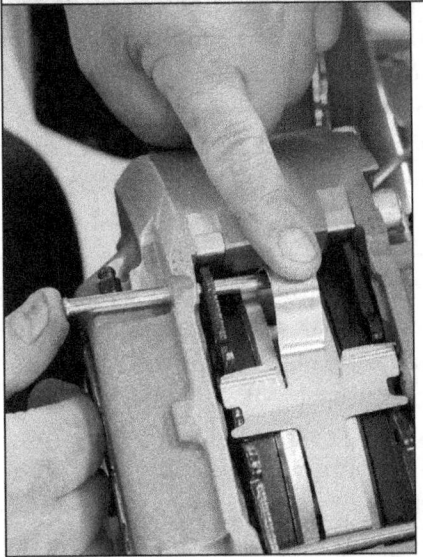

SSBC provides this disc pad anti-rattle retainer along with the pads and pins to hold the pads in place. Like the OEM disc pads and calipers, do not use any anti-squeak products. Your warranty will be void and caliper damage can result. I do the same trick, applying a light coat of high-heat silicone grease to the back of the pad.

3 Place Brake Hose

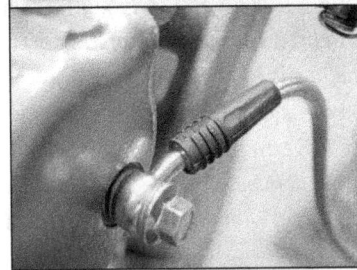

It seems simple enough: screw the new hose to the caliper and you are done. That kind of thinking can get you in trouble. I have found a few discrepancies in brake kits: the banjo bolt that goes through the hose must protrude 1/4 to 3/8 inch out of the fitting with the copper washers on both sides of the bolt. If the banjo bolt is too short, the threads can be ripped out of the caliper. If they're too long, brake fluid flow can be restricted. You must also pay careful attention to how the hose is routed, especially at the front where steering and rotating wheels can pinch or bind the hose. Check all of the hoses as you rotate the steering wheel from lock to lock with the Shark at road height.

4 Inspect Caliper and Rotor

This left front brake assembly is ready to stop this 3,400-pound Shark. The SSBC rotors are coated, drilled, and slotted for the ultimate in brake performance. I feel that this is the ultimate bolt-on brake kit for a Shark. The rotors are more than 1-inch thick with lightweight aluminum calipers. Keep in mind: drilled rotors eventually end up with spider cracking if used to their full potential. In a race environment, brake pad and rotor condition are checked before each event and brake fluid is serviced. Depending on your terrain, you may have to check your brakes more often even if you are not racing frequently.

5 Install Front Caliper

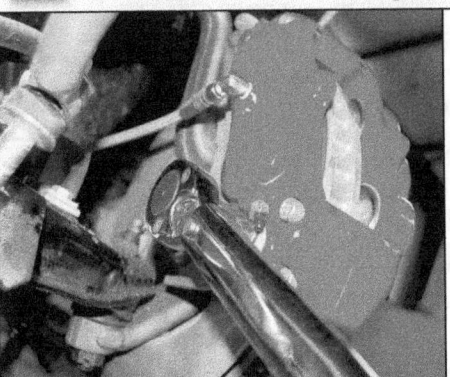

Wilwood makes an excellent OEM-style replacement caliper as shown on the front of this 1977 Shark. They provide the calipers, disc brake pads, hoses, and all required hardware. Overall, their caliper is slightly lighter than the SSBC unit; it also requires shimming to center the caliper on the rotor. A dab of Teflon sealer is applied to the 90-degree fitting's pipe threads before installing the fitting. I prefer to install the fittings after the caliper is installed and torqued to ensure correct hose placement.

6 Install Rear Caliper

Wilwood and SSBC use small-diameter rear caliper pistons to balance front-to-rear braking, as did General Motors. Wilwood supplies the braided stainless-steel hose for the caliper to trailing arm. Although it may look as if the hose is on top of the parking brake cable, it is not; be careful of hose placement. One nice feature of the hoses supplied with the Wilwood brake kit is the plastic coating that keeps corrosion off and limits abrasions to other components. Steel braided hoses can saw just about any metallic piece into two pieces over a long period of time. It is never a good idea to let uncovered stainless-steel hoses come into contact with any objects because of this.

7 Adjust Parking Brake

I prefer to have a parking brake: it beats having a wheel chock on a chain, especially if you have a manual transmission. First, the rotor must be aligned with the brake adjuster access holes in the spindle; second, make sure you have at least one lug nut holding the rotor flat on the hub. The rule is to tighten the star wheel until the rotor does not turn, then back off the adjuster seven to eight clicks. At best, when the brake shoes are in good condition with no grease on them, you can expect the parking brake to hold well enough to prevent rolling on a slight incline.

Wilwood

Wilwood has a different approach with their six-piston caliper offering; they place the caliper in the stock location on factory 12-inch-diameter rotors. They also powdercoat the two-piece forged billet aluminum bodied calipers. The major difference is that you could use your factory wheels if you prefer.

Some earlier Corvette wheels do not work without a spacer. Wilwood supplies stainless-steel braided hoses and national pipe thread fittings to connect to their calipers in the kit. When installed properly, pipe thread fittings do not leak, but keep in mind that it is easier to leave a fitting loose, which causes a minor seepage of fluid when using pipe thread fittings.

One major factor to consider is cost: a set of Wilwood D8-6 front calipers and rear set of D8-4 calipers with red or black powder coat is in the $1,600 range. Clear anodized calipers will shave about $400 off the cost of powder-coated calipers, leaving some money for drilled or slotted rotors at all four corners.

Vette Brakes and Products

On the other end of the spectrum, Vette Brakes and Products has a very dependable original-style caliper, pads, thermal-treated sport slotted rotors, stainless-steel braided hoses, and rear caliper-to-hose lines for all four corners of a Shark. The calipers are remanufactured cast-iron assemblies with stainless-steel sleeves and lip seal caliper pistons. All the necessary hardware is included for the installation, making it an easy afternoon project. This kit is very reasonable at $849 for the remanufactured calipers, and they come powder coated in numerous colors. This is the perfect kit for a street warrior and weekend competition enthusiast who is not worried about having a slick-looking caliper in open-spoke wheels.

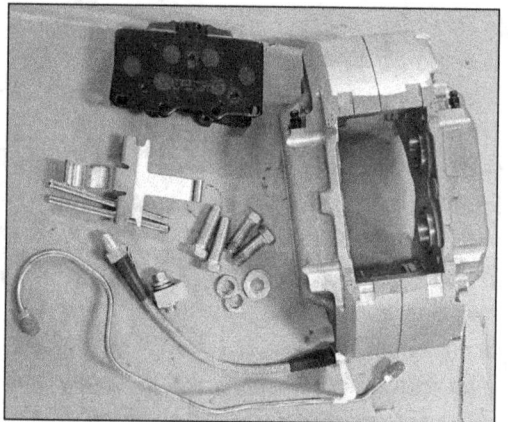

This all-aluminum, four-piston SSBC caliper is a direct bolt-on for a 1968–1982 Shark. Caliper piston size is similar to factory calipers for excellent brake balance right out of the box. Each caliper comes with the pieces shown for an easy installation. SSBC also supplies the stainless-steel hoses and proper fittings to connect to your original lines. The straight-thread fittings are a nice touch for high-pressure sealing long term. SSBC added a wear indicator squealer to the pads so you know the pads are low before rotor damage occurs. At about $800 an axle the calipers aren't inexpensive but well worth the investment long term and they come in different colors for open-spoke wheels.

CHAPTER 12

WHEELS AND TIRES

For many first-time owners of any car who have aspirations of building the ultimate performance machine, wheels and tires are the first purchase. This may be because you want your performance car to have a certain "look." And that drives the desire to put your hard-earned dollars and soul into it.

Wheels and tires are an important part of your performance Shark's ultimate equation. Developing a good overall plan is especially important because many other factors play into your purchase decision. For example, wheel offset and width depend on how far you go with chassis and body modifications. Brake rotor and caliper choice also play into which wheel works with your application.

Wheels

Wheel choices are mind boggling; seems although everyone has a set for a Chevrolet.

If you are an auto enthusiast you have probably changed wheels whether it was for a performance vehicle or not. So, many of us are aware of the top wheel manufacturers on the market, such as Weld Racing, Enkei, and American Racing. When the time comes to make a decision, you'll find that wheels are like everything else that is manufactured. You get what you pay for and top quality is not "cheap."

That is hard for many to believe. A point comes at which "too cheap" means inferior build quality and materials as well as inexpensive. Offshore wheels are a good example. Some are very good, depending on the country of manufacture. They are considerably

Shark ride height is essential for achieving the best handling characteristics and look. This 1979 sits 1½ inches lower in the front with the tire filling the wheel well just right. Even lowered, this Shark has 4 inches of ground clearance at its closest point. Wheel choice is the toughest part. Each vehicle and color seems to change the perspective. I like these painted five-spoke wheels for their racy but business look and easy-to-clean surfaces plus the 17-inch-diameter wheels helps high-speed cornering with less sidewall flex. This car toured the country attending shows and race events; over all the rough roads the only casualty was the front spoiler. You learn after replacing or repairing the front spoiler to back into parking spaces and approach steep driveways at an angle.

less expensive than the competitor's and it seems unbelievable, there probably is a reason. Do you want your life depending on them?

Wheel Width

For the 1968–1982 Corvettes, the maximum safe backspacing for front and rear is 4¼ inches. Modifications must be made to accommodate wider and deeper-offset wheels, some minor and some major. For example, to gain a mere 1/4-inch-deeper backspacing at the rear wheels, modifications must be made to the parking brake cable bracket on the trailing arms. (I discussed offset trailing arms in Chapter 10.) If those modifications have been made, you can go with a 4¾-inch offset.

Another area of concern as wheel width increases is the rear transverse spring. When assembling the rear suspension, it can be difficult to tighten the rear spring bolt due to tight clearances between the wheel's outer lip and the rear spring. Companies such as Van Steel offer shorter springs and modified trailing arms for this purpose. Now that coil-over shock assemblies are available, it makes more sense to do that conversion to avoid rear spring wheel clearance issues.

Fender flares are another way to get wide rubber under a Shark. Fender flares were the rage for most of the 1970s; but not today, mainly because they required major body surgery. Usually when someone goes for 12- to 13-inch-wide wheels they make the rear a narrowed solid axle with mini-tubs for drag racing. Shark owners who consider resale may find hat the fender flares limit sale potential due to the cost of restoring the fenders to the original look.

Stud Spacing

General Motors and a few other auto manufacturers use the same 5-on-4¾ lug stud pattern and spacing. BMW uses the same 5 x 4¾ pattern with a larger centering hub for broader coverage. The typical wheel manufacturer uses the larger BMW centering hub size to make the system easier to fit large groups of vehicles and save money.

Herein lies the problem with that simple formula: Wheels rotate with fewer anomalies when they are centered on the wheel hub, rather than using studs for the centering process. A few companies saw that problem and came up with hub-centric rings to center the wheels on the hubs properly.

This 1979 Shark has an aftermarket set of wheels replicated to look like the 1996 Corvette Grand Sport. Oddly enough they were originally replicated for a Chevy S-10 pickup or Blazer, the 17 x 8 wheel backspacing was correct, requiring no spacers for fitment. The BFGoodrich T/A KDWS 245/45ZR17 tires are a bit narrower at 9.5 inches tread width.

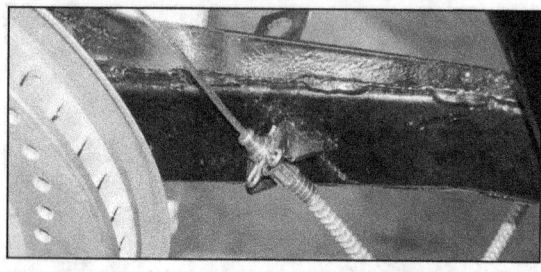

This parking brake cable–mounting tab is welded to the arm on all Sharks. Wheels with 4¼-inch backspacing clear the cable. However, in most cases the cable still runs close to the retaining clip and hits the wheel at 4½ inches of backspacing. The wheel's outer rim or drum position is offset relative to the wheel's center. Due to wheel hub placement, C3 wheels have positive offset with the center section of the wheel closer to the outside of the wheel. You will have to remove the brake cable and use a reciprocating saw to remove the mount.

This trailing arm was modified many years ago. The mounting tab has been welded on the top of the trailing arm. Now a 4¾-inch backspacing wheel can be used and no possible wheel damage will result. This modification allows a backspacing wheel of up to 5¼ inches at the trailing arm. Unfortunately the wheel lip rubs hard on the rear spring. To use a deeper backspacing wheel, companies such as Van Steel offer shorter width springs to accommodate up to the 5¼-inch backspacing wheel.

Another concern is frame rail and inner wheel well rub points after 5¼-inch backspacing is surpassed. Each case is slightly different because of the wheel hub and bearing stack-up. The only way to know for sure is to measure the available backspacing.

WHEELS AND TIRES

Spacer Adapter Ring Installation

1 Check Caliper-to-Wheel Clearance

For this example, there is no way to center the wheel or the spacer via the hub, and the studs are going to be too short. I use these inexpensive aluminum spacers for wheel fitment during chassis setup; they give me an accurate way to check caliper-to-wheel clearance. If you decide to use spacers such as these, please install longer studs to ensure that the wheel lugs have a minimum 1/4 inch of stud sticking through them. The chances are high that a wheel could come off because of the poor fit causing vibration and minimal lug nut thread purchase.

2 Install Wheel Spacers

If necessary this set of hub-centric wheel spacers make good sense with the longer wheel studs for proper wheel retention. The inner portion of the wheel spacer fits tightly over the original wheel hub while the machined outer ring fits into a Chevrolet stud pattern. You need to remove the brake caliper and rotor to install the longer studs, but it is the smart thing to do. Before you buy a set of used wheels, which is most likely why spacers are required, figure out the cost of the spacers and studs. You might find it fiscally smarter to buy new wheels with correct spacing.

3 Install Spacer Rings

These little jewels slip onto the original wheel hub and fit inside an oversized aftermarket wheel hub. They help ensure a smooth ride if the wheels fit tightly on the hubs. On the car, balancing equipment is used to smooth out a rough ride if you let the studs do the centering. Most dedicated tire and alignment shops have put their balancers in mothballs and few techs know how to use them. In extreme cases the tires have to be trued on the car to eliminate vibrations. The bad thing is, if the wheels are removed, all the expensive truing and balancing has to be done again.

Wheel spacers are rarely hub-centric; they are bolted on with lug nuts and center on the studs. These, of course, are the thicker spacers that allow enough room for the lug nuts and still allow the wheel sit flat on the spacer. Hub-centric wheel spacers are available and are considerably higher in cost because of the extra machining work required. If you need a spacer thinner than 1/4 inch, always check the stud length once the spacer and wheel are bolted up to the hub. You should have at least 3/4 inch in the lug nut for safety reasons. Any spacers more than 1/4-inch thick should have longer studs installed in the hubs. The best policy is to avoid spacers if at all possible.

Uni-lug wheels allow more than one wheel stud spacing. These wheels are difficult to install; couple that with larger-than-required center hub diameters and who knows where the wheel sits relative to center. You have to be extra careful with the elongated washers that cover up the large wheel stud holes; misplacing them can cause the wheel to rotate off-center.

This style of wheels are by far the most worrying to me and should be absolutely avoided when it's time to look for a set of new or used wheels. Used wheels can be a good deal if they are not bent; sometimes it is not obvious until the wheel is spun on a wheel balancer. If the wheels are inexpensive enough it may be worth chancing it. I prefer to negotiate after visiting the closest tire store to have the wheels in question spun on a balancer. Quite possibly the seller does not know the wheels are bent, so keep that in mind when considering used wheels.

Today there are usually numerous wheel repair shops in most major cities that straighten and weld broken wheels. I do not like the thought of driving at high speeds knowing a crack was welded up and then machined. The theory is good, but I would feel better possibly using one on a grocery getter, not my performance car. It really does not take much to

CHAPTER 12

bump and bend a wheel, so some minor straightening would not worry me. It's just the thought of a major reconstruction of the wheel that turns me off.

Wheel Diameter

Of course the latest trend is rubber bands on the tallest wheels you can possibly get. Many want the later 19-inch-and-larger-diameter wheels because they look "cool." The idea behind the larger diameter was to limit tire sidewall height and the resulting flex that occurs with the old-school 15-inch wheels.

That makes sense for a serious racer who wants the least amount of tire sidewall flex; street-driven vehicles need to compromise. As the wheel diameter increases and the tire sidewall decreases, so does ride quality. The 18-inch-diameter wheels for the Shark are the limit for me: they won't beat you up on rough road surfaces and still provide minimal sidewall flex and great handling capabilities.

By now you have most likely figured out that any and all performance modifications should be a balance of what works for both daily driving and a weekend performance event.

Lug Nuts

You have many choices when it comes to lug nuts: your main concern is that you use 7/16-20 thread nuts. Most aftermarket wheels use lugs with sleeves that go into the wheel's hub (and always a washer) to avoid gouging the wheel. Some aftermarket and all factory wheels use tapered seats to firmly hold onto the wheel; make sure you have the recommended lugs for your wheels. I look for the tapered-seat-lug wheels because of how easy they are to install and well they hold on to the wheel. A couple of pages back I mentioned hub-centric wheel benefits. Tapered-seat lugs are the best for allowing the wheel to center on the hub. This is important if you plan on any true high-speed driving.

Out-of-balance wheels and tires are bad on your suspension and chassis in general.

Chrome-plated lugs may look nice as long as you rarely remove them; each time the socket hammers on the sides of the lug the chrome begins to chip away. Race cars typically don't have pretty wheels or lug nuts; they are constantly removing them and it shows.

Gorilla Automotive has stainless-steel lugs that can take a beating and maintain a clean appearance. I have two sets: one for the street and one for race day to limit the amount of time the pretty lugs are removed.

Race lugs should have open ends to allow the race inspector to see that the studs are at the end of the lug nut. This is for your safety and the others around you. Always look over the lugs and studs for damage. I also require all the guys in the shop use a torque wrench to tighten lugs.

Hammering the lugs on with a large impact takes a toll on the lugs and studs; your brake rotors are also abused from the unequal pressure. Some may say, Well look at NASCAR! They hammer the wheels on as quickly as possible without even using the star pattern. They are using steel wheels with massive brake rotors and closely regulated air pressure on their impact tools.

The most important part is keeping the studs safe from stretching and the thread damage that can occur from over-tightening the lugs. You may be the one on the side of the road trying to loosen a stubborn lug nut one day; proper torquing makes an unhappy situation a bit better when the wheels come loose without using the biggest cheater bar you can find.

Wheel Fitment

Verifying fitment is an important part of the wheel selection process. I mentioned backspacing and the limitations of the Shark chassis. You also need to consider that the tires bulge beyond the wheel's inner or outermost edges. Brake calipers can also get in the way because they protrude beyond the outer edge of the wheel's mounting hub. Increasing the wheel's diameter beyond 15 inches usually helps caliper clearance for bolt-on aftermarket brake calipers. Many wheel companies now have templates that you can construct out of cardboard to check wheel clearance.

Wheel Upkeep

Now that you know what to look for on the mechanical side, the aesthetics come into play. That may seem easy enough: the wheel looks good and that's all that matters. You really should consider upkeep too, or those shiny wheels may be in rough shape before you ever get to drive the project on the street.

TECH TIP — Wheel Stud Installation

Replacing wheel studs is smart. After all, who knows how many times they have been hammered on with a big impact wrench? The newest Shark is 31 years old. How many times have the wheels been off? Over time the wheel studs get stretched and the threads become rolled over from numerous visits to tire shops. Changing them at all four wheel hubs is standard practice in my shop whether the Corvette sees Saturday night cruising or frequent weekends at the track.

Chances are you may need to replace the studs anyway for your local race sanctioning body. Make sure you read the rule book and understand what they want before making the change. Repeated stud changes are not good either: the stud becomes loose in the hub, making it difficult to tighten properly. ■

WHEELS AND TIRES

When wheel spacers approach 3/4 inch or more thickness, they are available to bolt to your existing wheel hubs using the factory studs, and then the wheel is placed onto studs that are in the wheel spacer. You must have machined areas in your wheels to have clearance for the existing studs and lugs. They also come in hub-centric versions for the best possible wheel balancing. These safely bolt your wheels on; however, they place more load on the wheel bearings with the added offset. The load is placed farther away from the wheel's center, particularly in later-model vehicles, but the bearing size is increased to accommodate the changes.

The owner of this vehicle ordered a set of wheels before the brake decision was made. I used this cardboard template to make sure the 13-inch rotor and caliper clear the 17-inch wheel. Moving the cardboard template around the rotor and caliper should leave a minimum .125 inch clearance between the caliper and inner wheel drum. Companies such as Baer Brakes have templates available to print out to check fitment. I did mine the old-fashioned way: I cut a piece of cardboard to fit inside the wheel and transferred it to the template used against the wheel hub. I went all the way to the wheel's outer edge so I could rotate the template with the wheel and check the entire circumference for any possible clearance issues.

The template was used because I needed to verify that the caliper did not have enough clearance to the wheel. Most brake manufacturers recommend at least 1/8 inch of clearance at all points from the wheel. If you change your brakes to a floating-caliper system, you must recheck the fitment of the caliper with new pads. This setup may take up more room and not fit under the wheels. When it's time to service the brakes you may discover that the wheel doesn't turn. I install two or three flat washers on the studs if I think the caliper is too close. Then I remove the washers one at a time until I know the caliper isn't gouged from the wheel; I can then use the appropriate thickness spacer.

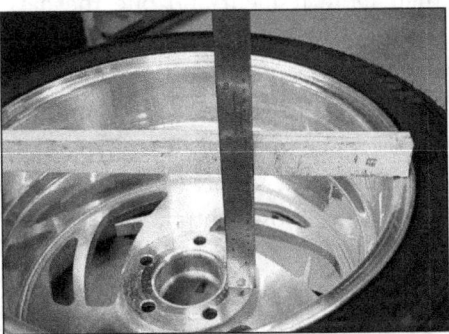

This is how wheel manufacturers measure wheel backspacing: place a flat object across the wheel's inside lip. I recommend removing the wheels from their packaging as soon as possible after receiving them and checking backspacing. More than once I have received wheels with different backspacing, always a minor discrepancy. However, it's too late to call after weeks or months have passed. Look the wheels over and handle the return immediately.

You need to know what the absolute outside of the tire sidewall is for an accurate clearance check. There can be a significant difference in the dimension depending on tire tread width versus wheel width, especially on tall-sidewall tires. As the wheels turn they can hit at numerous places and rub the sidewalls on the frame rail. The smart move is to find a wheel with the backspacing you need, mount a tire, and see how it all works.

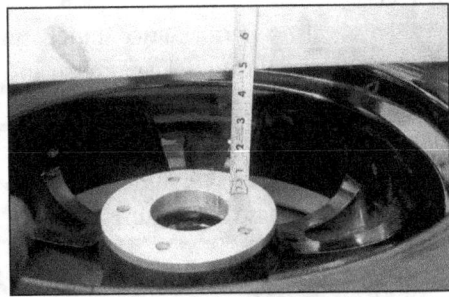

A wheel spacer has been installed. My straightedge is placed on the outer portion of the tire's sidewall for the ultimate backspacing measurement check. This aftermarket wheel just fits on the 1973 Shark. At 4¹¹⁄₁₆ inches of backspacing, there is just enough room to make it work with Shark chassis components. This 1973 Shark has coil-overs on the rear, and the parking brake cable mounts have been moved to the top of the trailing arm. This allows at least 1/8 inch clearance at all points.

Chrome-plated steel wheels rust no matter how well you take care of them. Chrome-plated aluminum, including black chrome, also corrodes over time. Raw aluminum is the easiest to take care of as long as you like the natural aluminum look that darkens as it ages. Polished aluminum is hard to take care of, and it requires constant polishing to keep up the luster. Clear-coated aluminum is typically easy maintenance, but it too has corrosion issues.

Wheel nicks and minor bumps undermine the chrome and whatever coating is applied, and eventually water makes its way in and rust/corrosion appears. The best policy is to buy what you like and take great care of them.

I have made a habit of removing the wheels on my personal car every time I change the oil. I wash the inside of the wheels to limit the brake dust's corrosive effects. After a good washing I apply a couple coats of wax to keep as much of the dust from adhering as possible. After implementing this policy, it requires little effort to clean the wheels.

This is also a performance thing. The slick inner wheel drums keep grease and dirt from sticking to them and the wheel balance is not affected. I avoid complex wheels with small crevices and difficult-to-reach areas that require plenty of extra time cleaning.

Tires

Wheels are important, but tires are everything when it comes to performance. What you run into is the overwhelming amount of available tires at many different prices.

Heat and G-Force Codes

Different diameters and widths are available to fit in the wheel well and be able to traverse bumps and turn the wheels without hitting the inner fender liners. Tire size matters more today than it used to. As the wheel diameters increase, tire choices become fewer for the 15- and 16-inch-diameter wheels. It's even getting difficult to find many sizes for 17-inch-diameter tires. That really good deal on a set of old-school wheels may not look so good when you're ready to buy the tires. You also need to understand the tire coding and the tires' capabilities.

The manufacturers also know that those long smoky burnouts can take out a set of rear tires at one event. Tire coding is used to give you an idea of the operating parameters of the particular tire you bought. For example, alpha codes ABC are used to inform you of the tire's capability to withstand heat at a particular speed range.

Temperature code A denotes the tire's capability to withstand speeds over 115 mph without heat buildup issues.

Code B keeps you in the 85- to 115-mph range at safe tire temperatures.

Code C temperature limits you to 85 mph and below. True performance tires typically do not have tread life warranties because the rubber compounds are used for better traction.

The traction codes are a suggestion of how well the tires grip the roadway. There are many variables to consider on the traction issue; pavement composition is one of the main variables.

Alpha codes are also used for the traction figures that measure the g-forces that the tire withstands under controlled testing. AA is the best, measuring at 0.54 and above on asphalt; the same tire has a 0.41 g-force rating on concrete. Alphas A, B, and C have lower g-force ratings. C has less than 0.38 on asphalt and 0.26 on concrete. My experience is the lower the g-force ratings, the longer the tread wear due to a really hard tire compound. The most important of all the codes or numbers is the speed rating if you plan on doing any real high-speed straightaways on road courses. Code V is for up to 149 mph, Z is for 149 mph, and Y is for the 200-mph club. If you take a cross section of one size of available performance tires, here is what you see. A Goodyear Eagle F1 GS-D3 maximum performance summer tire, for example, has a 280 tread wear, AA temperature, and an A traction rating.

A Michelin Pilot Sport PS2 maximum performance summer tire has the same traction and temperature with a lower 220 treadwear.

The Kumho Ecsta 4X ultra-high-performance all-season tire has the same traction and temperature ratings as the Michelin and Goodyear at almost double the tread life at 420. From experience I know that the Kumho may have longer tread life, but traction is not as good even though it has the AA rating.

The harder compound used to keep the tires around longer tends to make then more resilient and bite the pavement less. You should take your Shark to the road course to find the best tire for you. I tend to go for the best tires and brakes for competition. The drivetrain is important, but slippery tires may seem fun until you lose control.

Track/Competition Tires

BFGoodrich has some of my favorite street/track competition tires for the dollar as long as caution is used when driving in wet weather. Combine the wide width of the competition tires with limited water channels to relieve water pressure under the tire and around you go. They do a great job for the money with three choices for the serious street and weekend racer.

The g-Force Rival series has some tread to keep you going when some water is on the pavement. The g-Force R1 and R1S are better for the track and very limited everyday commuting unless the roads are dry. The g-Force T/A Drag Radial does a great job at the drag strip, and if you're careful you can drive your racer back and forth to work. One thing that I have noticed is these BFGoodrich tires are much better when they are new; after months of sitting around they become hard and traction suffers.

For those of you who are really serious about the best possible tire traction, Michelin Sport Cup tires are the ultimate. Their treadwear rating of 80 says it all: they stick well and can handle the temperature. Their grooved footprint lets you run in light rain safely. Most of us would never use these tires to their limit, especially on a factory Shark chassis. If you have gone the aftermarket purpose-built chassis route, these tires complement the handling.

I go with the Michelin Pilot Sport A/S for all-around performance and the occasional road course or autocrossing events.

However, before you buy a set go visit a local driving school and thoroughly understand how to drive, or you are spending dollars you really don't have to.

Tire Interference

The simple facts are that the overall tire diameter cannot exceed 25.75 inches and 10 inches wide or you have issues during turning. The fender outer lip hits or rubs on the frame rail at the rear of the front wheel. You have to modify the fender lip and limit the turning radius, which is not stellar now. Don't forget about trailing arm interference at the rear, 10 inches maximum here too. Always check for tire clearance with the wheel at ride height and when bottomed out or you may ruin an expensive set of tires.

Tire Pressure

All tires need valve stems and they are more important than many think. Every time the tires are replaced the valve stems should be too due to rubber degradation. Check the tire manufacturer's recommended pressures: some rubber valve stems do not meet this requirement, which is why I use metal valve stems. Rubber valve stems are cheap, and metal stems are slightly more expensive. Why chance the loss of a tire over a valve stem? I know we should all know this, but sometimes I find that tire shops do not routinely replace the stems. It's up to you to make sure they do. In the performance world, tire pressure is everything to maximize traction and handling. Checking tire pressure regularly is the key to good handling and tire life. The other important part of the equation is a good tire pressure gauge; many are available that vary widely in accuracy. Spend the extra dollars and get a good gauge and take care of it.

A couple of general rules: Don't go below the tire manufacturer's recommended lowest pressure, and always remember that tire pressures increase as the temperature increases. Low tire pressures create more heat as the sidewalls of the tire squirm around, causing friction and high-heat buildup. If you run any tire low on pressure, always check the sidewall for damage. Often you can see a ring around the middle of the tire's outer sidewall where the damage occurred. Tires with sidewall damage have sudden major blow-outs and the tire shreds.

Tire Balancing

Balancing a tire is simple but the technician must have the proper training. First, you need to know that there are two basic balancing procedures: static and dynamic.

Static balancing is the simpler; a wheel weight is placed on the light side of the tire, which worked fine for 3- to 4-inch-wide tires. As tire width increased, dynamic tire balancing was developed to balance the tire on the inside and outside of the wheel/tire assembly. Static-balanced wide-wheel/tire assemblies had a tendency to cause steering wheel oscillations as speed increased. The steering wheel moves back and forth like a fish nibbling on a line, which is why it is often called steering wheel nibble.

Dynamic balancing took the nibble away by placing weights on the inside and outside of the wheel. You may get your wheels dynamically balanced and find out that they only have one wheel weight on the inside or outside. That means the tires were very close to perfect balance, requiring only a minor bit of weight. High-end tires are apt to be this way, whereas inexpensive tires may require massive amounts of weight to balance.

The latest tire balancers let the operator choose between balancing methods, including where the weights are placed. Let's say you decide to use stick-on weights for the outside of the tire balance point. The balancer has a measuring device and you can place it where the weights are to be installed. This was a major breakthrough: now you can use stick-on weights accurately and have a dynamically balanced wheel/tire assembly.

Every wheel balancer has a calibration setup procedure to be used often. During my time on the balancer I calibrated after every 10 hours of operation per the manufacturer's recommendation. If you find that you have no success with tire balancing, it's probably best to move on to another shop.

If you have a nibble at the steering wheel and only one weight on the inside or outside, you found the problem. Cheap tires are difficult to balance

CHAPTER 12

because their casings are not as true as a quality tire. As the tire sidewall decreases so does ride quality, while cornering improves. Bouncing tires are rough on the suspension and shock absorbers from the rapid oscillations.

The simple clip-on wheel balance weight does not usually work and few shops want to look at them. Many aftermarket wheels do not have a lip suitable for the clip-on wheel weights. If there is a shop that uses clip-on weights, that is the best possible place to have the tire/wheel balanced.

Coated clip-on weights should be used on any alloy wheel to prevent corrosion and/or clear coat damage. If they use clip-on weights on the inside, they should also be coated to prevent wheel damage. That is a great question to ask when you begin the search for a reputable shop to do your tire work. If they don't know about coated wheel weights, I would be concerned about their commitment to quality. Coated clip-on wheel weights have been around for many years and by now all shops have access to them. They do cost a bit more.

Tire Wear

Tire wear can occur from many factors: incorrect alignment, worn shock absorbers, and worn suspension components (which affect alignment). Tires that wear smooth on the inside or outside have camber alignment issues. If the tires are wearing with rough irregular edges on the inside or out, there is a toe-in or -out problem.

Tires with scoops of rubber missing are bouncing on the pavement from worn shocks or an imbalance condition.

Wear at the center only is due to high air pressure or a tire that is too wide for the wheel.

Wear on both outer edges is due to low air pressure or a tire that is too narrow for the wheel.

You can expect to have smooth tire wear on the outside of the front tires from cornering. As positive caster increases, so does the wear on the outer edge of the tires. There is no way to prevent it except to avoid turning. Keep this in mind with your tire choice: Unequal wheel sizes front-to-back do not allow tire rotation, and tire life is shorter. Tire manufacturers have caught on to this situation and mention in their warranty that vehicles with two different-diameter or -width tires have a shorter warranty period concerning tire wear.

If possible I rotate my tires at every other oil change (7,500 to 10,000 miles) to keep the tire warranty in force. Rotating the tires flattens out the wear that occurs on the front tires and keeps them alive a bit longer.

Tire wear illustrations like these can point you in the right direction when troubleshooting suspension and steering issues. Before spending your hard-earned money on new rubber look over your tires carefully; they tell you the condition of your chassis. Wear on the outside of the tire tread indicates low pressure while inside wear indicates excessively high pressure. Wear on the inner or outer edges tells you there is excessive camber, toe-in, or toe-out issues. Feathering at the edges is pointing to a toe-in or toe-out problem. Bald spots denote a bad shock or out-of-balance tire, which you should have felt bouncing on the highway at speed.

CHAPTER 13

INTERIOR UPGRADES

When you discuss performance, few people think about their vehicle's interior. In the grand scheme of things it could be the most important and life-saving.

The most obvious item is seat belts to keep your backside in place during high-speed cornering. Installing good, high-quality seat belts with proper mounting is also very important.

Then, you need to consider seating to make sure you have the most advantageous positioning to operate the steering, transmission, and engine controls.

Highly visible gauges are important to help avoid engine and drivetrain damage, along with a reliable tachometer for those perfectly timed up or downshifts.

You might even consider some heat-proofing materials for driver comfort in the floorpan area. I'm not going to cover a killer sound system: the exhaust note should be more than adequate to replace the tunes.

Seat Belts

The 1968–1974 Sharks had fiberglass floorboards, then steel replaced the fiberglass. General Motors was concerned about burning fiberglass with the catalytic converters that were introduced in 1975. Lap seat belts were attached through the fiberglass floor to reinforcements riveted to the fiberglass floorpan, spreading the load out to better handle the high g-forces that occur during a crash. Shoulder belts were finally integrated with the lap belts in 1974; before that you fumbled around with latching two belts. Convertible shoulder belts were also optional until 1974.

The 1968–1974 Shark's original shoulder belt mounting points are not very good, even though they have reinforcement plates. Keep in mind that seat belts were in their infancy during the Shark era, and are too old to be safe by today's standards.

This Shark Bar is an alternative to shoulder seat belt installation. The bar is secured to the original GM shoulder belt harness retractor and the mount for the convertible top side hinge. The twin shoulder belts place the driver firmly in the seat with less chance of losing control during high-speed cornering. This bar does not qualify as a roll bar because it is only for secure seat belt mounting at the shoulder belts. For true safety in a rollover collision the bar must be mounted onto the chassis frame rail. The bar also requires at least two other mounting points far enough away to triangulate the load during a rollover.

Remember, you need the belts to keep you firmly in place during driving events or just some plain fun high-speed cornering. You need to focus on the driving chores, not holding on for dear life as you roll through a corner.

Most importantly, you need to be in the cockpit during a crash. I know some say, "Well, if they just were not in the cockpit they might have survived." All too often occupants are ejected from the vehicle and in some cases run over by their own car. I was wearing seat belts before it became mandatory due to my driving style and the slick seat

C3 CORVETTE: HOW TO BUILD AND MODIFY 1968–1982

preservatives causing you to slide all over the place. The seat preservatives are different, the seat belts are made better, and I'm still buckling them.

If you do not plan on road racing, autocrossing, or drag racing, you should at least look at replacing the existing belts or adding shoulder belts if they are not in place already. After all, your original seat belts are a minimum of 30 years old with weakened webbing and stitching.

Also, look at all the seat-belt mounting points and reinforcements before putting your trust in the belts. The body-mount cushions on the 1968–1974 Sharks should be checked and replaced if they are not in like-new condition. The 1968–1969 Sharks use a stout steel cable to connect the center seat belts to the chassis. The 1968–1974 Sharks also have a cable reinforcing the outer lap seat-belt mounting point.

Mounting Alternative

Vetteworks offers a Sharkbar series 3R rollbar-style harness for 1968–1975 convertibles. The rollbar-style harness bar is an enhanced shoulder belt mounting device using the original seat belt and a rear pillar mounting point. The most important attribute is that the bar allows the use of race-style shoulder belts and locates them at the optimum location for your safety.

This bar is not a legal rollbar for NHRA (National Hot Rod Association), SSCA (Simulated Sports Car Association), or NASA (National Auto Sport Association) participation; this is why it is important to research the info carefully before making any decision. The fact that the rollbar does not mount to the frame and has no front or rear bracing means it will not be a good situation in a rollover.

If you want to compete on any level, from a fun drag race event to sanctioned race events, need to know the safety regulations. For example, drag race safety inspectors limit your elapsed time and MPH if you have a convertible Shark without a rollbar. As speed increases, so do the number of safety requirements and the required inspections each time an event is attended.

Before you begin any rollbar or seat-belt modifications look into the safety requirements for your particular event. Remember, the inspectors are trying to provide a safe environment for all of those who participate; they are not picking on you. They are well versed in the knowledge of what it takes to keep you safe during the unthinkable. I always consider the others who lost their lives and what they have brought to the sport. Their ultimate sacrifice has made all racing events safer.

Competition Seat Belts

Seat belts used for competition have at least five mounting points, with the best having six mounting points. Having two shoulder belts keeps you firmly planted in the seat, and the use of the crotch or anti-submarine belt prevents you from sliding out from under the belts. An additional anti-submarine belt is used to capture your lower body at both legs to secure you tightly into the seat.

The belts are 3 inches wide, except the anti-submarine belts, which are 2 inches wide and should be certified by the SFI Foundation, Inc. There are two locking systems: a simple lever style or a cam lock similar to your everyday driver vehicle's seat belt.

The lever style costs less, but the downside is you have to fumble with five or six belts, putting them on the retaining post and then flipping the lever.

The cam lock allows you to slip each belt into one central latch, making it easier to operate. When you unlock the seat belts, a quick twist releases all the belts.

Shoulder belts can be secured at the rollbar by wrapping them around the bar, which is the most common for the street/strip environment. Bolt or snap-in seat belts are typically used for the lap and anti-submarine belt's retention at the existing seat-belt mounting points.

You may eliminate the factory belts and install race belts or add race belts to the factory belts at the same mounting points. This allows you to use the factory seat belts for everyday use and race belts at the track. Make sure you tighten the seat belts as the manufacturer recommends at each attaching point.

I know this sounds obvious, but please be aware of any edges that may cut or fray the seat belt. Once the webbing has been compromised it should be replaced. The belts are only as good as the installer and the mounts.

The use of a bar that allows shoulder belts is the minimum requirement for a street-driven Shark; the ultimate performance Shark should sport a minimum four-point rollbar with a shoulder belt bar. Most importantly, use the seat belts even for a short trip, it may save your life.

Rollbars

Ultimately, a good set of belts and a minimum four-point rollbar is the best choice if you really plan on pushing the envelope. The rollbar is an integral part of any four- or five-point seat-belt installation. True race shoulder harness seat belts have a strap over each shoulder that is securely mounted. The lap belts are wider to apply more surface area to your abdomen. A fifth belt is used as an anti-submarine device to keep you from sliding out and under the other four belts.

None of the belts do any good if they are not securely mounted. Worse yet, having one mounted better than the other could cause serious bodily harm,

INTERIOR UPGRADES

Air Conditioning

The true performance Shark builder out for every available ounce of power most likely does not consider A/C important. But it makes sense for Shark owners who end up on trips or tours with other performance vehicles. After long hours on the highway, comfort is important. Many opt for air-conditioning to make those long hours on the road less tiring, and it works even at the performance level. I build very few street/track cars that do not have A/C; after all, you just turn the switch off while you are competing.

An aftermarket A/C system has less weight and much greater efficiency than original factory units. Aftermarket A/C systems also use a low-drag A/C compressor, saving you fuel with very low-horsepower requirements to operate. Installing an aftermarket A/C system is not that difficult; it takes two to three days for the first-time installer.

Vintage Air systems are popular for ease of installation and efficiency. The kits are complete; the only thing to add is the refrigerant and possibly an A/C condenser fan to help cool the refrigerant during long idle periods. Your existing controls are modified to use with the new A/C system.

Another important aspect of the install is that Vintage Air units are an all-in-one assembly with heat and defrost. When defrost is selected, cold air is available to speed the process on warm days; much nicer than the original defrost system. Even the factory-air Sharks do not have this feature.

A Vintage Air aftermarket A/C system is installed on this 1968 model. It receives the defroster duct assembly. This Gen IV kit has it all (defroster, heater, and A/C) in one package. Remove the passenger-side map pocket and center gauge cluster to access the firewall and install the evaporator assembly. Follow the instructions carefully, especially about handling the evaporator unit around the electronic mode door actuators. Electronic motors control airflow and come close to the underside of the firewall/cowl during evaporator installation.

The Vintage Air kit includes a new control panel plate that modifies your existing control assembly. The use of electronic actuators and sensors makes the installation simple; it is much easier to install the console plate compared to the original equipment cables and hoses. You are required to disassemble your existing controller to make the changes (complete instructions for this complex original control assembly are included). Do not deviate from the instructions as to how the wiring should be connected directly to the battery.

or death, if they all let go. This is your life: you can enjoy it to the fullest with the knowledge that the belts are properly installed per the manufacturer's recommendations. You should also heed their replacement warnings, such as the webbing weakening in factory belts over time.

Another significant advantage when installing a four-point rollbar is rear-frame rigidity. The rear kick-up sections of the chassis are the weak points, allowing the frame to flex over almost any road surface. If you go to a six-point rollbar and tie the front section of the frame together with the rear chassis, rigidity is greatly enhanced. So much so that your choice of chassis suspension components should be considered to utilize the increased rigidity of the frame assembly.

The main concern is mounting the rollbar to the frame, not the body. The real trick is finding suitable mounting points for the seat belts on the rollbar assembly.

The problem with any rollbar is the lack of aftermarket availability. A few companies make Shark rollbars, but it is a very limited selection. Over many years of working solely with Corvettes, many of them Sharks, I have seen very few with any race-quality rollbars. I have never seen one in a T-top coupe and only a few convertibles have sported a rollbar.

Of course true race Sharks have rollbars, but few are driven on the street, probably due to their value. I have seen faux rollbars mounted to the fiberglass floor with self-tapping screws, and the occasional two-point mounted bar. My opinion of the faux rollbars? Chances are good that they will do more harm than good in a crash. The heavy metal will be ripped loose in a crash, and you will become tangled in the mess. The moral is, either spend the money wisely and do it right, or don't do it at all. Having a rollbar for show may cost you everything.

Autopower

Autopower performance driving equipment has one of the best selections of rollbars for a Shark coupe with and without the all-important shoulder belt bar. The shoulder belt horizontal bar is installed for correct shoulder belt installation; not all rollbars have this feature but they are highly recommended for race environments. Their product is a true race bar with four to six welded-in or bolted mounting points to the chassis for your safety.

Other options for their four- or six-point rollbar include an adjustable seat brace to keep the back of the seat from breaking rearward and the possible loss of vehicle control. They say specifically that they do have a street bar to give your car a true performance look and style; this bar, properly installed, is good for a rollover event but it's certainly not their best piece. You have to make the decision to look racy or truly be safe and racy.

Auto Weld

Auto Weld is another option for a ready-to-install rollbar and/or cage with many possible options. They start with a 4-point bar and go up to a 14-point cage assembly. They have a number of rollbar configurations that are ready to go. The tough part is you have to do some welding and some cutting of your floorpan for the installation. Their selection of four-point mounting rollbars makes the most sense for the do-it-yourselfer. Keep in mind that this is not going to be as easy as placing the rollbar in the car and doing some welding. Each car is different to some degree, and it requires patience and some ingenuity to make sure the installation goes well. Your life can be lost if you do not do the installation as intended by the manufacturer.

Roll Cages

The ultimate rollbar has 8 to 14 mounting points tying the frame at the front and rear to the roll cage with side bars to protect you in a side crash. Many purpose-built roll cages have removable side bars to aid in entry and limit occupant space.

Constructing a roll cage requires someone well versed in tubing requirements and a certified welder. Few Shark owners go this route because of the complexity of the project and the comfort-limiting factors. The tough part is that the roll cage requires the complete disassembly of the interior, including the dash pieces, to configure the tubes going through the firewall.

The best policy? If this is what you want, find a race shop to build the cage for the race sanctioning body that you plan on competing with. Rollbar or cage tubing is configured on the weight and use of each vehicle; this is why this should not be attempted at home. The race shop certifies the work and periodically requires inspections and recertifying to ensure your safety.

Seating

Proper seating position is as important as strapping yourself into the seats correctly. Bolsters should be strategically placed at the mid-section and thigh area to keep you firmly planted in the seat. Finding the correct seat is related to how your back and backside feel in the seat. Seat foam density requirements and thickness depends on how radical you went with the suspension stiffness.

Procar, Corbeau, and Sparco have some reasonably priced universal fit seats. Recaro manufactures an excellent seat, but the cost is significantly higher than the others. The majority of seat manufacturers have good information on their websites explaining seat dimensions.

Seat width is usually not an area of concern. However, placing the seat more than a couple of inches above the floor

INTERIOR UPGRADES

Many gauge options are available. Here custom gauge faces were made and the original speedometer and tachometer movements were used. I choose the 140-mph speedo face to replace the original 85-mph unit. Instrument restoration shops, such as Southern Electronics, can alter the faces for your application. They can give you a 200-mph speedo or one that increases your tachometer's redline. It is a good idea to listen to what they have to say about the changes and how they affect the numbering; for instance with a 200-mph speedo the numbers are small and very close together.

Autometer gauges deliver a true race car look and extreme accuracy. These gauges were installed into this original 1968–1976 center gauge cluster. Any 2 1/16-inch-diameter gauge fits into the center gauge cluster, including later 1977–1982 plastic center gauge cluster assemblies. The back of the gauges comes close to the defroster ductwork, especially with factory-air Sharks. Trimming the gauge-mounting studs provides just enough room for it all to work. If you decide on mechanical gauges 90-degree fittings must be used to plumb the oil pressure gauge.

can be a problem for anyone who is 6 feet and taller. General Motors modified the floorpan of the 1981–1982 Sharks to allow use of a power seat track assembly.

Sparco, Cipher Auto, Wedge Engineering, and Procar offer bolt-in seat tracks that are manually adjustable for the Shark. These are ready-to-go seat mounts for any of the universal seats available. Some use the original Shark Corvette seat tracks with an adapter track; others are straight bolt-on to your universal seats.

Make sure the seats are securely mounted to the floor. Reinforcements are required on the underside of the floor for 1968–1974 Sharks with universal seats that are to be mounted to fiberglass floorpans.

One well-thought-out item is that the majority of universal seats have places for the shoulder belts to be placed through the seat backs for optimum placement of the belts. The taller seat backs support your head in the event of a collision, especially any rear-end hit.

Lightweight seats also have wings on both sides at the upper seat back area to protect your head from a side collision.

They look good and come in just about any color.

Gauges

Monitoring your engine functions, RPM, and MPH are very important in the performance world. Shark Corvettes have a bit of an advantage from the start in the performance category with a complete set of decent-looking gauges from the factory. At least the most important gauges are there from the beginning and relatively easy-to-read placement.

Mechanical tachometers were used until 1974, and oil pressure gauges were also mechanical until 1973. The 160-mph speedometers were factory equipment until 1978; for a few years they dropped to 140 mph. In 1980, the Feds required 85-mph speedometers.

The large, almost 360-degree-sweep round speedometer and tachometer really looked race orientated until 1978, when a rectangular look was introduced. The entire Shark run had center–console mounted gauges that were informative.

The 90-degree sweep on the small gauges was not very accurate. The gauges available today are much more accurate and easy to read, especially when you opt for the 360-degree-sweep gauges.

In the past, true performance drivers rarely considered using any electrical gauges; mechanical was the way to go. Not so today, especially if you have a street/strip or weekend warrior project; electronic gauges are the most commonly used. They are more flexible during installation, with very few restrictions on placement or wiring concerns. Electronic components are more reliable, so it makes sense to use them for your project.

There are differences in electronic gauges. For example, Autometer has electronic gauges available using digitally controlled stepper motors that receive a signal from solid-state sensors.

Electronic gauges use 5-volt reference current with an internal voltage regulator for much greater accuracy. The digital gauges can be determined easily by the three wires required to operate them. The cost is higher, but well worth it, if accuracy is important to you. The cost to replace an engine is much higher than a good-quality oil or water temperature gauge.

Electronic gauges have single wires to transmit the varying resistance back to the gauge, which is how the original Shark electronic gauges operated. These work well, but they are susceptible to voltage variations. Another cost factor is the gauge sweep; 90 degrees is typical but 360-degree gauges space out the numerals and require more movement, increasing accuracy. The question is, should you spend the money to restore the original gauges that had moderate accuracy at best or replace them? Restoring the originals is not cheap if done professionally. Figure approximately $300 for the small gauges and add another $300 for the speedometer and tachometer.

Some choose to replace the small gauges, keeping the speedo and tach for their "look." All Sharks have 2-inch round gauges in the center console; fitting aftermarket gauges into them is not that difficult. The 1977–1982 Sharks have plastic center gauge cluster bezels that fit replacement gauges better than the pot metal bezel-type on early Sharks.

Over the years I have installed aftermarket gauges in numerous Sharks using mainly electronic gauges early on. Today many speed shop suppliers such as Summit Racing have gauge packs with all the gauges in one kit, which saves you a few dollars. The wiring is not too difficult with the majority of it already in place in the GM harness. Electronic stepper motor gauges have their own harness for each gauge, actually making it easier to install.

One thing to remember: using a 30-plus-year-old dash main harness to connect the new gauges could leave you with some inaccurate gauges. All electronic gauges use a resistance sensor to operate the gauge because as wiring ages so does the resistance, skewing the gauges' accuracy. Before you decide to use that old wiring you might want to do some resistance tests from the sensor to the gauge.

Steering Wheels

While it may seem that a steering wheel is not a performance item but more of an aesthetics issue, it's not. You must have a comfortable grip on the wheel at all times. Early Shark steering wheels were not that great as far as ergonomics are concerned: the thin wheel had grip issues for anyone with moderate to large hands. By 1977 General Motors had a decent wheel with a leather covering to hold on to. In 1976, Corvettes received a Vega steering wheel, which was not that bad as far as grip is concerned. But the stigma of it being from a Vega hurt its reputation.

The great thing is, just about any steering wheel bolts to the six-screw hub on the Shark's steering shaft hub. Early Shark steering wheels have the vertical spoke overlapping the horizontal spokes, requiring a lower area in the hub so the wheel sits flat. On a positive note, the majority of aftermarket steering wheels have a flat surface so replacing the wheel is a simple process.

Three-spoke wheels make the most sense with plenty of rigidity and easy-to-spot wheel position. Make sure you can comfortably grip the steering wheel for turning maneuvers. Looking cool is one thing; but no one wants to lose control because they couldn't hold on to the wheel.

Racers spend many hours making sure they are comfortable in their seat and can hold on to the steering wheel under high-g-force conditions. For instance, racers mark where the steering wheel is at when the wheels are pointed straight ahead to determine if they have had an alignment issue from an on-track incident. The same goes for your project: any steering wheel variation off-center is easily spotted with a three-spoke steering wheel.

Steering Wheel Removal

1 Remove Horn Switch, Spacer Ring and Shims

Many Sharks have tilt and telescoping steering columns, which have some special requirements during steering wheel removal. Three Phillips-head screws hold the horn switch to the spacer ring. Shims allow clearance for the telescopic locking ring, and these provide just enough clearance for the lock ring to turn without hitting the spacer ring. The shims are used so that the lock ring does not rub on the horn switch side. Typically all you do is note the shims and reinstall them in the same manner and check for binding. All major Corvette suppliers have shims, spacers, and screws.

2 Remove Lock Ring

Remove the two Phillips-head screws holding the lock ring to the telescopic lock ring inner screw. To remove the lock ring inner screw turn counterclockwise. For reassembly it may take a little practice to hit the correct adjustment of the inner screw and the outer lock ring. I run the inner screw in until it is tight with a screwdriver then place the lock ring tab in the middle of the travel available. When the adjustment is correct you are not able to telescope the wheel when the lock ring is full left; it should move easily when the lock ring is full right.

3 Remove Steering Wheel

Now the easy part. To remove the steering wheel, remove the six Phillips-head screws. Non-telescopic steering columns simply require horn switch removal. The six-hole steering wheel mount is how the majority of aftermarket steering wheels are held in place. Some do not have the additional six holes for the horn switch so make sure you know which you need. Companies such as Mid America Motorworks have specific steering wheels that are direct fit in many different styles.

Pedal Pads

For many years all you had available were rubber pedal pads; for years the only metal pedal pads available resembled a bare foot for the accelerator. Now you have race-bred metal pedal pads to keep your racing footwear where they should be: firmly planted on the brakes, clutch, or accelerator. Typically, aluminum is formed into the correct shape and raised areas are created to allow the best possible grip. The improved grip helps heel-toe shifting and keeps your foot on the brake if need be.

One of the best things is that this has to be one of the least expensive modifications you can do to really improve your driving prowess.

Safety Equipment

Although a fire extinguisher is not a performance item, the majority of race and/or show events require a fire extinguisher to be onboard your vehicle. Fiberglass burns quickly and ignites easily when just a little gasoline is added; I want a way out if the worst possible scenario occurs. The extinguisher should be placed as close as possible to the driver in case he or she needs to use it in the cockpit.

You need a fire extinguisher rated for B and C fires, preferably in a 2½-pound bottle. Just make sure you can get to it easily and that it is securely fastened to avoid a 5-plus-pound projectile on the loose in the cockpit. Fire extinguishers should be checked periodically for date of service and charge rate.

Helmets are always controversial; it seems that many people would rather die than use one. Roll cages and unprotected heads don't end up faring well in a violent event, whether it is a crash or rough roadway. Having your head bouncing around in between roll cage steel tubing can make for a severe headache at the very least.

Many race tracks have mandatory helmet requirements. Why take a chance with something that you really can't live without? Convertibles require a helmet once your elapsed time at the drag strip is lower than 11 seconds, at least at my local track. Your drag strip may have more stringent rules regarding the use of helmets.

You should also make sure your helmet meets Snell helmet safety standards for use in automotive racing events. If you are going to use protection, use the best possible.

Source Guide

American Powertrain
2199 Summerfield Rd.
Cookeville, TN 38501
931-646-4836
americanpowertrain.com

American Speed Enterprises
3006 Avenue of the Cities
Moline, IL 61265
309-764-3601
amerspeed.com

B&M
100 Stony Point Rd., Ste. 125
Santa Rosa, CA 95401
707-544-4761
bmracing.com

Be Cool
310 Woodside Ave.
Essexville MI 48732
800-691-2667
becool.com

Borgeson Universal
91 Technology Park Dr.
Torrington, CT 06790
860-482-8283
borgeson.com

Brad Penn
penngrade1.com

Canton Racing Products
232 Branford Rd.
North Branford, CT 06471
203-481-9460
cantonracingproducts.com

Challenger Engine Software
115 Jeanette Dr.
Granite City, IL 62040
618-797-1770
virtualengine2000.com

Chevrolet Performance
chevrolet.com

COMP Cams
3406 Democrat Rd.
Memphis, TN 38118
800-999-0853
compcams.com

Corvette Central
13350 Three Oaks Rd.
Sawyer, MI 49125
800-345-4122
corvettecentral.com

Dewitts Radiators
1275 Grand Oaks Dr.
Howell, MI 48843
517-548-0600

Earl's Performance Plumbing
1801 Russellville Rd.
Bowling Green, KY 42101
270 782-2900
holley.com

Edelbrock
2700 California St.
Torrance, CA 90503
310-781-2222
edelbrock.com

FAST
3400 Democrat Rd.
Memphis, TN 38118
877-334-8355
fuelairspark.com

Fuel Safe
1550 NE Kingwood Ave.
Redmond, OR 97756
800-433-6524
fuelsafe.com

Holley
1801 Russellville Rd.
Bowling Green, KY 42101
270 782-2900
holley.com

Hooker
1801 Russellville Rd.
Bowling Green, KY 42101
270 782-2900
holley.com

Keisler Engineering
2250 Stock Creek Blvd.
Rockford, TN 37853
888-609-0094
keislerauto.com

KWiK Performance
Springfield, MO
417-955-1467
kwikperf.com

Lakewood Industries
10601 Memphis Ave., #12
Cleveland, OH 44144
lakewoodindustries.com

Magnaflow
22961 Arroyo Vista
Rancho Santa Margarita, CA 92688
800-824-8664
magnaflow.com

Mid America Motorworks
17082 N. US Hwy. 45
Effingham, IL 62401
866-350-4540
mamotorworks.com

Midway Industries
2266 Crosswind Dr.
Prescott, AZ 86301
928-771-8422
centerforce.com

Moroso
80 Carter Dr.
Guilford, CT 06437
203-453-6571
moroso.com

NOS
1801 Russellville Rd.
Bowling Green, KY 42101
270 782-2900
holley.com

PerTronix Shortie Headers
440 East Arrow Hwy.
San Dimas, CA 91773
909-547-9058
pertronix.com

Petris Enterprises
809 West Willow St.
Scottsboro, AL 35768
256-259-2400
petrisenterprises.com

Professional Products
323-779-2020
professional-products.com

Racing Head Service
3406 Democrat Rd.
Memphis, TN 38118
901-795-7600
racingheadservice.com

Random Technologies
4430 Tuck Rd.
Loganville, GA 30052
770-554-4242
randomtechnology.com

Richmond
1208 Old Norris Rd.
Liberty, SC 29657
864-843-9275
richmondgear.com

Rick's Tank's
228 E. Sunset Rd.
El Paso, TX 79922
915-760-4388
rickstanks.com

Rock Valley Antique Auto Parts, Inc
Route 72 & Rothwell Rd.
Stillman Valley, IL 61084
815-645-2740
rockvalleyantiqueautoparts.com

Spal
1731 S.E. Oralabor Rd.
Ankeny, IA 50021
800-345-0327
spalusa.com

Speartech
3574 E. State Rd. 236
Anderson, IN 46017
765-378-4908
speartech.com

SPC Performance
4045 Specialty Pl.
Longmont, CO 80504
800-525-6505
spcalignment.com

S.P.E.C.
2490 Five Star Pkwy.
Bessemer, AL 35022
800-828-4379
specclutch.com

Speedway Motors
340 Victory Ln.
Lincoln, NE 68528
800-979-0122
speedwaymotors.com

Spiral Turbo Specialties
PO Box 186
Seville, OH 44273
330-321-1918
spiralturbobaffles.com

Stainless Steel Brake Corporation
ssbrakes.com

Stan's Headers
4715 Auburn Way N.
Auburn, WA 98002
800-962-6467
stans-headers.com

Street Shop
2270 Hwy. 31 S.
Athens, AL 35611
256-233-5809
streetshopinc.com

Tremec Transmissions
14700 Helm Ct.
Plymouth, MI 48170
734-456-3700
tremec.com

Van Steel
12285 West St.
Clearwater, FL 33762
800-418-5397
vansteel.com

Vette Brake and Products
7490 30th Ave.
St. Petersburg, FL 33710
800-237-9991
vbandp.com

Vetteworks Motorsports
3290 B St. NW, Ste. B
Auburn, WA 98001
253-373-4849
vetteworksonline.net

Vintage Air
800-862-6658
vintageair.com

Vortech Superchargers
1650 Pacific Ave.
Oxnard, CA 93033
805-247-0226
vortechsuperchargers.com

Weiand
holley.com

Wilwood Engineering
4700 Calle Bolero
Camarillo, CA 93012
805-388-1188
wilwood.com

Zip Products
8067 Fast Ln.
Mechanicsville, VA 23111
800-962-9632
zip-corvette.com

www.ingramcontent.com/pod-product-compliance
Lightning Source LLC
Chambersburg PA
CBHW081446070526
44586CB00019B/2256